Studies of the East Asian Institute,
Columbia University

The East Asian Institute is Columbia University's center for research, publication, and teaching on modern East Asia. The Studies of the East Asian Institute were inaugurated in 1962 to bring to a wider public the results of significant new research on modern and contemporary East Asia.

Studies of the East Asian Institute, *Selected Titles*

The Reluctant Dragon

Crisis Cycles
in Chinese Foreign Economic Policy

LAWRENCE C. REARDON

UNIVERSITY OF WASHINGTON PRESS
Seattle and London

A Study of the East Asian Institute,
Columbia University

Library of Congress Cataloging-in-Publication Data
Reardon, Lawrence C.
    The reluctant dragon : crisis cycles in Chinese foreign economic policy /
Lawrence C. Reardon.
        p. cm. — (Studies of the East Asian Institute)
    Includes bibliographical references and index.
    ISBN 0-295-98121-0 (alk. paper)
    1. China—Foreign economic relations.   2. China—Economic policy—1976-
3. Business cycles—China.   I. Title.   II. Series.
HF1604 .R4   2001   337.51—dc21   00-068321

客观的可能超过了主观的认识

主观的努力落后于客观的需要

Objective possibilities have exceeded
subjective understanding;
Subjective efforts lag behind objective necessity.

Premier Zhou Enlai, December 1955
(An antithetical couplet in response to Mao's first attempts at a Great Leap)

Contents

Preface

Academic analyses of China's foreign economic decision making are relatively rare, especially when contrasted to the myriad studies analyzing
Western governments' foreign economic policy. This is not surprising. The
Marxist-Leninist leadership, the various Chinese bureaucracies, and Chinese society have followed the traditional maxim that the truth must be shielded from
outsiders (*neiwai youbie*).[1] Even the most simple government policy documents
are classified for internal use (*neibu*) not to be revealed to foreigners; this is particularly true for documents or statistics concerning international relations or
foreign economic policy.

Although the Chinese have continued their policy of economic secrecy during the "opening" period,[2] foreign academics have made some progress in pry-
ing open the Chinese "black box." I conducted dissertation fieldwork in northern
and southern China between 1984 and 1988, with follow-up trips during the summers of 1990, 1992, 1994, and 1997. During the first two years of fieldwork, I
was granted a fellowship from the Committee for Scholarly Communication with
the PRC (CSCPRC) to study at Peking University's Economics College. At Beida,
I learned one of the most important lessons for any foreign scholar: how to work
within the Chinese system and collaborate with scholars and bureaucrats. By
1986, I was appointed a foreign expert in Shenzhen University's Economics
Department as well as a special researcher at the Research Institute for the SEZS,
Hong Kong, and Macao Economies at Jinan University. Enjoying the more
relaxed political atmosphere of the booming southern Chinese cities of Shenzhen
and Guangzhou, I applied the lessons learned at Beida to gain greater access to
policy makers, scholars, and research-quality materials.

As a special researcher at Jinan University, I participated in several conferences on Chinese foreign economic policy, including a small, two-day seminar
held during January 1987. The seminar participants, who included many of
Guangdong Province's best-known economists and policy makers, were tack-
ling very sensitive problems facing China's economic reforms and the special
economic zones (SEZS), including the establishment of a "socialist market econ-

omy." Just before the evening banquet, we were stunned by the news that Hu Yaobang had resigned from his post as leader of the Chinese Communist Party. The participants immediately began to discuss the implications of Hu's removal on the economic reforms and the Guangdong experiment.

Up to that point, the conference participants had freely discussed their contrasting views on China's reforms and had not disguised the various problems plaguing the SEZs or Guangdong's economic revolution. Yet, looking at the concerned faces around the banquet table, I suddenly realized that these protagonists of reform were now facing their greatest fear: a new political campaign against "bourgeois liberalism" during which they could possibly be condemned as Chinese traitors (*hanjian*). These researchers, some of whom I had closely collaborated with over the years, suddenly realized that I was present. By switching from Mandarin to Cantonese, they effectively isolated me from their conversation.

Although breaking through certain language, cultural, and political barriers to conduct research in the mainland, I faced barriers that remained insurmountable. In essence, I was still an "old foreigner" (*laowai*), who could rely on his "big nose" and U.S. passport to leave the country at any time. These senior Chinese researchers and policy makers at the 1987 conference had survived the Anti-Rightist Movement of the 1950s and the Cultural Revolution of the 1960s. They had witnessed how the Party had lavished praise on the risk takers of one period (*maoxianzhe*), only to revert to criticism and contempt during another period. They had learned to trust only close friends and family (*nei*); people on the outside (*wai*)—whether outside one's circle of acquaintances or outside the country—were unreliable.

With such concerns in mind, it would be impossible to recognize the countless number of teachers and friends in the United States and China who have supported and encouraged my work during the past two decades. I would, however, like to express my sincere gratitude to Professors Thomas Bernstein and Andrew Nathan at Columbia University. They have been excellent advisors, who continue to provide the critical insight and encouragement I have needed to complete this study. I can only hope to emulate their high standards of scholarly excellence.

I also gratefully acknowledge the faculty and staff of the East Asian Institute and the Political Science Department of Columbia University, who have given me generous moral and financial support. I thank Professors David Baldwin, Huan Guocang, N. T. Wang, and Madeleine Zelin for commenting on my dissertation, upon which this study is partially based. I have truly missed the intellectual stimulation and friendly camaraderie of the East Asian Institute, where scholars from various disciplines and regional specialties are afforded the unique opportunity to exchange ideas. With its acceptance of this study as one of the Studies of the East Asian Institute, the institute continues to provide strong support. I am profoundly grateful to Madge Huntington and Professor Carol Gluck for their sound advice and hard work in promoting the manuscript.

I learned much about the "real" China during my initial fieldwork in Beijing (1984–1986). I thank the CSCPRC for its financial and logistical support, as well as Peking University's Economics College and Foreign Students Office for their patience and assistance. I am also indebted to many foreign scholars in residence at Beida who taught me the ropes, especially Professor Pan Luli. In South China, I sincerely thank the faculty and students of Shenzhen University, where I was a foreign expert in the Economics Department between 1986 and 1988. I gratefully acknowledge the cooperation of Jinan University's Research Institute for the SEZs, Hong Kong, and Macao Economies; the Guangdong Academy of Social Sciences; the Universities Service Center; and China's SEZs Data and Research Unit of Hong Kong Chinese University. I am particularly indebted to Jordan and Cindy Pollack for their companionship and intellectual inspiration. I would also like to thank the Council for International Education Exchange, Ian and Elke Johnson in Beijing, and Professor Imai Hiroyuki of Lingnan College, Hong Kong, all of whom were helpful during my recent trips to China and Hong Kong.

At the University of New Hampshire, I am grateful to the Graduate School and the School of Liberal Arts for providing funding for three summers of research and to Professors Bernard Gordon and David Larson for their unfailing support over the years. I also want to thank several graduate assistants, who labored hard to carry out literature searches, helped me edit the text, and performed other assorted jobs. Nancy Hearst and Harvard's Fairbank Center have been indispensable during the past couple of years as I revised the manuscript. I also want to sincerely thank Lorri Hagman and Michael Duckworth of the University of Washington Press, Joanne Sandstrom and her meticulous copyediting, the anonymous reviewers of this manuscript, and those who commented on a 1998 *China Quarterly* article based on this manuscript.[3]

Finally, I wish to express my deepest gratitude to four extraordinary people. Dr. Dorothy Borg was the symbol of scholarly excellence and academic integrity for several generations of scholars around the world. I am deeply honored to have considered her my mentor and my friend. Of all my excellent language teachers at Columbia, Middlebury, and the Stanford Center, I especially thank Dr. Irene Liu. Her innovative teaching techniques and deep concern for her students have made her an irreplaceable asset to Columbia's China program. Lastly, I thank my parents, Rosemary and Larry Reardon. They collected and mimeographed materials, critically read my drafts, and tolerated the vicissitudes of a son who returned to the empty nest. They are the rock upon which I stand. I gratefully acknowledge the enormous debt I owe to these and other individuals.

This study presents one interpretation of China's foreign economic policy process from a Western political science perspective. Analysis of internal leadership speeches and the resulting government policies, however, does not guarantee an accurate representation of the "truth." In fact, the truth of any text cannot be found, since textual analysis is not a value-free endeavor. According to Hans-Georg Gadamer,

> The discovery of the true meaning of a text or a work of art is never finished; it is in fact an infinite process. Not only are fresh sources of error constantly excluded, so that the true meaning has filtered out of it all kinds of things that obscure it, but there emerge continually new sources of understanding, which reveal unsuspected elements of meaning.[4]

We carry out the process of understanding a text based on our preconceived notions. The very act of selecting, translating, and analyzing a document is determined by the academic and cultural traditions that define our horizons.[5] To understand horizons other than our own, Gadamer suggests that

> we self-consciously designate our opinions and prejudices and qualify them as such, and in so doing strip them of their extreme character. In keeping to this attitude we grant the text the opportunity to appear as an authentically different being and to manifest its own truth, over and against our own preconceived notions.[6]

Before undertaking fieldwork in China, I had been thoroughly trained in Western theories of international relations and international political economy. Firmly anchored in the American academic experience, I was immersed in a new and alien environment after arriving in Beijing in 1984. During the course of fieldwork and preparing this study, I continued to carry on a dialogue between my theoretical training and the Chinese texts to strip away my most extreme prejudices. This study thus tests my individual prejudices that form my horizon; it also redefines my understanding of Chinese policy making.[7] Readers must evaluate whether I have been successful in allowing the Chinese text to manifest its own truth.

I wholeheartedly welcome all criticism by "proffering a brick, in hope of receiving jade in return."

The Reluctant Dragon

Introduction

The legacy of the Third Plenum of the Eleventh Chinese Communist Party (CCP) Central Committee has been extraordinary. In late 1978 the Chinese leadership initiated an unprecedented series of dramatic economic reforms, which enabled China to sustain a phenomenal growth rate. During the last two decades, China's real gross domestic product (GDP) grew between 9 percent and 13 percent annually; China's foreign trade figures increased from the trivial amount of $1.94 billion in 1952 to $325.06 billion in 1997.[1] By opening to the outside world and liberalizing the domestic economic structure, China transformed itself into the third-largest and fastest-growing economy in the world.[2] With the incorporation of Hong Kong in 1997, China became the fourth-largest global trading economy, enjoyed the second-largest foreign exchange reserves, and managed the fifth-largest global equities and financial market.[3]

The Integration of China into the World Economy

One of the Third Plenum's greatest legacies has been China's gradual reintegration into the global economy. In the 1980s, mainland China obtained membership in the two major international organizations that promote international financial stability (the International Monetary Fund) and development (the World Bank). By 2001, China faced its last major hurdle to acceptance into the global economy—admission to the World Trade Organization (WTO).[4] As the primary organization dealing with international trade matters, the WTO requires all members to conform to international norms of trade behavior. The Chinese leadership accordingly approved several fundamental domestic and foreign economic reforms—such as reducing domestic protectionist measures and promoting a more transparent foreign trade system—to petition for WTO admission. If realized, compliance measures would represent for China an unprecedented, partial surrender of state autonomy to an international organization.

When initiating the opening to the outside world (*duiwai kaifang*) in the late 1970s,[5] Chinese leaders undoubtedly never envisioned signing international covenants on human rights or ensuring regional economic stability during the 1990s Asian crisis. Yet Chinese leaders have accepted such transaction costs to realize China's "manifest destiny" of assuming an important role in the new millenium's "uni-multipolar" system.[6] No longer do they consider themselves the "sick people of Asia" (*Dongya bingfu*), who for nearly two centuries were unable to defend their sovereignty against Western imperialist incursions. Instead, they envision a newly awakened Chinese dragon, along with their smaller Chinese siblings—Hong Kong and Taiwan—assuming a major global economic role by the early twenty-first century.

Western policy leaders have awakened to the potential power of the Chinese economic dragon, which in 1996 began to compete with a stumbling Japan to be the United States' most important foreign trade competitor.[7] Thus the advanced industrialized states are strongly motivated to encourage Chinese cooperative behavior in the international economy to moderate future trade conflicts. For these reasons, the United States, the European Union, and other WTO nations strenuously objected to China's violations of international norms of economic behavior—such as in intellectual property rights, the dumping of low-value merchandise on the world market, and the failure to extend "national treatment" to foreign investors—during WTO negotiations.[8] To guarantee continued compliance with such norms, WTO nations will need a greater understanding of the variables affecting Chinese foreign economic policy formation and implementation.

The Legacy of China's pre-1979 Foreign Economic Policies

Foreign academics conducting fieldwork in the People's Republic have published many valuable works on contemporary Chinese foreign economic policies.[9] Unfortunately, many of these studies, with several notable exceptions, either ignore or take only a cursory view of pre-1978 foreign economic policy.

They thus reinforce the widely held romantic view that Chinese leaders primarily pursued an autarkic development strategy based on a strict Maoist idea of self-reliance (*zili gengsheng*). Although acknowledging that Soviet technology imports jump-started Chinese economic development in the 1950s, this interpretation emphasizes the global isolation of the Chinese economy. The Cold War—specifically the UN trade embargo of the 1950s and the Sino-Soviet split of 1960—imposed an autarkic regime upon China that resulted in low trade dependency. Foreign trade thus "played a peripheral role at best" in economic development in the 1960s and 1970s.[10] The reversal of this splendid isolation occurred with the lifting of the U.S. trade embargo and the Central Committee landmark decision of late 1978, which enabled China to burst suddenly upon the world economic stage in the 1980s.

This study concurs with Perkins's argument that Chinese elites and not the international environment made a conscious decision in the early 1950s to limit dependence on foreign trade.[11] Second, while the international environment (bipolar conflict, the UN and U.S. economic embargoes, the Sino-Soviet schism) limited the policy options up to the late 1970s, it did not totally isolate China from the global marketplace. Beginning in the 1950s, Chinese elites imported large-scale turnkey plants from the Eastern- and subsequently the Western-bloc nations as well as welcomed limited investment from overseas Chinese beginning in the 1950s. Even during the Cultural Revolution, the Chinese revolutionary leadership operated the Guangzhou Trade Fair and used its financial and trading connections with Hong Kong. Many of these pre-1978 foreign economic policies and attitudes did not disappear with the advent of the Third Plenum, but instead were revised and expanded. Thus as Yahuda has pointed out, the Chinese indiscriminately used the term "self-reliance" "to describe a variety of different policies from virtual autarky to the importing of a wide range of agricultural products and industrial plants."[12]

Chinese leaders thus gained considerable knowledge and experience in dealing with the international marketplace during the pre-1978 period. By not analyzing such interactions, current Western studies unduly discount the legacy of previous interactions with the world capitalist economy. Such knowledge also can shed further light on the similarities and differences of the Chinese development model compared to the development paths of the other Asian developing economies. Most important, an understanding of China's protectionist heritage can explain its current reluctance to adhere to international norms of economic behavior.

The significance of this policy legacy became apparent to me while conducting dissertation fieldwork on China's opening policy.[13] Theoretically, China's post–1978 foreign economic policy should have heralded a new acceptance of the international market, which would supplant state planners in determining currency exchange rates and production, marketing, and investment decisions. China's export processing zones (EPZs), such as the special economic zones (SEZs) first authorized in July 1979,[14] should have reflected this new outwardly oriented strategy. Using their comparative advantage in labor and land to attract foreign capital, technology, and entrepreneurial expertise, the EPZs should have produced commodities competitive on the international market.

They did not. The most prominent symbol of China's bold experimentation with outwardly oriented development, the SEZs, exhibited many inwardly oriented development characteristics. Undoubtedly, a major reason for this incongruity was the influence of past policies. The SEZs were not a new, radical experiment, but the culmination of twenty years of experimentation with EPZs that was initiated by Zhou Enlai in 1960.[15]

Previous Western landmark studies, such as George Crane's *Political Economy of China's Special Economic Zones* and Michael Oborne's *China's Special Economic Zones,* underemphasized the legacy of inwardly oriented development and its influence on the formation of China's EPZ policy.[16] This legacy mandated strict controls on foreign direct investment and the continuation of high barriers against international environmental influences. As a result, the new Chinese EPZs were insulated from international market pressures; the domestic political and economic situation continued to determine EPZ policies. Only after 1982 did the Central Committee begin to lift the import substitution barriers and approve elements of an export-oriented strategy; not until 1995 did the Chinese leadership begin to terminate EPZ preferential policies as a precondition for WTO membership.[17]

Thus, an understanding of this pre-1978 legacy can explain many of the policy formation and implementation problems encountered by the EPZs and other foreign trade reform problems during the 1980s and 1990s.

Previous Interpretations of China's Foreign Economic Policies

The majority of openly published studies from mainland China provide little information about pre-1978 foreign economic policy. Like the reinterpretation of history following dynastic or ruling coalition change, Chinese studies of the pre-6.4 era (the pre-Tiananmen crisis of 4 June 1989) treat the 1978 Third Plenum as the beginning of civilized history, when Chinese reformers boldly broke "the shackles of leftist ideological tendencies, eliminated dogmatism and stagnation."[18] During the post-6.4 era, the Party has attempted to rebuild respect for the Party and Mao Zedong. The Party even promoted Mao as the initiator of China's opening policy.[19]

Although many Western accounts have been swayed by Maoist rhetoric concerning self-reliance, certain Western economists including Alexander Eckstein and Dwight Perkins have argued that technology and equipment imports made an important contribution to overall economic development.[20] Nicholas Lardy put these arguments in a global perspective.[21] Clarifying Eckstein's arguments about the importance of imports in China's early economic development strategy, Lardy argues that "the underlying strategy of import substitution adopted during the First Five-Year Plan changed relatively little right up to the eve of the reform period of the 1980s."[22] Lardy concurs with World Bank findings that China's previous development strategy insulated it from international market pressures and had a detrimental effect on such matters as material pricing, production of nonindustrial goods, and per capita consumption rates.[23] Yet the analysis lacks details of China's previous import substitution strategies, the politics of their adoption, and how they have influenced the implementation of post-1978 export-oriented development strategy.

Western political scientists have produced excellent studies of elite and factional conflicts over economic policy during the pre-1978 period but have paid little attention to conflicts over the role of the global economy in China's development strategy.[24] Exceptions include Yahuda's chapter analyzing self-reliance during the Maoist era, which outlines Mao's views and briefly describes differences within the elite.[25] Vindicating the utility of content analysis, Whiting thoroughly analyzed press reports to test whether China's turnkey plant imports in the 1970s became entangled in coalition politics.[26] Barnett's early 1980s work on China's modernization program provides an insightful analysis of the self-reliance debates in the 1970s.[27] Bachman as well as Lieberthal and Oksenberg explored the influence of the heavy industry coalition and the "petroleum group" on foreign trade policy formulation.[28] When analyzing China's pre-1979 automotive policies, Harwit identified major disagreements between the "pragmatists," who championed "rational industrial development," and the "Maoists," who emphasized the development of an indigenous automotive industry.[29] Van Ness argues that three different lines of development were proffered over a thirty-year period: socialist camp (1950–57), Third World (1960–70), and a modernization line (1978–83).[30] Solinger elegantly describes the crisis in China's relationship to the global economy, a crisis that energized China's leaders to readjust its moribund industrial strategy in the late 1970s.[31]

Building upon these previous works, this study presents a more comprehensive picture of pre-1978 foreign economic policies and the debates that they provoked.

The Cycling of Chinese Development Policy

While the international environment undoubtedly influenced China's adoption of an inwardly oriented development regime in the early 1950s, subsystemic approaches best explain the development regime and strategy choices from the late 1950s to late 1970s.[32] Chapter 1 explores why China did not embark upon a direct, evolutionary path toward outwardly oriented development like the Taiwanese and South Koreans during the 1960s and 1970s. China not only retained its inwardly oriented development regime, but alternated at various times between its traditional import substitution development strategy and a more extreme form of inwardly oriented development—semiautarky—that eliminated most economic contacts with the international economy, including the importation of foreign equipment, technology, and know-how.

To explain this antinomy of Chinese development, the study modifies the opinion-group approach originally proposed in Richard Lowenthal's seminal analysis of the "Communist dilemma."[33] Chinese inwardly oriented development strategies from the late 1950s to 1979 (dependent variable) were primarily determined by the disagreement between Chinese elites over the best path to self-reliance (independent variable). After the mid-1950s, elite coalitions coalesced around competing visions of inwardly oriented development: to use foreign economic policy to achieve self-sufficiency (import substitution) or to treat foreign economic policy as a supplementary and relatively dispensable tool of development (semiautarky). This basic difference resulted in a series of non–zero sum games, in which competing elite coalitions implemented their preferred vision of development without completely vanquishing competing ideas. This series of non–zero sum games constituted the primary determinant of China's inwardly oriented development regime up to the late 1970s.

Finally, the chapter argues that these non–zero sum games can be analyzed as a series of distinctive crisis cycles. Each cycle was initiated by a contending elite coalition (or contending coalitions), which used crises in domestic development to delegitimate the ruling elite coalition (or coalitions) and to readjust the previous development strategy (readjustment phase). While the previous policies were being modified or eliminated, the new ruling elite coalitions pursued novel solutions based on their preferred development vision (innovation phase). Such policies inevitably encountered problems or were perceived as creating chaos (implementation phase). If the contending elites were successful in linking the development strategy with national crisis, the ruling elite coalition (or coalitions) lost legitimacy. The crisis cycle thus started anew.

Chapter 2 empirically demonstrates that the international environment determined the PRC's initial adoption of an inwardly oriented development regime. Following the increase in bipolar tensions and the UN embargo, China sought preferential access to Soviet technology, expertise, and financing to strengthen national security. Yet beginning in the mid-1950s, certain Chinese leaders questioned the utility of the large-scale import substitution strategy. While the international environment continued to set boundaries of development strategy options, these internal debates within the Chinese leadership determined China's development path during the ensuing two decades.

Chapter 3 describes the 1959–66 crisis cycle initiated by the Great Leap Forward (GLF). After 1959, the post–GLF elite coalition gradually readjusted GLF policies by reducing production quotas and new capital investment.[34] During the policy readjustment phase, the post–GLF coalition introduced in 1961 the Eight-Character Plan, which was a mixture of administrative and remunerative measures. Such measures enabled China to repay its foreign debts, finance food imports, and continue its pre–GLF import substitution strategy, albeit on a far more limited scale. Having readjusted the economy, Zhou Enlai promoted his innovative views of China's long-term path of development—the Four Modernizations Program. In fall 1963, Zhou formally presented his alternative to Mao's "rash advance" approach to economic development by devising two fifteen-year plans to achieve the basic industrialization of China before the year 2000.

Chapter 4 analyzes the Cultural Revolution, which initiated the second crisis cycle (1966–71). Critical of the post–GLF's remunerative and administrative approach and the Four Modernizations Program, Mao with the help of Lin Biao's and Jiang Qing's coalitions promoted a wartime development strategy that reflected the "true meaning" of self-sufficiency. Revising Mao's GLF approach, they relied on normative means to tap the boundless energies of "Communist man." To promote a self-sufficient economy, the new leadership implemented a semiautarkic development strategy that eliminated the post–GLF's import substitution program, the foreign trade production incentive schemes, and the investment opportunities for overseas Chinese.[35]

The third crisis cycle was initiated after 13 September 1971, when Premier Zhou Enlai's new post–Cultural Revolution coalition readjusted the previous development strategy (chapter 5).[36] Prior to the Sino-U.S. rapprochement and the rise in the international oil price, Premier Zhou Enlai discarded the semiautarkic strategies of the Cultural Revolution to reimplement an import substitution development strategy.[37] This 4-3 Plan authorized the importation of chemical fertilizer plants, petrochemical plants, coal mine facilities, and electrical generation plants whose actual value exceeded $5 billion.[38] By January 1975, Zhou Enlai announced the revival of the Four Modernizations Program of 1963 that envisioned an industrialized China by 2000. To finance the strategy, the policy elites depended on higher petroleum export revenues as well as increasing export capacity. The policy elites thus issued administrative directives to improve the quality of Chinese exports,[39] to revive and expand the export commodity production bases (ECPBs),[40] and to reinstitute various remunerative post–GLF foreign trade policies, including the agricultural sideline bonus schemes.[41]

Chapter 6 describes the abbreviated fourth crisis cycle (1975–76), which was initiated by members of the CCP Political Bureau who opposed Zhou's post–1971 "normalization" policies and especially his import substitution development strategy. During the Anti-Lin, Anti-Confucius Campaign of 1974 and the subsequent November 1975 Campaign to Counterattack against Tendencies of Right-Deviation and Revocation, Jiang Qing's remaining politics-in-command[42] coalition—more commonly known as the Gang of Four—directly criticized Zhou Enlai's import substitution development strategy. Jiang Qing's coalition gradually convinced Mao that Zhou Enlai's anointed successor, Deng Xiaoping, was laying "the material foundations for capitalism" and was a "flunky for the imperialists who sold out the country and thus a traitor."[43] The abbreviated fourth crisis cycle is primarily noted for its policy readjustment phase, which culminated with Deng Xiaoping's ouster from power and the denunciation of his neomercantalist policies. However, Jiang Qing's coalition could not achieve elite consensus, and following Mao's death was replaced by a new coalition headed by Hua Guofeng in October 1976.

Chapter 7 shows how Hua Guofeng's accession to power and Jiang Qing's downfall in 1976 initiated the fifth crisis cycle (1976–78). During the policy readjustment phase, Hua immediately adopted deflationary measures and other policies to offset the economic problems in part created by Jiang Qing's bid for power. During the policy innovation phase, Hua championed his Ten-Year Plan, which mandated an import substitution program much larger in scope than Zhou's 4-3 Plan of the early 1970s.[44] To finance the new round of turnkey plant imports valued at more than $6.5 billion, Hua permitted the use of overseas Chinese capital and approved the limited use of foreign capital. Hua's grand development strategy, never realized, was subsequently readjusted during the April 1979 work conference.

Chapter 7 also discusses the proto-experiment with outwardly oriented development, which was initiated with Deng Xiaoping's reaccession to power. Deng's elite coalition believed that the Ten-Year Plan would bankrupt China.[45] Upon assuming power, Deng's post–GLF coalition readjusted the domestic economy, as well as the import substitution program. The new program reduced foreign equipment imports and technology transfer contracts, warmly welcomed foreign investment, and transferred greater foreign trade and investment authority to some cities and provinces.

To finance the remaining large import substitution projects and future technology and equipment imports, the new leadership coalition strengthened the foreign trade support measures implemented at various times since the early 1960s. These measures included priority access to production inputs for all export production units (Five-Priorities Policy);[46] various subsidized financial programs to provide liquidity to export industries (Foreign Trade Circulating Funds to Promote Export Commodity Production,[47] Investment Fund for Export Commodity Production,[48] Specialized Loan Program for Industrial Export Production,[49] and the Short-Term Foreign Exchange Loan Program);[50] the Foreign Exchange Retention Program to increase export industries' access to foreign exchange *(waihui fencheng)*;[51] a program for increasing the processing and assembly of imported materials for export *(yijin yangchu)*;[52] and a program for expanding China's export processing zones.[53]

In light of the readjustment of the national development strategy and the reduction in the state's capital investment funding, the leadership coalition substituted foreign capital for domestic investment. In addition to overseas Chinese capital, the new coalition expanded Hua Guofeng's experiment with foreign capital investment by tapping funds from commercial sources, foreign governments, and international organizations; promulgating State Council document 79.220, which among other measures included detailed regulations on processing and assembly and compensation trade; and adopting the joint venture law.

The new leadership also attempted to enliven the export sector to finance its import program by allowing some localities, enterprises, or individuals to "become better off before others." The new leadership hoped to "bring into full play" the strengths of China's major export regions by adopting State Council document 79.202, which outlined various export support and foreign trade decentralization policies to be nationally implemented; State Council document 79.233, which granted special foreign trade rights to Beijing, Tianjin, and Shanghai; and Central Committee document 79.50, which delegated greater authority to Guangdong and Fujian in the domestic economic and foreign trade sectors, including the establishment of SEZs in Shenzhen and Zhuhai.[54]

The study concludes that Chinese leaders enjoyed a high degree of policy autonomy and the capacity to carry out an inwardly oriented development regime, which was very similar to the East Asian experience. Yet the cycling between semiautarky and import substitution of the pre–1979 period was a uniquely Chinese experience. The cycling of development strategies delayed China's opening to the outside world and the adoption of an outwardly oriented development regime (chapter 7), thus qualifying any comparison with the "Asian miracle" paradigm.

While the cycling delayed China's adoption of a more outwardly oriented development regime, it did not condemn China to an unchanging loop of history. Elites incrementally learned from their policy successes and failures and implemented these changes when they had the opportunity. Mao's thinking gradually progressed from initially welcoming all foreign trade and investment, to restricting economic relations to the Soviet bloc, to minimizing foreign economic relations, and finally to acquiescing to greater connections with the Western marketplace. The post–GLF coalition incrementally learned over three decades that the inwardly oriented import substitution strategy suffered from diminishing returns on China's development. Thus, the economic policy initiatives proposed after 1978 are indicative of an outwardly oriented development regime akin to the Asian growth model.

An in-depth discussion of the primary and secondary sources, including an explanation for the various types of Chinese policy nomenclature has been included in appendix A and chapter 1. Unless otherwise specified, I have translated Chinese materials adopting the pinyin form of romanization; for Taiwanese names and places I use the Wade-Giles system.

CHAPTER I

The Domestic Determinants of Chinese Foreign Economic Policy

D uring the post–World War II era, developing countries considered foreign trade as a crucial element for economic growth.[1] Although facing far different circumstances, China joined the other East Asian economies in the 1950s in choosing an inwardly oriented strategy of import substitution. Yet China did not accompany Taiwan, South Korea, and the other high-growth Asian economies along the evolutionary road toward outwardly oriented development, but instead continued along a circuitous inwardly oriented path until the late 1970s.

The UN economic embargo undeniably affected China's adoption of inwardly oriented policies in the early 1950s. However, elite disagreement over the best path to self-reliance caused the two-decade continuation of inwardly oriented policies. Policy elite coalitions coalesced around a particular inwardly oriented strategy—import substitution or semiautarkic development—based on their different beliefs and experiences. Contending elite coalitions used crises to delegitimate existing policies and to implement their preferred development strategy. The resulting changes created a cycling of contending inwardly oriented development strategies; this cycling prevented the Chinese from enjoying the high growth rates experienced by "Asian miracle" economies.

Systemic Explanations of Chinese Foreign Economic Policies
Inwardly and Outwardly Oriented Development Regimes

Before World War II, most developing countries adopted—or were forced to adopt—primary export-led growth, which is based on the neoclassical doctrine of comparative advantage. By exporting their abundant raw materials and foods, developing countries theoretically used factors of production more efficiently, improved factor endowments (foreign investment, domestic saving, labor and skilled personnel), and stimulated development in other industrial sectors. To gain greater political and economic independence after World War II, many of these developing economies explored alternative growth strategies focusing on development of the country's industrial sector.[2] They subsequently adopted two industrial development regimes—inwardly and outwardly oriented development (table 1.1)—to achieve their ultimate goal of economic parity with the developed economies.[3]

These development regimes are based on two fundamentally different views of the international marketplace.[4] Inwardly oriented strategies treat the international market as a dangerous adversary whose influences on domestic economic growth must be controlled and in certain instances eliminated. The developing economy can achieve economic parity only by eliminating dependence on the developed economies through self-sufficiency. Outwardly oriented strategies take a more utilitarian view. Although the international market must be watched, it is regarded as a "partner in development," which provides an invaluable source of export revenue, technology innovation, and capital financing. Thus, domestic industrialization and economic parity can be achieved by becoming more integrated with the international market.

The two industrial development regimes also prescribe contrasting prescriptions for economic growth. Inwardly oriented strategies mandate explicit or implicit restrictions on foreign trade and investment activities to insulate the domestic economy from international environmental influences and to achieve self-sufficiency, which can be defined as the state's ability to control its internal economic affairs. A country's success in achieving such goals is dependent on its level of industrialization, geographic size, resource endowment, and government policies.[5]

The most extreme inwardly oriented strategy is autarky: A strict self-reliance strategy was the preferred solution to the extremely harmful influences of the international economy (see table 1.1, type 1). While economists assume that complete isolation can exist, Yahuda argues that "at no point during Mao's lifetime was the PRC truly autarkic in the sense of having no foreign trade at all"; Nai-Ruenn Chen describes China's policies of the 1960s as "import minimization."[6] The term "semiautarky" thus cumbersomely describes those periods when China severely restricted foreign economic relations but continued to import vital raw materials, technology, and equipment.

A less draconian type of inwardly oriented strategy involves import substitution. Virtually all economies have engaged in simple substitution of selected imported goods; certain developing economies have implemented a more comprehensive strategy of substituting intermediate goods (petrochemicals, steel), producer durables (machinery), and consumer durables (automobiles, television sets) for imports.[7] Theoretically, important substitution development is designed to protect the state's "infant industries" from international market competition until they achieve economies of scale and competitive strength (see table 1.1, type 2).[8] The state imposes high tariff barriers, import quotas, and other import restrictions to lower overall demand for imports. Through such policies, combined with vigorous regulation of foreign investment and extensive subsidies

TABLE 1.1 CONTRASTING TYPES OF INDUSTRIAL DEVELOPMENT
STRATEGIES

General Development Regimes	Examples
Inwardly Oriented Regimes	
1. Relatively closed economies with tight restrictions on trade and foreign investment	Burma (1962) Sri Lanka (pre-1976) USSR (pre-1986)
2. Highly protected economies, using administrative restrictions on imports, high tariffs (resulting in overvalued exchange rates), or both, but with attempts to promote development with some foreign investment capital	South Korea (pre-1962) India (pre-1991) Singapore (pre-1964) Taiwan (pre-1958) Brazil (pre-1964) Thailand (1971–1980)
Outwardly Oriented Regimes	
3. Export promotion, particularly for industrial products, but considerable use of protection and of government control of the economy	Japan South Korea (1962) Brazil (1964) Yugoslavia (1964) Hungary (1968) Thailand (1980)
4. Highly open economies with little protection against imports and few restraints on foreign investment, with little government intervention to limit poverty or guide investment, with considerable domestic intervention for social objectives	Hong Kong Chile (1973) Singapore (1967)

Source: Adapted from Sheahan, *Alternative International Economic Strategies,* 5; World Bank, *China: External Trade,* 4; idem, *The East Asian Miracle,* chap. 3.

for domestic industry, the state thus protects the national industries' monopoly of the domestic market. The overvalued exchange rate makes export activities unprofitable and enables the state to import industrial production technology and equipment for targeted industrial sectors. Unencumbered by international and domestic competition, these targeted industries produce goods for the domestic market that previously were imported. In essence, the state depends on the international marketplace in the short term to achieve autonomy or self-reliance in the long term.

An outwardly oriented regime is the second general type of development regime adopted after the late 1950s (see table 1.1, types 3 and 4). An outwardly oriented regime is based on Ricardian theories of comparative advantage and the Heckscher-Ohlin approach to international trade. Theoretically, developing countries enjoy comparative advantage in labor, land, or both and thus expand production of labor-intensive commodities for the domestic and export markets. Lacking capital and entrepreneurial ability, developing countries increase imports of capital-intensive products and progressively lift many protectionist barriers to foreign direct investment. Eventually, such countries adopt a more equitable pricing system for production inputs, reduce high exchange rates, and eliminate certain protectionist quotas and nontariff barriers.[9] Several economies, including Japan, Indonesia, Malaysia, Thailand, Taiwan, Hong Kong, and Singapore, took the further step of implementing an export-promoting strategy that regarded exports as the major engine of growth. They established various positive incentives to expand foreign trade (type 4), including export processing zones.[10]

While their overall goal is to promote economic growth, the two development regimes are based on two fundamentally different Weltanshauungs. An inwardly oriented regime is designed to strengthen the state's independence from the international economic system, which is chaotic and promotes inequality. By eliminating discriminatory measures against exports and foreign investment, an outwardly oriented regime promotes a greater integration with the international economy, which is considered a partner in development.

Alternate Explanations for an Inwardly Oriented Development Regime Choice

To understand Chinese foreign economic policy during the pre–1978 period, this study first analyzes why China, like so many other developing countries in the 1950s, adopted an inwardly oriented regime. Economic explanations for regime choice focus on the role of the market, which can either accelerate economic growth rates or suppress indigenous economic forces. Political explanations focus on the nature of power in the international system and the state's ability to pursue its interests. The latter, neorealist approach is the most appropriate explanation for China's development regime choice in the early 1950s.

ECONOMIC EXPLANATIONS FOR AN INWARDLY ORIENTED DEVELOPMENT REGIME

Neoclassical economists, who strongly adhere to theories of comparative advantage, emphasize the role of nonmarket forces in the choice of inwardly oriented strategies.[11] Such nonmarket forces must also include economists themselves, whose theories of the early 1950s and 1960s were based on "a mixture of touristic impressions, half-truths, and misapplied policy inferences" that contributed to an overemphasis of the infant-industry argument.[12] Therefore, in the 1950s many Latin American, South Asian, and Central and Eastern European economies implemented import substitution strategies that entailed the substitution of nondurable consumer goods and their production inputs. These economies continued to intervene in the marketplace by "deepening" the import substitution strategy to include the substitution of intermediate goods and other durables. Thus private entrepreneurs were unable to respond to international market demands to promote a transition to an outwardly oriented development regime.

According to another view, there is a discernible sequence of development strategies among the high-growth Asian economies; this sequence was first experienced by Japan from the 1870s to the 1920s. Reflecting their colonial past, many Asian economies initially were exporters of primary products; the Asian economies subsequently promoted inwardly oriented strategies of import substitution, which eventually were discarded in favor of outwardly oriented development.[13] Import substitution thus is considered a precondition for an outwardly oriented regime, whose adoption is hastened by higher domestic demand brought about by a more productive agricultural sector.[14]

An alternate economic explanation emphasizes the detrimental social and economic costs of comparative advantage. The Latin American school of development criticized primary-export-led growth strategies for condemning developing countries to languish perpetually in the periphery. Their growth stagnated because of weak international demand for raw materials and foodstuffs and the inability of international prices for primary products to keep pace with the manufactured import prices. Over time, countries relying on primary exports are unable to afford manufactured imports, and this inability in turn leads to underdevelopment.[15] During the 1950s, the UN Economic Commission for Latin America and the World Bank counseled developing countries to eschew primary-export-led growth and adopt an import substitution growth strategy.

POLITICAL EXPLANATIONS FOR AN
INWARDLY ORIENTED DEVELOPMENT REGIME

Such economic explanations fail to consider the influence of the international environment—especially the development of the Cold War—on the policy makers' decision to implement an inwardly oriented development regime. Certain international relations theorists, most notably Kenneth Waltz, argue that the international environment is the primary variable affecting foreign policy formation. They criticize subsystemic levels of analysis—such as domestic determinants (national styles, geographic position, the state, the bureaucracy) and decision-making theories (psychological approaches)—as "reductionist" approaches that do not possess sufficient explanatory power.[16] Systemic explanations thus focus on the general interactions between states, especially among the major players.

Two contending models have recently dominated the systems literature in the United States: neoliberalism and neorealism.[17] Neoliberals believe that states are constrained from military conflict by an increasingly complex web of regimes promoting cooperation.[18] Such views readily explain outwardly oriented development strategies—such as those adopted by Hong Kong, Taiwan, and South Korea—and help us to understand China's experimentation with outwardly oriented development strategies in the 1980s. Yet the low degree of interconnectedness between China and the world economy makes the neoliberal explanation for pre–1979 Chinese foreign economic policy inappropriate.[19] While initially imposed upon China, this low degree of interconnectedness became an idealized goal of Chinese policy makers, who feared systemic manipulation.

The second systems approach—neorealism—maintains that the world system is anarchic.[20] States pursue their self-interest by taking advantage of a public good (peace or free trade); such pursuit oftentimes results in major military or economic conflicts, such as World War II or the economic trade wars of the 1930s. Faced with such systemwide disturbances, the developing countries must adapt. To prevent increased interdependence whose asymmetrical structure would have a detrimental effect on their sovereignty, developing countries protect their economies by adopting inwardly oriented strategies—such as import substitution. By becoming more self-reliant, developing countries strengthen their chances of survival in the anarchic world.[21] This neorealist approach is the most appropriate explanation for China's initial adoption of the inwardly oriented development regime.

The first important case suggesting this hypothesis occurred during the early years of the new Soviet state. Following the conclusion of World War I, the victorious Western allies attempted to eliminate the Bolshevik threat to Russia and the rest of Europe. After expelling foreign forces, the Soviet leadership insured economic self-sufficiency by nationalizing the means of production, collectivizing the agricultural sector, using the Party to mobilize the state, and engaging in rapid industrialization.[22] Between 1921 and 1930, Soviet leaders, lacking finance capital, signed more than three thousand agreements with foreign capitalists ranging from Julius and Armand Hammer's Allied American Corporation to Germany's Junkers-Werke. By financing technology imports and transferring the most up-to-date Western technology, these foreign concessions became the essential component of the Soviet Union's initial import substitution development strategy. Western capitalism thus enabled the radical transformation of the Soviet Union's agricultural, industrial, and petrochemical sectors.[23]

During the 1930s and 1940s, systemic disturbances also disrupted economic relations between the major poles and the independent, developing states, especially in Latin America. With the severe systemic disturbance caused by the Great Depression, the economic trade wars of the 1930s, and World War II, Latin American countries could not import consumer and capital goods from their traditional European markets. These developing states thus turned to the United States to import the machinery and technology that could produce goods previously imported.[24] After World War II, the Latin Americans incorporated the inwardly directed import substitution program into an overall economic development regime.[25]

Many of the new, developing states established after World War II also resorted to inwardly oriented development as a result of the systemic disturbances occurring in the 1940s and 1950s. World War II accelerated the dismantling of the colonial system maintained during the nineteenth and twentieth centuries by the Europeans and the Japanese, who could no longer afford or were forced to relinquish their colonial possessions. Decolonization established myriad new, developing nations in Asia and Africa; these nations were concerned primarily with attaining political and economic power to guarantee their national sovereignty. Realizing the self-help nature of the international system and the necessity for sustained economic growth, developing countries signed bilateral and multilateral defense treaties or cooperative economic arrangements with a particular pole or sought collective support from other nonaligned states.

Such arrangements were crucial for the new economies in East Asia, which became involved in the systemic conflicts resulting from the transition to the new bipolar system. After June 1950, the Korean and Chinese civil wars were transformed from relatively contained, nationalist struggles into hostile, systemic struggles between the United States and the Soviet Union. Emerging from their colonial relationship with Japan and facing threats from the bipolar powers, the Koreas, Taiwan, and China became reliant on the two superpowers to reassert their nationalist political control and rebuild their war-torn economies.

The South Koreans and Taiwanese sought refuge with the United States, which extended comprehensive military protection to each ally through bilateral security treaties. In addition to military aid, the United States also provided extensive economic aid as well as access to the U.S. market, which was especially important for both the Taiwanese and South Korean economies emerging from fifty years of Japanese rule. During this colonial period, Taiwan and Korea had undergone primary-export-led growth by "venting" their surplus of primary goods, and thus more efficiently employed greater amounts of land and labor.[26] Embroiled in the titanic struggle between the two superpowers, the newly decolonized economies reestablished economic sovereignty by replacing primary-export-led growth with acceleration of national industrialization. Enjoying full access to U.S. technology and economic aid, Taiwan and South Korea thus adopted the Listian solution of substituting imports with domestic manufactures during the 1950s.[27]

Following in the footsteps of the late industrializing states,[28] Taiwan and South Korea initially concentrated on the domestic production of nondurable consumer goods, such as clothing and other textiles, that required limited capital investment and technology. Protected behind a wall of tariffs, quotas, and exchange controls, national producers enjoyed a monopoly in the domestic marketplace but were unable to expand exports.[29] This initial stage of import substitution undoubtedly diversified the structure of domestic production, increased the efficient use of abundant labor resources, promoted the diffusion of technology and management techniques, and encouraged domestic entrepreneurs.[30] Although a stepchild of the bipolar conflict, import substitution development provided Taiwan and South Korea with the industrial and managerial basis for their "outward leap" in the late 1950s.

This brief survey of the Soviet, Latin American, Taiwanese, and South Korean developmental experiences suggests that China's adoption of an inwardly oriented development regime was directly influenced by the bipolar conflicts of the Cold War period. One year after Mao Zedong stood atop Tiananmen's Imperial Gates and proclaimed the establishment of the People's Republic of China in October 1949, the Party was entering a particularly crucial period. While eradicating Nationalist forces on China's periphery, the CCP also stabilized the economy devastated by decades of civil war, the war against Japan, and hyperinflation. During this critical period of political and economic weakness, the Chinese became entangled in the Korean War. Following its formal isolation from the world capitalist marketplace for strategic goods, China adopted an inwardly oriented development regime—just as the Soviet and Latin American economies had during previous systemic crises.

Subsystemic Explanations of Chinese Foreign Economic Policies

The previous systemic argument remains the best explanation of China's initial foreign economic policies.[31] However, as the international environment changed after the mid 1950s, many of the East Asian economies—including South Korea and Taiwan—experimented with outwardly oriented strategies that treated foreign trade as an engine of growth. South Korea and Taiwan, along with other like-minded East Asian economies, grew "more than twice as fast as the rest of East Asia, roughly three times as fast as Latin America and South Asia, and twenty-five times faster than Sub-Saharan Africa."[32]

China did not enjoy such spectacular growth rates in part because the leadership did not follow the "Asian" path of outwardly oriented development. Between the 1950s and 1970s, China expanded its exports abroad and even considered following its Asian cousins along the outwardly oriented development path. At other times, China enacted a more extreme form of inwardly oriented development. Not until after 1979 did Chinese leaders take their first genuine steps toward outwardly oriented development by beginning the integration of China's coastal regions with the global economy.[33]

Why did the Chinese follow such a circuitous path of inwardly oriented development? Simply stated, there was a difference of opinion.

Measures to Analyze the Antinomy of Chinese Development (Dependent Variable)

To understand the dynamics of China's pre-1979 policies, one must differentiate between individual inwardly oriented strategies. To measure inwardly oriented development, economists normally have focused on the levels of protective tariffs, import quotas, and exchange rates.[34] In his 1992 study, Lardy primarily focused on four key measures of the Chinese import substitution strategy:

A centralized organization of foreign trade. The goal of the Ministry of Foreign Trade and its Foreign Trade Corporations was to finance a consistent supply of imports used "to overcome bottlenecks due to limited domestic production capacity," especially in the heavy industrial sector.[35]

An import pricing policy. Up to 1964, the state reduced the price of imported producer goods to facilitate import substitution project imports. After domestic producers began to provide the Chinese market with such goods, the pricing on competitive imported goods was practically doubled to protect domestic interests after 1964.

Stringent exchange controls and an overvalued exchange rate. The overvalued renminbi (RMB) reduced the cost of imported goods while it discriminated against Chinese exports. The Chinese continued to manipulate exchange rates for various imported goods, allowing some imported goods—for instance, goods ordered by the military—to continue to enjoy lower domestic pricing.

Foreign trade composition. The Chinese primarily imported produce goods such as "machinery and equipment, industrial raw materials and intermediate goods such as steel, [which] were critical to China's industrialization drive," although they did import grains in the early 1960s to relieve the famine situation.[36]

Using such measures, Lardy concurred with the World Bank and other economists that China adopted an "extreme example of import substitution" up to the late 1970s.[37]

Lardy's analysis can be further refined to distinguish between import substitution and semiautarkic strategies. Because they share the same overall goals of self-reliance and rely on similar protectionist policies, both strategies belong within an inwardly oriented development regime. However, they are fundamentally two different strategies within the same inwardly oriented development regime, especially their interpretation of self-reliance. With import substitution development, self-reliance is considered a long-term goal achieved by a planned import program; semiautarkic strategies achieved self-reliance in the shortest time possible with minimal foreign market interaction.[38]

Based on the works of Skinner and Winckler as well as Alexander Eckstein, this study has identified two instruments—remunerative-administrative and normative-administrative—that Chinese elites used for resource mobilization and allocation.[39] These two instruments are useful to distinguish between import substitution and semiautarkic development strategies.

Administrative methods are the basic bureaucratic tool used by policy makers in command economies. With state ownership of the means of production, policy elites formulate overall development plans that establish broad goals and quantitative targets. To meet plan goals, elites use administrative methods—ranging from bureaucratic fiat to negative sanctions—to regulate production inputs and output and prices in order to restructure economic sectors. Administrative techniques were first introduced in the early 1950s to the foreign economic sector, as the Chinese nationalized export industries and centralized foreign economic decision making. With the replication of Soviet planning systems in the early 1950s, Chinese policy planners formulated their First Five-Year Plan (FFYP) according to Soviet principles of "material balancing,"[40] including payments in kind for the massive importation of turnkey equipment, technical plans, and advice from the Soviet Union.

Yet Chinese planners learned that purely administrative measures were neither reflective of Chinese realities nor always effective in achieving economic growth.[41] In their search for supplementary tools of resource mobilization and allocation, policy elites—especially the technocrats and economists—championed a combination of administrative tools of mobilization and more market-oriented, remunerative measures.[42] Remunerative measures use material incentives—increases in wages, prices, privileged access to materials—to motivate producers. Thus in addition to the administrative instruments (prioritizing export production, establishing export production zones), Chinese elites increased state procurement prices of export goods and instituted various bonus schemes aimed at individual producers and state enterprises. The implementation of remunerative-administrative policies indicates a solid measure of the policy elites' acceptance of a relatively mixed, command economy. Thus elites acknowledged the logic of comparative advantage by advocating technology transfer and used market-oriented incentives to finance such imports.

Beginning in the mid-1950s, Mao Zedong discarded the Soviet ideal of balanced growth and market-based incentives to embrace more normative measures that mobilized the people's sense of nationalism and Communist ideals.[43] Mao criticized the Soviet model for its overemphasis on heavy industry, "technology and technical cadre."[44] Most important, Mao criticized Stalin for "his distrust of the people. . . . They believe technology and cadres decide everything. They emphasize specialization but not redness, cadres but not the masses. All these show that they walk on one leg only."[45] According to Mao, the Soviet Union did not "put politics in command and the mass line" but "one-sidedly stresses personal material interests, advocates material incentives, and promotes individualism."[46] Material incentives should not be directed to the individual, but "should be discussed in terms of collective interest, in terms of subordinating personal interests to collective interests, transient interests to long-term interests, and local interests to interests of the whole."[47]

Mao thus proposed a more balanced approach: "walking on two legs."[48] According to this Chinese version of "a thousand points of light," the Chinese people were "the determining factor in doing things."[49] With the proper indoctrination, the people could overcome any development obstacle.[50] They could be mobilized to pursue the national good and eschew all sense of self-interest. Market-oriented incentives were vestigial—and dangerous tools. Victory over capitalism lay not in selfish material interest, but in the mass line. Once harnessed, Chinese productive energies would break the chains imposed by Soviet-styled central planning and grow "more, faster, and better" than any other economy in the capitalist or socialist worlds (see chapter 2).

Although still dependent on the Soviets for large machines, precision instruments, and military technology, the Chinese increasingly could rely on themselves to foster economic development after the mid-1950s.[51] Arguments subsequently were proffered to adopt more autarkic policies, in which foreign trade was not eliminated but reduced to play a comparatively minor role. While debate and experimentation occurred during the GLF, elites eventually adopted a semiautarkic version during the Cultural Revolution: necessary imports, such as certain key raw materials or advanced military technology, could be financed with exports achieved through normative-administrative measures, such as the reemphasis on meeting planning targets, institution of widespread campaigns, and sloganeering. The implementation of such normative-administrative policies thus provides a reliable measure of the policy elite's acceptance of a relatively pure, command economy—one that did not need extensive foreign trade because it had already achieved a basic degree of self-sufficiency as well as one that used nonmarket, normative means to encourage the fulfillment of state quotas.

Based on these augmented measures, this study grossly categorizes Chinese economic development into the following periods:

1950–1958: large-scale import substitution based on the remunerative-administrative model

1958–59: proto-experiment with semiautarkic development strategy emphasizing normative-administrative tools while continuing an import substitution strategy

1959–66: period of small-scale import substitution relying on remunerative-administrative tools

1966–71: period of semi-autarkic development emphasizing normative-administrative means

1971–75: revival of large-scale import substitution based on the remunerative-administrative model

1975–76: attempted return to normative-administrative approaches to semiautarkic development

1976–78: period of large-scale import substitution that reaffirmed remunerative-administrative measures

1978–82: proto-experiment with an outwardly oriented regime while continuing a smaller-scale import substitution strategy[52]

Not surprising for a command economy, administrative means of resource mobilization and allocation dominated all eight periods. During periods of import substitution development, elites placed primary emphasis on remunerative means to augment administrative means; during periods of semiautarkic development, normative means augmented administrative means.

The elite leadership used the proto-experimental periods of 1958–59 and 1978–82 to test elements of the new strategy. During these initial experiments, elites evaluated and debated the results—such as a semiautarkic strategy after 1956 or an outwardly oriented strategy after 1978. The results of these debates did not guarantee the adoption of the new strategy. Semiautarky would not be fully implemented until the Cultural Revolution and only partially resurrected in the mid-1970s. Despite severe criticism, the majority of elites approved the initial experiments with outwardly oriented policies in the late 1970s–early 1980s; thus the new development regime was gradually adopted.

While grossly simplifying the political process, such periodization is a useful academic tool to describe the antinomy of Chinese development policy.

However, the periodization should not imply that Chinese politics was dominated by zero-sum games.

Explaining the Antinomy of Development:
An Opinion-Group Approach

Harry Harding has identified eight distinctive, subsystemic approaches that could
be used to analyze the changing role of foreign economic policy. The eight models can be divided into two subsystemic levels: the domestic environment level
(structural, normative, bureaucratic, generational, factional, and interest-group
approaches, which are mostly concerned with state structures); and the decision-making level (Mao-in-command and tendency approaches, which are concerned with the opinions and idiosyncrasies of the individual decision maker).
In addition, the public-choice approach provides another possible explanation
for the antinomy of Chinese development.[53]

Assuming that Chinese policy elites enjoyed both autonomy to formulate
development policy and the capacity to implement specific policies during the
pre-1979 period,[54] this study focuses on three possible explanations at the
decision-making level of analysis: a public-choice approach, Mao-in-command
approach, and the opinion-group (tendency) approach. The study argues that
the antinomy of Chinese development strategies was the result of differences
in opinion among the policy elites concerning China's best strategy to achieve
self-reliance.

PUBLIC-CHOICE EXPLANATIONS

The public-choice model, which has been developed by neoclassical economists
and game theorists since the 1950s, has dominated recent discussions in international political economy and influenced the Asian studies literature.[55]
Individuals are considered to be rational, rent-seeking egoists who eschew the
pursuit of the national good to pursue self-aggrandizement.[56] The national good
is compromised by individual leaders and policy elites pursuing their self-interested goals (the predatory state) or by distributional coalitions (the factional state).
Their "rational" rent-seeking activities often result in "irrational" policies that
inhibit national economic development by preventing the economy from adapt-
ing to new changes and reallocating resources.[57] Applied to the Chinese situation, the antinomy of development strategies resulted from policy elites pursuing
selfish interests or the detrimental influence of distributional coalitions.

A growing number of iconoclastic social scientists have leveled various attacks
on the public-choice approach, which often is described as the newest irrele-
vant fad in political science and one that lacks empirical testing.[58] Merilee Grindle
and John Thomas specifically argue that the public-choice approach cannot

describe or explain decision making in developing countries,[59] where policy elites retain a significant degree of policy autonomy. Unlike their U.S. counterparts, they define the policy agenda, debate the appropriateness of possible reform strategies, and make the final decision. In the case of China, the 1949 revolution dismantled Chinese distributional coalitions; the Party thus enjoyed autonomy until the decentralization policies reempowered regional coalitions in the 1980s.

As for arguments of a predatory state and self-interest, Chinese policy elites obviously were motivated to gain and maintain power; rent seeking is thus a credible explanation for behavior of elites confronted with overwhelming political opposition. Yet elites are not always motivated by self-interest; altruism can also be a motivation.[60] An ardent revolutionary fervor inspired the first generation of PRC elites, who were fully committed to establishing a strong, Communist nation. After the mid-1950s, they disagreed over the best methods to achieve the public good, based on their different life experiences and beliefs. Choosing their battles wisely, key elites expressed opposing views whenever the ruling elite lost legitimacy. Otherwise, to survive, they bent in the wind like a blade of grass on the top of a wall.[61]

Thus during periods when ruling elites lose legitimacy, the self-interest of opposing political elites (to gain and maintain power) can coalesce with the public interest (to establish a strong, independent nation).[62] "The Prince" will always desire to gain and maintain power. The key is to understand the background and differing experiences of the Prince to discover why he or she champions a particular policy path.

MAO-IN-COMMAND INTERPRETATIONS

Another possible explanation for development policy antinomy focuses on the nature of the Chinese leadership. Frederick Teiwes represents a zero-sum-game approach to Chinese politics. One player's gain is another's loss; interrated games result in one dominant player.[63] According to this Mao-in-command interpretation, elite political "games" were concluded by 1949. The sole "winner"—Mao Zedong—was the uncontested, preeminent leader of the Communist Party. As the ultimate arbiter of elite policy disputes, "the Great Helmsman" was solely accountable for the PRC's major political, economic, and social policies. Thus, Mao logically would have been responsible for China's inwardly oriented development regime, including the cycling between import substitution and semi-autarky.[64]

Such focus on Mao's preeminent role provides a parsimonious explanation for development strategy formation for the period up to 1956, the Great Leap Forward, and the Cultural Revolution. During these periods, Mao indisputably held power over the fate of millions—including the ruling elites. Yet the command school's interpretation of economic policy decision making is over-deterministic.

Mao-in-command interpretations ignore Mao's description of the 1956–57 period, during which he engaged in a strategy of "passive resistance."[65] Temporarily stymied by Zhou Enlai and Chen Yun, Mao eventually asserted his supremacy as the preeminent leader by breaking apart the Yan'an coalition and severely disciplining Zhou and others in 1958 (chapter 2). Mao subsequently implemented his vision for accelerating socialist transformation and industrialization, as well as promoting egalitarianism and self-reliance—the "general line" adopted at the second session of the Eighth Party Congress.

Secondly, Mao-in-command arguments do not give a satisfactory explanation for Mao's failure to reassume the state chairmanship.[66] In January 1958, Mao reiterated his desire first stated on 30 April 1957[67] to step down as state chairman so that he could spend full time on Party matters and for health reasons. While having previously withdrawn in 1953–54 to revise the constitution,[68] Mao by the late 1950s was attempting to promote a smooth transition of power.[69] However, Mao reminded his comrades that "in the future when the state has a critical need (*jinji xuyao*), I will reassume the duties of the state chairman as long as the Party approves."[70]

Although Mao and Chinese policy elites realized the impending economic chaos as early as October 1958,[71] Mao did not resume the state chairmanship. According to Bo Yibo, Mao criticized the other policy elites and himself at the expanded meeting of the Political Bureau at Wuchang on 21 November 1958 in preparation for the Sixth Plenum by stating,

> Under the guise of discussing ideological guidelines, we in actuality courted disaster (*wuxuming er shou shihuo*). Chairman Mao stated that he was most afraid of having committed the mistake of adventurism (*maoxian zhuyi*). Chairman Mao then made public his own views. He criticized the occurrence of "under the name of discussing ideological guidelines but in actuality courting disaster." He believed that in general everyone still did not possess enough understanding, nor grasp or skillfully operate objective laws. He furthermore stated that everyone including himself had committed a mistake of "rashness."[72]

Although implicating his fellow policy makers, Mao's partial self-criticism was one of his first admissions that the GLF was failing.[73] Conveniently forgetting that Zhou Enlai and Chen Yun had strongly opposed rash advance since 1956, Mao described "their" solution to China's development as "adventurist" and "rash"; Mao admitted that "their" stewardship over national economic policy had put the country in peril (*shihuo*).

However, having pushed aside the Yan'an coalition and assumed full control of the state and the economy, Mao was the leader responsible for implementing rash advance in spring 1958 and the subsequent deaths of millions of Chinese. As Mao stated later at Lushan,

> In 1958 and 1959, the main responsibility [for economic construction and industrial planning] was mine, and you should take me to task. In the past, the responsibility was other people's—[Zhou] Enlai, xx—but now you should blame me because there are heaps of things I didn't attend to. Shall the person who invented burial puppets be deprived of descendants? Shall I be deprived of descendants too [one son was killed, one went mad]?[74]

Faced with a potential economic disaster, Mao apparently did not desire to continue the state chairmanship. Thus by the end of the Sixth Plenum on 10 December 1958, the Central Committee approved "The Decision to Agree to Comrade Mao Zedong's Proposal That He Not Stand as the Next Candidate for the Chairmanship of the PRC"[75] and a partial readjustment of the GLF (*yasuo kongqi*),[76] including "The Resolution on Some Questions concerning the People's Communes," which publicly criticized the excesses of the GLF but not the basic spirit of the GLF.[77]

Mao made the tactical decision to retreat temporarily and was not dissuaded by the other policy elites.[78] After all, Mao had thoroughly criticized key elites who had opposed his previous attempts at rash advance in 1956, and had even forced Zhou Enlai to submit his resignation from his premiership in June 1958 (See chapter 2). While preserving Mao's reputation—and the Party's reputation—by acting as a Greek chorus of support in late 1958 and early 1959, Zhou Enlai, Chen Yun, and the other opponents of rash advance most probably were muttering "Huo gai" (Serves you right) under their breaths.

Following his partial self-criticism at the Sixth Plenum, Mao subsequently heeded the advice of his subordinates by "veering right" at the February–March Zhengzhou enlarged Political Bureau meeting of 1959. Mao asked Chen Yun to readjust GLF targets at the expanded Shanghai Central Committee meeting of March–April 1959.[79] After relinquishing the state chairmanship in April 1959,[80] Mao continued to veer right by approving regulations proposed by Deng Zihui, Li Xiannian, and Liao Luyan to allow private plots and private livestock, even though they contradicted the underlying collectivist tenets of the people's commune initiative. With Deng Zihui's assurance that such measures would not foster the development of capitalism, Mao even suggested that farmers should be given free time to devote to their private ventures.[81] Following the 15 June 1959 Central Committee meeting that criticized the GLF as unplanned and unbalanced, Mao boarded a train for Hunan to visit his boyhood home in Shaoshan, which he had not visited for thirty-two years. Like Chiang Kai-shek, who visited his ancestors' graves before escaping to Taiwan, Mao also visited his family plot, "placed the flowers on the grave, and bowed three times again."[82] Unlike Chiang, Mao quickly returned to fight the glorious fight.

As demonstrated during Peng Dehuai's failed attempts at criticism during the subsequent Lushan conference, Mao successfully maintained his mantle of preeminent leader and continued to review all documents issued in the name of the Central Committee with the support of Liu Shaoqi, Zhou Enlai, Deng Xiaoping, and Ye Jianying.[83] Yet even Teiwes concedes that "Mao often ceded to others responsibility for such specialized matters as economic planning."[84] He quotes Liu Shaoqi in 1961: "Chairman Mao concerns himself only with important state affairs. It is enough for him to propose to turn the whole country into a big garden and forestland. He has no time to solve this problem. . . . Therefore, I have to tackle it."[85]

Deng Liqun also made the comment in 1981 that "in reality, after 1958, [Mao] basically paid no attention to economic work." According to Schram, Deng was arguing that Mao did not care about "economics or economic reality," but about the "political and ideological dimensions of the economic system."[86] Thus although "enthusiastically" supporting Mao's GLF vision in 1958, key elites eventually readjusted economic policy following the deaths of millions that delegitimated Mao's development path.

Zhou Enlai's speech to the November 1963 supreme state conference perhaps best explains the relationship between Mao and the key policy elites during the post–GLF period. Zhou acknowledged Mao as the preeminent leader who set the general policy—such as the Ten Great Relationships, the "general line" of 1958 promoting the Great Leap, and "taking agriculture as the foundation and industry as the guiding force of the national economy"—while Zhou and others formulated the day-to-day policies. However, the analyst needs to go beyond the rhetoric. In the next paragraph, Zhou politely infers that Mao's search for the correct path of development resulted in "some mistakes and shortcomings" and that Zhou was responsible for cleaning up the mess.[87] Having learned his lesson in spring 1958, Zhou did not confront Mao directly over policy differences. Instead, Zhou strategically took the indirect path around Mao's disastrous economic stratagems to implement his own vision of development.

Thus, the post–GLF coalition did not challenge Mao's political preeminence.[88] They continued to respect Mao's political acumen and feared Mao's retribution, which had been inflicted on Zhou Enlai, Chen Yun, Deng Zihui, and of course Peng Dehuai. They desired to project the image of a united front when confronting the massive starvation at home and increasing hostility from their former Soviet allies. However, Lieberthal argues that the chaos of the GLF and the purge of Peng Dehuai at the Lushan conference "combined to unravel the political consensus that had held the Yan'an leadership together."[89] Having learned that direct opposition would result in dismissal, Zhou Enlai and others adopted a new tactic, indirectly questioning the efficacy of Mao's economic vision as defined by the GLF by promoting an alternate path based on remunerative-administrative strategies of economic development. Although successfully promoting higher steel production targets in 1960, Mao had reluctantly retreated from the GLF strategy by the Central Committee's Ninth Plenum of January 1961, which marked the end of the Great Leap;[90] he fully acknowledged his mistake on 30 January 1962 at the Seven Thousand Cadre Conference.[91] Realizing the changing attitude of his former Yan'an coalition partners, Mao recouped his losses, chose his compromises and disagreements carefully, and began once again to build support for his vision of economic development, which he increasingly interpreted as a problem of politics, not economics.[92]

The Mao-in-command school thus cannot adequately explain why remunerative-administrative measures continued to be implemented during the early 1960s.[93] Teiwes argues that Mao dominated the decision-making process and approved the post–GLF agenda, with the sole exception of Bo Yibo's Third Five-Year Plan. Teiwes characterizes Mao as generally not "pleased" during the post–GLF period, as "brooding" and "obsessed with a negative vision of degenerating revolution."[94] Yet this analysis is contradictory. If Mao was concerned with a "degenerating revolution" and was the preeminent leader, why didn't he more actively intervene to readjust the post–GLF economic development policy?

According to Teiwes, Mao was unable to identify the basic problem of the post–GLF policies and "indicate concrete ways of applying [class struggle] to many Party policies."[95] Mao admitted that he was not an economist[96] and was a "complete outsider when it comes to economic construction, and [understood] nothing about industrial planning."[97] Yet Mao was not oblivious to the political change in development approach. Assuming that Mao continued to be guided by the same ideological ideals that he championed during the socialist transformation period of the 1950s and later promoted during the Cultural Revolution, Mao must have recognized that the post–GLF coalition had reversed the GLF's normative-administrative approach in order to implement a "nefarious plan to dissolve the socialist economy and restore capitalism."[98] Reflecting on the series of agricultural, industrial, and other regulations drafted by January 1962, Mao stated,

> All these draft regulations have already been implemented or are being experimented with; they will be revised in the future—*some may have to be greatly revised.* . . . We must properly summarize experience and formulate a complete set of general and specific policies and methods suited to our conditions, so that they may progress *along correct lines.*[99]

Mao's approval of market-oriented tools was not the result of "intellectual incoherence" but of the lack of complete control over economic development policy.

Mao needed to join with other elite coalitions to "revise" policies "along correct lines" and thus eliminate the influence of "counterrevolutionary classes."[100]

Mao did not remain on the sidelines for long. He first focused on his primary policy concern—agriculture. While acknowledging the need to rectify his faults, Mao criticized the agricultural policies pursued by Liu Shaoqi, Zhou Enlai, Chen Yun, Deng Xiaoping, Peng Zhen, and others.[101] Mao's intervention eventually resulted in the revision of the Articles on the Agricultural People's Communes—which prevented the implementation of the household contract system—at the Tenth Plenum of the Eighth Party Congress in 1962.[102] While unable to prevent the adoption of the Seventy Articles of Industrial Policy, which promoted a remunerative solution to jump-start industrial growth,[103] Mao used rectification campaigns such as the Socialist Education Movement and the Four Cleanups after 1963 to discredit the remainder of the post–GLF policies and to promote his vision of development.[104]

To effect such change, Mao joined forces with two separate coalitions.[105] Mao sought support from Lin Biao and the People's Liberation Army (PLA) to block the initial draft of the Third Five-Year Plan and to adopt a more autarkic growth strategy (chapter 4). With the additional help of Jiang Qing's coalition, whose mission was to prevent the reemergence of a bourgeois culture, Mao achieved a full consensus over policy by 1966. Mao subsequently abolished the vast majority of the post–GLF development policies in order to reinstitute his normative-administrative approach.

Finally, the command school's explanation of the post-1971 period is also problematic. Although Mao continued to maintain his undisputed position as the preeminent leader, MacFarquhar argues that Mao's inability to detect Lin Biao's treachery resulted in a "disillusionment" that reached far beyond the Party elite.[106] In a situation somewhat similar to the late 1950s, Mao asked Zhou Enlai to reassume responsibility for the nation's economic development; Mao also approved the rehabilitation of some of the post–GLF coalition—including Deng Xiaoping and Chen Yun. Subsequently, the post–GLF coalition eliminated many of the normative policies of the Cultural Revolution.[107] During his remaining years, Mao became preoccupied with his succession, and thus issued fewer economic policy initiatives. According to his personal physician, Li Zhisui, Mao's rapidly declining health kept him from carrying out his preeminent leader's role during his last years.

A recent variant of the command school—at least in its discussion of the pre-1966 political system—is Avery Goldstein's application of systemic international relations theory to explain Chinese elite politics from 1949 to 1979. Ironically, Goldstein uses the most damning neorealist epithet—reductionism—to criticize available theories on Chinese domestic politics. Yet from a neorealist's point of view, Goldstein has committed the same sin by studying a subsystemic phenomenon—Chinese domestic politics. Nonetheless, Goldstein conducts a fascinating intellectual exercise that aptly describes certain elite dynamics of the pre-1966 and post-1966 era.

Unfortunately, his characterization of pre-1966 political dynamics as dominated by a hierarchical power structure in which consensus or "bandwagoning" takes place after debate is not reflective of the current wealth of information available to researchers. In the short term, bandwagoning certainly took place; it was a natural survival strategy for all members of the Chinese elite—including Mao Zedong.[108] However, Chinese policy elites did not change their basic Weltanshauung whenever they lost a debate. From spring to early winter 1958, Zhou Enlai praised rash advance in order to survive. Yet during the spring and early summer of 1959, after 1960, and after 1971, Zhou continued to promote the kind of planned and balanced development that he had advocated in the mid-1950s. While carrying out a policy of passive resistance during the 1956–57 period and in the early 1960s, Mao continued to refine his particular development strategy by focusing on energizing the mass line. Thus, Goldstein's "systemic" approach is an overdeterministic interpretation that fails to explain the continuity and evolution of elites' views on development.[109]

In summary, these zero-sum-game interpretations of Chinese elite politics oversimplify policy making during the Maoist period. While avoiding a crude, utility-maximizing analysis of the public-choice approach, they overpredict the effect of Mao's influence on policy formation during periods when Mao did not want to be in absolute command, especially in economic policy. Nor do they explain how policy elites who differed with Mao were able to enact their policies.

THE OPINION-GROUP (TENDENCY) APPROACH

A synthesis of the public-choice and Mao-in-command approaches suggests a third interpretation.[110] Mao Zedong and other policy elites enacted policies for the public good (strong, independent country) that in the long term ensured their self-interest (maintenance of power). Yet their disagreement over the means to achieve the public good resulted in a shifting among policy elites that in turn created a cycling of development strategies.[111]

Opinion-Group Approaches in Analyzing China. Attainment and maintenance of power is undoubtedly the underlying motivation of all decision makers, whether they be the Prince, Harry Truman, or Mao Zedong. Grindle and Thomas agree that policy elites "incorporate the concerns and orientations of a particular regime and are concerned to ensure its survival through their actions."[112] Yet elites are not pure utility maximizers, but leaders pursuing their perception of the national good. The primary variables affecting policy decisions are the "prior experience in the problem or area, professional expertise in a particular discipline, personal values, ideology or study, debate, and discussion among a group of individuals concerned with similar issues."[113] To understand the policy-formation process, the analyst must focus on the preferences and belief systems of the policy elites.

In advocating an opinion-group analysis of the Soviet policy process, Griffiths suggested that a decision maker's policy preferences result "partly in the structure of the environment in which the individual is embedded, and in reference to which he assesses the consequences of a given allocation."[114] Grindle and Thomas's emphasis on revealing the "embedded" preferences of individual decision makers adds a new twist to the opinion-group approach to politics, which focuses on informal groupings of people who are treated

> as sets of individuals who share common attitudes but who may or may not purposely be acting in concert. Concerted action is bound to occur, but its character is largely hidden, making it difficult to determine whether we are dealing with an aggregate, a loose coalition of like-minded actors, or the parallel unilateral articulations of virtually atomized individuals.[115]

In the China field, the opinion-group model has focused on the differing elite perceptions concerning the correct path of economic development. The model has included refined derivations of the Chinese two-line-struggle model, such as William Joseph's "veteran revolutionaries" and "cultural revolutionaries,"[116] as well as complex models advocated by Oksenberg and Goldstein (militant fundamentalists, radical conservatives, eclectic modernizers, and Westernizers), by Jacobson and Oksenberg (cosmopolitans and nativists), by Solinger (radicals, bureaucrats, and marketeers), by Harding (utopianists, developmentalists, and liberals; moderate reformers and radical reformers), by Van Ness and Raichur (Stalinists, social mobilizers, and market socialists), and by Yan Sun (affirmers, developers, and negators).[117]

Whether the models deal with two, three, or four contending opinions, their basic common denominator is the "Communist dilemma" first analyzed by Richard Lowenthal in 1970. Basing his arguments on the experiences of three underdeveloped Communist states—the Soviet Union, Yugoslavia, and China—Lowenthal argued that the elites' reliance upon "economic man" to accelerate the country's modernization inherently contradicts their second goal of cultivating "Communist man" to achieve a classless society. In 1970, Lowenthal predicted that the recurring policy conflict eventually would result in "the victory of modernization over utopianism."[118] Oksenberg praised the approach in 1987, describing it as "approaching the data with a dynamic model in mind, informed by historical and comparative perspectives."[119] Given the fall of the Soviet Union and the Eastern European Communist states as well as China's implementation of "market socialism," it seems appropriate to revisit Lowenthal's ideas.

Building upon Lowenthal's 1970s thesis and the Grindle and Thomas argument, this study argues that elites held divergent views on inwardly oriented growth and that these views were derived from the elites' previous experience with the capitalist marketplace. There was widespread agreement within the policy elite that China should pursue an inwardly oriented development regime, whose main goal was to achieve self-reliance.[120] Yet after China had undergone large-scale import substitution development during the FFYP, some Chinese elites—led by Mao Zedong—began to question this path based on the Soviet experience. Mao blazed a new path of development embodied in the Great Leap Forward and its emphasis on mass mobilization.

Mao subsequently joined with Jiang Qing's and Lin Biao's elite coalitions to promote a semiautarkic development approach that relied on Communist man. Advocates of this normative-administrative approach to development posit categories similar to Lowenthal and Harding's "utopians," Joseph's "Cultural Revolutionaries," Van Ness and Raichur's "social mobilizers," Jacobson and Oksenberg's "nativists," Yan's "negators," and Oksenberg and Goldstein's "militant fundamentalists" and "radical conservatives."[121] During their formative years, these policy elites had limited knowledge of the outside world, including in-depth knowledge of foreign economies. Despite their fascination with and increasing knowledge of the world outside China, many elites remained fearful of foreign exploitation and maintained a pessimistic if not hostile attitude toward the international environment.

As previously argued, Mao believed that China should primarily depend on its own capabilities and not on foreign assistance. Following the West's refusal to return Germany's Shandong colonies to China, Mao argued in July 1919 that China's salvation lay with the "Chinese people [who] possess great inherent capacities!"[122] As for Western technology, Mao argued in 1956 that Western "imperialism wants to keep its technology secret. No imperialism has ever designed anything for us."[123] The Chinese people were the key. The revolutionary experience in the Chinese countryside—especially in Yan'an—had taught them the importance of motivating Communist man as the primary means to develop China in an adversarial world.[124] Based on their personal experiences, Mao and others believed that their parochial approach to development was the most genuine Chinese path to self-reliance; they condemned the economist's manipulation of financing and planning schedules because in reality they did not understand it.[125]

Lewis and Xue argue that Mao Zedong's resentful attitude toward the Soviet Union in the 1950s was applied to all potential foreign allies, who were considered "competitors, not equals."[126] Thus when Nie Rongzhen reported in 1960 that the Soviets were refusing to provide China with technical help, Zhou Enlai responded by stating that China should turn to the West; Mao Zedong responded by stating that China should follow the true Leninist path of self-reliance.[127] In 1964, Mao further stated, "We cannot develop technology by taking the old road followed by foreign countries. We cannot crawl behind every step of other people."[128] Mao was not rejecting foreign technology, as some of his elite coalition colleagues did, but deploring the slavish attitude of the Chinese people toward foreign countries and technology. To Mao, the true source of technical innovation lay within Chinese people themselves; they were the key to developing a strong, independent China.

Whiting succinctly describes the Maoist desire of not "compromising social goals in order to maximize economic goals" in his 1979 study of turnkey plant imports during the 1970s.[129] Large-scale import substitution programs had several liabilities, such as the subversive influence of foreign technical advisors on Chinese soil, historical resentment of the reliance on foreigners to develop China, and the extensive costs of such turnkey plant imports on China's independence of the global community. In summary, Whiting argued that "these factors make foreign trade a potentially contentious topic from a political as well as an economic point of view."[130]

In stark contrast to such parochialism, after the late 1950s, elites who adopted a more remunerative approach to Chinese development called for a continuation of an import substitution strategy and the development of a mixed form of command economy.[131] Theirs was a more "pragmatically flexible" approach that promoted technological advance by importing foreign technology and equipment. Most of these elites also shared the Yan'an experience with Mao and hoped to build a classless society by mobilizing the masses. Yet they believed that such a utopian goal must gradually be achieved through a systematic process that in the interim must rely on remunerative-administrative tools. These policy elites to a qualified extent are similar to Lowenthal's "technocratic developmentalists," Harding's "developmentalists and liberals," Joseph's "veteran revolutionaries," Van Ness and Raichur's "Stalinists" and "market socialists," Jacobson and Oksenberg's "cosmopolitans," Yan's "affirmers" and "developers" and Oksenberg and Goldstein's "eclectic modernizers" and "Westernized Chinese." Many of the Yan'an "alumni" had studied or worked in a foreign capitalist environment whether abroad or in China. From personal experience, they learned not to fear economics and technical expertise, which must be utilized to achieve a modern socialist state.[132]

Marilyn Levine and others have documented the experiences of Communist elites who went to Europe and Asia during the 1920s.[133] They were a transitional generation who had witnessed the failure of the previous political order and were searching for the one road of national salvation. Initially placing their hope in Western technology,[134] many discovered Marxism as the one true road.

The shared experience of studying and working abroad undoubtedly influenced Communist elites such as Zhou Enlai, Zhu De, Deng Xiaoping, Li Fuchun, Nie Rongzhen, and Chen Yi. Not only did they form lasting bonds of friendship, but they also developed an understanding of the international political and economic systems.[135] Others such as Chen Yun gained extensive knowledge about the market economy from their experiences in preliberation Shanghai.[136] During his student days at the Communist University of the Toilers of the East (Moscow), Liu Shaoqi led the "practical workers," who emphasized practice as opposed to ideology and theory.[137]

These elites thus were more flexible in their views of China's development path than others in the leadership and championed both normative-administrative and remunerative-administrative tools to encourage China's economic growth.

Problems with the Opinion-Group Approach. The opinion-group approach does have certain inherent problems.[138] Referring to Parris Chang's *Power and Policy in China,*[139] Teiwes and Sun criticize the Orthodox "two-line struggle" approach as "generally suffer[ing] from superficial research" resulting in "descriptive rather than truly analytic" prose.[140] Teiwes and Sun thus have been motivated by "a certain frustration with the residual influence of the 'two-line struggle' model which we had hoped to demolish in various earlier works."[141]

However, opinion-group approaches should not be randomly categorized as adhering to Chen Boda's October 1966 views of the "two-line struggle."[142] Ironically, the two-line struggle is more similar to Mao-in-command interpretations. Adhering to classic zero-sum-game interpretations, both misrepresent Mao's role during the post–GLF period. Analysts today—including proponents of coalition politics—agree that Mao was never displaced as the preeminent leader and the symbol of Party legitimation.[143] Yet as previously argued, the Mao-in-command school does not fully account for Mao's limitations before the GLF or his frequent political disengagement after the GLF.

When viewed from a non–zero sum game perspective,[144] Mao was the preeminent leader, but not always engaged in the policy-making process. Elite coalitions, though powerful, could not exist independent of Mao. Thus, Mao and the top elites at various times compromised, co-opted, or sought stronger coalition allies to achieve their development vision. When viewed from a short-term perspective, such dynamics give the impression that the views of Mao or the top elites were contradictory or incoherent;[145] a longer perspective reveals certain underlying continuities.

This study's variation of the opinion-group approach could also be criticized as similar to the Chinese Communist *chengfen* analysis: one's class background forever will determine (one's) relationship to society. Such a dogmatic analysis fails to appreciate political expediency. While never directly confronting Mao, Chinese elites used different survival strategies during the GLF and the Cultural

Revolution.[146] Thus, the opinions of policy elites can be tempered by political circumstance (i.e., political survival). Grindle and Thomas agree that policy elites can be influenced by "societal pressures and interests, historical and international contexts, domestic economic realities, and bureaucratic capacity and compliance" and thus are not completely autonomous.[147] The analyst needs to investigate various factors that influence perception, including professional training and bureaucratic position, that produce similar perceptions of the state's goals. Opinion-group explanations need not be tautological if the analyst attempts to uncover the underlying influences on perception and then tests those findings against alternate policy explanations.

Unfortunately, the greatest problem in analyzing the "complete" Chinese policy maker is the continued lack of substantial information concerning personal background and perceptions. Analysts rely on autobiographical and biographical works,[148] various chronicles (*nianpu*) of the top elites,[149] collected speeches and writings, and Red Guard materials (see appendix A for a more complete discussion). Yet most sources fail to provide complete evidence linking opinions and beliefs to concrete policy actions.[150] While Bo Yibo's autobiography is a priceless analysis of one key economic policy maker's perceptions, the other biographies and chronicles greatly vary in quality. Li Zhisui's biography is limited by his professional position as Mao's physician, his close connection with Wang Dongxing,[151] and his inability to rely on his original journal entries. Ruan Ming's short account of the pre-1979 era is from the perspective of a theoretician outside the inner elite circles.[152] Internal journals such as *Dang de wenxian* often publish official documents and fascinating analytical analyses, whose sources are difficult to confirm. Finally, the Red Guard materials can be extremely enlightening, but also extremely biased. While more comprehensive than the newly issued volumes of Mao's *Collected Works,* the much heralded *Post-1949 Manuscripts of Mao Zedong* oftentimes only provides outlines of Mao's most significant speeches.[153]

This lack of primary sources seriously hinders a comprehensive testing of any approach, including an opinion-group approach. Thus, this study must rely primarily on the actual foreign economic policies and secondly on the collected works and biographies to infer how various groups shared particular opinions on development. Complete testing of the opinion-group model is thus deferred until more information is available.

The Cycling of Inwardly Oriented Development Strategies

Chinese elite coalitions coalesced around contending views of inwardly oriented development, which resulted in a cycling between semiautarkic and import substitution strategies during the 1960s and 1970s. The cycling of inwardly oriented development affected overall Chinese development and delayed the experimentation of a more outwardly oriented approach until the 1980s.

Discussion of the Theory of Cycles

Social scientists have been fascinated by the conceptualization of grand theories. Theories about cycles and trends are especially tempting because they describe and explain underlying causes that have determined world history and offer credible predictions of future world events in a fairly parsimonious fashion. Thus, there are economic theories propounding Kitchin inventory cycles lasting two to three years, Juglar business cycles lasting six to ten years, and the famous Kondratieff long cycles lasting forty to sixty years.[154] International relations and international political economy theorists have also proposed various cyclic theories, many of which eschew complicated subsystemic explanations.[155]

The Chinese were probably the first to philosophize about cycles, which have influenced political conduct and historical analysis since the Early Han.[156] Reportedly with Mao's approval, Lin Biao grafted the classical dynastic cycle argument onto Marxist dialectics.[157] Hua Guofeng linked the famines of 1960 with Liu Shaoqi and Deng Xiaoping's revival of agrarian capitalism. Mao's death on 9 September 1976 was directly linked to the horrendous Tangshan earthquake of 28 July 1976.[158] Even in the 1990s, Chinese ranging from bus drivers to secondary school teachers adhered to the concept of "great chaos leading to great order." Although premature, many Chinese thus believed that the catastrophic flooding in the summer of 1994 portended Deng Xiaoping's imminent demise.[159]

Cycle theory at the systemic level exaggerates the influence of the cycle or trend on national actors and unduly discounts the influence of other domestic determinants, such as elite conflict and bureaucratic foul-ups, on the decision-making process. Theorists working on the systemic level subsume inconsistencies in their pursuit of grand theory and avoid alternative explanations.

Economists, sociologists, and political scientists writing in the West have concentrated on more subsystemic catalysts for Chinese cycle theories. In analyzing the relationship between the Chinese elites and the peasantry, Skinner and Winckler "construct[ed] separate cycles for goals, power, and involvement, and then superimpos[ed] these cycles in order to study the pattern of coincidence among them." They determined that between winter 1949 and fall 1965, eight compliance cycles were completed; each cycle was composed of six specific phases: normalcy, mobilization, high tide, deterioration, retrenchment, demobilization.[160] While such meticulous categorization helped to differentiate individual cycle phases, the overall approach lacked parsimony.

Economists often have focused on variations of Chinese business cycles to analyze China's economic growth and have been particularly effective in analyzing and measuring cycle dynamics. Imai Hiroyuki has identified several different business cycle theories proposed by economists that have been applied to China. Alexander Eckstein adopted a harvest policy cycle, whose expansion period was initiated by good harvests and brought to a halt by either a poor harvest or excess demand for resources.[161] Barry Naughton applied Kornai's work on Eastern European centrally planned economies to focus on the demand for consumption goods. Imai's model incorporates both the demand for consumption goods and the role of exogenous factors such as harvest failures to explain nine Chinese business cycles since 1955.[162]

With the exception of Imai, these theories underemphasize politics as an exogenous influence on the investment cycle. Political scientists such as Lowell Dittmer, Sam Crane, and Susan Shirk focus on the relationship between economic and political cycles.[163] Others such as Richard Baum and Lucian Pye have analyzed the roles of either the elites or political factions on cyclic change.[164] Alternatively, the opinion-group version of Chinese cycle theories focuses on Weltanshauung. Chinese elites coalesce around a shared view of a particular policy path, yet their opinions are not necessarily put forward in a concerted fashion. In describing the "Communist dilemma," Lowenthal argued that all Communist systems are faced with a conflict between the competing goals of modernization and utopianism. Lowenthal argued that "throughout the history of these indigenous Communist regimes a kind of natural alternation in which periods of revolutionary upheaval are followed by periods of consolidation and economic progress, and these in turn by new revolutionary upheavals, though the alternation does not seem regular enough to be meaningfully described as cyclical."[165]

Lowenthal was not convinced that the antinomy of development goals produced cyclical changes of policies. Yet several political scientists using the opinion-group approach have subsequently uncovered evidence of such cycles; the most articulate has been Dorothy Solinger.[166] In analyzing Chinese commercial policies since the 1950s, Solinger argued that Chinese elites coalesced around three competing Weltanshauungs. She observed a policy cycling during which "bureaucratic approaches have repeatedly been followed by marketeer policies, which were then succeeded by radical initiatives. These in turn have been righted (in a double sense) by a return to bureaucratic modes."[167] In a separate study, Solinger outlined cycle dynamics; following the center's promulgation of a particular policy, self-interested actors at the grassroots who "are in general agreement with the aims of the policy" implement the policy.[168] Yet implementation is complicated by various

excesses and conflicts [that] in turn produced economic and social effects that central-level policy-makers could not fail to note. . . . No doubt at times negative social and economic feedback from a currently-pursued tendency provides those supporting a tendency that was out of favor with an opportunity to push their own policies. In other instances, it may be the case that the majority of the leadership as a whole finds such feedback a sufficiently significant trigger that a near consensus can be reached to shift policy back toward one of the other two tendencies.[169]

Solinger thus envisioned a continuous policy loop, in which negative feedback—or chaos—during policy implementation initiates policy readjustment or even legitimization of a new "winning" coalition.[170]

Thus, the opinion-group approach provides a strong justification for a cycling of Chinese policies. Lowenthal's theory can accurately describe and explain the antinomy of the modernization and utopian approaches in foreign economic policy; in retrospect, it accurately predicted the eventual predominance of the modernization view. Expanding on Solinger's work, this study further argues that the alternation of approaches is regular and measurable.

Characteristics of Chinese Crisis Cycles

No matter how enticing the explanatory power, cycle theories must be thoroughly tested. In the mid-1970s, Andrew Nathan criticized the derivative nature of Western cycle theories, which he believed reiterated the Chinese Manichean view. To justify the downfall of Chinese elites such as Liu Shaoqi, Maoist polemicists oftentimes interpreted Chinese post-1949 politics as a zigzag "struggle between the two classes, the two roads and the two lines."[171] Nathan feared that Western cycle theories continued to impose this superficial view of the development process, which he characterized as a learning model in which policy options were "so multiform and complex that the choices are really more than two, and might best be regarded as infinite."[172] While Winckler ably responded to Nathan's various criticisms,[173] current cycle theories must take advantage of the greater variety of available policy documents and the four and a half decades of Chinese policy change to heed Nathan's call to analyze the dynamic learning aspects of the Chinese policy process.

Speaking in 1963, Zhou Enlai observed that China had experienced three policy stages (recovery, development, and readjustment) since 1949.[174] Using an opinion-group approach, this study builds on Zhou's observations to hypothesize that these policy stages were components of a larger policy cycle. Each cycle was initiated by the perception of crisis—hence the term, "Chinese crisis cycles." The perception of crisis not only spurred policy makers to change current policies, but also to experiment with new and innovative policies, many of which were improved versions of past initiatives.

THE PERCEPTION OF CRISIS

Pye and Solomon argue that the fear of chaos is a uniquely Chinese phenomenon, resulting from the need of consensus and the existence of factional conflict.[175] Yet policy makers in the developed and developing world fear that any crisis will devolve into chaos. Neo-Marxists and statist advocates have argued that crisis is often the catalyst for major public policy changes, especially in developing countries.[176] According to Grindle and Thomas, crises involve all the top policy elites, who are pressured to enact dramatic change to prevent total political or economic disorder. Consequently, they often adopt innovative reforms that can change the basic direction of the state.[177]

East Asian economies often reacted to impending economic crisis by changing development regimes and strategies. Kent Calder argues that crisis has been the primary catalyst for "domestic, non-industrial innovation in Japan . . . rather than the routine lobbying of corporatist interest groups (either business federations or labor unions) or even the strategic planning of the state." Citing previous works in the American and European fields, Calder argues that crisis was a major catalyst for change in highly bureaucratized, developed economies, "such as France, China, and Japan in the postwar period, [when] institutional conservatism often inhibit[ed] major innovation in the absence of crisis."[178]

For the most part, the conservative nature of Chinese and Japanese policy makers compels them to avoid chaos. Tsou Tang thus has defined crisis in the Chinese policy process as "denot[ing] dangers so imminent or problems so pressing as to raise the question of survival, and which in the view of a group of people are beyond their ability to avert or resolve by means of their usual ways of thinking and acting."[179] Yet in light of the positive role crisis can have in the policy process, Tsou Tang's definition needs a small refinement. Dorothy Solinger points out that the Chinese compound characters for crisis (*weiji*) includes the character for peril (*wei*) and the character *ji,* which can be interpreted as opportunity. The threat of crisis facing Chinese elites in the late 1970s "legitimated the rejection of past [development] strategies, admission of their failure, and . . . one could say even pressed . . . political elites to unify around a new policy, a major economic shift."[180] Thus, any crisis can pivot favorably and result in an improved situation; just as easily, any crisis can devolve into utter chaos (*luan*)—a condition in which the political order and stability of the country is under threat (Tsou's "total crisis").

Chinese policy makers have not needed Western pundits to reveal the positive aspects to crisis. In discussing the need to recentralize the material management system in the early 1960s, Li Xiannian questioned whether the recentralization would cause an economic crisis. Admitting that a certain degree

of chaos was inevitable, Li also argued that "through chaos order will be achieved
(*youluan daozhi*)."[181] During the Cultural Revolution, Mao Zedong used crisis
to route out all "capitalist demons" from the Party, the government, and among
the people; in his infamous talk of August 1967, Lin Biao argued that "chaos is
necessary and normal."[182] Thus, elites have used the perception of crisis and
impending chaos as a policy tool to effect drastic policy changes within China,
including the replacement or elimination of particular leading Party elites.

The perception of crisis and the appropriate policy response was dependent
on the Weltanshauung of particular Chinese elites. Those elites who championed
a more remunerative-administrative approach to development measured crisis
in terms of concrete economic performance indicators and the Party's control
over the economy and the state. In 1959, the GLF crisis subsequently led to Mao's
temporary retirement to the second line in economic policy making. The threat
of a military putsch and the death of Lin Biao allowed Zhou Enlai to gain greater
control over economic policy after 13 September 1971, while the possible
revival of the chaotic Cultural Revolution enabled Hua Guofeng, Ye Jianying,
Li Xiannian, and Wang Dongxing to arrest the politics-in-command coalition
in 1976. Persuaded by Deng Xiaoping and Chen Yun of impending economic
chaos, Chinese elites lost confidence in Hua's new Great Leap Forward. Hua
was ousted and the new elite approved the Eight-Character Plan to readjust the
Chinese economy.[183]

Proponents of normative-administrative approaches viewed chaos from a
Maoist ideological point of view. While they championed "economic marvels"
such as Dazhai, Maoist ideologues were not as concerned about concrete economic performance data and efficiency. To paraphrase Deng Xiaoping, adherents to a Maoist approach did not care if the cat could catch the mouse as long
as the cat was the right color—red. Thus by 1966, Mao convinced the military
and the Party that the remunerative policies of the post–GLF coalition had infected
the top Party echelons. In 1974–75, the politics-in-command coalition used similar fears of capitalist revival to criticize the "new Confucius"—Zhou Enlai—
and his anointed successor, Deng Xiaoping.

THE POLICY READJUSTMENT PHASE

This perception of economic or ideological crisis marks the beginning of the
policy readjustment (*tiaozheng*) phase of the Chinese crisis cycle. Solinger
defined economic adjustment in terms of a specific industrial policy that was
adopted between 1979 and 1982, while this study looks at various instances of
economic readjustment implemented over time and is not restricted to industrial policy.[184] Prybyla's differentiation between socialist economic reform and
adjustment does not adequately reflect the intricacies of the Chinese policy-
making process.[185] Prybyla's definition of adjustment appropriately describes

the changes in policy necessary to implement economic reform, yet does not consider the policy adjustments necessary to initiate economic reform. Several Chinese sources see a more intimate relationship between the two concepts, with adjustment being the core of the reform process.[186]

During the readjustment phase of the Chinese crisis cycle, the new elite coalition adopts certain emergency measures to reduce the most adverse effects of the previous strategy. Proponents of the remunerative-administrative approach focused on emergency economic measures. Liu Shaoqi and the post–GLF coalition enacted a series of economic emergency measures after the spring of 1959 to counteract the GLF, although they did not completely readjust the GLF strategy until 1961 because of the fallout proceeding the Lushan conference. After assuming control in 1976, Hua Guofeng took a little more than one year to readjust the economy following the abortive coup of the politics-in-command coalition. At the 1979 April Work Conference, Li Xiannian announced that the readjustment period would take at least three years, during which time there would be readjustment of the economic plan, "proportional imbalances," and Hua's large-scale import substitution program (chapter 7).[187]

During the readjustment phase of the Chinese crisis cycle, proponents of the normative-administrative approach focused on mobilizing the Party and the masses to identify "wrong thinking." Beginning with the Four Cleanups in 1963 and culminating with the Cultural Revolution in 1966, Mao Zedong initiated a series of campaigns to renew a socialist ethic among the people, especially by emulating the PLA's devotion to Mao Zedong Thought. These campaigns were an implicit attack on the policies of the post–GLF Party leadership and the state bureaucracy, which by the later stages of the Cultural Revolution were discredited, suspended, or eliminated.[188] Jiang Qing and the politics-in-command coalition used similar campaign methods in the early and mid-1970s to attack Zhou Enlai and Deng Xiaoping's development approach.

While carrying out emergency measures to counteract potential political or economic crisis, any new elite coalition used the readjustment phase to build consensus within the coalition and the Party.[189] Contending elites during the 1977–78 period were engaged in extensive private conversations and letter writing to build a consensus within the Political Bureau (chapter 7). Once achieved, the coalition used work conferences, the Party plenum, and the expanded Party plenum to persuade other Party elites within the Central Committee that the previous development strategy would result in political or economic chaos—or both. If successful, the contending coalition gains political legitimacy and the right to eliminate previous policies. This new consensus would be transmitted to the Party's grassroots organizations, which in turn used a corrupted, top-down version of the mass line approach to mobilize the people.

Consistent with the non–zero-sum interpretation of Chinese politics, delegitimation was not always comprehensive or conclusive. Tsou Tang argued that Mao's domestic and foreign policy failures of the late 1950s

> produced not only criticisms of these policies but also a questioning of specific elements of Mao's thought. . . . The doubters of Mao's thought also resorted to the method of verbally reaffirming its validity but refusing to be guided by it in practice. . . . The dissidents tried either to insulate certain areas of activities from the influence of the ideology or even to establish therein values and norms not in harmony with the Maoist doctrine.[190]

Despite such doubts, elites never completely criticized Mao or the GLF in the early 1960s. According to William Joseph, elites feared that such criticism would threaten the Party's overall legitimacy.[191]

In light of Joseph's explanation, the post–GLF coalition's attempt to implement the Four Modernizations development approach in 1963–64 failed because of the post–GLF coalition's inability to discredit Mao's development approach (See chapter 3). During the 1971–73 period, Joseph argues, the contending elite coalition—the "Cultural Revolutionaries"—prevented the "veteran revolutionaries" from completely vilifying the Cultural Revolution; during the post-1976 period, Hua Guofeng's "Whatever" faction initially prevented Deng Xiaoping's "Practice" faction from declaring the Gang of Four as ultraleftists.[192] The opinion groups' inability to delegitimate an opposing development strategy is indicative of the non–zero sum game dynamics of pre-1978 Chinese politics.

POLICY INNOVATION PHASE

Having initiated the readjustment of the previous development strategy, the elite coalition entered the second phase of the Chinese crisis cycle: policy innovation. During this second cycle phase, the new elite coalition rallies support for a new or revised development strategy based on a shared philosophy of establishing a strong, self-reliant country.

Reflecting their concern over concrete economic results, the adoption of a remunerative-administrative approach is usually marked by impressive programs presented by the Party as new, innovative economic initiatives. Thus during an early 1963 visit, Zhou Enlai promised to transform Shanghai into the leading center for Four Modernizations reform by liberalizing local foreign technical and equipment imports (chapter 3). By the September 1963 Central Work Conference, Zhou had gathered sufficient support to present his Four Modernizations strategy, which offered an alternate path to the GLF by envisioning a modernized industrial economy by the end of the century. Zhou Enlai also rallied support for his large-scale import substitution plan (the 4-3 Plan), which was first outlined publicly in January 1973. On 18–23 February 1978, the Central

Committee approved Hua Guofeng's Ten-Year Plan for Developing the National Economy, which was more grandiose than the development strategy of Zhou Enlai announced five years before. During the following spring and summer, the post–GLF coalition gained initial support to experiment with outwardly oriented development.

In contrast, elites promoting a normative-administrative approach to inwardly oriented development cared little about new economic programs. They desired to develop a revolutionary praxis that would eliminate false consciousness. Following the Great Leap, the basic framework of development was embodied in Mao Zedong's writings, which had been popularized in the "Little Red Book." Having co-opted or eliminated the post–GLF leaders and policies, the adherents of the normative-administrative approach used the Cultural Revolution to transform Maoist theories into a Maoist praxis. The masses were urged to study Marxism–Leninism–Mao Zedong Thought at all times of the day so that their thoughts and actions harmonized with a Maoist revolutionary praxis. Once achieved, the masses would realize the correctness of the Maoist path of development.

POLICY IMPLEMENTATION PHASE

The third phase of the Chinese crisis cycle, policy implementation, is the most complicated. Both the normative-administrative and the remunerative-administrative approach employed campaigns to encourage producers to fulfill and exceed state procurement quotas or to energize Communist man to produce more for the collective good. Lieberthal argued that the large nationwide campaigns of the 1960s and 1970s had primarily "sociopolitical" objectives, such as those championed by proponents of the normative-administrative approach.[193] Yet, no matter the type, campaigns were unable to overcome several implementation problems.

The development strategy itself might create long-term economic disruption, such as the GLF disasters. Policy implementation can also generate ideological opposition—such as Mao's objections to the post–GLF policies or Jiang Qing's objections to Zhou Enlai's policies of the 1970s. Although the ruling elite coalition might adopt interim policy readjustments (policies that Prybyla defined as economic adjustments), their intervention might not prevent contending elite coalitions from fostering a growing perception of economic or ideological crisis. If contending elites are successful, the growing fear that the crisis could lead to widespread chaos delegitimates the ruling elite coalition. At this point, the Chinese crisis cycle renews itself.

There is an intimate relationship between the process of implementing policy and the decay of elite coalitions. Policy elites enjoyed both autonomy and capacity to formulate and implement foreign economic policy during the pre-

1979 period. However, the central government's authority was not absolute during that entire period. The actions of Chinese bureaucracies, regional distributional groups, and local Party officials undoubtedly influenced the policy formation process, but eventually any policy could be overridden by Mao, the Party, or the central government. While discussing the 1959 foreign trade plan, Li Xiannian admitted that certain central bureaucracies and localities had changed the plan without consultation. Li reasserted that only the Ministry of Foreign Trade and its associated departments—with approval of the Central Committee—had the right to formulate the foreign trade plan. He stated that "one department cannot revise the plan on its own. Whenever a situation arises in which a department revises the plan on its own, comrades in the various provinces can refuse to implement it."[194] And of course, Mao eventually used the PLA to contain and dissemble the Red Guards during the Cultural Revolution.

Research of post-1979 foreign economic policy also indicates that a key intervening variable affecting implementation was the decentralization of power. While providing Guangdong and Fujian Provinces with greater autonomy after 1979, Beijing was constantly dealing with bureaucratic or regional distributional coalitions that delayed policy implementation or distorted policy intent. Likewise, local Guangdong Party officials approved thirty-seven compensation trade agreements in 1978, even though Hua Guofeng had blocked their authorization in State Council document 78.139 (see chapter 7). Rent-seeking behavior brought about a crisis in development strategies in late 1981, resulting in a policy readjustment and a split within the post–GLF coalition.[195] Such behavior did not suddenly appear after 1978.[196]

Until more-substantial evidence can be discovered, this study will continue to assume that the pre-1979 policy elites enjoyed autonomy in formulating and the capacity to implement a coherent foreign economic policy. Thus, Party elites during the pre-1979 period were able to counter regional or bureaucratic distributional coalitions' attempts to influence the policy process.

Conclusion

To summarize, World War II and the subsequent bipolar conflict compelled many developing economies, including Korea, Taiwan, and China, to adopt an inwardly oriented development regime during the 1950s. To reduce dependence on the international market, developing countries engaged in large-scale import substitution that promised to reduce long-term dependence on foreign imports and to encourage domestic growth. Less dependence empowered decision makers from Asian and African countries that were struggling to dismantle their colonial economic structures and assert sovereignty.

Initially facing extreme systemic pressures from the United States and the

United Nations, China adopted a large-scale import substitution development strategy. Foreign training and the importation of turnkey plants, equipment, and technological information provided China with the basic tools to establish a strong, self-reliant economy, which was a source of economic and political power.

While the international environment continued to determine the general parameters of Chinese foreign economic policies during the 1960s and 1970s, Chinese elites determined the specific development strategy and its foreign economic policy component. China was a "strong" state, whose leaders enjoyed both autonomy and capacity to implement their vision of inwardly oriented development. However, the state's ability to prevent self-interested behavior at the lower levels did not preclude conflicts within the central Party leadership. The differing beliefs and experiences of the twenty-five to thirty-five top policy elites[197] within this strong state resulted in a growing disagreement after 1956 about the correct path of economic development and the formation of opinion groups that coalesced around a particular view of development. Disagreements among these opinion groups over the best path to self-reliance condemned China to a cycling within the inwardly oriented development regime between import substitution and semiautarkic strategies beginning in the early 1960s.

CHAPTER 2

Antinomies of Chinese Development, 1949–1958

The major systemic changes caused by World War II and the subsequent bipolar conflict compelled the Chinese policy elites in the early 1950s to adopt an inwardly oriented development regime. China subsequently engaged in one of the largest import substitution programs to be carried out by any developing country. The success of its First Five-Year Plan (1953–57), which mandated inwardly oriented development based on capital-intensive industrialization, accelerated China's progress toward self-sufficiency. China thus became less vulnerable to international pressures generated by the bipolar conflict.

Yet by the mid-1950s, systemic constraints on Chinese foreign economic policy diminished as Western Europe, Japan, and to a lesser extent the United States, altered their economic embargo on mainland China. The international environment—principally the continuation of U.S. Cold War policies toward China—defined parameters that limited the choices opened to Chinese policy makers. Yet such systemic variables were not the primary influence on Chinese policy makers' choice of specific inwardly oriented development strategies and their foreign economic policy components during the next two decades. Instead, the primary influence was the increasing division among the elites concerning China's correct path of development.

China's Adoption of an Inwardly Oriented Development Regime, 1949–1956

The Early Period of the PRC-Soviet Economic Relationship

The Chinese Communist Party looked upon the Soviet Union as its major source of economic materials, financing, and inspiration even before the Korean War. In July 1946, two months after the Soviets had completed the wholesale dismantling of the vast Manchurian infrastructure during their 1945–46 occupation, the newly "liberated" areas of northeast China undertook trade discussions with the Soviet Union.[1] Overcoming Soviet anxieties about "foreign relations problems" and the trade mix, the Chinese Northeast Trade Corporation began

TABLE 2.1 VALUE OF NORTHEAST REGION IMPORTS, 1947–49
(dongbeibi, 100 million)

	1947		1948		1949	
	Amount	%	Amount	%	Amount	%
Cotton yarn and cloth	31.756	65.2	47.892	41	5.301	29.3
Silk, wool, linen	2.298	4.7	7.440	6.4	.527	2.9
Oils	4.099	8.4	13.746	11.7	1.220	6.7
Telecommunication	1.119	2.3	16.656	14.2	2.246	12.4
Metals and products	.327	0.7	7.107	6.1	1.506	8.3
Machinery	.149	0.3	2.406	2.1	.112	0.7
Medical equipment	.374	0.76	3.811	3.2	1.315	7.2
Rubber shoes etc.	1.003	2.04	5.702	4.9	1.649	9.1
Paper products	1.735	3.5	3.858	3.3	.521	2.8
Chemicals	.977	2.0	3.856	3.3	2.436	13.4
Food and beverages	1.826	3.8	2.062	1.7	1.178	6.5
Other	3.052	6.3	2.390	2.1	.134	0.7
Total	48.715	100	116.926	100	18.145	100

Source: *Shangye hezuo cankao cailiao,* [Reference materials on commercial coopera-
tion] (Liaoning: Liaoning Danganguan Dongcai Dongcaiwei Dangan, n.d.) v. 581, as
cited in Meng Xianzhang, ed., *Zhongsu maoyishi ziliao,* 1991), 543–4.

in November 1947 an exchange of Chinese grains and meats for Soviet textiles
as well as industrial, military, and transport equipment, all of which were vitally
needed by China's military and civilians (table 2.1).[2]

By 1949, the new Chinese leadership was anxious to regularize its foreign
economic relations, especially with the Soviet Union.[3] Based on the successful
Sino-Soviet economic exchanges in northeast China, Liu Shaoqi outlined the
Soviet Union's crucial role in Chinese development, stating,

> It is very clear that the aid to be given by the Soviet Union, Eastern Europe
> and the proletariat classes of various countries will be very important to the
> Chinese proletariat and to China's economic development. I consider this aid
> to be in the following categories: (1) their experience; (2) technological aid;
> and (3) financing. In addition, there also must be a set amount of economic aid
> given to provide materials in certain areas. If this type of aid is sufficiently
> large enough, China can progress along the socialist road at a faster pace.[4]

"Secretly" leading a delegation that included Gao Gang (Political Bureau member and secretary of the northeast bureau) to Moscow in June 1949, Liu Shaoqi told Stalin of China's intentions not only to study the Soviet organizational, planning, and educational system, but to formalize cross-border trade. Following a month of negotiations, Liu Shaoqi signed a one-year trade agreement with the USSR's Georgi Malenkov on 30 July 1949;[5] similar exchanges took place along the northwest border in Xinjiang Province.[6] Confronted by a domestic economy weakened by decades of warfare and an increasingly hostile United States, Chinese leaders subsequently signed the Treaty of Friendship, Alliance, and Mutual Assistance on 14 February 1950 followed by several bilateral trade, investment, and financial agreements—including an agreement to provide the Soviets access to the Changchun railroad as well as the Dalian/Lüshun ports in northeast China for a limited period.[7]

To finance import needs, Zhou Enlai signed a $300 million preferential loan agreement at a 1 percent interest rate. The money was to be distributed over a five-year period beginning on 1 January 1950; repayment would begin on 31 December 1954 and be completed by 31 December 1963.[8] Chinese leaders planned to procure Soviet military hardware, electrical power stations, equipment for metal and equipment manufacturing plants, mining equipment, and railroad and other transport equipment. Stalin reportedly intervened to keep the interest payments low by ordering, "On average the interest on loans to the various new democratic countries in southeast Europe will be 2 percent. Because of the wars and economic devastation, interest on China's loans will be a bit lighter."[9]

Publicly, the Chinese stated that they had found a military and economic ally who would "act in accordance with principles of equality and mutual benefit, mutual respect of national sovereignty and territorial integrity, and noninterference in internal affairs."[10] *People's Daily* praised the one-year trade agreement for its fairness and concern for promoting Chinese development, unlike most pre-1949 arrangements, which were "exploitative tools for the imperialist colonization of China."[11] Privately, there was concern that the new agreements revived an older exploitative relationship, one that the Communist leaders from the Yan'an period had long endured.[12] Mao reportedly was upset with the overall arrangements, including the establishment of joint ventures in shipping and aviation as well as oil and ore production in Xinjiang;[13] Mao quite probably knew that China's loan was $150 million less than the credit line Stalin granted to Poland in 1949.[14] Chinese nationalists were also upset. In an internal Party directive dated 30 March 1950, Liu Shaoqi reported that

the news of the Sino-Soviet signing of the two joint stock company agreements involving Xinjiang petroleum and nonferrous metals has caused a very great commotion among Beijing students. They are suspicious that the two agreements might harm China's sovereignty. Many Youth League members are raising doubts and difficult questions for discussion. They have asked for an explanation. Some even have cursed Soviet aggression and the traitorous People's Government, while others preferred to tear up their Youth League membership than submit to the will of the People's Government.[15]

Such nationalistic concerns—which border on xenophobia—foreshadowed problems encountered not just with the Soviets after 1956, but also with China's interactions with the world during the following decades, such as the 1999 bombing of the Chinese embassy in Belgrade.

The Effect of the Korean Conflict on China's Development Strategy

THE IMPORT SUBSTITUTION STRATEGY AND "LEANING TO ONE SIDE"

After branding China as an aggressor state in the Korean conflict, the United Nations imposed an embargo on strategic exports in May 1951. Subsequently, the North Atlantic Treaty Organization (NATO) states (minus Iceland) and Japan formed the China Committee (CHINCOM) within the Consultative Group Coordinating Committee (COCOM) to impose stricter limitations on Western trade with China and North Korea than that imposed on other Soviet-bloc countries.[16] The United States, the primary initiator of the embargo, established a more draconian embargo of both strategic and nonstrategic goods to China.[17] To guarantee the embargo's effectiveness, the United States linked trade restriction compliance to the Marshall Plan funds received by fourteen Western allies.[18] Although these restrictions were partially lifted by the mid- to late 1950s, their influence had a profound effect on China's foreign economic policy.

Zhou Enlai and the Government Administration Council (the forerunner of the State Council) had already discussed the reduction of trade with the United States as early as August 1950. Zhou urged a greater centralization of foreign economic policy and a renewed emphasis on foreign exchange. Zhou argued that the state had to intervene in the leasing of foreign ships to export agricultural goods rotting in local warehouses; the earned foreign exchange would then be used to import industrial materials.[19] He furthermore urged that the private sector should be strongly "encouraged to import automobiles, petroleum, and even railroad equipment so that such privately held capital would be guided toward developing domestic production and transport systems."[20]

Following China's intervention in Korea, the Chinese leadership consolidated its management of foreign trade under the Ministry of Trade, strengthened customs procedures, and instituted import and export licensing procedures (*xukezheng*).[21] Military units as well as large and medium-sized state and privately owned enterprises were forbidden to purchase imported materials, except under extraordinary circumstances.[22] Eventually, the Chinese leaders "eradi-

cated" Western trade and financial interests on the mainland;[23] by the mid-1950s
they had assumed complete control over all import and export activities.[24] As
Zhou Enlai stated in his political report to the third session of the Chinese
People's Political Consultative Congress presented on 23 October 1951, the
embargo actually "accelerated the process of recovering China's complete economic sovereignty."[25]

In addition to accelerating the centralization of foreign economic activities,
the Korean conflict increased the immediate need for military production technology. The Chinese leadership originally had set aside a portion of the $300
million Soviet loan to prepare an invasion of Taiwan, starting with the May 1950
occupation of the Danshan Islands east of Shanghai.[26] After the outbreak of the
Korean War, the Chinese leadership allocated an even larger portion of the original loan as well as procured entirely new loans on 1 February 1951 to finance
the importation of Soviet military production technology and military equipment, including the provisioning of sixty Chinese infantry divisions.[27]

Such efforts were crucial. Zhou Enlai later described the national munitions
industry as "not in any way able to satisfy the needs of national defense in terms
of munitions variety, quantity, and sophistication."[28] In view of the new wartime
requirements and China's inability to produce modernized weaponry or munitions, the Chinese invited a second Soviet delegation to evaluate China's military needs in the aircraft, automotive, shipbuilding, and military armaments
industries; Nie Rongzhen was in charge of coordinating planning.[29] Such efforts
undoubtedly were indispensable to Chinese successes on the Korean battlefront
and to its military modernization efforts—including the explosion of the Chinese
nuclear weapons in the 1960s.

A comprehensive understanding of the PRC's development experience thus
should consider both the military and economic import substitution projects,
especially since the Chinese and Soviet economic leaderships considered both
plans as linked to a certain extent.[30] Fortunately, Arthur Lewis and Xue Litai
have already provided in-depth studies of the Sino-Soviet strategic cooperation
during the 1950s.[31] For the purposes of this study, it should, however, be remembered that many military import substitution projects contained dual-use technology that became fundamental to China's economic development—such as
the development of the ubiquitous Liberation (Jiefang) brand trucks.[32]

It is also important to analyze the two efforts in a comparative perspective.
Although reliable budgetary figures are unavailable, the Central Committee's
policy (*fangzhen*) during the Korean conflict was "simultaneously to fight [the
enemy], stabilize [the state], and construct [the economy/culture]" (*bianda, bian-
wen, bianjian*). According to Zhou Enlai, this policy ensured that expenditures
for economic construction would always be greater than military expenditures;[33]
Mao Zedong argued for an even greater proportion of expenditures to be spent

on civilian construction in his "Ten Great Relationships" speech of 1956.[34] This emphasis on domestic economic construction has been maintained throughout the PRC's history, with the possible exceptions of the late 1957 period, when civilian technology imports were sacrificed to import nuclear technology,[35] and the Third Front period between 1964 and 1971 (see chapter 3).[36]

The final effect of the Korean conflict was to impel the Chinese leadership to seek a long-term solution to China's economic development needs. Comments made by Mao Zedong, Liu Shaoqi, and Zhou Enlai indicate that the top Chinese leadership was aware of the developmental experience of the Soviet state, which although initially isolated later gained access to foreign investment and implemented a development strategy based on import substitution. Liu Shaoqi even argued in an internal Party document in 1950 that

> to utilize foreign capital to promote China's industrialization, it will be necessary under the appropriate conditions to sign joint contracts and even concessionary contracts involving certain enterprises, joint ventures and even joint stock companies not only with the Soviet Union, but also with the newly democratic countries and even certain capitalist countries. During the New Economic Policy after 1921, several concessionary enterprises were both proposed by Lenin and established in the Soviet Union.[37]

Just as the Soviets faced the Western forces helping the White Army, the Chinese perceived threats to their national sovereignty when confronted by opposing UN forces in Korea and Taiwan as well as an economic siege imposed by the UN embargo.

It was under such international pressures that the PRC began to construct a modern Chinese economy. In early 1950, after Mao and Zhou returned to Beijing, Li Fuchun remained in Moscow to enlist Soviet economic aid by "obtaining first the [Soviet] design plans, and then and only then submitting accurate and necessary goods orders."[38] Subsequently, the Soviets signed contracts to design or renovate fifty Chinese industrial projects between 1950 and 1953, including thirty in northeast China, six within Shanhaiguan, five in Xinjiang, and one in Inner Mongolia.[39] While ordered to cooperate closely with the contracted Soviet experts who were hired to supervise various construction projects,[40] Chinese units were also required to use domestically produced materials and personnel whenever possible to reduce the high costs.[41] The Chinese leaders thus from the beginning were somewhat wary of the expense and overreliance on foreign aid; whenever possible, they desired to increase the Chinese "content" of this exchange relationship.

As in the early 1980s, "special" Chinese students, such as Zhou Enlai's adopted son Li Peng, were sent to study in the Soviet Union;[42] beginning in 1952, Chinese students, scientists, engineers, and bureaucrats were chosen based on their "political qualifications, vocational skills, and health."[43] Although unable to study abroad, Mao wrote in the early 1920s that he "advocate[d] a policy of studying abroad in a big way" and especially wanted to go to the Soviet Union because it was "the number-one civilized country in the world."[44] Having studied in Moscow before 1949, Liu Shaoqi stated that "sending [the Chinese students] to study in the Soviet Union is a form of investment. You need to invest in order to construct an industrial sector, and the very first investment is in the training of cadre."[45] Liu Shaoqi thus took a special interest in the affairs of the Chinese students sent to the Soviet Union; his son, Liu Yunruo, studied aviation electronics at the Moscow Aeronautical Institute.[46]

Yet despite the claims of socialist brotherhood and solidarity, Soviet help was not free. China was required to export to the Soviet Union various types of foods and agricultural products, mineral products, and textiles (table 2.2).[47] Following Khrushchev's suggestions, the Chinese even developed an indigenous rubber industry, which eventually was established in Hainan with the help of a 70 million ruble (old) loan from the Soviets.[48] Despite the Soviet technical aid to renovate steel factories, electrical generating plants, and even hospitals, the Central Finance and Economy Commission reported on 9 February 1952 that the northeast had "a long way to go before recovering to the levels achieved during the Japanese occupation in terms of equipment."[49] More help was needed to transform China into a strong, self-sufficient country able to stand up to the American "imperialists."

There was an initial debate whether China should follow the Soviet example of import substitution development based on importing heavy industrial turnkey plants and technology or develop light industry, which in turn would produce capital to be reinvested in the heavy industrial sector.[50] The Chinese leadership eventually decided to formulate the First Five-Year Plan based upon the Soviet import substitution development model;[51] Yeh argues that China's heavy industrial import substitution model actually was more radical because of its increased emphasis on industrial investment.[52] Such increased investment during the FFYP not only accelerated the pace of industrialization, but allowed China to be more independent of the Soviet Union by developing its own economic and military-industrial complex.[53] Implemented between 1953 and 1957, the FFYP thus authorized the importation of a large number of turnkey plants and technology from the Soviet Union; these became known as the "156 projects."

During an enlarged meeting of the Central Committee's Political Bureau in February 1951, the leadership decided to establish a six-person Small Group including Zhou Enlai, Chen Yun, Bo Yibo, Li Fuchun, Nie Rongzhen, and Song Shaowen to plan the FFYP.[54] From August 1952 to April 1953, Li Fuchun negotiated the plan's details in Moscow and invited comments from Soviet planners, who increasingly expressed their fears of Chinese impetuousness. During Zhou

TABLE 2.2 CHINESE COMMODITY EXPORTS TO THE
SOVIET UNION, 1950−52 (rubles, 1 million [1961 value])

	1950		1951		1952	
	Amount	%	Amount	%	Amount	%
Raw agricultural products	60.5	35.1	77.7	26.0	112.5	30.2
Foodstuffs	20.0	11.3	20.7	6.9	50.1	13.8
Nonferrous and alloy metals	18.4	10.7	41.2	13.8	65.8	17.7
Textile yarns, semifinished	15.3	8.9	27.2	9.1	35.0	9.4
Industrial textiles	n.a.	n.a.	3.2	1.1	13.3	3.6
Animal byproducts	9.0	5.2	15.4	5.1	28.8	7.6
Chemicals	1.5	0.8	1.1	0.4	2.1	0.6
Arts and crafts	n.a.	n.a.	n.a.	n.a.	0.3	0.1
Total	124.7	72%	186.5	62.4%	307.9	83%

Source: Sladkovskii, *Istoriia Torgovo-ekonomicheskikh Otnoshenii SSSR s Kitai*, 204, 222, 255, as cited in Meng Xianzhang, *Zhongsu maoyishi ziliao*, 582.

Enlai's visit to Moscow in September 1952, Stalin reiterated his willingness to provide China technology, equipment, and loans, but added that China's projected gross value of industrial output (GVIO) had to be reduced from 20 percent to 15 percent per year.[55] Bo Yibo reports that "although these views primarily were based on the Soviet experience, they basically were relevant to the Chinese situation at that time. We referred to their views when making a fairly substantial revision of the draft plan."[56] After readjusting certain projected rates of growth, the Chinese leadership adopted the FFYP, which devoted 50 percent of total industrial investment outlays (RMB 12.8 billion out of RMB 25.03 billion) to the import substitution projects.[57]

On 15 May 1953, the Chinese signed the agreements with the Soviets initiating one of the largest transfers of technology in history.[58] The Soviets agreed to provide China with ninety-one new import substitution projects, including large iron and steel complexes, metallurgical industries, electrical generating plants, and petrochemical, automobile, and tractor factories worth 3−3.5 billion rubles, the majority of which were imported between 1956 and 1957.[59] In this way, Mao Zedong stated, the Chinese people will, with their efforts to learn from the advanced experience and latest technical achievements of the Soviet Union, be able to gradually build up their own powerful heavy industry. This plays an extremely significant role in China's industrialization in its gradual transition to socialism and in the strengthening of the camp of peace and democracy headed by the Soviet Union.[60]

With the 50 projects agreed to during the first three-year period, the 91 projects agreed to in May 1953, and an additional 15 new industrial projects initialed during Khrushchev's October 1954 visit commemorating the PRC's fifth anniversary,[61] China signed a total of 156 import substitution project agreements by the end of 1954 (150 projects were actually constructed).[62] Although the six "people's democracies" in Eastern Europe also participated in building 68 industrial projects,[63] Zhou Enlai warned the Poles in 1955 that the Soviets would continue to be their primary foreign supplier for the indefinite future.[64] Thus the leadership signed agreements for 55 new industrial projects worth 2.5 billion rubles during Mikoyan's visit in April 1956 included in the FFYP and 78 turnkey industrial plants worth $1.25 billion during Zhou Enlai's visit to Moscow in February 1959 for the Second FYP.[65] Yet as will be described in the following section, controversy ensued over this expansion of the import substitution program.

These turnkey projects not only strengthened the civilian economy, but also enhanced military power. Of the 150 turnkey projects that actually underwent construction during the FFYP, Bo Yibo states that 44 turnkey projects expanded China's military industrial infrastructure, including military aviation (12), military electronics (10), military armaments (16), aerospace (2), and shipbuilding (4).[66] Ivan Arkhipov, who was the "manager" of the Soviet aid to China, estimated that roughly 30 percent of the 250 import substitution projects undertaken by the Chinese in the 1950s were devoted to the military sector.[67] In addition, the Chinese government sent eight thousand Chinese scientists and technicians to the Soviet Union for educational training, invited more than seven thousand Soviets to China as "foreign experts," and signed several major scientific and technical exchange agreements with the Soviets.[68] As Naughton has pointed out, this "investment in human capital [was], in some ways, even more important" than the investment in physical capital because it permeated all levels of China's infrastructure.[69]

Chinese planners hoped that this tremendous transfer of equipment and technology would reduce their reliance on foreign equipment and military arms imports from 40 percent during the FFYP to 30 percent during the Second FYP (1958–62).[70] China's dependency on Soviet and Eastern European commodities such as textiles and light industrial goods were necessary for the short term during the renovation of China's war-torn economy.[71] Yet after 1953 and China's economic recovery, planners' long-term goal was to achieve self-sufficiency in industrial and agricultural production.[72] China thus reduced imports of Soviet light industrial goods and drastically increased the importation of turnkey projects, equipment, and technology (table 2.3).[73]

The import substitution strategy embodied in the FFYP was quite successful. According to Rawski, the import substitution projects successfully produced electric locomotives at 39 percent of import cost, as well as cheaper metallurgical equipment (33 percent cheaper), railway carriages (50–67 percent), freight cars (30–76 percent), automatic blast furnaces (59 percent), coke ovens (38 percent), and seamless steel tubes (33 percent).[74] Planners thus had correctly predicted that these projects and equipment imports would "gradually establish our own formidable heavy industrial and national defense industrial sector and [have] an extremely important role in China's industrialization and progress toward socialism."[75] The import substitution program formed the backbone of China's post-1949 industrial development.[76] Naughton adds that this wholesale transference of technology and know-how contributed to an "enormous savings in time and expense" and allowed China to avoid damaging inflation and delay policy debate till the mid-1950s.[77]

MAINTENANCE OF THE IMPORT
SUBSTITUTION DEVELOPMENT REGIME

Many of the institutions and rules for China's new inwardly oriented development regime had been established by the early 1950s and remained basically unchanged until the late 1970s. Chinese leaders expanded centralized control of trade and specific import/export licensing procedures first adopted in December 1950; by the mid-1950s, private import/export firms were transformed into joint state-private enterprises, which in turn were converted into state-owned enterprises.[78] By March 1951, the Government Administration Council had also agreed upon the basic foreign economic policy direction of the state;[79] the Barter Trade Control Regulations promulgated a few days later most fully embody these principles:

> If at all possible, virtually all imports will precede exports.
>
> No favorable trade balance will be built up unintentionally.
>
> Strategic exports, if allowed to be sold to the capitalistic countries at all, will be exported only in exchange for the most essential imports.
>
> The monopolistic position of the country as a buyer or seller, as well as any temporary market advantage it may enjoy, will be exploited to the full in order to assure the country of the best terms of trade possible.[80]

Thus China used administrative measures and tariffs to restrict exports to the capitalist states,[81] while at the same time implemented a friendly foreign trade

TABLE 2.3 SOVIET COMMODITY EXPORTS TO CHINA, 1950–60
(rubles, 1 million [1961 value])

	1950	1951	1952	1953	1954	1955	1956	1957	1958	1959	1960
Machinery	37.2	98.8	140.9	145.2	179.0	206.6	274.3	244.4	286.2	537.8	453.5
Equipment sets	0.9	30.9	36.6	44.3	83.8	127.4	195.3	188.1	—	—	—
Petroleum products	8.7	33.0	25.6	36.4	35.5	58.4	64.0	68.6	69.6*	93.6*	90.9*
Rolled steel	n.a.	n.a.	n.a.	35.6	47.2	48.3	39.3	19.3	33.1	26.5	33.4
Chemicals	2.6	2.4	1.1	0.9	1.0	1.3	0.6	1.1	1.1	1.9	2.8
Paper	3.6	10.0	14.9	8.0	5.6	6.5	5.1	2.7	2.8	2.0	1.9
Cotton goods	3.6	13.3	2.9	0.4	1.5	—	—	—	—	—	—
Stationery	n.a.	n.a.	n.a.	1.9	2.7	4.2	4.5	5.4	6.5	4.9	3.6

Source: Sladkovskii, *Istoriia Torgovo-ekonomicheskikh Otnoshenii SSSRs Kitai*, 204, 222, 255, as cited in Meng Xianzhang, *Zhongsu maoyishi ziliao*, 581, 583, 585.

* Includes both petroleum and petroleum products

strategy toward its socialist brothers that sought trade balance rather than trade advantage. To offset rising international prices for necessary imports, China increased the value of the old RMB from 42,000 to the dollar set on 13 March 1950 to old RMB 22,380 on 23 May 1951;[82] the Ministries of Commerce and Foreign Trade began discussions on 29 September 1952 to raise the exchange value of the RMB even further. Private exporters were asked to export certain goods at a loss; in compensation, the state allowed them to retain a larger percentage of profits earned from imports. The higher RMB value thus allowed the Chinese to import needed technology and equipment from abroad cheaply—a prerequisite for any country implementing an import substitution strategy.[83]

Yet the Chinese were left with a high price tag for the Soviet turnkey projects and equipment imports.[84] The UN economic embargo had hindered overseas Chinese investment in China, thus contributing to a major shortage in hard currency reserves,[85] which were already low because of the Nationalists' removal of the pre-1949 reserves to Taiwan. Like many developing countries, China depended on foreign remittances as a major source of hard currencies. According to the "Report on Problems of Overseas Chinese Remittances" issued by the Overseas Chinese Affairs Committee and the People's Bank of China in 1955, between 1950 and 1954, Chinese living abroad remitted more than $600 million, which exceeded half the foreign exchange earned by trade with the West. However, "there [was] a continuous drop in overseas Chinese remittances since 1952. Receipts in 1954 were only equivalent to 70 percent of those in 1951. The major reason for the drop [was] the serious encroachment upon overseas Chinese remittances."[86] Such "encroachments," according to Wu Yuan-li in one of the first Western scholarly treatments of the post-1949 economy, included U.S. financial controls and the harsh treatment accorded overseas Chinese landlords during the initial land reform movement. Wu argued that the controls on remittances to the Chinese mainland and Hong Kong denied "up to 40 percent of the normal flow of inward remittances" to the new regime.[87] Such controls on remittances limited China's ability to finance import substitution projects. To renew the flow of remittances, the State Council thus issued an order (*mingling*) to all cadre in 1955 that they "must thoroughly understand the utility of overseas Chinese remittances and adopt the appropriate attitude."[88]

Having already assumed a long-term loan from the Soviet Union for $300 million in 1950, the Chinese again approached the Soviets for a new long-term loan;[89] the Soviets agreed to lend 520 million rubles (new) at 2 percent interest in 1954.[90] China also relied increasingly on the export of Chinese goods to pay the import bill, following the recovery of the Chinese economy and establishment of a more centralized economic planning structure. Similar to the February 1950 Soviet loan repayment terms, the 15 May 1953 trade agreement obligated China to export strategic goods such as 160,000 tons of tungsten ore, 110,000 tons of copper, 30,000 tons of antimony, and 90,000 tons of rubber as well as various foodstuffs each year between 1954 and 1959. Unable to obtain new Soviet export loans, the Chinese thus financed new import substitution projects after 1955 with raw materials and manufactured goods needed by the Soviet Union.[91]

Adoption of the Import Substitution Regime in Retrospect

The Chinese leadership considered the cost of the large-scale import substitution strategy to be worthwhile. China, like the Soviet Union in the 1920s and Taiwan and South Korea in the 1950s, was faced with severe international military and economic pressures. The UN embargo in the early 1950s had cut off normal economic interchange with their traditional Western markets. To become economically strong, China had to achieve economic self-sufficiency in the fastest manner possible. The Chinese thus turned to the Soviet Union and its Eastern European allies to implement the large-scale import substitution development strategy.

The import substitution strategy made China very dependent on the equipment, technology, and development capital of the Soviet Union in the short term. Yet Chinese leaders hoped that in the long term, turnkey plants and technology would enable China to become economically independent not only of the Soviet Union, but of the entire international market place as well.

The Debate over the True Chinese Development Path, 1956–1958

While the systemic level of analysis provides the strongest explanation for China's initial adoption of an import substitution development regime, it is less persuasive as an explanation for China's continuation of inwardly oriented development. From the mid-1950s onward, the effect of the previous systemic disturbances—World War II and the bipolar conflict—on China's economic development abated as Western Europe and Japan "defected" from the UN embargo effort. According to Alexander Eckstein, the U.S. decision to continue the embargo "circumscribed [China's] choice as to quality, models, types, and price much more than would otherwise have been the case." Yet its effect on China's overall development was minimal, except in military procurement and access to long-term credit financing.[92]

During the next two decades, the Chinese confronted several new systemic changes—a split within the world Communist movement, Sino-U.S. rapprochement, and the oil price increases of the 1970s. These changes in the international environment continued to define certain parameters (direction of trade, the foreign trade export commodity mix, and access to overseas Chinese remittances) within which China's decision makers formulated development strategy.[93] Yet subsystemic variables would primarily affect the continuation of the inwardly oriented development regime and the significant changes in Chinese foreign economic policies.

After an initial debate, Chinese leaders supported the Soviet-style large-scale import substitution development strategy as embodied by the FFYP. Yet this uniform agreement on development was short-lived. By December 1955, Mao initiated a debate on the best path toward socialist industrialization, which would bring an early end to import substitution development. Zhou Enlai, Chen Yun, and Zhu De opposed Mao's initiative and sought to continue China's economic relationship with the Soviet Union as well as build new economic and financial ties with Western market economies and overseas Chinese capitalists. By the Eighth Party Congress of September 1956, Zhou and Zhu had gained the tacit support of the other major economic policy players, including Liu Shaoqi, Li Fuchun, Li Xiannian, and Bo Yibo.[94] However, their two-pronged approach appears to have been defeated after the Third Plenum in fall 1957, when Mao began to "persuade" the key policy elites to accept the Great Leap Forward and its rash advance (*maojin*) approach to industrialization and self-reliance.[95]

Mao Zedong's Call for Chinese-Style Development

MAO'S CALL FOR RASH ADVANCE, 1955

According to Bo Yibo, Mao first questioned the Soviet model of development in 1955.[96] Bo states that

> after Stalin's death, several incidents within the Soviet Union made the Chinese Central Committee gradually perceive several problems with Stalin and the Soviet experience. These incidents included the exposure of Beria, the rehabilitation of several important unjust and faked cases, the strengthening of agriculture, the debate revolving around plans to regard heavy industry as the key, the change in attitude concerning Yugoslavia, and the rapid replacement of Stalin's chosen successors, etc.[97]

Unhappy with the low economic growth rates in 1955 and the projected growth rates, Mao rejected Stalin's path to economic development and began to promote a Chinese style from which the Soviets could learn. According to Mao, "The masses demanded rapid development."[98]

On the afternoon of 5 December 1955 at Zhongnanhai's Western Pavilion, Liu Shaoqi informed 122 Party central and military leaders of Mao's directive concerning the upcoming Eighth Party Congress. According to Bo Yibo's recollection,

Chairman Mao said: "We must use this current period of international truce and international peace to once again strive to accelerate our development and bring about the early completion of socialist industrialization and socialist transformation." *While guaranteeing the fifteen-year plan, China also must strive to exceed the goals of the fifteen-year plan beforehand.* Regarding preparations for the Eighth Party Congress, Chairman Mao proposed, "Our core idea must be to emphasize opposition to right-deviation and to conservatism." We can assume that when the day comes that we go to war, we will be faced with tremendous problems if we have not accelerated construction; affected a transformation of agriculture, private industry, and enterprises; or have not developed industry. Thus, we must be opposed to conservatism in all our work. Chairman Mao stated: "We can proceed along several paths. After comparing them, we must select the most reasonable and correct path." The conventional path takes a very long time and results in few accomplishments. This is the conservative path. Every aspect of our work is lagging behind in development. Quite a few of our comrades are taking the conservative path. Industrial sectors should not be self-satisfied, and must step on the gas. Otherwise, both flanks will be ahead of the main corps of troops, which will not be able to catch up. The objective reality of development is not balanced. Constant breaching of equilibrium is a good thing. Don't promote balance in your work. Those units that do have a problem.[99]

China could not wait for "women with bound feet" (*xiaojiao nüren*) who advocated "balanced" development, but had to take advantage of the ten- to twelve-year window of peace to develop as fast as possible.[100] Mao thus advocated that "we must hurry and achieve faster, greater, and better results in all work projects." The operative words were "faster, greater, and better"; the policy became known as "rash advance."[101]

Thus when discussing their long-term development needs with the Soviets, Li Fuchun projected that China would have a Gross Value of Industrial and Agricultural Output (GVIAO) of RMB 467.5 billion by the end of the Third Five-Year Plan (1967), which was an increase of 43.1 percent over original estimates. Instead of producing 18 million tons of steel by the end of the Third FYP, China would produce 24 million tons; instead of 650 billion *jin* of grains, China would produce 1 trillion *jin;* instead of 56 million *dan* (one *dan*=50 kilograms) of cotton, China would produce 120 million (Bo Yibo states 100 million); instead of 280 million tons of coal, China would produce 300–320 million tons of coal (Bo Yibo states 330 million).[102] By 1967, the country would eliminate illiteracy along with every living rat, sparrow, fly, and mosquito.[103]

The Soviets were dumbfounded.[104]

To prevent such rash advance, Zhou Enlai and Chen Yun agreed with Li

Fuchun's suggestion to modify Mao's initiative by adding "more economically" to Mao's call for "more, faster, and better" development.[105] Zhou Enlai also regarded the new long-range targets as "not official, and it could be said that they are not to be written in documents. It is much preferable that the numbers be low, and that you criticize me in the future as being a rightist. Backwardness is our reality."[106] By June 1956, Zhou and Chen Yun agreed to oppose rash advance directly.[107] Almost exactly two years later, Zhou was forced to submit his resignation to the Political Bureau's Standing Committee. They did not accept.[108]

Thus began the first extensive debate between the elites over the PRC's correct economic development path. Characteristic of the non–zero sum nature of Chinese elite politics, elites agreed to agree, disagree, or compromise. Unlike future differences of opinion, however, this initial debate was characterized by a relatively open exchange of ideas between elites. Western scholars supporting various interpretations already have provided in-depth analysis of the actions taken by Mao, the economic elites, and the bureaucracies.[109] This study will concentrate primarily on the fifteen-year plan to make China an industrialized state by continuing along the Soviet path of import substitution. Discussions of this long-term plan and the continuation of the import substitution development program sparked a prolonged internal debate over the import substitution development model that lasted until Mao's death in the mid-1970s.

ZHOU ENLAI AND ZHU DE DEFEND
LONG-TERM IMPORT SUBSTITUTION DEVELOPMENT

January–February 1956 was a crucial period in Chinese long-term economic planning. In light of the upcoming Eighth Party Congress to be convened in fall 1956, the top leadership was preparing China's long-term agricultural, scientific, and industrial development plans,[110] formulating the Second Five-Year Plan, and revising the 1956 economic plan.[111] Thus in April 1956 they signed agreements with the Soviets for fifty-five new import substitution development projects and initiated new discussions on long-term economic cooperation. While preparing for these plans and negotiations, Zhou maintained his stance that China could only begin to achieve scientific and industrial parity by the end of the Third Five-Year Plan—or 1967. To that end, Zhou proposed 188 new industrial projects that would need Soviet or Eastern European assistance.[112]

While agreeing that modernization could and should be accelerated, Zhou opposed Mao's December 1955 initiative to realize industrialization in the short term. More important, Zhou and others reinforced the idea that China could not finish the industrialization process by itself. While leading a Chinese delegation to Moscow in February 1956, Zhu De stated that instead of closing the door on the international marketplace, China needed to increase exports that met international demands in order to increase imports. He further criticized the autarkic vision by stating, "We don't want to close the door [on the world economy] and drive ourselves nuts with these small niceties (*xiao taotao*)."[113] Zhu De thus continued to travel throughout the country in 1956 and 1957 searching for new export sources and management methods that would increase exports, which in turn would finance the import substitution projects. In April 1957, Zhu De submitted a report to the Central Committee outlining the various problems in export production and procurement in which he stated, "Whether to serve our country's socialist construction endeavors or to strengthen international exchange, our foreign import and export work must be greatly strengthened and developed."[114]

Zhu De's interest in foreign economic policy is not surprising. Although a military man, Zhu De was part of the "international" generation; he left for Europe in 1922 when he was thirty-six. Zhu De pursued Zhou Enlai from Paris to Berlin, where Zhou sponsored Zhu De into the Communist Party.[115] Zhu De thus shared a similar international experience of the Communist movement and understanding of global economic development. He promoted greater integration with the global economy as early as 1949, when he stated that not only should "China conduct business with the Soviet Union and all democratic countries," "but also conduct business with Japan and America." "Because of the globalized nature of all production, we need theirs and they need ours."[116] This truly was a prophetic statement, and would underlie Zhu De's actions of the 1950s and 1960s.

Zhou pointedly stated his objections to Mao's vision in his political report presented to the seventeenth meeting of the Standing Committee of the Chinese People's Political Consultative Congress on 6 February 1956. According to Zhou,

> The transition period is composed of two different "transitions." One transition refers to the socialist transformation of agriculture and handicrafts as well as capitalist industry and commerce. This transformation basically can be completed within three years. Of course, this timing is much sooner than we originally had thought, and the transition will definitely not be completed within the new period. The second transition is the gradual realization of the socialist industrialization of the state. Putting the two types of transitions together constitute the total scope of the state's transition. . . . There are two types of thinking concerning socialist industrialization. One type contends that industrialization can be completed ahead of schedule; the other contends while one can expand the scale and quicken the pace, this does not constitute completing industrialization ahead of schedule. We cannot casually propose the slogan of early completion of industrialization. Very possibly, it will take longer than the three five-year plans already proposed to complete industrialization.

It is better to be prudent because we still do not grasp the [complexity] of industrialization. In order to be prudent, there is nothing wrong with maintaining our original idea of having a somewhat longer transition period. It is currently said that we have already entered socialism. This is worth thinking about, because if we have already entered a socialist stage, then we have already completed construction. In addition, if we have already completed building socialism, then we have eliminated exploitation and poverty. According to Lenin, we also will have eliminated ignorance, achieved a high cultural level, etc. Thus, China has only begun to enter socialism.[117]

Some delegates criticized Zhou's political report for not discussing the early completion of China's industrialization. Without naming Mao, Zhou characterized such proposals as "without any foundation" and "mixed up"; proponents of such an approach needed to be more realistic when it came to the actual industrialization of China.[118] Less diplomatically, Zhou directly refuted Mao's 6 December 1955 position that "it is very possible for a nation to become socialized without being industrialized."[119]

These actions do not fit with Li Zhisui's description of a weak-kneed, opportunistic Zhou Enlai or Teiwes's characterization of Zhou as practicing "careless politics."[120] This is Zhou Enlai the revolutionary, who had fought Mao in the 1930s and was now fighting for his vision of development. At the 8 February 1956 State Council meeting, Zhou agreed with Mao that socialist transformation could be accelerated. While Zhou concurred that "industrialization [could also] be accelerated, we cannot say that it can be completed earlier than planned." Slogans alone could not bring about the complicated process of economic industrialization, which required capital, technology, and expertise that China lacked.

In December 1955, Zhou initially devised an antithetical couplet describing his support of Mao's initiative: "Objective possibilities have exceeded subjective understanding; / Subjective efforts lag behind objective necessity."[121] Two months later Zhou also prescribed a solution: "Leaders have been running a fever. Let's wash their faces with cold water to wake them up a bit." To follow China's true path of development, leaders had to "seek truth from facts."[122]

A CROSSROAD IS REACHED: A CHINESE OR A SOVIET/WESTERN PATH TOWARD DEVELOPMENT?

Faced with adamant opposition to an acceleration of China's industrialization and strong support for the import substitution strategy, Mao initiated an attack on the core ideology of the FFYP, the Soviet model of development. Perhaps in this way, Mao hoped to affect the Chinese attitude toward negotiations with the Soviets on near- and long-term economic cooperation, including the upcoming import substitution agreement to be signed in April 1956. Mao thus ordered Bo Yibo to arrange for thirty-four ministries and commissions to present a general oral overview of the economy and the FFYP from 14 February to 22 April 1956.[123] Eleven days into this process, at the Soviets' Twentieth Party Congress, Nikita Khrushchev delivered his secret denunciation of Stalin; its suddenness and intensity shocked the Chinese leadership.[124] This was an opportune moment for Mao to denigrate the Soviet model and push for his alternative of a more, faster, and better approach that disdained balanced growth.

Zhou attended several rounds of the first review in February involving heavy industry. Whether attempting to cooperate with, co-opt, or circumvent Mao's initiative, Zhou agreed that it was appropriate to reevaluate the Soviet model based on the experiences gained over the past several years. On February 25, the day after Khrushchev's secret speech,[125] Zhou began to present his solution to China's true path of development. Zhou stated that "to improve construction, we should send people to study the technology of the capitalist countries, and study the experiences of every country. [Chinese leaders] must have a bold vision."[126] Zhou expanded upon his "bold vision" on 4 March while attending a conference on capital construction and wages. Reinforcing Zhu De's 5 February 1956 reference to the "open door," Zhou stated,

> We must open the door. We must not only ask progressive and moderate states, but also backward and even reactionary states to come to China, and increase meetings between peoples. In this fashion, the state will benefit. On the other hand, we must be more enthusiastic to send people abroad. China is a backward country. How can we rid ourselves of economic and cultural backwardness? We need to realize the realities of China, and then comprehensively study and master the strengths of other peoples. Take grain production for instance. Japan produces high-quality rice, while the United States and Canada produce high quantities of wheat. Thus we must pay close attention and study them. Not only should we study the Soviet Union and the new democratic states, but the capitalist states and the Afro-Asian states as well. We must study any strong point of any country. The capitalist political system is decadent and backward. However, it can't be said that they don't have any strong points.[127]

Zhou proposed a two-pronged strategy: maintain a balanced import substitution development model based on Soviet equipment and technology as well as explore economic and technical cooperation with Western countries.[128] Zhou argued,

> We must first and foremost study the Soviet Union, which is the most advanced socialist state. This is a distinct point, about which we cannot afford to waver. Just because we have stated that the Soviets made a mistake at the Twentieth

Party Congress to criticize Stalin doesn't mean that we shouldn't study the Soviets.[129]

Zhu De concurred, and argued in an April 1956 discussion of Mao's Ten Great Relationships that trade with the Soviet Union and Eastern Europe should be increased so that China could acquire the technology and equipment for Chinese development.[130]

Nevertheless, Zhou was in basic agreement with Mao that there should not be blind adoption of the Soviet experience.[131] When speaking to János Kádár, the newly appointed leader of Hungary the following year, Zhou argued that

the Soviet experience has its positive and negative aspects. Their experience with socialist construction is positive. However, after studying their experience, one cannot blindly adopt it, but must adapt it to the conditions of one's country. There is also some good to be found in its negative aspects. After understanding the negative aspects, one not only won't use them, but can avoid fewer circuitous routes and not repeat the Soviet mistakes.[132]

Besides balanced, planned growth, another positive aspect of the Soviet experience was the Soviets' import substitution development experience. Thus on 7 April 1956, Li Fuchun and Mikoyan signed agreements initiating fifty-five new import substitution industrial projects worth 2.5 billion rubles and establishing a railroad line linking Lanzhou with the Soviet Union.[133]

As for expanding economic cooperation with the West, Zhou at the very least had the continued support of Zhu De and the minister of communications, Zhang Bojun. Three days before the signing of the Soviet import substitution agreement in April 1956, Zhu De stated that "we must make the necessary preparations" for expanding trade relations with the capitalist states, including the United States.[134] While speaking with Japanese political leaders in May 1956, Zhou Enlai argued that it would take decades for China to become an advanced industrialized state. China still needed Soviet aid, but it also needed "to import many pieces of industrial equipment and materials." Thus, China could not afford to "close its door" to "Western economic cooperation and aid."[135] During his meeting with a New Zealand delegation, Zhou, in an effort to promote greater economic interchange with the capitalist economies, repeated the critique of the closed door approach to development; he reiterated this position in his May 1956 meetings with another Japanese delegation and an Australian reporter and again in his July 1956 encounter with an Austrian delegation.[136]

Zhang Bojun, whose ministry controlled a variety of Hong Kong–based enterprises such as the China Merchants' Steam and Navigation Company, supported Zhou's initiative at the June 1956 National People's Congress (NPC) meeting by suggesting the development of the southern Guangdong port of Zhanjiang to facilitate trade with the overseas Chinese in Southeast Asia.[137] Twenty-two years later, this same ministry would propose establishing a somewhat similar zone north of Zhanjiang in Shekou, which eventually became the Shenzhen Special Economic Zone (see chapter 7).

Overseas Chinese and Western participation became even more crucial when the chairman and vice-chairman of the Soviet Planning Commission on 17 August 1956 informed Li Fuchun in Moscow that the Soviets

> could not guarantee a supply of equipment as requested by China because of tight metallurgical supplies and labor strikes. They thus hoped that the Chinese comrades could understand Soviet problems. On 1 September, the Soviet Central Committee formally replied to the Chinese Central Committee. They believed that the national economic growth rate stipulated by China's Second FYP draft was too hurried (*jinzhang*). The correct method would be to consider the real possibilities in carefully determining the development speed of the national economy. The reply clearly stated: China has asked for Soviet technical help in constructing 109 new enterprises during the Second FYP period. The Soviet Union will do its utmost to meet this request, but the needed equipment can only be supplied after 1961 (some projects can be supplied in 1960). It is not possible to consider the supply of equipment any earlier.[138]

The formal Soviet response was made two weeks before the opening of the Eighth Party Congress. Luckily for Zhou, the delay of Soviet turnkey projects did not detract from Zhou's economic triumph at the congress. However, it did reinforce the need to find a second source of import substitution equipment and technology. During a State Council Standing Committee meeting in October, Zhou observed,

> We must eliminate parasitic views (*yilai sixiang*), and strive for Soviet help. If the Soviet Union has troubles or plays rear guard in certain areas, then we must rely on ourselves to figure out a way. We must primarily be self-sufficient, and strive for foreign help. Of course, it is great if we had Soviet help, but if we don't, then we still will construct socialism. It is not that we don't respect or want to unite with the Soviet Union. Help from the Soviet Union is important, but the deciding factor is the Chinese people. This and respecting and uniting with the Soviets are two different matters. We not only want to go after help from socialist states, but also want to study things from capitalist and Asian countries.[139]

Thus for China's modernization to succeed by the Third FYP Zhou believed that China had to develop economic relations with the West as soon as possible.

Mao concurred that Chinese experts could be sent to study Western technology and even popularized the phrase "study from foreign countries,"[140] which duplicated the Chinese Communist elite's experience abroad in Europe and Japan during the 1920s. Mao was not as enthusiastic as Zhou or Zhu De about seeking extensive economic cooperation with the Soviet Union or the West. Self-reliance was the true path of economic development and could be achieved by tapping the phenomenal strengths of its people. Bo Yibo relates that after listening to the oral reports from the ministries and commissions on heavy industry in the spring of 1956, Mao directed,

> We must study the advanced experiences of all countries. We must send people to capitalist countries to study technology, no matter if it is England, France, Switzerland, or Norway.[141] As long as they want our students, we'll go! However, we don't want to be superstitious when studying the Soviet Union. We must study the correct, not the incorrect things. The Soviet Union's Internal Affairs Ministry is not controlled by the Party; the military and enterprises implement "a system of one-man management."[142] . . . We do not want to study these things. . . . Thus, we must be very specific when studying the Soviet Union. We do not want to study the Soviet example when we carry out land reforms or transformation of industry or commerce. Comrade Chen Yun is responsible for finance and the economy. He will not study certain things. In summary, we must overcome myths, whether they are about China or about foreign countries. Likewise, future generations must overcome myths about us.[143]

Mao recognized that China still needed the Soviet Union's aid to manufacture large machinery and precision instruments as well as to develop China's strategic forces.[144] He also acknowledged that China could learn from the West's technological prowess, and he later helped to develop economic ties with Japan and Western Europe.[145] Yet compared to Zhou Enlai and Zhu De, Mao was far more critical of the Soviet and Western development models, especially their emphasis on comparative advantage, which was the antithesis of self-reliance.[146] In essence, Mao was attacking the legacy of the opium wars of the 1840s—a defeatist Chinese attitude that the outside world was better. To Mao, this was a dangerous and self-destructive myth. China could "vi[e] with the teacher" to promote a new path of development that "is even faster and better than the Soviet Union and the European nations."[147]

A few days later, Mao Zedong directly criticized the Soviet model in his speech "On the Ten Great Relationships," which was delivered to the 25 April 1956 expanded meeting of the Political Bureau.[148] According to Bo Yibo, Mao delivered two versions: the first version was more critical of the Stalinist model. In "Taking the Soviet Case as a Warning," Mao criticized the blind copying of Soviet agricultural policies ("Soviet grain production still cannot surpass the highest levels of the Tsarist era"), the Soviet concentration of legal powers in the central government ("American states have legislative powers. . . . [American] imperialism is definitely bad, but there are reasons why [America] has become such a developed country. We need to research its political system"), Soviet treatment of non-Communist parties ("With only the Communist Party left, they very seldom hear conflicting views"), and counterrevolutionaries ("People's heads are not like chives, cut them off and they will grow back") as well as the general lack of Soviet support of the CCP ("When speaking of Stalin, we become absolutely enraged [*sanduzi huo*]. But we still believe he was 30 percent mistaken, 70 percent successful"). Mao was especially critical of the Soviet emphasis on heavy industry and emphasis on the military-industrial complex ("Now is a peaceful period; it is not good to have the proportion spent on military expenditures too high").[149]

China needed to forge its own model of development by increasing the proportional expenditures for agriculture and light industry, increasing economic decentralization—including the dissolution of "one-man management" in China's factories—and increasing the role of small- and medium-scale industries.[150] While many of China's economic elites agreed with these positions,[151] Mao also criticized Stalin's overemphasis on administrative tools at the expense of more-normative methods—such as the mass line. Mao later in 1956 argued that Stalin "abandoned some of Lenin's things, deviated from the orbit of Leninism, and became alienated from the masses, and so on."[152] Disregard of the mass line thus had contributed to the 1956 rebellion of Hungarian "counterrevolutionaries."[153] To inoculate against the Soviet infection that had spread to all walks of life, from the sciences to literature, Mao initiated the Hundred Flowers campaign.[154] In late 1956 he also directly criticized "some of our comrades [who] have precisely, one-sidedly looked upon the Soviet Union as perfect."[155] China could be better than the Soviet Union by using normative measures to promote faster development and higher-quality goods.[156]

It also appears that Mao was less enthusiastic concerning the expansion of economic cooperation with capitalist countries. Before 1950, Mao Zedong held a more positive attitude toward the international economy, arguing during the Sino-Japanese War that China could not afford to close its door to the outside world.[157] In March 1949, Mao reported to the Central Committee that "so far as possible, we must first of all trade with the socialist and people's democratic countries; at the same time we will also trade with capitalist countries."[158] If the Red Guards had been evenhanded in investigating the capitalist bourgeois attitudes of the Chinese elites, they would have discovered the following excerpt from Mao's political report of 24 April 1945 titled "On Coalition Government":

> Large amounts of capital will be needed for the development of our industries. They will come chiefly from the accumulated wealth of the Chinese people, and in a lesser degree from foreign assistance. We welcome foreign investments

if such are beneficial to China's economy and are made in observance of China's laws. What is beneficial both to the Chinese people and foreigners is that China, after winning a firm internal and international peace, and instituting thorough political and agrarian reforms, will be able to develop her large-scale light and heavy industries and modernized agriculture. On this basis we shall be able to absorb vast amounts of foreign investments. A politically backward and economically impoverished China will be unprofitable not only to the Chinese people, but also to foreigners.[159]

Such thinking allowed the establishment of Soviet joint ventures in Xinjiang in 1950.

Yet times change. Whether because of nationalist protests against the Soviet joint ventures or the nationalization of foreign investment following the imposition of the UN embargo, the promotion of foreign investment as an engine of development ended by the early 1950s. Mao excised his positive comments on foreign direct investment from the 1954 and 1967 English editions of his *Selected Works*.[160] By early 1957, Mao stated that China "should do business with [all peace-loving nations and peoples]. . . . However, under no circumstances should we entertain any unrealistic idea."[161] Mao was not rejecting the second half of the stated policy to "rely mainly on one's own efforts, while striving to make external assistance supplementary" (*zili gengsheng weizhu, zhengqu wai-huan weibu*);[162] Mao's caution in 1957 echoes similar statements made by Zhou Enlai and Chen Yun during this time.[163] Before the Cultural Revolution, Mao commented on the necessity to study capitalist "advanced science and technology as well as management techniques";[164] in 1964, Mao even argued the need to reduce food grain imports in order to "use the foreign exchange thus saved to buy more technological equipment and materials."[165] Yet there is no evidence to indicate that Mao advocated a continuation of a large-scale import substitution development strategy in the civilian economic sector.

Mao instead promoted a strategy of "walking on two legs," which he defended in December 1958 as

a theory of the unity of opposites within the realm of dialectics. Marx's theory on the unity of opposites made great progress in China in 1958 which, under the premise of preferential development of heavy industry, included the simultaneous promotion of industry and agriculture, of heavy and light industries, of central and local industries, of large, medium, and small enterprises, of small plants using indigenous methods and large plants using foreign methods, of native and foreign methods, and simultaneous development in other fields. . . . Both indigenous methods and modern methods are simultaneously promoted. There are plants using both Chinese and modern methods. Were not Chinese methods used at T'ang-shan and Huang-shih-kang? Are there also small plants using foreign methods? In general, it is very complex. Some of these [combinations] are considered wrong and may not be practiced in some nations of the socialist camp. We permit them; we consider them proper here. Is it better to permit them or not to permit them? We have to wait a few years and see. However, for a nation like ours, which is extremely poor, it is all right to use some indigenous methods to build small plants. It will be too monotonous to concentrate only on big projects.[166]

To compensate for the "one-legged" nature of the FFYP industrial development model that ignored the mass line and overly concentrated on large industry, Mao argued for expansion of medium and small industrial plants. In January 1957, Mao stated, "We need big [industrial] plants, but not too many. We need small plants even more, the more the better."[167] The key to walking on two legs was the mass line, which could be more effectively implemented within medium and small plants; he later argued that "of the more than twenty million tons of pig iron produced in [1959], one-half was turned out by medium and small mills."[168] According to Mao, China would see accelerated growth if it followed the mass line and emphasized medium and small production units.

Mao's attitude toward large production plants was similar to his attitude toward foreign technology—useful, but not essential for development. To accelerate development and achieve self-sufficiency, Mao believed he must compensate for the FFYP's bias against indigenous technology. Mao argued in the early 1960s:

We will adopt advanced technology. But we cannot, because of this, negate the inevitability of backward technology in certain periods of time. Since the beginning of history, in revolutionary wars, it has always been people armed with inferior weapons who defeated those armed with superior weapons. During the civil wars, the anti-Japanese war, and the War of Liberation, we did not exercise power over the whole country and we did not have modernized arsenals. If we must have the newest weapons before we fight, then this is tantamount to disarming ourselves. . . . At present, we are still not advocating universal automation. We should discuss mechanization, but we should not do it excessively. *Excessive discussion of mechanization and automation will make people have contempt for semi-mechanization and production by native methods. There have been such tendencies in the past. Everybody one-sidedly went in for new technology and new machinery, massive scales and high standards. They looked down upon native methods and medium sized and small enterprises.* . . . As to large scale and foreign ways, we also must do it by relying on our own efforts. In 1958, we proposed the slogans of exposing outworn myths and doing everything by ourselves. Facts prove that we still can do it by ourselves. In the past, backward capitalist countries, relying on the application of new technology, catch up in production with advanced capitalist countries. The Soviet Union also relied on the application of advanced technology in catching up with capitalist countries. To be sure, we also will, and can, do the same.[169]

Note the ambivalence toward advanced technology in Mao's argument. Foreign advanced technology was important, but China was not quite ready to use it. The mass line approach depended on the small and medium-sized factories, many of which used indigenous technology. According to Mao, "The correct method is that every country should develop its industry to the fullest extent so as to strive for regeneration through one's own efforts, and do it independently as much as possible so that it will not depend upon others as a matter of principle."[170] While Asian countries were importing advanced technology and capital in their search for their rightful place in the global division of labor, Mao was advocating a far more inwardly oriented development strategy. To Mao, the catalyst for growth could be found at home, within the Chinese people themselves. The key was the mass line.

Mao's ambivalence is indicative of a growing opinion among certain Chinese elites that China should pursue a more autarkic development path. According to Li Xiannian as well as Wang Xiangli's account in *Dang de wenxian*, "certain" elites in 1956 began to interpret "self-reliance" as a "reject[ion] of seeking foreign assistance and helping to supply each other's needs."[171] They believed that China should "close the door in order to promote construction, and manufacture everything that China needs." According to Wang, the proponents of this autarkic strategy had a more conservative interpretation of self-reliance, one that regarded the development of foreign trade to be anathema to China's true development path. They rejected the notion that all countries need to conduct foreign trade to develop. More seriously, they failed to understand that by relying solely on Chinese-based technology, "a huge gap would indeed grow between China and global advanced technology levels."[172]

The identity of these elites remains unclear. But the rebuttals of Zhou Enlai, Zhu De, and Li Xiannian during the period indicate the serious nature of the debate. This study posits that during this proto-experiment with autarkic development, such testing and debating were indicative of attempts to change the fundamental development strategy.

The Eighth Party Congress of September 1956 marks an end to the first round of development debate. Zhou Enlai's balanced economic growth approach temporarily eclipsed Mao's more, faster, and better initiative.[173] While co-opting many of Mao's themes expounded in the Ten Great Relationships—such as the relationships between the interior and the coastal regions and larger and smaller enterprises—Zhou's report on the Second FYP firmly squashed Mao's December 1955 initiative to accelerate industrialization.[174] Zhou argued that basic completion of "a comprehensive industrial system [would occur] approximately within the period of the three five-year plans." Echoing his 1953 argument that China needed to set up an industrial system separate from the Soviets,[175] Zhou cleverly painted proponents of accelerated industrialization as having a "parasitic view (*yilai sixiang*) that we need not build our own comprehensive industrial system, and can rely wholly on international assistance." In other words, if there was an attempt to terminate the import substitution strategy ahead of schedule, China would have no choice but to import necessary goods and materials from abroad. By the end of the FFYP, China still needed to import 40 percent of its machinery and equipment from abroad, and it required at least two more five-year plans to establish a domestic machine-building and metallurgical industry, as well as carry out "the mining and refining of rare metals, the establishment and expansion of an organic synthetic chemical industry, the peaceful utilization of atomic energy, etc."[176] Without such industries, China could not become self-sufficient.

Zhou then restated his vision of a two-pronged approach to implement China's import substitution strategy by attacking autarkic development proponents:

> Another view, that we can close our doors and carry on construction on our own, is wrong too. Needless to say, the establishment of a comprehensive industrial system in our country requires assistance from the Soviet Union and the People's Democracies for a long time to come. At the same time, it is also necessary for us to develop and expand economic, technical, and cultural exchanges with other countries. Even when we have built up a socialist industrial state, it will be inconceivable that we should close our doors and have nothing to ask from others. Facts show that economic and technical cooperation among the socialist countries will continue to expand. Concurrently, economic, technical and cultural relations with other countries will certainly expand day by day with the growing strength of the people fighting for peace, democracy and national independence in many countries, and the gradual relaxation of the international situation. Therefore, the isolationist view of socialist construction is also wrong.[177]

Ye Jizhuang, the minister of foreign trade, subsequently proposed that China should dramatically increase its exports.[178]

Mao apparently cooperated with the expansion of Western economic contacts. Yet after Mao renewed his more, faster, and better approach under the GLF rubric at the Third Plenum of September–October 1957, criticism of the import substitution approach reappeared (see below). During the Cultural Revolution and the anti-rightist movements of the 1970s, the proponents of a more autarkic approach dominated. Mao's call to augment Chinese resources (*tu*) with Western technology (*yang*) became blurred and forgotten.[179] Hence,

Mao's 1949 comments on the need to trade with capitalist countries were excised from later editions of the *Selected Works*.[180] Those elite coalitions supporting Mao's vision of development in the 1960s and 1970s—such as the politics-in-command coalition headed by Jiang Qing—argued that advocates of foreign trade and technology were committing treacherous acts. While Mao had not proposed such a strict autarkic stand, he also did not attempt to stop such criticism in the 1970s (see chapter 6).[181] Thus the xenophobia of the Cultural Revolution partially had its roots in this 1956 debate over import substitution and the acceleration of industrialization.

Tapping the Capitalist Marketplace and the Overseas Chinese

CHINESE PERCEPTION OF A MORE TRANQUIL INTERNATIONAL ENVIRONMENT

By 1956, the systemic conditions that had brought about China's initial adoption of an inwardly oriented development had changed. Although still facing a containment web of American bilateral and multilateral military agreements around their periphery, China was not as threatened territorially following the Korean armistice of July 1953, the Geneva conference of 1954, and the end to the first Taiwan crisis in 1955. According to Bo Yibo, the Political Bureau believed that the international situation by 1956 had "ameliorated" and the possibility of war was low. Bo states that

> two major international conferences had a major impact. The first was the Asian-African conference held at Bandung in April 1955, which proposed the Ten Principles to Promote World Peace and Cooperation. The second was the Geneva conference held between April and July 1954, which brought about the Indochinese truce.[182] The success of these two conferences gradually strengthened world peace and cooperation; imperialism would not dare to use force lightly. The Central Committee gradually believed that the international situation had ameliorated by the end of 1955 and the beginning of 1956. The Political Bureau believed that within the short term there would not be an invasion of China or a world war. There possibly would be ten or more years of peace. Premier Zhou's report to the Second Plenum of the Eighth Party Congress delivered on 10 November 1956 was based on the following idea: "Comrade Mao Zedong proposed at the Political Bureau meeting that we slow the growth of national defense industries and strengthen our emphasis on the metallurgical, machinery and chemical industries to build a good foundation; on the other hand, we should develop nuclear weapons, guided missiles, remote controlled equipment and long-range aircraft; other areas need less emphasis (*The Collected Works of Zhou Enlai*, 2:236)."[183]

As for the Poznan strike in Poland and the Hungarian revolt of 1956, Bo states that the Political Bureau saw these events primarily as the result of Khrushchev's complete denunciation of Stalin and failures of the Eastern European Communist parties to control dissent. Bo does not treat the incidents as systemic threats from the Soviet Union, although he states that the unrest in Eastern Europe caused worker and student strikes in China.[184]

Thus, as external systemic pressures subsided, China enjoyed a greater flexibility in selecting the level of involvement with the international community. Emerging from its wartime, defensive position, China developed its external relations with other Asian and African developing states, such as during the Bandung conference of April 1955. With the announcement of its Five Principles of Peaceful Coexistence in foreign policy and Zhou's unprecedented tour of Asia and Eastern Europe from November 1956 to February 1957,[185] China attempted to discard its reputation as an aggressor state and international pariah and to portray itself as a responsible member of the international community. Chinese diplomatic actions were welcomed by many developed, Western economies, which reciprocated by loosening international restrictions on China's foreign economic activities.

ESTABLISHING CONTACTS WITH THE WESTERN MARKETPLACE: JAPAN AND WESTERN EUROPE

From the beginning, the Beijing leadership attempted to diversify its foreign economic relations.[186] Even before the imposition of the economic embargo, Chen Yun suggested in August 1949 that the Chinese must take advantage of the "contradictions between imperialist countries: if you do not want to do business with us, [others] will." Chen Yun argued that any embargo could be circumvented by funneling trade through Hong Kong, Tianjin, Dalian, and Manzhouli, as well as by finding foreign business people to sell Chinese goods indirectly.[187] The Chinese government subsequently encouraged the Western Europeans and Japanese to "defect" from any concerted Western embargo by "dangl[ing] the supposedly unlimited prospect of expanded trade."[188]

Because of its precarious position in Hong Kong, the British government did not fully plug up all the trading loopholes, including the transshipment of goods through Hong Kong.[189] The Chinese used the British pound as their unit of account and to a certain extent as their unit of payment for foreign trade with nonsocialist states. The Chinese also used London to conduct their large-scale commercial shipping business, to market their commodities on the international market, and to obtain international insurance.[190] For countries such as France that did not enjoy direct political or economic relations, the Chinese Committee for the Promotion of International Trade was established in May 1952 to encourage bilateral trade.[191] Thus by the end of 1954, China had established official trade relations with more than sixty countries and rapidly expanded its global trade from Southeast Asia to Western Europe (table 2.4).[192]

With the easing of international tensions by the mid-1950s, Chinese global economic relations began to flourish, in part because of U.S. acquiescence to a larger role for China in the world economy. New research reveals that U.S. policy flexibility allowed the Europeans and Japanese to defect from the Chinese embargo and at the same time prevented a renewal of the Chinese civil war. Nancy Tucker argues that President Dwight Eisenhower and Secretary of State John Foster Dulles designed the 1954 mutual defense treaty with Taipei to restrain Chiang Kai-shek from reconquering the mainland. While insulating itself from right-wing Republican criticism, the Eisenhower administration pursued a two-Chinas policy whose eventual goal was recognition of the PRC.[193]

According to Tucker and Qing Simei, Eisenhower was the key moderating influence in U.S.-Chinese relations. Instead of pursuing the aggressive roll-back strategy advocated in National Security Council document 68 of 1950, Eisenhower believed that international trade with the West could become a wedge that would weaken the solidarity of the world Communist movement. While Eisenhower realized that the United States could not become directly involved in such trade, he would approve an expansion of Sino-Japanese trade. Even in the middle of the Korean conflict, the Japanese signed private trade accords with the Chinese beginning on 1 June 1952; by 1953, the Japanese government permitted Chinese trade representatives to reside in Japan and even extended diplomatic privileges to China by 1955.[194] The United States had the ability to prevent the expansion of Sino-Japanese economic ties even though Japan's sovereignty had been restored with the signing of the peace treaty in San Francisco in 1952.

Yet Eisenhower quietly allowed the trade. In justifying his decision to his cabinet, Eisenhower stated in August 1954 that "some Japanese trade with her Communist neighbors should be encouraged and would set up influences behind the iron curtain [that] would hurt Russia rather than help the Soviets because it would turn Peiping away from Moscow and create a friction between the Communist countries."[195] Consequently, there was an exponential expansion of Sino-Japanese trade from $35 million in 1954 to $83 million in 1955 and $128 million in 1956 (see table 2.4).[196]

Unsuccessful in their attempt to influence U.S. policy toward China, the British government unilaterally rejected the U.S.-imposed embargo on strategic and nonstrategic goods on 29 May 1957; the Japanese officially relaxed the embargo on 10 July.[197] Instead of pressuring the British to change their position, as the United States had during the Suez crisis of 1956, Eisenhower supported the British and eliminated the special "China differential" of embargoed goods (i.e., CHINCOM). COCOM rules would be applied equally to China and to other Soviet-bloc

TABLE 2.4 SELECTED CHINESE FOREIGN TRADE STATISTICS, 1954–59
(U.S. $1 million)

	Japan		Britain		West Germany		USSR		Indonesia	
	Imports	Exports	Imports	Exports	Imports	Exports	Imports	Exports	Imports	Exports
1954	14.6	20.6	46.1	24.6	13.2	7.5	705	587	4.6	2.8
1955	25.1	58.2	64.6	40.1	10.3	9.0	1,120	670	13.3	9.0
1956	63.7	64.7	63.3	49.2	19.2	11.7	762	762	26.0	29.3
1957	55.1	59.7	58.4	43.9	45.9	11.5	618	747	27.6	21.2
1958	48.1	32.5	128.2	75.7	155.2	31.0	640	899	38.8	52.4
1959	n.a.	n.a.	105.9	91.1	129.3	25.6	979	1,118	60.0	69.1

Source: Zhongguo Duiwai Jingji, *Zhongguo*, sect. 4, pp. 18, 19, 58, 67, 68.

countries; the change allowed the Western economies to export to China greater numbers of strategic goods, such as machine products, locomotives, and electric generators. Obviously, this was a fortuitous turn of events for Zhou Enlai, who described U.S. policy in early 1957 as constantly fluctuating between mild and strained attitudes.[198]

While the command economies enjoyed the greatest proportion of Chinese foreign trade, the market economies enjoyed a higher growth rate in volume of trade from the mid-1950s onward. Sino-British trade doubled between 1957 and 1958 from $102 million to $203 million, while Sino–West German trade during the same period more than tripled, from $57 million to $186 million (see table 2.4). In July 1958, Eisenhower waived the Wartime Trading with the Enemy Act to allow U.S. multinationals based in Canada to trade with the PRC.[199] Within the Eisenhower administration, Robert McClintock of the Policy Planning Staff even went as far as proposing a general "Pacific settlement" on 31 December 1957; the settlement would have permitted the PRC's admission to the United Nations and the signing of a regional peace pact that guaranteed the neutrality of Taiwan, Indochina, Korea, and Tibet. Such an arrangement would have allowed the United States to have a more open economic relationship with the PRC that would "intensify existing and potential areas of conflict or divergence of interest between the USSR and Communist China."[200]

Eisenhower hoped that international trade would lure China away from its socialist brothers and generate a peaceful evolution to a more democratic state. Although the United States officially continued its Cold War economic containment policies of China until 1972, Alexander Eckstein concluded in 1966 that "the U.S. embargo is practically of no economic significance, for China has been and is currently able to obtain virtually all the goods she needs from other countries at no significant additional cost. Therefore, the embargo has only a symbolic meaning."[201] Zhou thus was successful in gradually implementing his two-pronged approach to develop economic relations with both the socialist and capitalist economies.

THE HONG KONG "SPRINGBOARD" TO FOREIGN TRADE AND INVESTMENT

Hong Kong was and remains today the portal through which China engages the world marketplace. Despite the British colonial government's attempts to restrict Chinese trade activities in the early 1950s, the Chinese leadership sidestepped such restrictions by exerting greater centralized control over Chinese organizations already based in Hong Kong.[202] On 28 June 1951, the Central Finance and Economy Commission issued a directive outlining the following emergency steps to deal with British restrictions and the embargo:

Trade work should be refocused on southern China. The Finance and Economy Commissions in southern China should organize the relevant departments to organize business people to use Hong Kong as a springboard to engage in a lot more small-scale trading. Many small sales will add up to large volume. We must strengthen the commodity exchange system and make sure that no gaps exist. We must strengthen our work against smuggling [and] prevent the illegal export of pig bristles, mineral ores, and other important exports. The settlement of export exchange accounts temporarily will not be changed.

In the financial sector, we will temporarily cease the issuance of new purchasing certificates when trading with European capitalist countries. As for certificates already issued, we must adopt different methods according to the different circumstances. We must change the previous methods of issuing new purchasing certificates in conducting trade with Hong Kong. Further notice on the actual measures will be issued by the bank. These plans of the Central Finance and Economy Commission are extremely timely and necessary to break the American imperialist embargo and expand trade with capitalist countries while guaranteeing the safety of our funds.[203]

By using small-scale transactions through Chinese enterprises based in Hong Kong and adopting nontraditional means of payment, China hoped to sidestep British restrictions.

Despite such measures, the embargo and China's internal socialist transformation did have an immediate effect on Hong Kong's development. According to Szczepanik, entrepôt trade dropped by 35 percent between 1951 and 1952; the embargo directly affected Hong Kong's transshipments of natural rubber and latex, synthetic rubber, petroleum, steel, transport equipment, and machinery. With the imposition of Chinese trade controls, Chinese demand for foreign goods through Hong Kong was drastically reduced, only to revive after 1955.[204] In addition to the reduction in trade, Hong Kong business people also suffered from socialist transformation. While having reassured the Hong Kong banking community in November 1949 that the new Chinese government would protect certain Chinese banks in conducting business on the mainland,[205] the Chinese leadership proceeded to nationalize not only foreign assets, but also those of the mainland industrialists. Consequently, many Shanghai and Guangzhou industrialists joined the 1.24 million refugees who had fled to Hong Kong since 1945.[206]

Zhou understood that he was facing a serious problem in Hong Kong. It was crucial for Zhou to gain the assistance of overseas Chinese living in Hong Kong and abroad to implement his two-pronged approach in 1957. Yet these were precisely the people who had become increasing disenchanted with the new regime.

Zhou Enlai thus apologized during his speech to Shanghai industrialists and business people on 28 April 1957. Zhou admitted that mistakes had been made in the past and that "our policies were a bit too inflexible." Zhou reassuringly argued that "because Hong Kong is still under British rule and is a pure capitalist marketplace, we cannot and should not cause it to become socialist. Only by completely running Hong Kong within the capitalist system will it survive and develop, which is very helpful to us." The Hong Kong people should not worry about their future, but instead concentrate on running their businesses well. Just as Hong Kong people could return freely to the mainland, mainlanders could travel to Hong Kong, as well as return as long as they "loved their country."[207] As a result of Zhou's policy, millions of immigrants fled across the Shenzhen River into the New Territories during the next couple of years. While forcing British authorities to develop new housing estates, this immigration wave also provided cheap labor to fuel Hong Kong's leap into the international economy.[208]

Zhou hoped that his apology would win over the Hong Kong capitalists, who in turn could play a major role in China's development. During his speech, Zhou stated that "in the past we cooperated with Hong Kong's national bourgeoisie, and in the future we can still cooperate with Hong Kong entrepreneurs." Zhou argued that the Chinese entrepreneurs should be encouraged to stay in Hong Kong, which could be used as a base not only to expand business abroad, but also develop economic ties with the mainland. Thus, "Hong Kong can become our base for making economic connections with foreign countries, for attracting foreign capital and earning foreign exchange." To guarantee their support, Zhou promoted several measures that cushioned Hong Kong and the overseas Chinese from feeling the full brunt of domestic political campaigns, such as the Anti-Rightist Campaign following 8 June 1957.[209] In the battle with Taiwan for the hearts and minds of the Chinese living in Southeast Asia, the leadership approved several initiatives to protect and advance the rights of overseas Chinese.[210]

The use of foreign capital and investment was a touchy subject in "New China." The 1949 revolution had "liberated" China from the control of the world's "monopoly capital"; even the establishment of joint ventures with the Soviets had touched off nationalist demonstrations in 1950.[211] Yet facing the extreme costs of economic development, Zhou believed that foreign capital and investment was crucial. During his January 1957 visit to Poland, Zhou Enlai stated that "in principle" it was fine to borrow capital from Western countries, as long as it was done on an "equitable basis."[212] Upon his return, Zhou and Zhu De began to lay the groundwork for introducing foreign capital and investment into China. According to Wang Xiangli, Zhu De sent Mao and the Central Committee a letter that argued as follows:

> China must fully utilize the two export bases of Hong Kong and Macao. Hong Kong and Macao are free ports, which allow frequent commodity transactions among countries. China can use the two as springboards to get our commodi-

ties transshipped to every place in the world. . . . Hainan Island is geographically close to Hong Kong and Macao. It has plenty of mineral resources, and
a large variety of aquaculture products and economic crops. Its shipping routes
expand in all directions, and many of its ports can be expanded to handle cargo.
This is one of China's excellent export bases. We should vigorously concentrate all of our energies to carry out development work without delay.[213]

Zhu De thus argued the merits of expanding exports through Hong Kong and
Macao, as well as developing Hainan's export capabilities.

However, capital was needed to develop Hainan and other coastal areas. Zhou
Enlai had the solution. During the forty-fourth meeting of the State Council on
6 April 1957, Zhou argued that "we don't have enough foreign exchange. We
can unearth some hidden strengths by having a couple of people go to Hong
Kong or abroad to borrow capital and pay a bit of interest in order run a factory
or other endeavors."[214]

This proposal coincided with Zhou's initiative to expand individual economic
freedoms. In discussing Bo Yibo's report on the 1957 economic plan at the forty-
fourth State Council meeting, Zhou argued that

> while the main current should be socialism, a smaller one can be to provide
> some freedoms, which will help the development of socialism. This method
> can be adopted in industry, agriculture, and the handicraft industries. In my
> opinion, this can be accomplished in all sectors with the exception of the rail-
> roads, which would be difficult to manage. For instance, the pedicab drivers
> and street peddlers can take responsibility of their own profit and losses. In
> addition, in areas where 96 percent are working in a cooperative and the remain-
> der is self-employed, let the remainder stay self-employed. We can allow pri-
> vately run schools to remain open. In just about every field—industry, labor,
> commerce, education with the exception of the military—we can allow a lit-
> tle bit of freedom and private management. There can also be some privately
> managed endeavors in the cultural field.[215]

For the overseas Chinese, Zhu De's and Zhou's initiatives translated into the
overseas Chinese gaining the legal protection to invest in China and establish
their own schools by August 1957.[216] China considered Chinese living abroad
to be Chinese citizens, who could be trusted to invest fairly in the domestic economy. Thus, Zhou avoided direct criticism of having "sold out" China.

Consequently, the leadership approved the establishment of overseas Chinese
investment enterprises (OCIES), which harnessed the investment capital of
Chinese living in Southeast Asia to promote domestic economic employment
and growth. The success of the first OCIES established in Fujian (1952) and
Guangdong (1955) persuaded the leadership to expand the concept nationwide

by 1957.[217] Overseas Chinese investors naturally focused their investment in their *laojia* (ancestral hometowns) in Guangdong, Fujian, Zhejiang, and Guangxi, where they also built schools and other infrastructure projects. Supervised by the Overseas Chinese Investment Company, the OCIEs grew to number 318 private enterprises (*siying qiaohui ye*). Compared to today's foreign-invested enterprises, the OCIEs played a minor role in transferring management and technological skills.[218] Their value and output were relatively small: the OCIEs had a market capitalization of about $560,000 (66 percent of which belonged to overseas Chinese investors) and generated a total of $52.81 million of overseas Chinese remittances by the late 1960s.[219] Yet the OCIEs were an important learning experience, which became invaluable after the late 1970s.

ADAPTING TO THE WESTERN MARKETPLACE

Chinese policy makers realized that new foreign economic policies were required to compete in the capitalist global marketplace. After the Soviets had reduced their orders for clothes and for woolen and knitted goods in the late 1950s, the Chinese turned to the Japanese and Western European markets. Chinese foreign trade planners were forced to change "the export product production process so that production levels, quality standards, variety, color, and other requirements more suit[ed] the demands of the capitalist market."[220] To improve the marketing of Chinese exports, the leadership inaugurated the first export commodity trade fair, held in Guangzhou during spring 1957.[221] This biannual event became the most important conduit for exports to the West for the next twenty years. Thus, the change of trade direction to the international capitalist marketplace determined the types of goods exported and the methods of marketing.

In 1957 policy makers also began to discuss the foreign trade program by which imports would be used to produce exports (*yijin yangchu*). In his April 1957 report to the Central Committee, Zhu De argued that "the most basic problem facing current foreign trade is access to raw materials." Export procurement was problematic because there was a high domestic demand for the raw materials and various problems within the domestic supply network.[222] Zhu De had suggested his solution in February 1957: China should "import raw materials, which in turn could be processed into semifinished and finished goods." For example, China could import flax or cotton yarn that could be processed and resold abroad. He suggested that there were "benefits to selling the sweat of one's hard work."[223] It was thought that this was an excellent way to increase foreign exchange by "importing raw materials, equipment, and technology from abroad, processing [the material] into a finished product, and then exporting it."[224] While the program was to become a major source of foreign exchange, it was not "explicitly proposed to be implemented" until the withdrawal of Soviet advisors in 1960.[225]

Again it was Zhu De who revived the concept, when he submitted a report to the Central Committee in January 1961 again proposing the program.[226]

Although the Chinese leadership previously had decided not to consider a large-scale export strategy until the early 1960s, when China could produce more exportable items,[227] they doubled or tripled their trade with U.S. allies during the 1950s. Yet trade with the West diminished somewhat in 1959. Eckstein notes two reasons for the reduction in trade: a diversion of exports to the Soviet Union in 1958–59 to finance a doubling of Chinese import substitution development projects from the Soviet Union and the growing effect of the Great Leap Forward on export procurement (see chapter 3).[228] After overcoming the economic chaos of the Great Leap and the break with the Soviet Union, the Chinese leadership took advantage of their new access to Western markets in the early 1960s to diversify their sources of foreign technology and financing. Yet this growing interchange was inhibited by a changing attitude toward all foreign countries caused by the Cultural Revolution. To understand China's extreme interpretation of self-reliance, one must look at subsystemic causes, specifically the search for a true Chinese path of development.

Mao's Second Attempt to Accelerate Economic Industrialization: The Great Leap Forward

THE SOURING OF SINO-SOVIET RELATIONS
AND THE EFFECT ON THE DEVELOPMENT DEBATE

Zhou's implementation of a two-pronged import substitution strategy to develop China encountered major difficulties beginning in fall 1957. Internationally, there was a growing uneasiness in Sino-Soviet political relations. Domestically, Mao had grown tired after two years of "passively resist[ing]" the anti–rash advance policy, which entailed "not read[ing] [the Political Bureau's] documents," reports to the NPC, or the budgets, which he was "press[ed]" to sign.[229] Beginning in fall 1957, Mao began to coerce the leadership to support his vision of economic growth—the Great Leap. As a result, a growing Greek chorus chanting the praises of rash advance grew louder; facing severe reprimand and possible removal, Zhou and the other elites acquiesced to Mao's will.

In the aftershock of the Polish and Hungarian incidents of 1956 and an internal leadership struggle, Khrushchev had sought Chinese support by approving the New Defense Technical Accord in October 1957. "Moscow agreed to supply China a prototype atomic bomb, some missiles, and major industrial equipment related to China's nuclear weapons and missile programs."[230] Yet the Chinese leadership became increasingly concerned with Soviet "great-nation chauvinism."[231] By August 1958, Mao refused Khrushchev's request to allow the Soviets to build a telecommunications station or to lease bases in Lüshun that would support a joint submarine fleet, which according to Mao was an attempt "to have control over [the Chinese] coastline and blockade us."[232] The Chinese leadership also refused to participate in the Soviet "socialist division of labor" schemes as embodied by the Council for Mutual Economic Assistance (COMECON).[233] Three months after abrogating the October 1957 nuclear weapons cooperation agreement, the Soviets in September 1959 publicly acknowledged for the first time uneasiness with the Chinese by declaring neutrality during the first serious Sino-Indian border dispute.

Mao also was increasingly concerned that Dulles's January 1953 pronouncement that communism could be defeated by adopting a strategy of "peaceful evolution" (heping yanbian) was coming true. Mao believed that the Soviets had already become revisionists. In September 1959, Khrushchev had failed not only to support the Chinese in the Sino-Indian border dispute, but had agreed at Camp David to a reduction of 1 million Soviet troops and to diplomatic talks to resolve Berlin's status.[234] Thus by November 1959, Mao reprinted Dulles's 1953 speech for a small conference and began to alert the Chinese leadership to the potential dangers.[235] The Chinese publicly responded on 22 April 1960 by publishing "Long Live Leninism" in the Chinese Communist Party chief theoretical journal, Hongqi; the article was an indirect criticism of Khrushchev and his revisionist policies.[236]

Such tensions inevitably affected Sino-Soviet economic relations. While the massive transfer of Soviet technology and equipment during the 1950s laid the foundation for China's future industrial development, many in the Chinese leadership—especially Mao Zedong—were unhappy with Sino-Russian economic relations. There had been the inevitable conflicts with the Soviet foreign experts in China and various problems in the management of the four Sino-Russian joint venture operations.[237] Mao's disdain for the Soviet emphasis on balanced growth and technical experts spewed forth at the Party's Chengdu conference in March 1958. Mao revived his criticism of the Soviet development model, stating that China's adaptation, especially in industrial and planning management, had been too dogmatic (jiaotiao zhuyi). The Chinese needed "to do away with blind faith, eliminate old thinking, and bring into play their creative spirit."[238]

Domestically, Zhou Enlai's and Chen Yun's vision of balanced economic development initially came under indirect attack with the issuance of the Directive to Organize All Efforts to Prepare the Attack against Rightist Elements on 8 June 1957. According to Goldman, the directive not only resulted in the attack of up to 700,000 Chinese intellectuals during the Anti-Rightist Campaign, but "marks Mao's abandonment of the intellectuals as the key to economic development and his increasing concern that educated youth, the next generation of leaders, had insufficient revolutionary consciousness."[239] Yahuda adds that such anti-intellectualism also negatively affected attitudes toward foreign experts and their contribution to China's development.[240] During the summer and fall of 1957, Mao's vision of rash advance thus gained in strength at the expense of Zhou Enlai's and Chen Yun's vision of balanced growth.[241] The stage was set for the Great Leap.

Mao's accelerated approach relied on the indomitable strengths of Communist man, who had the ability "to walk on two legs" to achieve self-reliance.[242] Mao criticized the leadership's relatively conservative policies of 1956: an economic revolution had not been accomplished, while a political and ideological revolution was absent.[243] Mao's solution was rash advance through mass mobilization. Mao proudly boasted to the leaders of sixty-four Communist and Workers' Party representatives on 18 November 1957 that within fifteen years, China's steel production would exceed Great Britain's;[244] by 22 July 1958, he ordered (*pishi*) that China exceed Great Britain's steel production "within two to three years, two years if possible."[245] Foreign technology could be used, but China's development did not have to reproduce the Soviet path, which had relied on foreign experts and large-scale import substitution during its initial phases. Mao's solution was to mobilize the Party and the people to carry out a massive political campaign to complete massive water conservation schemes and reach the unrealistic steel quota, a goal that resulted in the establishment of backyard steel mills.[246] Thus, the Soviet Union and the other socialist states could learn something from China—that politics and not economics was in command.

"KILLING THE CHICKEN TO SCARE THE MONKEY"

Whether swept along by Mao's enthusiasm, pursuing personal advancement, or just fearful of opposing Mao, the majority of China's elites eventually agreed with Mao that "rash advance = Great Leap = Marxism" (*maojin = Yuejin = Makesi zhuyi*).[247] Lieberthal attributes Liu Shaoqi's support of the GLF to an attempt to secure the state chairmanship, while Deng Xiaoping's wholehearted support for the mass line is attributed to his long association with Mao Zedong's faction within the Party.[248] In recounting his support of the GLF, Bo Yibo appears to have been primarily influenced by the Deng Zihui incident of 1955. As director of the Rural Work Department, Deng Zihui directly opposed Mao's acceleration of agricultural collectivization and instead promoted a slower, more market oriented approach.[249] As a result of his opposition to Mao's vision of economic development, Deng Zihui failed to gain a seat on the Political Bureau during the Eighth Party Congress in 1956.[250] In addition, Bo undoubtedly was cautious following his experience of being accused of "rightist opportunism" in August 1953, when he barely missed being charged with making "mistakes of the political line" (*dai luxianxing*).[251] MacFarquhar adds that Bo had been a close ally of Liu Shaoqi, who was strongly supporting Mao's rash advance initiative.[252]

To reduce the State Council's influence in economic policy, MacFarquhar argues, Mao greatly strengthened the economic role of the Party Secretariat under Deng Xiaoping.[253] Following Mao's criticisms at the Nanning conference in 1958, Li Xiannian apparently made the appropriate self-criticisms in spring 1958. Mao subsequently co-opted Li Xiannian by appointing him to the Party Secretariat, along with Li Fuchun, the chairman of the State Planning Commission, who escaped major criticism.[254] Mao could thus treat them as pliant "team players."[255] In agriculture, the independent-minded Deng Zihui was bypassed in favor of Tan Zhenlin, who was not only appointed a member of the newly empowered Secretariat, but to the Political Bureau at the Fifth Plenum on 25 May 1958.

This left two major opponents within the State Council who had continued to sidetrack and eventually oppose rash advance in 1956 and 1957: Chen Yun and Zhou Enlai. During the Nanning conference in January 1958, Mao directly criticized Zhou Enlai and Chen Yun to remind those who had previously opposed the rash advance of the necessity of supporting the Great Leap.[256] In his address to the opening session the Eighth Party Congress in September 1956, Chen Yun had advocated a more remunerative approach to Chinese development, based more on market regulation and production incentives.[257] As acting premier during Zhou's diplomatic tour abroad from November 1956 to February 1957, Chen Yun was responsible for continuing the attack on rash advance.[258] Chen Yun also was one of the most senior proponents of the Soviet model, having assumed overall responsibility for the FFYP and the Soviet import substitution strategy.[259] Following Mao's criticism, Chen Yun made a self-criticism at an expanded meeting of the Political Bureau on 18 February 1958 and again in May.[260] As a consequence, Chen Yun was not elected along with Li Fuchun and Li Xiannian during the Fifth Plenum of 25 May 1958 to the Party Secretariat, which had been granted a larger role in the economic decision-making process. Other than promoting increased steel output and the backyard furnaces, Chen Yun apparently remained silent.[261]

Finally, Mao confronted his most powerful adversary in implementing rash advance. Several days beforehand, in Hangzhou, Mao could no longer contain his anger over the economic policies and blew up at Zhou and Bo Yibo;[262] at Nanning, Mao grilled Zhou by asking, "Aren't you against rash advance? I am against those against rash advance!"[263] Zhou Enlai's response to Mao's attack was very similar to his response at the Zunyi conference in 1935, when Mao took command of the Party by attacking Zhou and others for the fall of the Jiangxi Soviet.[264] As in 1935, Zhou "sincerely" admitted his mistakes. On the night of 19 January 1958, Zhou admitted to having committed a "vacillation of direction and mistakes," and subsequently lost his influence in economic policy formulation.[265] After Mao dismissed Zhou as foreign minister in February and described any action against "rash advance" as being "anti-Marxist,"[266] Zhou recanted his actions by describing "the lessons he had learned."[267] During the Hankou conference in April 1958, Mao described " xxxx" as "a member of the political bureau for forty years, but he divorced himself from the masses and did not set foot in one plant or one rural village. His good point had been visiting everywhere in the field, and he was known as a traveler."[268]

Thus during the second session of the Eighth CCP Congress in May 1958, Zhou promised that he would

1. Let correct ideology guide practical work, and combine vocational work with politics.

2. Support the Party's leadership.

3. Take the mass line, and along with other people responsible for central government work spend four months of the year getting in touch with reality and being closer to the people.

4. Raise his work style, and have the courage to fight against countercurrents and unhealthy trends.

5. Look up to (*xiang*) Mao Zedong for study.[269]

Nonetheless, Zhou, Chen Yun, Li Xiannian, and Bo Yibo again were forced to make a self-criticism.[270] Responding to Mao's 26 May 1958 letter proclaiming the correctness of the term "Great Leap," Zhou composed a self-criticism that he sent to Mao, in which he stated that

my overriding concern at the time was to protect socialism and attack rightists. Based on the actual results of construction, I confirmed that the construction of 1956 was a Great Leap in development and abandoned the mistaken appraisal that it was rash advance. However, at that time I was not consciously aware that being against rash advance was a mistake in policy [*fangzhenxing de cuowu*].[271]

Luckily for Zhou, he still had courageous friends within the Central Committee. On the same day that Zhou composed his criticism, Peng Zhen wrote a report to Mao stating that Zhou Enlai had devised the term "Great Leap." Mao must have been embarrassed: he had just composed a letter suggesting that "a first-order Ph.D. should be conferred on that scientist that discovered this very important slogan (the 'Great Leap')."[272]

In his final move of contrition, Zhou offered to resign his premiership at the expanded meeting of the Political Bureau on 9 June 1958, just as he had resigned as chair of the Military Affairs Commission twenty-three years earlier. Although the Political Bureau did not believe resignation was necessary, Zhou continued to play the penitent. As promised, Zhou traveled up to the Shisanling Reservoir project, where he harnessed himself to a cart for two days and hauled rocks out of the construction site. He also actively promoted the mass line, such as calling for an increase in agricultural and industrial production quotas in August 1958.[273] Yet the full extent of Zhou's trials and tribulations were kept secret from the Party's rank and file. Only now do we fully understand the wrath of Mao and the lessons he inflicted on Zhou, Chen Yun, Li Xiannian, and Bo Yibo.[274] Only now can we begin to understand why the elites supported the GLF.

Bo Yibo's description of his thinking during the Great Leap perhaps is representative of the pressure confronting these elites. While attending an 18 June 1958 Standing Committee meeting held around Mao's pool at Zhongnanhai, Bo Yibo recounts that "Chairman Mao stated that he approved the raise in the steel production quota. I was also impassioned. In addition, I had just completed a self-criticism for opposing rash advance, which would make any disagreement difficult to sustain. I thus agreed to raise the steel quota."[275] Tong Xiaopeng, who became head of the Prime Minister's Office in April 1958, analyzed the situation in 1958 most succinctly:

> Because he had such a lofty reputation within the Party, everyone venerated Mao Zedong. Although many of his criticisms had no basis in reality, Zhou Enlai and the other high-ranking cadre had no option but to sing Mao's tune. It was almost as if one could not ask for an explanation or make an observation. One just over and over again made verbal self-criticisms, wrote self-criticisms, and had no recourse but to say things contrary to one's convictions. None of the high-ranking cadre within the Party could put forward their own views. Not only was this not internal Party democracy, but in reality a situation was created where only one person laid down the law. Some comrades said with deep feelings that after the Nanning conference, the atmosphere within the Party became increasingly tense. Mao Zedong had put himself somewhat above the Political Bureau, and it was difficult to imagine that he had ever discussed problems with other members of the Political Bureau on an equal basis. Internal Party life was becoming abnormal. I think this is the true reflection of the actual situation.[276]

While Lieberthal has argued that Mao's actions at the Lushan conference had disrupted the free exchange of views among the Yan'an coalition,[277] it seems that Mao had already broken those rules beginning in 1955 and had totally eliminated them by early 1958. Mao had successfully coerced the Standing Committee and the Party to support his utopian vision of development. These elites had to find other means to promote their particular development path, methods that could not be interpreted as directly challenging Mao's authority. To extend MacFarquhar's comments about Zhou, these elites had "dedicated [their lives] to the revolution and [did not allow] considerations of 'face' to prevent [them] from continuing to contribute to that cause."[278]

Mao hoped that this proto-experiment with semiautarkic development would be a shining example of the Chinese path of development—one that would overcome the criticism of the Soviet planners[279] and surpass Soviet growth rates of the 1920s and 1930s.[280] Such results not only would impress Khrushchev—who also did not believe China could achieve such growth—but also increase China's standing within the world Communist movement.[281] Mao later would describe 1958 as the key turning point, in which "we decided to make self-reliance our major policy, and striving for foreign aid a secondary aim."[282] Having abolished the "voting machine" within the Political Bureau, Mao was now in full command of the state and the economy.

THE GREAT LEAP AND FOREIGN ECONOMIC POLICY

The growing attack on Zhou Enlai and Chen Yun and the subsequent adoption of the GLF strategy had a definite effect on the two-pronged import substitution strategy. Bo Yibo states that major criticism of Zhou's economic policies really began during the Third (enlarged) Plenum of the Eighth Party Congress meeting between September 20 and October 9, which according to Teiwes "began an important shift in policy."[283] When discussing the Soviet model, Mao's final speech, "Be Activists in Promoting the Revolution," copies almost verbatim Zhou Enlai's comments to the visiting Hungarian leader Kádár on 4 October (see above). However, Mao further posed the question, "Can't we avoid the circuitous routes taken by the Soviets, and develop faster and produce higher quality goods than the Soviets? We must fight for this possibility."[284] Mao then excoriated the year and a half period of opposition to rash advance,[285] thus indirectly implicating Zhou Enlai and the economic elites.

Perhaps not wanting to throw the baby out with the bath water, Zhou Enlai attempted to moderate the critique of the Soviet model and thus preserve the two-pronged import substitution model of development. Zhou urged that a conference be held to celebrate the fortieth anniversary of the October Revolution. Thus while Mao was in Moscow proclaiming that "the East Wind is prevailing over the West Wind," the Chinese elites at home discussed "the theme of Sino-Soviet friendship, that the Soviet Union is the core of socialist unity. We especially want to emphasize studying the Soviet Union, studying how to join their experience with China's realities and be against dogmatism."[286] Perhaps responding to both Khrushchev's announcement that the Soviet Union would overtake the United States within fifteen years and Zhou's conference, Mao telephoned from Moscow further criticizing the previous policies against rash advance and again promoting the faster-growth agenda.[287]

Despite Mao's domination at the Third Plenum, Zhou continued to fight for the two-pronged development approach. While holding discussions with the Polish ambassador on 31 October 1957, Zhou stated,

Our basic policy is self-reliance—to develop industrial and agricultural production, to rely on help from the Soviet Union and the brotherly countries, to
develop trade with the Afro-Asian nations based on the principle of equality
and mutual benefit, to develop trade with European countries not carrying out
the embargo policy and peaceful neutral states. At the same time, we cannot
put too much hope on trade with the imperialist countries.[288]

This fight for a two-pronged development approach was basically lost. However,
a more ominous battle was once again looming on the horizon.

During the Third Plenum, Zhu De responded to a "fairly significant number
of people who one-sidedly supported self-reliance, and that China should produce every little thing that it needs."[289] In February 1959, Li Xiannian described
these proponents of a more autarkic approach as

some comrades [who] have a biased understanding of the policy to "rely mainly
on the domestic economy, while making the foreign marketplace as subsidiary"
and "rely mainly on one's own efforts while striving to make external assistance supplementary." We are a socialist country, and we are a large country
with over six-hundred million people. Of course, we must be self-reliant in our
development; we must primarily satisfy the needs of the domestic market. Yet
it is not right to think that foreign trade work is unimportant, or to regard external assistance as insignificant, or that the expansion of exports is not essential.[290]

However, as Zhou Enlai and the other major elites promoting import substitution development were put under growing pressure, it was up to Zhu De to
rebuff this renewed autarkic initiative. In his speech at the Third Plenum's closing session, Zhu De argued, "We must fight to expand exports and imports, so
that we gradually become a large importer and exporter (*dajin dachu*)."[291] Zhu
De justified his position on 6 December 1957 to the National Conference of
Foreign Trade Bureau Chiefs by arguing,

Foreign trade is an important task for our Party and country. It is an important
component of China's socialist construction. If we want to build, we need to
import technology, equipment, steel, and other necessary materials. If we do
not have these materials, there will be problems with China's construction.
Foreign trade work also is one of the important foreign policy links that reflects
China's task of protecting and fostering human development. Protecting world
peace is a very important task, and the development of trade can bring about
long-lasting peace. With a long-lasting peace, trade will definitely grow even
further.[292]

Perhaps Zhu De's strongest support for the import substitution strategy came
the day before the crucial Nanning conference, during a 10 January 1958

expanded meeting of the Political Bureau. Zhu De argued that the leadership "must break free from the mistaken idea that we must carry out a policy of closing down the country to international intercourse in constructing socialism and purely pursue self-sufficiency in any endeavor we carry out in China." He also stated, "The idea of a national closing down of the country to international intercourse (*minzu biguan zishou*) and a national isolation to develop the economy is against the objective laws of the internationalization of economic life that was already begun early in the capitalist period."[293]

Analysis of the 1957 and 1958 import mixture reveals that Zhu De was partly successful in limiting the effect of the autarky debate (table 2.5). There is a dramatic drop in the percentage of Chinese imports devoted to machinery and equipment imports, from a high of 62.8 percent in 1955 to 45 percent in 1958. Part of this percentage drop is due to the increased demand for industrial raw material imports to supply the import substitution projects coming on-line. However, one can also detect a perceptible drop in the overall growth rate in the value of machinery and equipment imports by the later part of the decade, especially during the 1955–58 period. Yet in 1959, with the signing of the import substitution agreement with the Soviets, the percentage of machinery and equipment imports rose to 52.8 percent.

Despite Zhu De's partial success, not everybody approved of his tactics. In essence, Zhu De fought off the proponents of autarkic thinking by harmonizing foreign economic policy with Mao's rash advance philosophy. China was to become a big importer and big exporter. Localities would no longer need planned export goals emanating from Beijing, but instead would take the initiative to expand all export opportunities no matter how detrimental they could be to domestic market supplies or international market stability. Yet, according to Li Xiannian, Zhu De's *dajin dachu* policy

> did not take into account the special characteristics of foreign trade work nor objective reality that the capacity of the foreign market cannot be increased rapidly. At the same time, this policy did not consider actual possibilities for the domestic supplies of export materials. Contracts were signed to export a large number of goods. More often than not, these contracts could not be fulfilled. This policy was a mistake.[294]

In his 11 May 1959 speech that called for a readjustment of China's foreign trade policy, Zhou Enlai severely criticized the Great Leap in exports for being too divorced from economic realities.[295] Of the 117,000 contracts signed with capitalist countries in 1958, nearly 5,000 were abrogated partly because of China's inability to meet contractual obligations. As for the remaining contracts, China subsequently had to catch up to meet export obligations and thus was unable to exploit new export opportunities in 1959.

TABLE 2.5 CHINESE IMPORT COMMODITY COMPOSITION, 1950–81
(U.S. $100 million)

Year	Machinery and equipment		Industrial raw materials		Agricultural production materials		Means of sustenance	
	Amount	%	Amount	%	Amount	%	Amount	%
1950	1.31	22.5	3.45	59.2	0.10	1.7	0.97	16.6
1951	4.21	35.1	5.27	44.0	0.26	2.2	2.24	18.7
1952	6.22	55.7	3.49	31.2	0.28	2.5	1.19	10.6
1953	7.62	56.6	4.53	33.7	0.25	1.8	1.06	7.9
1954	6.97	54.2	4.50	35.0	0.41	3.1	0.99	7.7
1955	10.88	62.8	4.82	27.8	0.56	3.2	1.07	6.2
1956	8.37	53.6	5.07	32.4	0.88	5.6	1.31	8.4
1957	7.90	52.5	5.21	34.6	0.74	4.9	1.21	8.0
1958	8.50	45.0	7.86	41.6	1.24	6.5	1.30	6.9
1959	11.20	52.8	8.10	38.2	1.0	4.7	.90	4.3
1960	9.70	49.7	8.13	41.6	0.80	4.1	.90	4.6
1961	3.30	22.8	4.98	34.5	0.67	4.6	5.50	38.1
1962	1.72	14.6	4.12	35.1	0.64	5.5	5.25	44.8
1963	1.22	9.6	4.76	37.6	1.11	8.8	5.57	44.0
1964	1.69	10.9	5.90	38.2	0.99	6.4	6.89	44.5
1965	3.58	17.6	8.08	40.1	1.76	8.8	6.75	33.5
1966	5.02	22.3	9.19	40.9	2.03	9.0	6.24	27.8

(continued on next page)

TABLE 2.5 (*continued*)
(U.S. $100 million)

Year	Machinery and equipment		Industrial raw materials		Agricultural production materials		Means of sustenance	
	Amount	%	Amount	%	Amount	%	Amount	%
1967	4.06	20.1	9.29	46.0	2.01	9.9	4.84	24.0
1968	3.03	15.6	9.49	48.8	2.50	12.8	4.43	22.8
1969	2.17	11.9	10.43	57.2	2.44	13.3	3.21	17.6
1970	3.69	15.8	13.36	57.4	2.20	9.5	4.01	17.3
1971	4.84	21.9	11.63	52.8	2.04	9.2	3.54	16.1
1972	5.57	19.5	14.62	51.1	2.51	8.8	5.88	20.6
1973	7.88	15.3	28.26	54.8	3.26	6.3	12.17	23.6
1974	15.85	20.8	37.95	49.8	3.85	5.1	18.54	24.3
1975	24.06	32.1	34.17	45.7	5.70	7.6	10.94	14.6
1976	20.37	30.9	32.99	50.2	3.75	5.7	8.67	13.2
1977	12.77	17.7	37.23	51.6	4.92	6.8	17.22	23.9
1978	19.03	17.5	62.72	57.6	6.89	6.3	20.29	18.6
1979	39.57	25.2	78.67	50.2	9.23	5.9	29.28	18.7
1980	53.75	27.5	86.20	44.1	14.25	7.3	41.30	21.1
1981	51.05	26.2	76.69	39.4	14.09	7.2	52.99	27.2

Source: Zhongguo Duiwai Jingji, *Zhongguo*, sect. 4, p. 10.

The rush to increase exports also resulted in shoddily produced goods and the inability to adapt to changing international market demand. Soviet consumers had sent more than 280 letters complaining that the previously excellent Chinese products were now defective, including the Happy (Xingfu) brand pen, which either leaked or did not work. Zhou tartly commented that these Happy pens were no longer "happy" and should never be sold—even to Chiang Kai-shek! In another case, Zhou cited China's producers of scented cotton prints, who continued to increase exports even though the Hong Kong craze for the material had died down. Finally, the decentralized atmosphere of the Great Leap allowed a plethora of trade missions to be sent abroad, while delegations to foreign trade fairs exhibited machinery that did not work. In summary, Zhou argued that China's reputation in the international marketplace had been severely compromised during the GLF export push.

Thus, while keeping the door to the outside economy open and the autarkic wolves at bay, Zhu De's tactics of making China a big importer and big exporter resulted in the same logistical and political problems inherent in the rest of the GLF program. By 1959, Chinese leaders were scrambling to readjust the GLF foreign trade strategy and to cope with looming foreign trade procurement problems.

Conclusion

By the early 1960s, Mao was unable to pursue his utopian dreams. As MacFarquhar has argued, "The economic crisis constrained Mao's options. He had led a forced retreat on the communes, and allowed his colleagues to devise a series of plans for the industrial front, the common characteristic of which was the restoration of the status quo ante the GLF."[296] These elites did not challenge Mao for political leadership, even during Mao's weakest period of leadership in January 1962 during the Seven-Thousand Cadre Conference.[297] Nevertheless, they did promote an economic recovery program that was the antithesis of the Great Leap's utopianism.

After Nanning, Zhou Enlai and others adopted a far more obsequious attitude toward Mao. They never again dared to challenge him directly, with the exception of Peng Dehuai during the 1959 Lushan conference. By bending in the wind and taking advantage of Mao's desire to remove himself from the drudgery of the day-to-day activities of the state, these elites continued to pursue their beliefs about China's true path of development. Zhou Enlai, Zhu De, and other senior elites who had lived and studied in Europe and Japan as well as those who had an in-depth understanding of economic practice believed that autarky would not enhance self-reliance, but would be a detriment to building a strong, socialist economy. In the 1960s, these elites and others thus agreed that self-

reliance was an important goal, but that China could achieve this only by relying on Western technology and trade (see chapter 3).

More important, if one can delve beyond the GLF rhetoric, Zhu De's support
for a large-scale import and export policy signifies a more cosmopolitan outlook on development. Zhu De wanted to engage the global political economy
and use foreign trade as an engine of development. Yet even Zhou was not ready
to discard his inwardly oriented import substitution development approach to
cultivate an outwardly oriented development strategy, which had found root in
the Japanese, Taiwanese, South Korean, and Hong Kong economies during this
period. Zhou compared China's policy of peaceful coexistence and nonexpan-
sionism with foreign trade policy, which also "was not outwardly expanding.
China's foreign trade policy is not akin to capitalist foreign trade policy."[298] Zhou
Enlai might have learned the efficacy of Zhu De's outwardly oriented approach
following the recovery of China's economy in the 1960s. However, the debate
with autarky advocates had not ended.

Thus the origins of the antinomy of Chinese development lies in the fundamental disagreement among policy elites after 1956 about the best approach to
achieve a self-reliant, strong state. Mao learned from his mistakes of the GLF.
With the support of Jiang Qing and Lin Biao, Mao revived the normative-administrative approach in the 1960s. No longer adopting an ambivalent attitude toward
foreign trade, Mao was persuaded to pursue a more autarkic approach, which
was implemented during the Cultural Revolution and during a short period in
the mid-1970s. After overcoming the worst effects of the GLF and the Sino-Soviet
schism of 1960, the post–GLF coalition used the remunerative-administrative
policies to finance a limited import substitution strategy by importing turnkey
plants from European and Japanese suppliers, thus taking advantage of the 1957
loosening of the UN embargo.[299] By the early 1970s, Zhou Enlai revived the
post–GLF import substitution approach, which was expanded by Hua Guofeng
in the mid- to late 1970s. This antinomy of development strategies resulted in
a cycling of the two inwardly oriented strategies and thus delayed China's implementation of an outwardly oriented development regime.

CHAPTER 3

Neomercantilism versus Self-Sufficiency, 1959–1966

Beginning in 1959, an emerging elite coalition faced with the largest economic dislocation since liberation initiated steps to reject the Great Leap Forward strategy. Although the Eight-Character Plan was a lengthy and not entirely successful process, by 1963 the post–GLF coalition had readopted an import substitution strategy. Embodied by Zhou Enlai's Four Modernizations program, China's new long-range strategy envisioned a modernized economy by the end of the century.

Before reimplementing the import substitution strategy, the coalition desperately needed to finance grain imports to feed China's starving millions. They also had to repay foreign debts, especially to an increasingly estranged Soviet partner in development. The leadership thus proposed several innovative export promotion policies in the early 1960s, including the establishment of export commodity processing bases (ECPBs), the forerunner of the contemporary SEZs. These successful strategies financed debt repayment as well as the import substitution program based on imports from the Western capitalist economies.

The Economic Crisis, 1959

One year after Zhou's humiliating apology for blocking rash advance, students and teachers at Peking University were making soup from tree leaves (*yezitang*).[1] According to the Central Committee's emergency directive of 26 May 1959, many urban areas had exhausted their monthly allotment of edible oils (peanut oil, soybean oil, cottonseed oil, vegetable oil, sesame oil); the monthly industrial allotment of 40 million *jin* could not be maintained.[2] The adjusted planned grain quota for 1959 had been only 62 percent fulfilled; pork, jute, tobacco, oil-bearing crops, and sugar production were down 13–22% from the previous year.[3] Although Beijing attempted to readjust the GLF policies by requiring more grains from the countryside, Bernstein argues that this intermediate readjustment of the GLF resulted in nearly 30 million dead Chinese.[4] A drastic readjustment of the GLF strategy was necessary to end the massive starvation and death.

Chinese leaders had various explanations for what Alexander Eckstein was to call the "Great Crisis" (1959–61).[5] They all agreed that the GLF caused production scarcity that adversely affected supplies for the domestic and foreign markets. In an opinion submitted to the Central Committee just before the second Zhengzhou conference of February–March 1959, Li Fuchun, Li Xiannian, and Bo Yibo stated,

> The supply of certain manufactured goods for daily use and materials for agricultural production currently are in short demand. This shortage of raw materials principally is the result of not encouraging a diversified rural economy and reducing output of local and specialized products. In addition, some industrial enterprises, which originally produced goods and raw materials used to manufacture goods for daily use, were converted to produce other goods.[6]

Whatever the cause, the resulting chaos discredited the Great Leap approach. Zhou Enlai and the other members of the first line of the Chinese leadership—Liu Shaoqi, Zhu De, Chen Yun, Deng Xiaoping—proceeded along a protracted path to readjust the strategy and formulate a new development approach.[7]

Initial Policy Readjustment, 1959–1961

The Second Great Leap and the Delay in Domestic Economic Policy Readjustment

In January 1959, Chen Yun attempted to convince Mao that the 1959 production quotas could not be achieved; as a result, "some comrades" accused Chen Yun of harboring "rightist tendencies."[8] Following the Seventh Plenum and Liu Shaoqi's assumption of the state chairmanship in April 1959, the new leadership coalition implemented various emergency measures[9] and began to end the GLF proto-experiment with autarky.[10] Admitting the "unbalanced" nature of rash advance, the Central Committee in May 1959 reduced the steel quota from 16.5 million tons (which had previously been reduced in April 1959 from the originally planned 30 million tons) to 13 million tons. The grain quota was reduced from 105 million tons to 50 million tons in July 1959.[11]

Disregarding Mao's criticisms of the previous year, Zhou attacked the GLF approach during an 11 June 1959 meeting of the Central Committee Secretariat and while meeting Soviet experts on 26 June 1959. Mao and Li Fuchun joined Zhou in echoing similar criticisms during a 13 June 1959 Political Bureau meeting.[12] The Central Committee meeting of 15 June 1959 even agreed that "the GLF's major problem was [that policies promoting] an overall equilibrium and a planned, proportional developing economy had not been carried out."[13] The Central Committee thus officially opposed rash advance. On 29 June 1959 just before the official opening of the Lushan conference, Mao Zedong agreed with

Chen Yun's position to "arrange the markets before we go into capital construction" and to concentrate on "putting agriculture, food, housing, public utilities, and transportation into good order" (*yao xian anpaihao shichang, zai anpai jichu. . . . yao ba yi, shi, zhu, yong, hang wugezi anpaihao*).[14]

The readjustment of the GLF strategy was not completed until after 1961. Bo Yibo ironically described the problem more than thirty years later:

> In formulating the 1960 plan, there had been thought of continuing to complete comprehensive balancing and leave some margin in the plan, based on the readjustments of the previous year. But influenced by the struggle "against rightist tendencies" of the 1959 Lushan conference, the heads of many comrades became inflamed, and there was just no way to carry out readjustment.[15]

While tactically taking a rightist turn during the previous six months, Mao Zedong seized upon Peng Dehuai's criticisms at the Lushan plenun to turn leftward once again and to criticize the opponents of rash advance.

The emerging elite coalition was unprepared for Mao's assault. When initially asked about Peng Dehuai's 14 July 1959 letter to Mao, Zhou Enlai responded, "Oh, well, that really isn't anything" (*Na meiyou shenme ba*).[16] Having learned their lessons the previous year, Zhou and the other Party elites strategically decided to join Mao in the short term to criticize Peng and praise the GLF. During the enlarged Seventeenth Supreme State Conference, Zhou praised the Great Leap, whose successes "proved the absolute correctness of the policies put forward by the Party and Chairman Mao concerning the general line and the policy to move forward on two legs."[17] Bo Yibo's "head" was also "inflamed"—his calls for a "Great Leap" in the 1960 coal output apparently resulted in major coal shortages by the third and fourth quarters of 1960.[18]

Despite these actions, the emerging post–GLF coalition in actuality was playing the game for the long run. They realized that economic readjustments were necessary, but they delayed overall implementation because of their unwillingness to challenge Mao and suffer the fate of Peng Dehuai. They thus acquiesced to Mao's desire to pursue high steel output and formalize Maoist management techniques, such as those adopted at the Anshan iron and steel complex.[19] The new post–GLF coalition quietly continued to readjust other economic sectors—such as the foreign economic sector. And they bided their time until they could effectively end the GLF–including the Anshan charter.[20] Unfortunately, their delaying tactics resulted in a second Great Leap; as Yang Dali has pointed out, the subsequent political bandwagoning among the inflamed local Party officials resulted in higher death rates in China's rural areas in 1960.[21]

The subsequent catastrophes enabled Zhou Enlai to attack the excesses of the anti-rightist campaign and the continuation of the Great Leap strategy. Zhou then proposed a comprehensive economic readjustment beginning with discussions of the State Planning Commission's 1961 plan in August and September 1960.[22] Zhou Enlai, Nie Rongzhen, and Chen Yi effectively called for the end of the anti-rightist campaign, including an end to discrimination against expertise.[23] Thus, the sacrifice of tens of millions of people enabled the new elite coalition to pursue a more stable economic development path.

Initial Foreign Economic Policy Readjustment: The First Squeeze, Secondly Replace, Thirdly Exceed Policy

Despite his inability to effect a comprehensive economic readjustment, Zhou Enlai began to implement readjustment of the foreign economic sector in late 1958. His actions provide an insightful look into the dynamics of Chinese coalition building.

While the Sixth Enlarged Plenum was discussing a partial readjustment of the GLF during November and December 1958 (*yasuo kongqi*), Zhou Enlai commented to the secretary of the Hong Kong/Macao Work Committee,

> One point must be made clear. There will not be a Great Leap Forward in exports. From now on, we can consider reducing somewhat our commodity exports to nationalist countries with whom China maintains a relatively antagonistic relationship. We can also increase prices. However, in general we cannot dump our goods on foreign markets, monopolize the exports of certain goods, or take advantage of political privileges. We must promote self-reliance, and primarily focus on the domestic marketplace.[24]

Zhou immediately put forward his readjustment agenda during a December 1958 Minister of Foreign Trade (MFT) conference. Zhou argued for gradually increased foreign trade to reflect "objective realities," supplying the export market only after meeting China's domestic development needs, and trading with the imperialist states as long as such trade benefited China.[25]

Subsequently, Zhou built a coalition of like-minded elites who agreed with his approach toward development and foreign trade, including Bo Yibo, Chen Yi, Chen Yun, Li Xiannian, and Ye Jizhuang.[26] Although concurring in theory that domestic market supplies should be given priority, Zhou and Li feared that proponents of an autarkic path would prevent fulfillment of all international market obligations.[27] Zhou and Li thus argued for recentralized administrative control over foreign economic policy. China thus could meet its international obligations as well as finance a new round of import substitution projects from the Soviet Union.

Promptly following the Second Zhengzhou Plenum and Mao's "veering to the right" on agricultural collectivization, the Central Committee readjusted the foreign trade plan on 8 February 1959.[28] Concurrently, the Party Secretariat honored all foreign trade contracts concluded in 1958.[29] To regain authority lost during the Great Leap, Zhou reasserted Beijing's control of foreign trade, arguing that the fulfillment of the State Export Plan must take precedence over local export desires.[30] The State Council thus imposed direct controls over the procurement, sale, allocation, storage, and foreign trade of thirty-eight commodities, including grain, edible oils, cotton, and cotton textiles.[31]

To guarantee procurement, the Central Committee approved Five-Priority (*wu youxian*) status to all exports on 18 March 1959. The plan thus provided "priority to all export commodities, priority in production and processing, priority in access to raw materials and packaging supplies, priority in procurement, and priority in transportation."[32] Li Xiannian argued in April 1959 that future domestic economic and foreign trade plans should seriously take into account "the needs of national economic construction and foreign policy."[33] Citing a July 1954 Central Committee decision,[34] Li proposed to redirect all commodity supplies (with the exception of grains and oils) from the domestic to the export sector.

With the readjustment of the foreign trade sector, Zhou hoped to finance the disrupted Second FYP and its large-scale import substitution development strategy. The Soviets had announced in 1956 that they could not immediately supply China's request for 109 new industrial import substitution projects because of "tight metallurgical supplies and labor strikes" (see chapter 2). However, Zhou signed a $1.25 billion (approximately 5 billion rubles) economic agreement with Khrushchev on 7 February 1959. In exchange for Chinese exports, the Soviets agreed to provide plans, equipment, and technological help to establish 78 industrial and power-generation projects that ranged from large-scale chemical factories to machinery plants.[35]

Directly criticizing the GLF's rash advance approach, Zhou revived his original 1956 idea that China's industrial development would be initially completed by the end of the Third FYP—or 1967. By December 1959, he conceded that it might be delayed until the Fourth FYP in 1972.[36] The agreement demonstrated Zhou's success in checking the autarky advocates and redirecting the enthusiasm of the GLF advocates so that again China could promote a more balanced import substitution industrialization strategy. It also demonstrates how important Zhou's readjustment of the foreign trade strategy was in February 1959.

To formalize the readjustment initiatives, Zhou delivered a major speech on 11 May 1959 to various provincial and municipal finance and trade secretaries as well as leading cadre from seventeen state council ministries. On the same day that Chen Yun proposed a reduction in steel targets, Zhou argued against an autarkic interpretation of the slogan "Domestic market is the priority, while the foreign market is supplementary" (*Neixiao weizhu, waixiao weibu*). Zhou argued that the foreign market continued "to play a very important role in China's development and construction." The import substitution strategy was responsible for

China's production of 9 billion kilowatt hours of energy, which increased China's electrical power capacity by one-third over 1958. To finance continuation of the import substitution strategy, cadre needed to place full priority on exports and ensure that their quality and quantity met contractual agreements. Prices had to be set according to international demand. Participation in trade fairs and foreign delegations was to be limited.[37] In this way, Zhou hoped to eliminate the bad practices adopted during the Great Leap period as well as earn enough foreign exchange to finance the import substitution strategy.

However, these administrative readjustments could not overcome the growing economic disasters encountered during the second and third quarters of 1959. According to the Central Committee's emergency directive of 26 May 1959, China was obligated to export 34.8 billion *jin* of edible oils during the first three quarters of 1959 to repay its foreign debt. China had exported only 60 million *jin* by the end of April 1959. The new economic leadership thus decided that

> it would be better to have one area without supplies than four areas. . . . [Thus] from June till September, there will be a temporary cessation of supplies to the countryside . . . so that the export needs of the reduced supplies of edible oils can be fully guaranteed and that supplies which are absolutely necessary for urban areas and industry can also be appropriately guaranteed.[38]

The Central Committee went beyond Li Xiannian's suggestion of 27 April 1959 by redirecting domestic grain and oil supplies to the export market.[39] The Party thus deprived Chinese farmers of oils used for daily cooking to fulfill export obligations; suburban areas were encouraged to grow their own edible oil crops and grains.[40] Yet these draconian measures were unable to prevent shortfall in export supplies. By the third quarter of 1959, the state could meet only 66.4 percent of its planned export commodities, resulting in the export of only 65 percent of the planned RMB 7.9 billion worth of commodities.[41] Emergency readjustments were required.

Based on Zhou's 11 May 1959 speech on foreign economic policy,[42] the Central Committee and the State Council issued an emergency directive on 26 October 1959, inaugurating the First Squeeze, Secondly Replace, Thirdly Exceed (Yi Qi, Er Xiang, San Chao) policy.[43] The policy "squeezed" from the domestic economy "all commodities which [had] not met the export plan and whose domestic consumption [could] be reduced or eliminated." Secondly, it mandated the "replacement" of any export commodities that could not be procured on the domestic market by other obtainable, exportable goods. Thirdly, the policy obligated production units to "exceed" their planned export quota (see appendix B). The policy also reinforced the five-priority status to all exports adopted on 18 March 1959. Finally, the leadership appointed Yao Yilin, the vice-minister of finance and trade, to oversee policy implementation. As a result, the

1959 planned foreign trade procurement quota of RMB 9 billion was exceeded by 115 percent, and the actual planned export total of RMB 7.92 billion was exceeded by 102 percent.[44]

Nineteen sixty was a different story. The First Squeeze, Secondly Replace, Thirdly Exceed emergency directive of 26 October 1959 only temporarily resolved the country's export procurement problems. According to a February 1960 report of the State Council's Office of Finance and Trade,

> The agreed upon export figure with the Soviet Union was 4.717 billion rubles in 1959. Originally, we would have had a favorable trade balance with the Soviets. However, the Soviets exceeded deliveries of complete plant sets and equipment by over 200 million rubles and [our side] added an additional order for 36 million rubles of goods. It was already too late in 1959 to repay with exports. We now owe the Soviet Union 300 million rubles [worth of goods].[45] Thus by the beginning of 1960, the Chinese had incurred the maximum trade payments deficit (300 million rubles) agreed upon with the Soviets.[46]

The foreign trade structure could not respond to unanticipated changes in demand. More ominously, China could not repay the Soviet Union or other creditors. During the previous decade, the Chinese borrowed 7.6 billion rubles (old; 1.7 billion new rubles) to finance the purchase of technology and equipment for its large-scale import substitution development strategy.[47] They also borrowed 5.6 billion old rubles (1.2 billion new rubles) from the Soviets between 1950 and 1955[48] to buy war material, and owed 580 million old rubles (130 million new rubles) in interest. In addition, China still had not met contractual obligations to deliver exports to several other foreign countries.[49]

China did not have enough goods to export. By July 1960, China had fulfilled only 38 percent of its 1960 export quota. The Ministry of Foreign Trade reported in August 1960 (see appendix D) that

> as of July 25 (1960), only 43.3 percent of the original quota for the annual export commodity procurement plan and only 38 percent of the original annual export quota had been achieved. Yet the original annual import quota already was fulfilled by 52.7 percent. According to this rate, the deficit toward the Socialist countries would reach RMB 1.7 billion to 2 billion by year end; debts owed to the Soviet Union would reach RMB 1.4 billion to 1.6 billion; debts owed to our brotherly countries in Eastern Europe could reach RMB 300–400 million. This is a serious political problem confronting the whole Party.[50]

The situation was a profound embarrassment to the leadership, especially during this early period of the Sino-Soviet confrontation. The Chinese already had a 300 million ruble trade deficit with the Soviets for 1959. The Chinese admitted that between 1959 and 1961 they were unable to export to the Soviets "as large a quantity of agricultural produce and processed products as before."[51] Therefore, the Chinese leadership had to negotiate a temporary repayment moratorium for RMB 1.21 billion in trade debts incurred in 1960.[52]

To complicate matters even further, China remained committed to its international obligations with the Communist and developing world. While the Chinese death toll was ominously rising, the CCP continued to provide North Korea with loans, grain, rubber, and cotton textile machinery;[53] to the Albanians, the Chinese provided 50,000 tons of wheat between August and December 1960;[54] for the Cambodians, the Chinese built small-scale steel complexes, machine factories, and other infrastructure projects.[55] By 1962, Zhou Enlai estimated that China had agreed to provide RMB 6.9 billion in foreign aid projects (80 percent to North Korea, North Vietnam, Mongolia, and Albania; 20 percent to the developing countries).[56] Approximately 53 percent of this amount was spent during the 1961–64 period.[57]

While delaying or eliminating certain projects, Zhou remained committed to the foreign aid program. He argued that strengthening the Communist and developing world would "reinforce its ability to combat imperialism."[58] As the schism in the Communist world became more acute, Chinese aid programs no doubt strengthened ideological alliances. Thus, Zhou and the leadership allowed the Chinese people to starve in order to feed the Albanians and North Koreans.

Administrative solutions were not sufficient. Based on their experience of 1959, policy elites looked to remunerative solutions to guarantee export procurement.

Policy Readjustment (Second Stage): The Eight-Character Plan

The Sino-Soviet Split and Domestic Policy Innovation

By 1961, the post–GLF coalition could initiate a comprehensive readjustment designed to feed the Chinese people and to ensure quotas in the domestic and export sectors. The new strategy reduced new capital investments including the scale of the import substitution program, introduced stronger macrolevel management of production inputs, and mandated various production incentive schemes. Yet the post–GLF coalition was hampered by two important factors.

Chinese elite first needed to tackle the economic implications of the Sino-Soviet Schism following the withdrawal of Soviet advisors between 28 July and 1 September 1960. According to Zhou Enlai, the economic sectors most affected were "construction projects, technology cooperation, specialized military technology, peaceful nuclear energy projects, technical cooperation projects with the East Europeans, foreign students, propaganda, various international meetings, China's foreign interactions, foreign trade, etc."[59] The CCP Central Committee later accused the Soviets of "unscrupulously [withdrawing] the 1,390 Soviet experts working in China, [tearing] up 343 contracts and supplementary contracts concerning experts, and [scrapping] 257 projects of scientific and technical cooperation, all within the short span of a month."[60]

Second, the coalition had to contend with a recalcitrant Mao Zedong. Although "retired" to the second line, Mao Zedong successfully intervened to prevent the adoption of innovative agricultural initiatives in 1961 and 1962. Yet Mao's preoccupation in building coalition support within the PLA and ideological circles allowed the post–GLF coalition to implement remunerative measures in the industrial and foreign trade sectors.

The post–GLF coalition nonetheless established a nationwide consensus regarding a three-year readjustment of the national economy, including reduced financial outlays and credit. The Eight-Character Plan was the lodestar for the policy readjustments and innovation. The plan was initially discussed during the formulation of the 1961 economic plan in August–September 1960.[61] Officially approved by the Ninth Plenum of the Eighth National Party Congress (14–18 January 1961), the plan was not fully implemented until after the Lushan conference of August–September 1961.[62]

The Eight-Character Plan completely rejected the GLF domestic development strategy. The plan stipulated that "every industrial and construction project should be readjusted, consolidated, supplemented and have higher expectations of success (*tiaozheng, gunggu, chongshi, tigao*)."[63] Industry was to "concentrate on increasing product variety, raising quality, paying attention to equipment repair and spare parts, increasing new product research, development and trial manufacture, and speeding up new technology for national defense." Capital construction would "be concentrated on small and medium-sized [projects], be completed in order of importance, [and] continue to be reduced in its overall scope. . . . [Except for certain exceptions], all construction not related to production [would also] be halted."[64]

Fiscal realities and starvation thus had forced a change in the domestic development strategy. Backyard furnaces and large-scale import substitution construction projects were no longer considered affordable. Although Mao was not overtly criticized, it was clear that Mao's vision was defunct. During the Seven Thousand Cadre Conference of January–February 1962, Mao finally took full responsibility for the GLF debacle.[65] The new development strategy now focused on a recentralized foreign trade system that was insulated from the domestic economy and that provided material incentives to individual producers to stimulate their enthusiasm to produce.

Foreign Economic Readjustment: Eat First, Construction Second

"EAT FIRST"

Before achieving consensus on the Eight-Character Plan, the Central Committee on 8 August 1960 issued The Emergency Directive for the Whole Party to Make

Great Efforts in the Campaign for Foreign Trade Procurement and Export. This document established the agenda for foreign trade reform in the early 1960s, including two important guidelines for readjustment: (1) under centralized control by the state, imports would be approved according to the state's repayment capability (*liangshou weiru*);[66] and (2) imports were to be prioritized according to the principle "Eat first, construction second." To alleviate massive starvation, the Central Committee first focused on grain production. As Chen Yun stated at the time, "The most dangerous situation is not to have food."[67]

Contrary to the GLF's concentration on heavy industrial production and unrealistic grain quotas, the Eight-Character Plan treated agriculture as the foundation of the Chinese economy. As emphasized by the 1961 State Economic Plan Report, all economic sectors would contribute to increasing the annual agricultural production rate to 10 percent for 1961. Production inputs were guaranteed by expanding cultivated land; diverting labor, cadre, and 1.5 million tons of steel to the "agricultural front line"; increasing domestic fertilizer production to 4.5 million tons; and importing 1 million tons of fertilizer from abroad.[68]

Such traditional administrative methods were insufficient. Faced with natural disasters affecting 650 million *mu* in 1959 and 980 million *mu* in 1960,[69] Zhou Enlai decided on 30 December 1960 to import 1.5 million tons of grain to "relieve scarce grain supplies and stabilize the domestic market and help grain production."[70] In discussions with a North Vietnamese delegation in January 1961, Zhou explained that China had been a net exporter of grains for fourteen years. However, China was "forced" to import grain in 1961 "because we had focused too much on industrialization" and encountered natural disasters since 1958.[71]

Li Xiannian oversaw grain imports as head of the Central Work Group for Receiving and Transporting Imported Grain (Zhongyang Jinkou Shiliang Jieyun Gongzuozu).[72] Describing the imports as a necessary, temporary measure, Li hoped to prevent "chaos" in Beijing, Tianjin, Shanghai, Liaoning, and other areas suffering from two years of natural disasters as well as to "guarantee the farmers' enthusiasm to produce."[73] Li Xiannian initially proposed to spend $300 million to import 5.2 million tons in 1961 and $280 million to import 3–3.5 million tons in 1962.[74] To circumvent the U.S. embargo, Chen Yun—the most senior planner overseeing the grain import scheme—suggested importing U.S. wheat via France.[75]

However, with the terrible droughts plaguing Sichuan, Anhui, and Hubei, China expanded its grain imports in 1961 to 6.3 million tons. Beijing already had planned to spend 50 percent of foreign exchange earnings on grain imports for 1962. The actual amount was increased to finance 5.1 million tons in 1962 and 4.88 million tons in 1963.[76] Li Xiannian argued that grain and raw material imports were "a temporary measure that the state will gradually change following the recovery and improvement of domestic agricultural production."[77]

However, the logic of the international division of labor was addictive. By 1964, grain production levels had nearly regained the levels achieved in 1957. Yet Li Xiannian observed that the dramatic population increase had actually reduced the amount of average grain consumption of China's farmers, which on average was 400 *jin* per year, versus approximately 420 *jin* in 1955.[78] China needed to import grains for "another two or three years, which would be beneficial to the recovery of economic crops, increase production of light industrial products, reduce the discrepancy between the two-price system [planned prices and open-market prices] and increase fiscal revenue."[79] Consistent with a more "economic" approach to development,[80] grain imports would be criticized during the Cultural Revolution as not consistent with "self-reliance."

"CONSTRUCTION SECOND"

The post–GLF foreign economic strategy rejected the nascent autarkic policies of the Great Leap, alleviated the agricultural disaster, and took a long-range view of industrial development. Policy makers initially reduced investment in large-scale capital import substitution imports to strengthen investment in the agricultural sector—including agricultural machine-building and chemical-industry projects and nitrogenous fertilizer plant imports.[81] According to Lardy and Lieberthal, promotion of the import substitution projects clearly rejected the Maoist self-reliance policy and "the Maoist concept of 'walking on two legs' in which small-scale plants with less advanced technology were developed simultaneously with modern facilities."[82]

While agricultural import substitution projects could relieve food shortages, Chinese planners also had long-term goals. Li Xiannian had stated that a continuation of grain imports should only be implemented if it "didn't seriously affect the importation of needed equipment and new technology."[83] Following the economic upturn of 1963,[84] the post–GLF coalition reimplemented the import substitution program, yet with some obvious changes. They reoriented the import substitution program toward the Western marketplace to import comprehensive technology and equipment projects so that China could become fully modernized by the end of the century.

Chinese planners first had to wean themselves from Soviet imports (table 3.1). In August 1960, Li Fuchun argued that "while the greatest possible help from abroad should be obtained in socialist construction, the Party has consistently held that we should mainly rely on our own efforts. This was so in the past and will be even more so in the future."[85] While agreeing with the self-reliance approach, Zhou Enlai predictably adopted a different tactic. Responding to Marshal Nie's 3 July 1960 report on Soviet unwillingness to provide military and civilian technology, Zhou reiterated his two-pronged strategy to import from the Soviets and the West first enunciated in 1957.[86]

TABLE 3.1 SELECTED CHINESE FOREIGN TRADE STATISTICS, 1960–71
(U.S. $1 million)

	Japan		Britain		West Germany		USSR		Indonesia	
	Import	Export	Import	Export	Import	Export	Import	Export	Import	Export
1960	0.2	—	104.5	82.0	94.2	19.5	845.2	818.8	39.7	34.3
1961	14.5	21.6	46.3	57.8	33.7	13.4	291.7	536.3	36.7	46.8
1962	42.2	31.6	32.0	60.2	38.0	21.4	210.9	490.7	39.8	29.0
1963	64.4	64.8	42.9	72.7	15.5	31.2	194.3	406.8	42.6	48.9
1964	160.8	141.3	69.7	101.6	26.2	41.5	133.6	311.6	62.4	47.2
1965	261.8	192.4	123.1	135.5	67.7	58.9	185.8	221.7	43.8	65.1
1966	333.8	269.4	203.8	139.1	120.6	64.5	164.7	140.4	16.4	0.3
1967	304.3	233.7	219.4	129.9	207.7	63.6	55.9	55.5	—	—
1968	334.9	204.9	176.3	118.5	214.3	64.5	59.2	32.9	—	—
1969	381.8	200.8	283.6	119.9	171.7	74.8	27.0	27.2	—	—
1970	582.7	223.8	385.6	103.9	205.5	69.5	24.1	23.2	—	—
1971	594.4	281.4	166.2	123.6	157.5	73.3	68.3	80.9	—	—

Source: Zhongguo Duiwai Jingji, Zhongguo, sect. 4, pp. 18, 19, 58, 67, 68.

The Chinese thus attempted to reconcile their differences by "solemnly [affirming their] desire to have [the Soviet advisors] continue their work in China and expressed the hope that the leaders of the CPSU [Communist Party of the Soviet Union] would reconsider and change their decision."[87] Symbolizing his desire to continue trade with the Soviet bloc, Zhou Enlai promised the Czech ambassador in September 1960 that their bilateral economic relationship would "improve within two to three years."[88] The Russians reciprocated by offering food assistance (a loan of 1 million tons of grain and 5 million tons of Cuban sugar), rescheduling the 1960 trade debt to be repaid interest-free within five years, and even offering joint production of the MiG-21.[89]

With Zhou Enlai's sudden departure from Moscow on 23 October 1961 and the failed delivery of Soviet imports for 1961, the Chinese confronted a "new situation after the 22nd CPSU Congress." The leadership "firmly [swore] not to build up any new debts with the Soviet Union or the Eastern European countries."[90] Thus from 1960 to 1966, imports from the Soviet Union fell by more than 80.5 percent (see table 3.1); from Czechoslovakia by 74.5 percent; from East Germany by 64.1 percent; from Hungary by 48.2 percent; and from Poland by 38.9 percent.[91] To compensate, the leadership increased investment in coal, timber, metallurgical, and petroleum industries from 30.6 percent in 1960 to 58.8 percent in 1962.[92] Always the pragmatist, Zhou continued to keep the door to the Soviet Union unlocked and to temper rash actions.[93]

The Soviet withdrawal left the Chinese with 201 industrial turnkey projects in various stages of completion. For certain projects, China would "completely rely on its own strengths to overcome problems." The Chinese waited until the 1980s Sino-Soviet rapprochement to complete other projects.[94] One important military import substitution project was not put on hold—the nuclear bomb. Foreseeing potential problems, Mao Zedong and the Chinese military had been preparing a self-reliant path since 1958.[95] On 3 November 1962, Mao approved Luo Ruiqing's report to establish the Fifteen-Member Special Commission under Zhou Enlai's leadership to overcome the myriad problems in developing the Chinese bomb.[96] China's first nuclear explosion on 16 October 1964 was not a total victory of the self-reliance policy, although it was portrayed as such. Evidence shows that during the second meeting of the Fifteen-Member Special Commission, Zhou Enlai argued that China could import needed technology from the capitalist countries.[97]

Because of the growing conflict with the Soviet Union, Zhou abandoned his two-pronged development approach of 1957 and leaned toward the capitalist marketplace. An analysis of the relative growth in imports from Western market countries, especially during the 1964–66 post–GLF expansion period, is evidence of this decision (see table 3.1).

Perhaps the greatest change occurred in Sino-Japanese relations. After the signing of the Korean armistice, Japan vied with Great Britain to be China's primary foreign trade partner. However, by May 1958, this growing economic relationship withered following the defilement of the PRC flag during a Chinese exhibition in Nagasaki. Zhou Enlai accused the Kishi government of supporting Chiang Kai-shek.[98] The newly appointed foreign minister, Chen Yi, accused Japanese Prime Minister Kishi of "blatantly destroying the Sino-Japanese trade agreement and having carried out a malicious and insulting attack on China."[99] All contacts between China and Japan were subsequently suspended.

It now is clear that Mao's attack on Zhou Enlai during the spring of 1958 strongly influenced Zhou's and Chen Yi's exaggerated response to the Nagasaki incident of May 1958. While admitting in the same month that opposition to rash advance had been "a mistake in policy," Zhou did not want to be subject to a more serious charge of betraying the Chinese people (*maihan*).

Following Zhou's vindication on economic policy after December 1958 and the Soviet withdrawal of advisors, Zhou Enlai reengaged the Japanese in August 1960. He set forth three basic principles to the political relationship:

> The Japanese government and the Chinese government would not be hostile to one another but would have friendly relations.

> The Japanese government could not follow the Americans in plotting to establish "two Chinas." The Chinese government would recognize only one Japan, would never try to promote two Japans, and would always regard the Japanese government as its primary partner in any negotiations.

> Japan could not place obstacles in the way of normalization of Sino-Japanese relations. China would always encourage, support, and aid normalization of Sino-Japanese relations.

Furthermore, Zhou stated that a renewed economic relationship could be established through bilateral government agreements, nongovernmental contracts, and special consideration for individual cases.[100]

While the new Ikeda government immediately imported more than $100 million worth of Chinese goods in 1960, tensions did not really abate until after the 1963 Chinese decision to reinstitute its import substitution development strategy. China dramatically expanded Sino-Japanese trade; as a result, trade liaison offices were exchanged in 1964, and Japan became China's major foreign trade partner in the mid- to late 1960s.[101] To Zhou, Japan was the perfect substitute for the Soviet Union. As he commented to a visiting Japanese delegation in 1964,

> China basically has all the raw materials needed by Japan. Japan can provide China with many varieties of technology and equipment. China has a popula-

tion of 670 million and Japan has 100 million. Both have large markets. As both markets increase in economic strength, their needs will increase. Thus, the opportunities of providing what the other needs will become even greater.[102]

Except for the doubling of China's population, this statement still appropriately reflects the current Sino-Japanese economic relationship.

Policy Innovation: The Four Modernizations Program

With the reorientation toward the Western marketplace and the gradual economic recovery, Zhou Enlai and the post–GLF coalition again addressed the industrialization issue that had recently torn apart the Yan'an coalition. In 1963 Mao's protégé, Chen Boda, proposed reviving the GLF to enable China to surpass the U.S. and Soviet economies within twenty-three years.[103] To prevent a GLF revival, Zhou proffered his grand vision to achieve a strong, independent China. It has become known as the Four Modernizations Program.

During the late 1970s and early 1980s, the term "Four Modernizations" became a ubiquitous slogan that the post–Maoist leadership used to legitimize economic policy initiatives. By the mid-1980s, the slogan was replaced by terms such as "Opening to the Outside World." However, the slogan's political significance remains understudied in the West. The Four Modernizations concept represents Zhou Enlai's alternate vision of economic development, which emphasized economic planning and remunerative policies, expertise, foreign technology, and import substitution.

According to Cao Yingwang, the concept of the Four Modernizations has a long history.[104] Premier Zhou first proposed to modernize industry, agriculture, communications and transportation, and defense in his government work report of 1954.[105] Following Mao's general call for scientific culture during the Hundred Flowers campaign and for a reemphasis on national defense in 1959,[106] Zhou added "scientific culture" to the Four Modernizations goals by folding communications and transport modernization into overall industrial modernization. Thus during a conference of Heilongjiang cadre held in December 1959, Zhou called for modernization of industry, agriculture, scientific culture, and defense.[107] Zhou formally described the strategy as the Four Modernizations at a National Work Conference on Culture held on 4 January 1960.[108]

Zhou more boldly proffered an alternative to Mao's economic development approach during the early 1960s. In April 1961, Zhou argued that China needed "a new understanding" of an "independent industrial system." He indirectly criticized Mao's emphasis on steel production as based on the standards of the 1930s and 1940s. Arguing that times change, Zhou described a future dominated by "nuclear energy, electronics, and jet engines," whose production required China "to pursue a Great Leap in quality, product variety, standardization, and technology."[109] Zhou rejected the broad anti-intellectual tendencies of the anti-rightist campaign and the Great Leap's walking-on-two-legs approach, in which "Central Committee directives inspired ordinary citizens to act like scientists and experts, and ill-equipped Party cadre became embroiled in the heady world of advanced science and technology."[110]

Instead, Zhou praised intellectuals, "the vast majority of whom are willing to be led by the Party and are willing to use their specialized knowledge to serve socialism."[111] The Party needed to embrace intellectuals, as well as science and technology, whether it was developed at home or abroad. Zhou thus argued in 1962 that "China's strategic policy is to obtain self-reliance, whether it is in carrying out the revolution or in construction. However, there is a process that must be undertaken."[112] China could not afford to carry out an autarkic policy: "it is impossible to close the door to the outside world in order to implement communism."[113]

In light of the disaster in agriculture and industry resulting from the Great Leap, the global technological revolution, and the preliminary negotiations over China's Third Five-Year Plan,[114] Zhou began in 1963 to lobby for support of his alternative to the Maoist development model. Traveling to mainland China's most cosmopolitan city, Shanghai, to celebrate the Spring Festival in January 1963, Zhou spoke to a gathering of scientists, artists, and Party stalwarts. Directly invoking the liberal attitudes of the Hundred Flowers Movement, Zhou announced that the Four Modernizations strategy would focus on the modernization of agriculture industry, national defense, and science and technology. To win over his audience, Zhou hoped aloud that Shanghai would "become China's leading advanced city."[115]

The next day, Zhou continued to emphasize the Four Modernizations in his speech to the Science and Technology Work Conference formulating the Ten-Year Science Plan (1963–72).[116] Zhou argued:

> In the past, China's scientific foundation was very weak. The key to building China into a strong socialist state by modernizing agriculture, industry, national defense, and science and technology is the implementation of science and technological modernization. . . . Our Four Modernizations must be carried out simultaneously and enhance each other. We cannot wait until industrial modernization is completed to engage in agricultural, national defense, and science and technology modernization. We are below the world's advanced levels. But we can study advanced experiences and utilize new scientific and technological breakthroughs. In this way we can expand our world and accelerate our advancement. Of course, we can't avoid meandering a bit, but we can reduce such wanderings. We must try hard to catch up, and we can catch up. We

shouldn't follow in anybody's footsteps, because we will always lag behind. Our scientific and technological development will meet the standards of the 1960s only if we simultaneously seek truth from fact, progress in an orderly fashion (*xunxu*), make mutually beneficial efforts and try hard to catch up. Only in this way can we catch up relatively quickly to advanced world standards.[117]

Zhou's speech was a blatant reversal of the GLF approach. He enticed the assembled Shanghai intellectuals and cadre by promising that they could import any necessary equipment, raw materials, or library materials from abroad as well as recruit the needed technological experts or staff. In this way, Zhou hoped that Shanghai would lead China down the new modernization path.

These actions were duly noted by Zhou's opponents: in April 1963, Jiang Qing first began to use culture to criticize opponents of Mao's economic vision, and Chen Boda praised the GLF.[118] However, Zhou took advantage of the "timely" sinking of China's first domestically produced ocean-going cargo ship in May 1963 to suppress the arguments for a return of the GLF development. After steaming out of the Shandong port of Qingdao, the prophetically named ship, *The Great Leap,* ran against submerged reefs and quickly sank. According to Zhou, the disaster diminished China's international reputation. Had the ship been outfitted with proper radar and sonar devices and accurate positioning equipment imported from abroad, it might not have sunk.[119] Interestingly, Jiang Qing used this same issue to flame the debate over import substitution development a decade later (see chapter 6).

To acquire such technology, raise living standards, and improve national defense, Zhou argued in fall 1963 for a different interpretation of self-reliance. China needed to become self-reliant, especially following the Soviet withdrawal of advisors. By the end of the FFYP, China could design and build small to medium-sized factories and produce a variety of production inputs. By the Second FYP, China was fairly self-sufficient in producing petroleum products and had made great advances in its chemical industry, radio technology, and steel and precision equipment manufacture. Yet Zhou argued that the current concept of self-reliance was based "on the wartime period when little construction was undertaken in the liberated areas."[120] In a British television interview, Zhou argued,

> When we talk about self-reliance, we definitely do not mean autarky or a closed-door policy [*zigei zizu, biguan zishou*]. No country in the world can produce everything that it needs. But if you don't produce goods that you are capable of producing, then what will you use to trade with others [for the things you need]?[121]

In late summer 1963, after several months of rallying support within the state and Party, Zhou proffered a new development strategy innovation. In August,

Zhou chaired a committee drafting a Central Committee document on industrial development. Blocking Chen Boda's proposal to reinitiate the GLF, Zhou proposed the Four Modernizations Program, which mandated the completion of China's industrial modernization by the end of the century.[122] Lacking support within the post–GLF coalition, Mao abandoned Chen Boda's call for accelerated development and approved Zhou's continued readjustment plans by the September 1963 work conference.[123]

After modifying the timetable for modernization,[124] Zhou presented the September work conference with his Four Modernizations plan, which harked back to the long-range planning of the mid-1950s (chapter 2). There would be two fifteen-year programs: during the first fifteen years (1965–80), China "basically would establish the beginnings of an independent, national economic system and industrial system"; during the second fifteen-year program (approximately 1980–95), China "by the end of the twentieth century would complete the building of a strong socialist state that enjoyed a modernized agricultural sector, a modernized industrial sector, a modernized national defense sector, and a modernized science and technology sector."[125] In retrospect, these two plans seem eerily prophetic.

Building on the successful readjustment of the national economy mandated by the Eight-Character Plan, Zhou thus presented his alternative to Mao's rash advance approach of the Great Leap. When speaking to representatives from five special conferences called by the Central Committee and State Council on 12 October 1963, Zhou described the Four Modernizations Program as an attempt

> to find China's road to construct socialism. Marxism provides broad principles for socialist construction, such as a planned economy and proportional development. However, we still must develop our own specific road through experience and according to China's general line and general policy. We must work out the details and create our own experiences. Up to now we have not achieved a successfully comprehensive approach to socialist construction. . . . [In implementing the Fifteen-Year Long-Range Plan], we currently lack on-the-spot investigation and research. Without this basic tool, we will have to revise our plan many times.[126]

Zhou was promoting neither Communist man nor pure self-reliance. The plan was the solution to China's modernization problems.[127]

For Zhou, another important key was the Western marketplace. After repaying its foreign debt and completing its economic readjustment by 1965, China could afford to finance new import substitution projects. While COCOM regulations prohibited advanced technology and equipment imports, the technology-control regime did not restrict desperately needed midlevel technology or surreptitious procurement through Hong Kong or other third parties.[128] Besides,

TABLE 3.2 SELECTED CHINESE EXPORT/IMPORT FIGURES, 1960–71
(U.S. $100 million)

Year	Exports		Imports	
	Total	% change	Total	% change
1960	18.56	−17.9	19.53	−7.9
1961	14.91	−19.7	14.45	−26.0
1962	14.90	−0.1	11.73	−18.8
1963	16.49	10.7	12.66	7.9
1964	19.16	16.2	15.47	22.2
1965	22.28	16.3	20.17	30.4
1966	23.66	6.2	22.48	11.5
1967	21.35	−9.8	20.20	−10.1
1968	21.03	−1.5	19.45	−3.7
1969	22.04	4.8	18.25	−6.2
1970	22.60	2.5	23.26	27.5
1971	26.36	16.6	22.05	−5.2

Note: Percentage change is based on the change from the previous year.
Source: Zhongguo Duiwai Jingji, *Zhongguo,* sect. 4, pp. 3, 4.

Zhou believed that the huge China market with nearly one-quarter of the world's population was very attractive to Western capitalist markets, which were burdened by smaller, more-competitive markets.[129] Li Xiannian thus announced that "China's [policy] direction is to import more industrial equipment. Originally, we imported turnkey plants and equipment from socialist countries. Now, we must import them from capitalist countries."[130]

After a year of carrying out feasibility studies, Zhou in April 1963 reinitiated his import substitution development approach by approving the Plan to Carry Out Discussions for Complete Plants.[131] By July 1963, Zhou suggested that China spend $50 million per year for seven years ($100 million during the readjustment period up to 1965; $250 million up to 1970) on the importation of foreign technology and equipment (table 3.2).[132]

To start the process, China paid $22 million to import a Vinylon factory from Japan to increase textile production in June 1963; the agreement also included a long-term Japanese loan to finance imports.[133] Between 1963 and 1966, China imported fifty-one import substitution projects from Western countries: fourteen industrial machine-building projects, thirteen metallurgical equipment projects, thirteen chemical industry projects, three oil equipment projects, two construction material processing-equipment projects, two light industrial projects, two geological survey equipment projects, one electrical equipment project, and one printing project.[134] China also signed thirty-three other technology exchange accords with the West that resulted in eighty-four import substitution projects.[135] To encourage China's change in policy direction, Japan, Britain, West Germany, and other Western market-countries offered to help underwrite China's growing trade with the West. For instance, up to the mid-1960s, the Chinese took advantage of $260 million in Western export credits (of which 70 percent were extended terms) to pay for the fifty-one complete plant and equipment imports and paid only $13 million in interest.[136]

Ironically, China's most prized example of the spirit of self-reliance—the Daqing oil field—was not only discovered with the help of Soviet and Hungarian geologists in 1960, but the Daqing refinery completed in 1963 relied on imported foreign equipment.[137]

Financing China's Grain Imports and the Four Modernizations: Adapting to the Capitalist Marketplace

The post–GLF coalition enacted dramatic changes in foreign trade to realize the transition to the capitalist marketplace. During the first full year after the Sino-Soviet schism, Li Xiannian warned that many localities and departments did not understand the dynamics of the capitalist marketplace. Echoing a phrase made famous by Zhou Enlai, Li Xiannian characterized the Western business people as "not tolerating outstanding accounts. If we do not comply with the contract, we will lose our credit, which will be dangerous."[138]

The Central Committee thus approved directives ancillary to measures first taken in the late 1950s. A circular was issued on 30 November 1962 stating that "we must especially pay close attention to our Hong Kong and Macao exports."[139] The leadership issued a second circular on 23 February 1963 reiterating the importance of the Guangzhou Trade Fair. Six years after its inauguration, the biannual event was bringing in "over one-third of the amount of money earned yearly in export trade with the capitalist markets."[140] The Ministry of Foreign Trade ideologically justified the fair as an effective "propaganda forum for [Chinese] foreign policy and the achievements of socialist construction." In their general report on the autumn 1963 fair, the MFT thus ordered foreign trade departments to "consider the successful running of the trade fair as a regular, important task. The vice–party secretary or provincial vice-governor of every province, city, and autonomous region will be put in day-to-day charge of the trade fair work of his area."[141] This underlined the fair's entrepôt role in facilitating trade expansion with Western markets.

Finally, there was a further attempt to improve export quality and composition to reflect Western market demands. At the May 1961 Specialized Conference on Foreign Trade, Li Xiannian and Chen Yun noted the need to improve the quality and variety of industrial exports.[142] At the National Foreign Trade Conference held 5–27 September 1963, the conferees suggested that with

> the reduction of export products to the Soviet Union and Eastern Europe, our guiding idea for supplying export products should be: Greatly develop production of products suited for export to the capitalist markets [and] further raise product quality and variety to suit the characteristics of the capitalist market.[143]

Unfortunately, it would take more than thirty years for China to learn that the White Elephant brand had a different connotation in the West.

Financing China's Grain Imports and the Four Modernizations: Recentralizing Foreign Trade

While continuing to strengthen administrative means to guarantee export procurement begun in 1959, the post–GLF coalition also developed innovative remunerative measures. Through an emergency directive of August 1960, the Central Committee centralized authority over foreign trade. One of the most significant administrative measures was the upgrading of a temporary foreign trade office set up in 1959 under Bo Yibo. Based on another emergency directive on 10 August, the Central Committee authorized the establishment of the Three-Person Foreign Trade Command Post: Zhou Enlai (head), Li Fuchun, and Li Xiannian. The command post directly controlled all aspects of the export procurement and export process. In January 1960, to coordinate "foreign trade liaison work," the leadership also established the Bureau for Economic Relations with Foreign Countries (Duiwai Jingji Lianluo Zongju), which was controlled directly by the State Council.[144]

The post–GLF coalition believed that the decentralized nature of the Great Leap Forward was in large part responsible for the chronic shortages. Li Xiannian argued for a completely reorganized foreign trade system in May 1959. The state needed to dismiss incompetent foreign trade officials and prevent the rechanneling of foreign export goods to the domestic marketplace.[145] Li Xiannian thus made three important suggestions in May 1959:

> 1. In principle, it is better to separate domestic and foreign trade organizations. After separation, the domestic and foreign trade organizations might argue with each other. However, if they do, their individual viewpoints will become more deeply apparent, enabling both sides to resolve their differences and reach an understanding. This is not a bad result. Every local Party Committee must decide whether to separate the two. However, if the Party Committees decide to make the division, they must wait until the fourth quarter [1959] or the beginning of next year in order to avoid any interference with the fulfillment of this year's

export plan. Prefectures and counties ought to have specialized organizations or at least full-time cadre managing foreign trade work.

2. Whether or not domestic and foreign trade organizations are separated, foreign trade warehouses must be independently established with independent accounting systems.

3. Local Party Committees, such as in Shanghai, Guangzhou, Tianjin, and other places, must reorganize their coastal foreign trade organizations. Foreign trade is an international-oriented unit—*foreign* is the operative word. Personnel must have stronger political qualities. Those who don't meet such standards must be transferred. Of course, this work must be based on the principle of finding truth from fact.[146]

The establishment of a separate foreign trade system as advocated by Li Xiannian in 1959 became very problematic. It would return to haunt the foreign economic sector during the Cultural Revolution.

One of the most sensitive sectors to separate from the domestic economy was the production and acquisition of material used to produce commodities (*shengchan ziliao*), including key export commodities.[147] According to Li Xiannian, control over the entire material management system from 1957 onward had been "too decentralized, too dispersed, and too much power given to lower levels (*xiafang de guoduo, guokuan, guoxia*)."[148] In 1960, the State Economic Commission established a "multilevel material management organization and a material supply network . . . that would uniformly organize and manage the procurement, supply, and allocation of the means of production." Thus on 18 May 1960, the Central Committee approved the establishment of the General Bureau for Material Management (Wuzi Guanli Zongju). Within three years the bureau established a new material management system that provided "unified leadership and management to the sales and business organizations and personnel of all production departments." Offices (*ting*) and bureaus (*ju*) also were established from the provincial to county levels.[149] The leadership thus hoped that a centralized system (*xitong*) would rationalize the procurement process and strengthen the planned economy.[150]

Yet, according to Li Xiannian, it was not an easy task. Unlike the recentralization of the banking and finance systems as mandated by the Eight-Character Plan, recentralization of the material management system was far more difficult. "Everyone ha[d] control over materials, including the General Bureau for Material Management, every locality, every enterprise, even every small enterprise."[151] Thus, it took a series of central work conferences and expanded meetings of the Political Bureau in 1962 to bring about a consensus that recentralization would not cause "chaos."[152]

Mirroring measures adopted in the domestic material-management system, the leadership asserted stronger macrolevel management of materials needed for export production. One year after the establishment of the General Bureau for Material Management, raw materials used in export production continued to be short in supply. The State Planning and Economic Commissions suggested

> that each area redistribute its [raw materials] to resolve [problems in export production supplies] from the 1961 quota already distributed to the localities, cleaning up stockpiled materials and using those materials assigned to postponed or terminated capital construction projects.[153]

On 30 June 1961, the State Council approved in principle the proposal of the MFT to establish a materials management organization (*cailiao guanli jigou*) directly under the MFT. The original MFT proposal envisioned a more independent supply system dedicated to export production. Yet perhaps reflecting the difficulty of recentralization, the State Council's directive reasserted the principal role of "central and local departments responsible for production and supply of export products." The role of the MFT's materials management organization thus was to "assist production and supply departments, and organize arrangements for the supply of important raw and processed materials and packaging materials needed for export products."[154]

After 1961, Li Xiannian's goal of establishing a more independent foreign trade system was gradually realized. Following the slogan "Four united into one" (*Si he yi*), the MFT established a separate foreign trade system that combined commerce, purchasing, supply and marketing cooperatives, and foreign trade.[155] This system undoubtedly created turf battles between overlapping bureaucratic authorities.[156] Lower-level cadre on occasion acted without applying for instructions from higher bodies (*qingshi baogao*).[157] By 1963, several provinces attempted to eliminate the independent foreign trade system.[158]

It remains unclear whether such infighting had a profound affect on forming or implementing foreign economic policy. The post–GLF elite coalition continued its policy of centralized control over foreign trade through the mid-1960s.[159] Yet the separate foreign trade system would be criticized during the Cultural Revolution as an attempt to "set up an independent kingdom" and would be eliminated by 1970–71 (see chap. 4).

Financing China's Grain Imports and the Four Modernizations: "Number One Priority to Exports"

According to a Zhou Enlai directive, the Three-Person Foreign Trade Command Post was to give "number one priority" to exports (*chukou diyi*).[160] Zhou's export guideline was accomplished by "in general subordinating domestic consumption to foreign sales" (*neixiao yiban fucong waixiao*). As outlined in a 1961 Office of Finance and Trade report, China would "first emphasize the export of goods and second emphasize imports, [would] use imports to develop exports and achieve a balance between imports and exports" (*xianchu houjin, yijin yangchu, jinchu pingheng*).[161]

EXPANDING THE *YIJIN YANGCHU* PROGRAM

Proposed by Zhu De in 1957 but not fully implemented until 1961 (see chapter 2), the basic strategy of the program to increase the processing and assembly of imported materials for export was straightforward: to guarantee export procurement and raise the amount of foreign exchange receipts derived from exports. A nationwide procurement, export, allocation, and transportation campaign (*shougou, chukou, diaoyun yundong*) was launched to raise the value-added content of export commodities; another initiative sought to increase gold production.[162]

Li Xiannian was particularly supportive of the program. Speaking to the National Foreign Trade Planning Conference in September 1963, Li stated,

> The program to use imported materials to develop exports [*yijin yangchu*] is an important method to expand exports. Practice has shown over the years that this is a feasible and correct policy. We must continuously summarize our experiences and use all means possible to actively expand this work. The program can be implemented in two ways: First, we can process imported raw materials into commodities for export; secondly we can process imported raw materials into commodities or directly import some commodities that subsequently can be exchanged with the countryside for other exportable items. In implementing the program, the Ministry of Foreign Trade must be given greater latitude within the allowable limits of the plan. This will greatly enliven business and increase foreign exchange earnings for the state. The Ministry of Foreign Trade will draw up regulations for the program, which must be complied with after receiving approval from the Central Committee.[163]

Li Xiannian thus added a new twist to the program: using imports of commodities to "bribe" agricultural producers to sell particular export commodities to the state. Such remunerative approaches were expanded during the early 1960s but ended up in the dustbin during the Cultural Revolution. Li Xiannian needed to wait sixteen years to realize his hope that the program would be fully legalized.[164]

REMUNERATIVE MEASURES: INCREASING THE ROLE OF THE INDIVIDUAL PRODUCER

In 1960, the PRC mostly exported unprocessed and processed agricultural commodities (table 3.3). To ensure their procurement, the leadership implemented policies analogous to those in the domestic economy. These included the stabilization of the agricultural economy by increasing the role of the individual

TABLE 3.3 CHINESE EXPORT COMMODITY COMPOSITION, 1950–81
(U.S. 100 million)

Year	Agricultural sideline products		Processed agricultural sideline products		Industrial and mineral products	
	Amount	%	Amount	%	Amount	%
1950	3.18	57.5	1.83	33.2	0.51	9.3
1951	4.13	54.6	2.38	31.4	1.06	14.0
1952	4.88	59.3	1.88	22.8	1.47	17.9
1953	5.69	55.7	2.65	25.9	1.88	18.4
1954	5.53	48.3	3.18	27.7	2.75	24.0
1955	6.51	46.1	4.01	28.4	3.60	25.5
1956	7.01	42.6	5.15	31.3	4.29	26.1
1957	6.40	40.1	5.03	31.5	4.54	28.4
1958	7.03	35.5	7.33	37.0	5.45	27.5
1959	8.50	37.6	8.75	38.7	5.36	23.7
1960	5.75	31.0	7.85	42.3	4.96	26.7
1961	3.09	20.7	6.84	45.9	4.98	33.4
1962	2.89	19.4	6.84	45.9	5.17	34.7
1963	3.99	24.2	7.07	42.9	5.43	32.9
1964	5.37	28.0	7.49	39.1	6.30	32.9
1965	7.37	33.1	8.02	36.0	6.89	30.9
1966	8.50	35.9	8.87	37.5	6.29	26.6
1967	8.39	39.3	7.75	36.3	5.21	24.4
1968	8.41	40.0	8.03	38.2	4.59	21.8
1969	8.24	37.4	8.62	39.1	5.18	23.5
1970	8.29	36.7	8.52	37.7	5.79	25.6
1971	9.55	36.2	9.20	34.9	7.61	28.9
1972	10.77	31.3	14.10	41.0	9.56	27.7
1973	20.80	35.8	23.00	39.5	14.39	24.7
1974	25.30	36.4	20.73	29.8	23.46	33.8
1975	21.50	29.6	22.61	31.1	28.53	39.3
1976	19.46	28.4	22.41	32.7	26.68	38.9
1977	20.96	27.6	25.74	33.9	29.20	38.5
1978	26.91	27.6	34.14	35.0	36.40	37.4
1979	31.57	23.1	44.86	32.9	60.15	44.0
1980	34.19	18.7	53.97	29.5	94.56	51.8
1981	36.81	17.6	54.62	26.2	117.50	56.2

Source: Zhongguo Duiwai Jingji, *Zhongguo,* sect. 4, p. 7.

farmer to the detriment of the commune and the increase of producer incentives by raising the state procurement price and by instituting various bonus schemes. Thus while simultaneously regaining macroeconomic control over the economy and the foreign economic sector, the post–GLF coalition regarded the individual, rent-seeking producer as its secret weapon to achieve production quotas.

To reverse the GLF collectivist trend and to relieve the acute agricultural labor shortages, the Central Committee adopted several important policy innovations. On 15 May 1960, the Central Committee transferred the commune labor force from capital construction projects back to the agriculture sector; 60–65 percent of the commune workers were to devote full time to agriculture and husbandry (80 percent and more during the busier periods).[165] Second, the Central Committee issued the Emergency Directive Letter on Current Policy Problems in Agricultural People's Communes on 3 November 1960; it declared that the production brigade and not the commune was the basic unit of account. The directive thus "asserted the [brigade's rights] over labor, land, farm animals, and agricultural tools." It criticized the egalitarianism and indiscriminate transfer of resources mandated by the GLF development strategy. Finally, the letter approved a greater percentage of accumulation to be allotted to the individual commune members.[166] The Central Work Conference held the following month strongly supported the new role for commune members. It legitimated household sideline and handicraft production, increased the size of individual plots to 7 percent of arable land, and privatized hog production.[167]

According to Li Xiannian, such innovations were necessary to offset Great Leap policies, which "committed the mistake of setting high procurement quotas in grains and other agricultural products"; this "serious commandism dampened the farmers' enthusiasm and harmed agricultural production."[168] The Central Committee thus "greatly lowered unified state purchases and state quotas (*tonggou paigou*) of grains and of other important agricultural commodities. It simultaneously [compensated for the loss] by importing a large amount of grains." Sales and purchases of grain, edible oils, pork, and other agricultural products could even be negotiated.[169]

Thus, the Central Committee guaranteed to a certain extent the brigade's and individual farmer's rights over agricultural inputs. According to Chen Yun, this was a primary solution to stabilizing the entire economy. He argued that

> "fertile water doesn't leak into outsiders' fields." . . . Now the peasants are still very poor. If we leave more to the peasants, actually they will not just consume it but they will still want to sell some of it. There will be more goods if there is more flexibility. . . . The problem now is that we are too strict, as more and more kinds of things come under unified control, and less and less

is procured. If we are more flexible, there naturally will be more things procured after production is developed. . . . To stabilize the market, the key is to
import grain.[170]

The result of these measures was the limited emancipation of the agricultural
producer, which would not be fully realized until the post–GLF coalition
returned to power after 1979.

REMUNERATIVE MEASURES: PRODUCER INCENTIVES

The second relevant theme of the new development strategy in agriculture was
to boost producer incentives by increasing the state procurement price and instituting various bonus schemes. Such incentives would "be beneficial in encouraging the farmer to produce" agricultural goods that were not as profitable as
other agricultural and cash crop production; it also compensated the beleaguered
farmer, whose share of the agricultural accumulation during the GLF period "was
relatively low."[171]

A price rise was first agreed upon on 11 November 1960. The Central Committee approved the Office of Finance and Trade plan to raise by 14.33 percent
the unified procurement price of six edible oil crops (peanut, soybean, sesame,
rape seed, tea oil, and tung oil). Prices were raised again on 15 January 1961
along with grain, hog, poultry, and egg procurement prices, and it was hoped
that farmers would divert their production to these scarce agricultural goods.[172]

The 11 November 1960 decision also approved a bonus of 10 percent of the
grain unified procurement price to be awarded any area that had exceeded the
set grain procurement quota (*jiangshou banfa*).[173] In 1961, other bonus schemes
were implemented in which the state offered farmers desired goods in exchange
for desired commodities (*huangou banfa*).[174] For example, between 1961 and
1962, the state awarded a bonus of 35 *jin* of grain for every 50 kilograms (*yi
dan*) of cotton and 20 *jin* of grain for every 50 kilograms of shelled peanuts,
sesame seeds, or flue-cured tobacco.[175] Such economic levers coerced the newly
"freed" farmers into diversifying production and producing goods most needed
by the state.

Similar measures also were adopted in the export sector. The export procurement price took as its base the domestic procurement price. Thus, the domestic price increases also applied to products intended for the export market. Later
the State Council approved a separate foreign-trade procurement price (*waimao
shougou jiage zhengce*). The policy stipulated higher procurement prices for
goods whose quality, variety, or packaging exceeded that of similar goods
intended for the domestic market.[176]

As in the domestic economy, the leadership instituted a bonus scheme in 1961
to stimulate production of a variety of agricultural sideline products for export.[177]

On 20 March 1961, Li Xiannian spoke at a Central Work Conference on methods to overcome the current economic problems. Confronted with a projected bill of nearly $600 million for imported grain to feed the burgeoning urban population, Li suggested that the following "effective economic measures" be taken:

1. While importing grains, a portion should be set aside to reward the planting of economic crops, for expanding pig or livestock production, etc. In this fashion, not only can we guarantee exports, but we can stabilize the domestic market and withdraw money from circulation. We must fundamentally resolve the problems in grain production and gradually reduce grain imports.

2. We must appropriately raise the procurement price for all small agricultural sideline products or agricultural handicraft products that the state needs. The sale price for these items on the agrarian market has been set so unreasonably above the set state-owned commercial price that they absolutely cannot be procured.

3. In addition to rewards of grain, we can also use rewards of material goods needed by the farmers (for instance, a farmer who sells one *jin* of eggs could be provided with several *liang* of sugar, etc.). Contracts can be signed with farmers that stipulate that for the sale to the state of a particular product, the farmer would be supplied with the needed material good. In addition, the prices for some products needed in industry, handicraft industry, and for domestic consumption can be lowered somewhat in price as long as it is according to an overall pricing policy. This will be beneficial in procuring the agricultural sideline products needed for export.[178]

Production of economic crops needed to be increased because they were the foundation of China's light industrial economy and export production. Without an increase, Li warned that there would be "major problems in next year's light industrial production, in market supplies, and in exports" and that the standard of living for China's farmers would decline.[179]

As Li Xiannian had suggested in March 1961, the state initially offered grain to producers of six economic crops—tea, silk, peppermint oil, apples, oranges, and shelled walnuts. By 1962, foreign trade companies offered the producer a variety of bonus items in exchange for the procurement of 108 export commodities. With farmers entranced with the idea of receiving bonuses of scarce items such as cigarettes, silks, and tennis shoes, the successful scheme was implemented throughout the early 1960s. Chinese analysts consider it a major reason for export procurement successes after 1961 (table 3.4).

In addition, in 1964 the Ministry of Foreign Trade and the Chinese People's Construction Bank allocated RMB 600 million for the Specialized Loan Program

TABLE 3.4 SELECTED EXPORT PROCUREMENT AMOUNTS, 1960–63

Item	1960	1961	1962	1963
Live hogs	1,040,000	480,000	1,000,000	1,430,000
Frozen pork*	75,000	11,000	19,000	31,000
Poultry	12,280,000	6,380,000	9,580,000	13,140,000
Live fish*	20,000	11,900	15,800	—
Fresh shrimp*	49,000,000	24,000,000	91,000,000	—
Vegetables*	163,000	127,000	195,000	—
Oranges*	77,000	38,000	46,000	—
Apples*	116,000	46,000	75,000	—
Tea**	2,484,000	1,405,000	—	1,557,000

Source: Tan Qingfeng, Yao Xuecong, and Li Shusen, eds., *Waimao fuchi shengchan shijian,* 18–19.

*tons

***dan** (50 kilograms)

for Industrial Export Production (Chukou Gongyepin Shengchan Zhuanxiang Daikuan).[180] Export taxes remained nearly nonexistent and only applied to peanut oil, peanuts, peppermint oil, and menthol.[181]

Case Study: ECPB Policy Implementation, 1960–1966

In early 1960, Premier Zhou Enlai issued a directive stating, "It is very necessary for the Ministry of Foreign Trade to establish export commodity production bases and to carry out their basic construction."[182] The Ministry of Foreign Trade accordingly held a National Foreign Trade Work Conference on 4–20 April 1960 to formulate plans for establishing the ECPBs. The ministry subsequently submitted a report on 1 June and received Central Committee approval on 30 June 1960.[183]

According to the June report, the ECPBs were to promote "self-sufficiency, increase production, encourage economy of resources, . . . combine current needs with long-term intentions, [and] establish processing bases in areas of raw material production" (see appendix C). The report mandated five different types of production bases; the Ministry of Foreign Trade was to develop immediately certain key bases and to provide them financial assistance. Zhou subsequently ordered the Ministry of Foreign Trade to formulate plans for the directive's implementation.

Reflecting the overall turn toward centralization, the post–GLF coalition desired to centralize or "basify" (*jidihua*) the production of the most important export commodities. Vice-Premier Chen Yun proposed in 1961 that "all export commodities should have production bases" (i.e., ECPBS) to ensure quality and competitiveness. He criticized some Chinese exports as not meeting the specifications and being "of poor quality and lack[ing] a good reputation in the international market." Chen Yun reminded his audience of the "vitality" of the international marketplace:

> There is not just one country but there are many countries. In the competition between each other, commodities of good quality and low price will find a market. To win the competition, those who trade can only follow the needs of customers, not subjective decisions made by the producers. To export more, we must organize production and manage well the bases for export commodities according to the requirements of the international market. . . . To ensure exports we must work on commodity bases.[184]

Export production thus could be guaranteed, and export commodity specifications and quality could be standardized.

While echoing similar pronouncements in Taiwan and Korea during the late 1950s and 1960s to establish EPZS, China's version was not part of a coherent strategy to confront the international marketplace. The establishment of the ECPBS was the first step to insulate export production from domestic economic disruption. The Chinese EPZS were more akin to their domestic cousins established in the late 1950s to guarantee food production for the urban areas. After submitting the Report on the National Conference on Agricultural Sideline Products and Arts and Craft Production in Large Urban Areas, held in Shanghai in June 1959,[185] Li Xiannian drafted a Central Committee directive that placed a major emphasis on establishing agricultural sideline production bases (*fushipin shengchan jidi*).[186] Situated in the surrounding suburbs, the urban production bases encouraged "self-sufficiency in [agricultural production], with outside help as a supplement."[187] These suburban areas primarily were responsible for raising vegetables, while the outlying regions would produce grain, cotton, and oil-bearing crops and engage in animal husbandry, and fisheries. Urban organizations, factories, schools, and military units also were required to become self-sufficient in agricultural sideline products.[188]

As early as December 1958, the Central Committee encouraged even urban areas to experiment with establishing self-sufficient urban communes.[189] By March 1960, Zhou Enlai had changed his mind and supported their establishment;[190] by mid-1960, 190 large urban areas had approved 1,064 urban communes that contained nearly 77 percent or the areas' urban population (55 million people).[191] While the urban commune idea ultimately failed, remnants of the urban agricultural sideline production bases policy could still be seen in Beijing's Haidian district in the post-1979 period. Unfortunately for those of us who jogged a loop from Peking University through the rice paddies to enter the back door of the Summer Palace, these urban farms have been replaced by sprawling housing complexes erected during the urban construction explosion of the late 1980s and 1990s.

After the Central Committee approved the ECPB policy in summer 1960, policy implementation did not proceed as originally anticipated. A few agricultural sideline, local, and specialty commodity bases (*chukou nongfu tute shangpin jidi*) were established.[192] For instance, a "five materials" (*wu liao*) production base was established on Hainan Island to produce oil crops, spices, goods and materials, beverages, and seasonings. A hog production base was constructed in Henan Province, while an export base was launched in the Bohai reclamation area, and specialized factories were established (*zhuanchang*). To coordinate these activities, the Ministry of Foreign Trade established a Bureau for Production Bases (Shengchan Jidiju).[193] Vice-Premier Chen Yun even gave his hearty endorsement to the ECPB policy in a widely quoted May 1961 speech. Chen Yun hoped that export bases would be established within eighteen months and would become the major producer of export commodities that exceeded $200,000–300,000 in value and that were competitive on the international market.[194]

Yet these bases did not play a substantial role in Chinese foreign economic strategy during this early period.[195] Chinese scholarly treatments mention ECPB policy failure yet fail to clarify the "various reasons [why the policy] did not flourish."[196] Only by analyzing the economic directives issued at the time can one offer a plausible explanation.

In comparison with the other export promotion schemes, the cost of implementing the ECPB policy was high. The ECPB policy called for the establishment of a series of export bases, export factories, and workshops. There was little money for new capital expenditures under the readjustment policies of the Eight-Character Plan. Besides, the other export promotion schemes, especially the agricultural bonus scheme, were more simple and yielded quicker returns for less investment. Second, the establishment of bases for export commodities required the creation of an independent production system. The implementation of a separate system would take time and involve intense bargaining among the various bureaucracies involved; as mentioned previously, the Ministry of Foreign Trade had already encountered difficulties in establishing its own separate production system.

Considering the need for an inexpensive and quick solution to its foreign export procurement problems, the post–GLF leadership emphasized the other export promotion schemes. According to Li Xiannian, the leadership agreed at the July 1963 Central Work Conference on Finance and Trade that there are some commodities that can be procured for export according to regular procurement channels. The Ministry of Foreign Trade does not need to establish bases for these products. There are some commodities that are difficult to supply for export purposes. The Ministry of Foreign Trade must establish bases for these products. Bases will be developed for commodities in demand by the international market. In summary, foreign trade export bases will be developed according to particular circumstances. In some instances, they can be increased; in others, they can be reduced. Yet they cannot be dismissed altogether.[197]

Thus, only a few ECPBs were established in the 1960–66 period of economic recovery and expansion. After 1964, Chinese leaders became less concerned about innovative ways to finance an import substitution development strategy. Their attention was drawn to more ideological matters and the building of the Third Front.

Conclusion

The post–GLF coalition saved China from the economic disaster of the Great Leap. Mao's use of normative means to increase production had resulted in tens of millions of deaths. Although they were avowed adherents of the command economy and administrative approaches, the post–GLF economic policy coalition had proved the efficacy of additional remunerative methods to increase production. They accepted the necessity of appealing to the people's profit motive—especially if it meant an extra pair of rubber galoshes—to repay Soviet debts and grain imports. They also continued to believe that the international market was an important source of technology and expertise that would accelerate China's progress along the path of self-reliance.

Yet this Four Modernizations path of development was short-lived. With the support of Lin Biao and Jiang Qing's elite coalitions, Mao recovered complete control over economic development policy by 1966. The post–GLF coalition's remunerative-administrative approach to economic development subsequently was declared a capitalist poison pill designed to destroy China's socialist revolution. Having learned that the GLF methods of mobilizing the population were not as effective, Mao used international threats to mobilize China. A more militaristic economic development path was promoted that required only a minimal foreign economic policy.

CHAPTER 4

Chaos and the Cultural Revolution, 1966–1971

During the Cultural Revolution (1966–71), Mao Zedong recovered full political control over the Party and the state. Strongly critical of the economic policies adopted in the post-1959 period, Mao, with the support of Lin Biao and Jiang Qing's coalitions, altered the domestic development strategy to support a wartime economy. The new strategy as epitomized by the Third Front reflected the "truc meaning" of self-sufficiency, whose goal was to achieve a form of economic autarky. They thus eliminated the small-scale import substitution program based on Western capitalist technology and equipment as well as the post–GLF export promotion schemes.

The Ideological Crisis of the Mid-1960s

Because of the post–GLF economic reforms, China steadily increased its exports after 1961. Chinese leaders repaid the country's foreign debts, financed grain imports, and instituted a small-scale import substitution development program. Yet the relative growth rate for exports and imports, which had been increasing since 1961, began to drop precipitously after 1966 (see tables 3.2, 2.5, 3.3).

What caused this precipitous drop? Developed economies more than doubled their trade with the developing world during the 1960s. China also enjoyed a doubling of agricultural and semiprocessed exports to the West.[1] Because of China's limited involvement in Vietnam, the United States never sought to reimpose a UN economic embargo or convince Western allies to suspend their trade with China.

Domestically, export procurement problems did occur during the Cultural Revolution, but they were not as serious as implied by post-1976 accounts. Urban chaos, especially the internecine conflict within the Red Guard movement, affected industrial production and capital construction.[2] The State Planning Commission on 29 April 1967 suggested "an increase [in] the importation of some steel, used steel, and chemical and industrial raw materials" to compensate for a drop in the domestic production.[3] Exports of heavy industrial products, in turn, fell from the post-1949 high of $549 million in 1966 to $354 million in 1970;[4] the percentage of gross export value derived from industrial and mineral products dropped from 30.9 percent in 1965 to 21.8 percent in 1968 (see table 3.3).

The Cultural Revolution did not have as great an effect on the countryside. Because of the post–GLF emphasis on agricultural production, grain production reached its post-1949 high of 214 million tons in 1966, increasing to 239.9 million tons by 1970; cotton production also reached its post-1949 high of 2.337 million tons in 1966, dropping a bit by 1970 to 2.277 million tons.[5] The amount of foreign exchange earned by raw and processed agricultural exports was fairly close to its post-1949 high of $850 million reached in 1959 (table 3.3). Except for fruit production, which was not a "politically tasteful" crop, agriculture fared so well that the State Planning Commission suggested in 1967 "the reduction of 500,000 tons [1 billion *jin*] from the planned annual import of 3.5 million tons of grain. . . . [That will translate into] a savings of approximately $40 million. This roughly can buy 100,000 tons of steel and 300,000 tons of used steel [from abroad]."[6]

Thus, the production situation during the Cultural Revolution was the antithesis of that in the early 1960s. Instead of increasing foreign grain imports to overcome domestic shortages, the Chinese increased steel imports. Instead of offsetting reduced agricultural exports with industrial exports, the Chinese during the Cultural Revolution effected a large increase in agricultural exports (raw and processed agricultural goods) to compensate for the reduction in industrial exports (see tables 2.5, 3.3).

During the famine period of the early 1960s, agricultural procurement was consistently problematic. Afterward, procurement eased as agriculture production flourished. During the post–GLF period, Chinese leaders were burdened with the politically sensitive Soviet debt. By the time of the Cultural Revolution period, the Soviet debt had been paid, and export loans owed to Western creditors were relatively small.[7] Thus, Chinese leaders in the mid-1960s were facing a less burdensome foreign and domestic economic problem. Foreign trade growth rates were not reduced by the international environment or by domestic economic shortages.

An ideological difference among the elites was the primary cause for the reduction in foreign trade. According to Bo Yibo, Mao feared that post–GLF policies were leading to "peaceful evolution." Khrushchev and the Soviet revisionists had infected eight members of the Chinese Central Committee, including Political Bureau member Peng Dehuai, who had challenged Mao during the Lushan conference.[8] With the 1966 issuance of the Circular of May 16, Mao Zedong finally criticized "those representatives of the bourgeoisie who [had] sneaked into the Party, the government, the army and various cultural circles."[9]

Supported by Marshal Lin Biao and his PLA as well as Jiang Qing and her like-minded Party ideologues, Mao finally attacked bourgeois elements of the Party who were leading the country to ideological chaos.

Mao thus exposed "the sinister schemes and tricks of [these] power holders of the Party," including most of the architects of the post–GLF economic recovery and expansion policies—Liu Shaoqi, Deng Xiaoping, Bo Yibo, and Chen Yun.[10] Second, Mao "carr[ied] out investigation and study on certain irrational things done in the past concerning economic affairs"—including the export promotion policies of the early 1960s.[11]

Readjustment of Foreign Economic Policy: Sweeping Away All Ghosts

To sweep away undue "worship of foreign things" and reassert Chinese nationalism, China's connections with the outside world were severely criticized. Shanghai people were attacked for wearing Western-style clothes or hairdos. The Bund was stripped of its colonial heritage, including the brass lions crouching in front of the former Hongkong and Shanghai Bank. Western- or Japanese-sounding street or building names were replaced by patriotic labels, such as the Anti-Revisionist Building or the People's War Hotel.[12] In Beijing, the Dutch chargé d'affaires was a prisoner within the embassy for nearly six months; the Soviet embassy was besieged by thousands of demonstrators; parts of the British compound were set ablaze. In retrospect, the Chinese demonstrations following the 1999 bombing of the Chinese embassy in Belgrade were tame.[13]

Mao and the politics-in-command coalitions considered the post–GLF domestic economic reforms as "irrational" measures designed to restore capitalism (*fubi zibenzhuyi*).[14] Within the foreign economic sector, the export promotion policies were vilified as "against the principle of self-sufficiency," "setting up independent kingdoms," or policies of "national betrayal." Most policies and measures were suspended.[15]

The first promotion policy to come under attack was the bonus scheme, which was officially eliminated by 1972 (table 4.1).[16] "Revolutionary China" would not repeat Stalin's mistake of creating "a high salary stratum." Politics were in command (*zhengzhi guashuai*); "one only [needed] to use spiritual encouragement and not material incentives" to stimulate production.[17] By the First Plenum of the Ninth Party Congress, Mao Zedong argued that "carrying out any material incentive scheme, bonus system, etc. is akin to putting profits in command. This is not promoting the principle of putting proletarian politics in command."[18]

As a result, the Specialized Loan Program for Industrial Export Production (Chukou Gongyepin Shengchan Zhuanxiang Daikuan) was suspended by

TABLE 4.1 NUMBER OF AGRICULTURAL PRODUCTS INVOLVED IN THE
PRODUCTION INCENTIVE BONUS SCHEMES, 1963–69

Year	Agricultural products for the domestic sector	Agricultural products for the export sector
1963	169	48
1964	161	51
1965	144	57
1966	139	39
1967	129	39
1968	80	27
1969	80	27
1970	—	0

Source: Tan Qingfeng, Yao Xuecong, and Li Shusen, eds., *Waimao fuchi shengchan shijian,* 19–21.

1970.[19] The programs allotting foreign exchange to localities (*waihui fencheng*)[20] and using imports to develop exports (*yijin yangchu*) were also canceled.[21] In addition, the overseas Chinese investment programs inaugurated in the 1950s were suspended. Raising interest rates on overseas Chinese remittances had been a useful tool since the late 1950s to increase foreign exchange reserves.[22] On 24 September 1966, a report to the CCP Central Committee suggested that "the preferential interest savings rates on overseas Chinese remittance accounts should be lowered."[23]

The Overseas Chinese Investment Company "was set up in the late 1950s and early 1960s . . . with investment offices in twelve provinces, cities, and autonomous regions [and] had attracted a total of $52.81 million of overseas Chinese remittances."[24] The company was severely criticized for its "capitalist management ideas in attracting overseas Chinese remittances" and closed by 1970.[25] The operations of 318 private enterprises with overseas Chinese remittances (*siying qiaohui ye*) in Guangdong, Fujian, Zhejiang, and Guangxi, whose market capitalization was valued at about $560,000 (66 percent of which belonged to overseas Chinese investors), were frozen and eventually nationalized on 8 May 1972.[26] The fear of "having any relationship abroad" (*haiwai guanxi*) also resulted in the disbanding of schools established for returning overseas Chinese, such as Jinan University outside Guangzhou.[27]

Mao's new development strategy clearly did not support the ECPB idea. The Ministry of Foreign Trade was criticized for implementing programs "against the principle of self-sufficiency" and of "setting up independent kingdoms."[28] A definite contradiction thus existed between the new development strategy and the ECPB policy; the basic ECPB idea was to establish an independent production center promoting export production. Based on the Maoist strategy's decentralization policy, it can be assumed that the ECPB program was canceled and the few operating bases turned over to local authorities. On 26 September 1970 the National Foreign Trade Planning Conference approved the "transfer [of] MFT industries to the localities, [and implementation of] dual leadership with primary management responsibilities given to the localities."[29] Like other ministries,[30] the MFT relinquished its "independent kingdom" by 1971.

Mirroring the fate of one of its major early supporters, Chen Yun, the ECPB idea was assigned to the dustbin with other bourgeois capitalist notions of the post–GLF period.

Policy Innovation:
The Maoist Development Strategy and the Third Front

Politics-in-Command Path to Development

As argued in chapters 1 and 2, Mao Zedong's normative-administrative approach to economic development was the complete antithesis of the post–GLF's remunerative-administrative approach. Instead of profit motives and economic efficiency, Mao sought other ways to tap the tremendous potential of the Chinese people, who when selflessly united in a common purpose, could overcome any obstacle in China's road to self-sufficiency (see chapter 1).

While continuing the normative-administrative approach first used during the GLF, Mao had learned from his previous mistakes. Mao continued to de-emphasize—although did not totally eliminate—administrative methods. He never again called for the achievement of grandiose goals such as the GLF's attempt to surpass the United States and Britain in steel production.[31]

Instead, Mao emphasized normative tools to liberate the productive force of Communist man. In an internal Party communication issued in March 1959, Mao blamed the failure of the GLF on "the leading cadre of some units, nearly all of whom were divorced from the masses, acted arbitrarily, and only believed themselves and not the masses when handling problems. They were completely indifferent to the mass line."[32] During the Cultural Revolution, Mao focused on purifying the people's ideology by championing the idea that "politics can assault all others" (*zhengzhi keyi chongji qita*). By emphasizing the mass line and class struggle, the Party and the military could eliminate the "Three Great Differences (between city and countryside, worker and peasant, and mental and manual labor)."[33] With the masses unfettered by selfish elitism, their vast productive forces could be tapped.

Mao had also learned from the GLF that the masses need to be truly motivated. The solution: a foreign threat.

The Third Front

In looking back at the mid-1960s, Bo Yibo argues that the Chinese leadership "overestimated the threat of war. This led to an overaccelerated deployment of Third Front[34] construction and an overextension of projects."[35]

Two major variables affected the Chinese leadership's "overestimation": the desire to eliminate contradictions and prevent the rise of Soviet revisionism, and the preparation for a possible war against the United States and the Soviet Union. Up to the May–June work conference of 1964, the domestic variable played the key role; following the conference, Mao used the perception of international threat to de-emphasize the Four Modernizations strategy and legitimate a Third Front strategy of economic development.[36]

ELIMINATING CONTRADICTIONS

Mao's emphasis on egalitarian struggle had major implications for China's development strategy. Just as self-reliance resulted in a more decentralized, self-reliant government structure from the provinces to the communes,[37] self-reliance was the guiding theme of foreign economic policy. Mao strongly disagreed with the Soviet belief in comparative advantage among the socialist states because it was the antithesis of self-reliance. Mao argued,

> This is not a good proposition. We will not even go so far as to propose it to our provinces. We advocate overall development. We will not say that there is no need for each province to produce goods which it can depend on other provinces to supply to meet its needs. We want all provinces to do as much as possible in developing all kinds of production, so long as they do not militate against the overall situation. . . . We are advocating that under a plan of unification for the whole country, each province does its own thing as much as possible. As long as the raw materials are there and the market conditions are there, as long as they can obtain raw materials locally and sell their products locally, they can do as much as possible what they are able to do. Previously, we were afraid that after the various provinces developed all kinds of industry, industrial products would find no buyers, like in such cities as Shanghai. Now, it does not appear to be the case.[38]

Although recognizing the limitations of smaller provinces such as Qinghai and Ningxia, Mao argued that the large provinces should become self-reliant and that interprovincial trade should be suppressed.

Mao subsequently promoted a more egalitarian distribution of state investment funds to eliminate the contradiction between the rich coastal regions and the backward interior. During the 1950s, Mao publicly complained that the economic infrastructure was too focused in China's coastal areas. Mao had severely criticized "trickle-down" theories,[39] in which the coastal areas continued their historical role as China's primary economic powerhouse and recipient of new capital construction funds. Mao thus proposed in his Ten Great Relationships that "more than ninety percent of [new factories were to] be built in the interior."[40]

Privately, Mao in the mid-1950s did not intend to sacrifice the coastal areas "like some comrades, who feel that war is coming and in preparing their position for war want to restrict the coastal area." Instead, Mao refuted the Soviet emphasis on heavy industrial production inherent in the FFYP and promoted light industrial production, 70 percent of which was situated along China's coast.[41]

Zhou Enlai concurred with Mao's April 1956 initiative by agreeing that an interior development plan was possible and should be pursued. But Zhou was more open about his opposition to "the tendency of paying less attention to or even restricting coastal industrial development." Under the current world situation, he said, a world war would "be delayed or possibly even avoided." Thus, China "should not overlook being prepared; we also don't want to be too much intimidated by Dulles and become passive." China should "utilize well coastal conveniences to develop industry, accumulate capital, increase qualified personnel and raise the technology level. . . . By using coastal development to stimulate interior industrial development, we will help and support interior industrial development."[42] Zhou's alternate trickle-down approach to domestic development was reminiscent of the coastal development strategy of the 1980s. It took more than eight years before there was any dramatic redirection of state investment toward the interior. However, instead of a trickle, there was a deluge of investment to the interior.

PREVENTING SOVIET REVISIONISM

Until Mao's 6 June 1964 speech, the post–GLF coalition had not considered the international situation to be critical. According to John Holdridge, the United States clearly stated its lack of territorial ambitions during the Sino-U.S. ambassadorial talks in Warsaw. Alan Whiting had convinced Secretary of State Dean Rusk to avoid the southeastern Chinese border in order to prevent another Chinese intervention such as in 1950.[43] As for the Soviet threat, Lin Biao could not persuade the post–GLF coalition to prepare a Third Front during his 29 January 1962 speech at the Seven Thousand Cadre Conference.[44]

While helping to draft the Third FYP (1966–71), Bo Yibo relegated defense spending to third on the list of priorities, despite the Sino-Indian border war of the previous year.[45] In several speeches leading up to the Central Party Work Conference of May–June 1964, Li Xiannian failed to even mention defense spending, but instead called for a continuation of the import substitution development strategy.[46] As late as 21 May 1964, the Central Committee and the State Council approved a report from the Small Group on Overseas Chinese Remittances that claimed that China could exceed the planned target of $120 million in overseas Chinese remittances for 1964. In agreeing to the report, the Central Committee and the State Council stated that the goal was possible "because the international situation is even more advantageous to us."[47]

The post–GLF coalition thus perceived the international environment as generally favorable in early 1964. Consequently, the Third FYP draft focused on resolving the problems of "eating, wearing, and using." Bo Yibo defined the underlying strategy of the plan as focusing on

> eating, [which] is grains; wearing, [which] is textiles that also encompasses nylon and plastic products [such as nylon socks, plastic shoes, shoe soles, etc.]; and using, [which includes the production of] ordinary household furniture, ordinary kitchen tools and utensils, thermoses and other commonly used industrial products, but not refrigerators or television sets. We must develop the basic industries and carry out the necessary defense construction. In sum, number one priority must be given to "eating, wearing, and using," number two priority to basic industries while number three priority must be accorded to national defense. This is the direction to developing industry and is the direction taken by the national economic plan.[48]

The draft plan continued the post–GLF strategy based on remunerative-administrative measures, and it focused on strengthening the production of consumer products. In doing so, the draft plan allotted 70 percent of all investment to China's traditional industrial region—the coastal areas.[49] Overall, the draft was consistent with the long-term aims of Zhou's Four Modernizations development program announced in 1963, which continued to use large-scale import substitution development to realize a modernized Chinese economy by the end of the twentieth century.[50]

The drafting of the Third FYP offered Mao a prime opportunity to attack the post–GLF coalition. As Mao stated in the Ninth Polemic issued in July 1964, the Communist Party and China were facing "a matter of life and death" in "prevent[ing] the emergence of Khrushchev's revisionism in China."[51] Mao had taken the initial step in March 1961 to reenter the first line of decision making in order to stop the adoption of the household contract system (chapter 1). Having consolidated the support of the PLA via Lin Biao's propaganda campaign in the early 1960s, Mao Zedong focused on society at large and used the Socialist Education Movement to attack indirectly the post–GLF's policies in 1963. Thus, Mao's intervention at the work conference of 1964 can be viewed as a further step to discredit the post–GLF coalition.

While pursuing his self-interest—undisputed power—Mao at the same time was motivated by altruism. Mao strongly believed that the normative-administrative approach constituted the best path to self-reliance (*zili gengsheng*), which is the primary goal of any inwardly oriented development regime. Having learned his lesson during the GLF, Mao became fixated on resolving contradictions within Chinese society. Mao thus sought to alter the post–GLF's vision of economic development based on remunerative-administrative norms and to focus on the impoverished interior. He undoubtedly believed that the country was threatened by the international situation during the spring and summer of 1964. But to paraphrase a Chinese saying, Mao considered the Third Front as a way to kill three birds (to discredit the post–GLF coalition and its Four Modernizations strategy, to resolve the contradiction between the coast and the interior, and to strengthen the country's defenses) with one stone (*yiju "san" de*).

Apparently perceiving weakness within the post–GLF leadership, Mao went on the offensive during spring 1964. Zhou, who had been traveling in Asia and Africa between December 1963 and March 1964, had been separated from internal elite dynamics. He thus was unable to consolidate support for his Four Modernizations approach presented the previous year or to counter Mao's developing alliance with Lin Biao and Jiang Qing's coalitions. According to Li Zhisui's account, Mao also took advantage of Liu Shaoqi's sudden contraction of tuberculosis. Mao thus initiated the attack on the ruling elites, whom Mao described as "lords [who] live in luxury and comfort." Mao denied the ruling elites—but not himself—access to their personal physicians, thus complicating Liu Shaoqi's road to recovery. Li Zhisui quotes Mao as saying, "What's everyone so excited about? If [Liu Shaoqi] is sick, then let him take a rest and have the doctors treat him. This has nothing to do with you [Li Zhisui]. Let other people handle it."[52]

Liu's illness and Zhou's alternate views perhaps explain Mao's remarks at a March 1964 meeting:

> In the final analysis, are some people ill or is their revolutionary will declining? Or did they go dancing six times a week? Or is it love of beauty but not country? Some say they are so sick that they cannot do their work. Can an illness be that bad?! . . . Like certain comrades, in the final analysis, do they love beauty or country? In my view, when we ask them to do XX, they may not necessarily be able to do it well. We should give them a "prime minister." For many years we have advocated going out to do investigation and study. But they did not go out. They have been engaging in industry for so many years yet they do not know what industry is. They do not understand machinery or equipment: what can they do?![53]

Exploiting such weaknesses in the spring of 1964, Mao sought direct support from Jiang Qing and Lin Biao's coalitions in launching a surprise three-pronged attack on the post–GLF coalition during the period leading up to the work conference. As previously noted, Jiang Qing in April 1963 attacked the current craze of ghost plays, especially *Li Huiniang,* whose story could be interpreted as an attack on the GLF.[54] Mao followed up Jiang Qing's attack by severely criticizing the cultural bureaucracy in June 1964 and implying that a purge might be necessary to avoid Hungarian-style revisionists.[55] At this stage of the drama, it is especially fascinating to understand Mao's growing alliance with Lin Biao and the PLA. Although he had opposed those "comrades" who in the mid-1950s saw enemies around every corner, Mao now collaborated with them in an attempt to regain full control over the state, especially economic policy.

While Zhou Enlai endured Mao's attacks in May 1958, Lin Biao was elected vice-chairman of the Central Committee and a member of the Standing Committee; following the Lushan conference of 1959, Lin Biao replaced Peng Dehuai as the leader of the PLA. Within the Party, Lin Biao was a strong voice for Mao Zedong and his utopian vision of development, especially during the Seven Thousand Cadre Conference of 1962, during which Mao was directly and indirectly attacked by the members of the post–GLF coalition.[56] Within the PLA, Lin spearheaded the campaign to glorify Mao Zedong Thought. According to Lin Biao, "In our time, Mao Zedong Thought is the pinnacle of Marxism-Leninism" and "studying the collected works of Mao Zedong is a shortcut to studying Marxism-Leninism."[57] Lin Biao thus promoted the Maoist ideological approach by advocating the "four firsts: put the human factor first; political work first; ideological work first; and living ideas first."[58] To promote Maoist ideas throughout the state, Lin Biao began the process of intermeshing the military with Party affairs and with finance and economics bureaucracies (*xitong*)[59] as well as working to militarize the entire Chinese population by June 1964.[60] Lin Biao thus became an extremely important ally in Mao's attempt to regain full control of the military, the Party and the state.

Just before the opening of the May–June work conference, Lin Biao authorized the publication of two important propaganda tools. On 25 April 1964— two weeks before the opening of the conference, the headquarters of the PLA's General Staff issued a report signed by Luo Ruiqing stating that China's industry, population, and infrastructure were too concentrated in the large coastal cities.[61] The PLA asked that the Central Committee adopt effective measures to prevent destruction of China's war-making capability from a sudden aerial attack. Second, the General Political Department of the PLA complied with a Lin Biao directive to edit the *Mao zhuxi yulu* (Quotations of Chairman Mao), which was published for the first time on 1 May 1964. These snippets of wisdom originally had been printed in the *People's Liberation Army Daily;*[62] by the height of the Cultural Revolution, hundreds of millions of Chinese worshiped this PLA-inspired collection that became a sacred text comparable to the Bible, Koran, and Torah.

Taking advantage of the post–GLF coalition's weaknesses, as well as armed with the PLA report and the Little Red Book, Mao successfully persuaded the post–GLF coalition to support the Third Front initiative. The Central Committee thus established on 6 June 1964 the Party Committee on National Defense (Guofang Gongye Dangwei) and the Military Defense Industry Political Affairs Department within the Central Committee (Zhongyang Guofang Gongye Zhengzhibu), which directed Third Front construction.[63]

A balanced assessment of Lin Biao is very difficult. Ever since Lin's attempted military coup in September 1971, the Chinese have literally airbrushed Lin Biao out of contemporary Chinese history. As a strong supporter of Mao, he probably had been upset with the post–GLF coalition and the low budget priority assigned to the PLA during the early 1960s. While all military bureaucracies engage in contingency planning, Lin Biao willingly aided and abetted Mao by exaggerating the threat facing China in April 1964. To gain the Party's and the country's support for Mao and the PLA, Lin Biao continued to exaggerate the threat throughout the 1960s; the exaggeration culminated with his apparent instigation of the Sino-Soviet border clashes of 1969.

Using International Threat to Change the Development Strategy

Countering Zhou's Four Modernizations strategy, Mao attacked the post–GLF coalition's draft plan before attending the Central Work Conference on the Third FYP that met during May and June 1964. In his earthy manner, Mao offered alternative priorities for the Third FYP: "Agriculture and national defense are your fists, while basic industries are your ass. You have to make sure that you have powerful fists, and a firm ass."[64]

The assault culminated in his 6 June 1964 speech to the conference. Mao thoroughly criticized China's Soviet-styled planning model, "which has become a force of habit with us and it seems hard to change."[65] Instead, Mao argued that China should adopt a more wartime economy by building a vast military infrastructure in the interior provinces. Originally published in *Wansui,* crucial parts of Mao's speech can be filled in by Bo Yibo (in italics):

> Moreover, we should consider war and make strategic plans. Party committees in various localities should not manage civil affairs alone and ignore the military, should not manage money alone and ignore guns. As long as imperialism exists, there will be a threat of war. *We are not the Chief of Staff for imperialism. Who knows when he will fight. The final victory in the war will not be decided by nuclear weapons, but by conventional weapons. . . . We must con-*

struct an industrial base in the Third Front. We can also build a few military industries in the First and Second Fronts. Every province must have military industries so that they can make their own rifles, submachine guns, light and heavy caliber machine guns, mortars, bullets and explosives. We can rest assured if they have all these things. This does not mean we no longer care about the seacoast which must also be well guarded so that it can play the role of supporting the construction of new bases. *We must accelerate the construction of the Panzhihua Steel Industrial Base. However, we cannot do a sloppy job of it. If Panzhihua is not built, we won't be able to sleep at night. . . . If you don't build Panzhihua, I'll get on my donkey and go there to hold a meeting; if you don't have the money, you can use my [book] royalties to build it.*[66]

Mao was not rejecting nonindigenous technology—such as the use of chemical fertilizers or foreign technology. In fact, Mao called for their continued use—but as supplementary tools. Mao placed far greater emphasis on the mass line, self-reliance, and the development of indigenous methods so that China could be prepared for war.

During the May–June 1964 central work conference, Mao gradually convinced the post–GLF coalition to make defense spending the country's second-highest priority. By his 6 June speech, Mao apparently convinced them that defense spending should be as important as eating, wearing, and using;[67] Bo states,

> Chairman Mao's speech struck a sympathetic response among all the assembled comrades. Everyone endorsed his position, believing that while simultaneously strengthening agricultural production and finding a solution to the people's eating, wearing, and using, construction of the third front must be made and that combat readiness must be stepped up. From that time on, the winds of war blew ever gradually stronger.[68]

To convince the Chinese elites of increased international tensions, Mao attacked the Soviet Union in July, calling into question the legitimacy of Soviet revisionist leadership and their right to control Siberia.[69] This attack culminated with the July publication of the last of the nine anti-Russian polemics, titled "On Khrushchev's Phony Communism and Its Historical Lessons for the World." These polemics were used not only to convince the world Communist movement of the superiority of Mao's path, but to remind the Chinese policy elites that Khrushchev was endangering the world Communist movement by promoting a capitalist restoration.[70]

Offering a counterstrategy to the Four Modernizations, Mao strongly supported the Third Front strategy and convinced the post–GLF coalition of its necessity two to three months before American actions at the Gulf of Tonkin. To solidify support, Mao thus manipulated the perception of war—not necessarily with the

United States but with the Soviet Union. In Holdridge's opinion, Chinese leaders during this period were beginning to see the Soviet Union as their greatest threat: China's newly established medium-range ballistic missiles were aimed toward the Soviet Union, not at U.S. bases in Asia.[71] Before the U.S. bombings of the North Vietnamese torpedo bases and oil depots, the Chinese Office on Defense Industry had already delivered its report on Third Front construction to Zhou Enlai.[72]

American actions at the Gulf of Tonkin thus were not the primary catalyst to the adoption of the Third Front strategy, but a tool used by Mao to reinforce his arguments.[73] Mao took full advantage of the uncertain international situation confronting China along all its borders to justify the redirection of capital construction funds to the interior regions.[74] Mao even sent a letter to Chen Boda on 27 August 1964 calling for the termination of the SPC unless dramatic changes were made; his intervention eventually resulted in the establishment of the Small Planning Commission (Xiao Jiwei).[75] And the post–GLF coalition agreed. On 19 August 1964, Li Fuchun, Bo Yibo, and Luo Ruiqing argued that all current construction projects be reduced or eliminated, and new projects concentrated in the Third Front.[76] The report, submitted two weeks after the Gulf of Tonkin, obviously reflected the elite's concern and desire to rally to national defense.

ZHOU'S ATTEMPT TO REDEFINE THE THIRD FRONT APPROACH, 1965

Faced with such an overwhelming assault from Mao, Lin Biao, and Jiang Qing, the post–GLF coalition had no recourse but to accept Mao's call to adopt a wartime development strategy during May–June 1964. Zhou Enlai thus directed the provinces to follow Guangdong's example of promoting Third Front construction and directed the SPC to increase national defense spending within the plan, especially in the southwest.[77] However, the post–GLF coalition was not truly convinced that the Third FYP should transform China into a wartime, autarkic economy. Zhou continued to promote the Four Modernizations approach, including import substitution development, in his government work report presented to the NPC on 21 December 1964.[78] On 12 April 1965, Zhou argued in an expanded meeting of the Political Bureau that China should develop the Third Front projects as well as continue to implement his long-range industrial development strategy.[79] The next day, the Central Committee agreed that

in 1965, *China must fully take advantage of the current, relatively favorable international conditions* to import new technology from capitalist countries in order to accommodate the domestic economic situation and meet construction needs. The key focus will be on equipment and technology for the metallurgical, mining, automobile, machine tool, instruments and meters, and electronics industries as well as meet the mechanical engineering needs of Third Front construction. Of the three methods of importing technology [import turnkey plants, import individual pieces of equipment, and purchase technological materials], we must put even greater emphasis and investigation on the latter two methods.[80]

While the Central Committee reduced capital construction investment to RMB 17 billion and reduced the emphasis on certain Western imports because of a lack of foreign exchange,[81] they remained unconvinced that the international situation was critical and that China needed to fully implement a wartime economy. Thus when an American F-104 was shot down over Hainan on 20 September 1965 and another U.S. plane over Guangxi on 5 October, the Chinese did not regard the intrusions as prelude to war and responded in a very low key.[82] Consequently, Zhou attempted to co-opt Mao's initiative by proposing a two-track development strategy emphasizing the development of both the civilian and the military economies. This amalgamation of plans—the "Four Guarantees: guarantee of war preparedness; guarantee of foreign aid; guarantee of the Third Front; and guarantee of key point projects"—was expanded by December 1965 to include agriculture.[83]

The post–GLF coalition's adoption of this intermediate policy readjustment of the development strategy was too late. Mao had found a ready ally within the State Council, Yu Qiuli, the minister of petroleum.[84] Along with Gu Mu, the vice-chairman of the State Planning Commission; Lin Hujia of Zhejiang; and Jia Tingsan, the vice-mayor of Beijing, Yu Qiuli was appointed to head the Small Planning Commission. In his 27 August 1964 letter to Chen Boda, Mao had already hinted at this action, which was an attempt to circumvent Li Fuchun of the State Planning Commission and Bo Yibo of the State Economic Commission. After July 1965, Yu Qiuli's Small Planning Commission immediately redrafted the Third FYP to place first priority in the third front, thus substituting Mao and Lin's strategy of promoting a wartime economy for the plan's underlying theme of promoting Zhou's Four Modernizations development strategy.[85]

Although Yu Qiuli would be attacked during the Cultural Revolution,[86] Yu played an important role in preventing the post–GLF coalition's attempt to emphasize a two-track development strategy in 1964. Yu's timely intervention in the economic planning bureaucracy ensured the success of the Third Front initiative. Expanding upon a Maoist directive, Lin Biao made sure that military-related industries ranging from steel mills to ball bearing plants as well as supporting units were in or relocated to remote regions safe from foreign invasion, such as the interior mountains or desert regions, or deep within caves.[87] Everyone became involved in war preparations, as extensive underground tunnels, subways, and bomb shelters were excavated throughout China's major cities.

Naughton roughly estimates that the Chinese spent more than RMB 140 billion to build the Third Front industrial complex between 1963 and 1975.[88] Such a massive redirection of capital investment and expertise had a particularly detrimental effect on the industrial development of coastal China, especially in the southeast border areas around Hong Kong, Taiwan, and Vietnam as well as the northeast and northwest borders with the Soviet Union. These areas were turned into military buffer zones bereft of any transborder trade.[89]

Maoist Foreign Economic Policy

Mao essentially believed that the 1950s import substitution program had fulfilled its purpose of updating China's civilian industrial infrastructure. If China needed chemical fertilizers or machinery, the primary solution "was to turn to small-scale enterprises in rural areas rather than to larger plants often imported from abroad and located in urban industrial centers."[90] In addition, Mao was putting into place a wartime economy with the establishment of the Third Front; China could not afford to become dependent on foreign producers and foreign technology. Relying on the inventiveness of the Chinese people, China had to develop the domestic market by itself; China did not need to assume new foreign debts or to continue export policies implemented since the late 1950s–early 1960s. Consequently, there was a perceptible drop in the growth of foreign trade between 1966 and 1969 (see table 3.2), especially with certain key countries such as the Soviet Union (see table 3.1). However, there is no evidence to suggest that Mao advocated a completely autarkic policy during the Cultural Revolution.

Unable to realize his Four Modernizations strategy, Zhou Enlai indirectly lobbied for an import substitution strategy by continually emphasizing China's technological backwardness. After the Ninth Party Congress, Zhou called for balanced growth between domestic economic and military industrial development.[91] In one case, Zhou ironically pointed out that China could make a hydrogen bomb, but could not produce a semiconductor.[92] Even though Mao had directed that China develop its own color television production line in 1969, three years later Chinese research and production units still had not produced one.[93] Zhou suggested a very limited import substitution strategy to import electronics equipment to improve one sector crucial to military modernization—radio.[94] At least one other import substitution turnkey project was ordered, while delivery of several previously agreed upon contracts were completed.[95] Zhou thus kept the door to the outside world somewhat ajar and continually argued against a complete autarkic approach, including direct criticism of "closed doorism" (*guanmen zhuyi*) in 1970.[96]

Although China no longer imported large-scale import substitution projects, Yu Qiuli and Zhou did implement a policy of mutually exchanging needed goods in international trade (*hutong youwu*),[97] which approved the import of scarce raw and processed materials as well as specific technical items.[98] As the Soviet, Japanese, and Western European import substitution projects were coming on-line in the 1960s,[99] the industrial projects needed various types of steel, nonferrous metals, and chemicals as well as machinery to produce the tractors and fertilizers needed for the domestic market. Many of these raw materials had to be imported from abroad. As for grains, the leadership could not forget the starvation of the GLF period or the burgeoning Chinese population and continued to import chemical fertilizers and grains from abroad.[100] But Mao had stated that "it is very dangerous to depend upon foreign countries or other provinces for the things that you eat."[101] The leadership thus reduced grain imports from 6.4 million tons in 1966 to 3.8 million tons in 1969. Thus, the foreign trade figures for the Cultural Revolution period show a relatively modest reduction in the growth of trade (see Table 3.2).[102]

To finance these crucial imports, the revolutionary leadership could only partly depend on the foreign currencies and securities uncovered and expropriated by the Red Guards.[103] The revolutionary leadership depended on the month-long, biannual Guangzhou Trade Fair to export Chinese goods as well as their financial and trade connections with Hong Kong. They thus took a series of steps to ensure that the fair, Hong Kong, and the Ministry of Foreign Trade would remain relatively untouched by the chaos of the Cultural Revolution.

The Cultural Revolution leadership recognized the Guangzhou Trade Fair as a major source of foreign exchange and as "an important front for propagandizing Mao Zedong Thought." Yet the leadership needed to adopt extreme measures to ensure the successful opening of the biennial event, especially during the first two years of the Cultural Revolution. During the initial mass movement to Destroy the Four Olds (old ideas, old culture, old customs, and old habits) of summer–fall 1966, Guangzhou's Red Guards planned to smash the antiques and burn the wall hangings adorning the entrance hall of the Guangzhou Trade Exhibition Building. Although the State Council posted a bulletin (*bugao*) at the exhibition center's entrance, Zhou Enlai's plea lacked power; it took the personal intervention of Liao Chengzhi to prevent the destruction of the exhibition hall's antiques.[104] To prevent further problems during the opening of the spring 1967 trade fair, the Central Committee, State Council, Central Military Commission, and Central Cultural Revolution Group jointly issued a five-point directive preventing the "seizure of power" (*duoquan*). With Mao's approval, the revolutionary leadership temporarily halted all Four Large (*sida*) activities (speaking out freely, airing views fully, holding great debates, and writing large-character posters) at the fair and any units directly related to it.[105]

Yet because of his experience of the previous year and the increasingly violent activities of the Red Guards, Zhou Enlai increasingly became concerned that the local Guangdong revolutionaries would ignore Beijing's directives. Zhou subsequently wrote a personal letter to Mao Zedong and Lin Biao outlining his fears that the chaos in Guangzhou would "be extremely detrimental" to the opening of the spring 1967 trade fair.[106] On the morning of 14 April 1967, Zhou flew to Guangzhou to ensure an uninterrupted opening. Zhou pleaded with the local Red Guard factions during a meeting at the Sun Yat-sen Memorial Hall not to interfere with the fair or to struggle against the local military or the Party leadership.[107] Zhou was partially successful: foreign businesspeople were only required to "study and recite *Quotations from Chairman Mao Tse-tung* before each trade negotiation session, to sing Chinese revolutionary songs, and to take part in demonstrations by the Red Guards."[108] This is in contrast to the foreign technicians servicing the import substitution projects of the 1960s. Some were treated as foreign agents, and either sent to prison or confined to their hotels.[109]

Following the Wuhan incident of 20 July 1967, radical Red Guard factions used weapons stolen from local PLA munitions depots to clash with each other and the PLA throughout China. By August, the May 16 rebels (*wuyiliu bingtuan*) had seized the Ministry of Foreign Affairs building in Beijing and torched the British diplomatic compound.[110] Equally violent was the situation in Guangzhou, where, according to Ezra Vogel,

> rail transport was disrupted and food shortages developed. Buildings were encircled, stormed, and gutted by fire. Bus service on many routes was discontinued as people walked long distances to work. People were afraid to go out at night because of the fights and the hoodlums, which were beyond police control. Student Red Guard groups clashed several times at Sun Yat-sen University, the major headquarters of student activists. Although it is impossible to estimate the total scope of the clashes, first-hand Red Guard accounts reveal that many thousands were involved in fighting in Canton [Guangzhou], that several thousand were injured and hundreds killed.[111]

Following this upsurge in internal chaos, Jiang Qing reluctantly made a self-criticism; Mao Zedong along with the Central Cultural Revolution Small Group finally agreed that the civil war within China's urban areas had to be controlled.[112] After September 1967, the more radical members of the Central Cultural Revolution Small Group were purged, and the Chinese military, as it had done countless times during previous centuries of political and economic chaos, took direct control over Chinese society.[113]

The situation was so tense in Guangzhou by fall 1967 that it was decided to delay the October 10 opening of the trade fair for one month. Following Premier

Zhou's negotiations in Beijing's Great Hall of the People, representatives of Guangzhou's Red Guard factions signed An Announcement to the People of the Guangzhou Area on 14 November 1967. The factions agreed to allow the trade fair to open; the PLA in turn issued orders for all Red Guard factions to turn in their weapons and to return to their units.[114] Foreign businesspeople probably had no idea of efforts made on behalf of the fall 1967 trade fair, which succeeded in completing deals worth $406 million.

Following the intervention of the PLA across China, the Central Committee, State Council, Central Military Commission, and Central Cultural Revolution Small Group were assured of a successful spring 1968 Guangzhou Trade Fair. They issued a second circular on 8 March 1968, stating,

1. The Guangzhou Export Commodity Trade Fair is an important international front to propagate Mao Zedong Thought. However, it must be remembered that we cannot force our views on others.

2. The Guangdong Provincial Party Committee (Shengwei) and the Ministry of Foreign Trade will send representatives to make up the Leading Committee on the Guangzhou Export Commodity Trade Fair of Spring 1968.

3. From March 20 to May 20, the Guangzhou Export Commodity Trade Fair and directly related units such as hotels [the Dongfang Hotel; Guangzhou Hotel], inns, and theaters will not carry out the Four Large activities.

4. With the determined support of export supply areas and suppliers, foreign trade departments must work vigorously to obtain export supplies.[115]

Not only was the spring 1968 trade fair a success; China's tallest building at the time—the Guangzhou Hotel—opened. Standing twenty-seven stories tall and overlooking a major square and the Pearl River, the hotel had been severely criticized by the Red Guards as a private project of the despised Guangdong Party leader Tao Zhu, who had petitioned the State Council in 1965 to build a new hotel for foreign businesspeople attending the trade fair. Because of Zhou Enlai's direct intervention, the Guangzhou Hotel opened without incident on 12 April 1968.[116]

Although some trade representatives in China were targeted and even accused of spying,[117] the Guangzhou trade fair remained a relative island of peace and a major tool of Chinese foreign economic policy during and after the Cultural Revolution period. According to Chae-jin Lee, a steady number of businesspeople attended the biannual fair, averaging 7,000 businesspeople per event between the spring fair of 1966 and the autumn fair of 1970. Despite the Sino-Soviet border clashes and Lin Biao's call to mobilize for war in 1969, the invited participants no longer had to participate in Red Guard demonstrations, but could directly engage in more professional trade negotiations.[118] Following the fall of Lin Biao and the unfreezing of Sino-U.S. relations, attendance at the

Guangzhou fair more than tripled, to over 20,000 participants after 1970, although the numbers of actual businesspeople has been estimated at about 9,000.[119] Earnings at the trade fair remained fairly constant during the Cultural Revolution (fall 1966, $481 million; spring 1967, $418 million; fall 1967, $406 million; fall 1970, $500 million); they more than tripled following the fall of Lin Biao and the reinitiation of the import substitution large-scale development strategy in the early 1970s (fall 1972, $1 billion; fall 1973, $1.587 billion).[120]

In addition to safeguarding the Guangzhou Trade Fair, Zhou attempted to reduce the Cultural Revolution's adverse effects on the foreign trade system. In June 1967, Zhou accused Guangzhou trade officials and representatives from two Ministry of Foreign Trade Red Guard factions of attempting to usurp Mao's authority. With the imminent death of Minister of Foreign Trade Ye Jizhuang, Zhou argued that the factions within the Ministry of Foreign Trade should "not capture, kidnap, or beat up cadre, should not crash into meetings, hold criticism meetings of over three hours, or force people into the 'airplane position' (*pengqishi*)."[121] Zhou later implored factions within the Ministry of Foreign Trade not to copy the example of the Ministry of Foreign Affairs by stealing PLA weapons or plundering the ministry's cash reserves.[122]

Zhou continued to maintain steady vigilance against the incursions of the Cultural Revolution on China's remaining foreign trade system. He blocked a Red Guard attempt in Xiamen to prevent the docking of a British cargo ship,[123] ridiculed the "naïve idea of the Red Guards" that China should only export goods that serve the working classes,[124] checked "ultraleftists" who argued that trade with foreign capitalists would make the Chinese spirituality more materialistic,[125] and criticized the promotion of Mao's slogans on export packaging or on banners carried by Chinese cargo ships entering foreign harbors.[126]

Zhou was most worried that the Cultural Revolution would severely disrupt the economic life of Hong Kong.[127] Responding to calls in July 1967 for the armed take-over of Hong Kong, Zhou countered that such actions would not serve the long-term interests of China.[128] Although such a military take-over did not occur, pro-Communist revolutionaries in Hong Kong incited widespread demonstrations in the British colony that were encouraged by mainland Chinese newspapers from June to September 1967. By January 1968, Zhou was arguing that these measures had been a mistake.[129] After the Ninth Party Congress in 1969, militant attitudes toward Hong Kong gave way to more utilitarian concerns. Zhou ordered the Xinhua News Agency, which had been China's "eyes and ears" in Hong Kong, and the Bank of China to begin to study Hong Kong's political, economic, and social situation in order to understand the international economic situation.[130]

Primary and secondary sources are unclear about problems within other segments of the export sector. Lee reports that the Japanese were unable to procure

Chinese coal and corn in the late 1960s; Chinese statistics do show a drop in overall coal exports, from 3.97 million tons in 1966 to 1.46 million tons in 1969.[131] By 1970, China again began to increase imports of crucial raw materials and the machinery necessary to supply domestic development (see table 2.5). A jump in demand for imports in 1970 put undue strain on domestic sourcing; without the necessary exports to finance the imports, China incurred a hard currency deficit in 1970.[132] The Central Committee admitted that "problems [were] occurring in export 'sourcing,'" and reinstated the program of using imports to develop exports, one of the only post–GLF policies to be revived during the Cultural Revolution.[133] The Chinese immediately imported raw cotton, which was subsequently spun into cloth for export.[134] Unfortunately, further analysis of the period is hampered by a lack of information.

Conclusion

Ironically, the success of the post–GLF incentive policies for producers and small-scale import substitution program enabled Mao Zedong to change the path toward self-reliance. By the beginning of the Cultural Revolution, many of China's production levels were at their highest levels since 1949. Mao and the politics-in-command coalitions thus could freely tap the ideological fervor and fears of foreign invaders to mobilize the people.

The result was internecine warfare.

CHAPTER 5

Resurrecting the Four Modernizations, 1971–1974

From a political economic view, the Cultural Revolution ended with Premier Zhou reassuming responsibility for the routine affairs of state on 13 September 1971 following the death of Marshal Lin Biao (the 9.13 incident).[1] As in the early 1960s, Zhou Enlai and the rehabilitated post–GLF coalition readjusted the development strategy to overcome the after-effects of Mao's ideological foray. However, instead of agricultural devastation or foreign debt repayment,[2] the post–GLF coalition tackled significant industrial and export problems.

Zhou subsequently resurrected the large-scale import substitution development strategy embodied by the 1963 Four Modernizations Program. He reconstituted the Ministry of Foreign Trade's export production system (*xitong*) and the export promotion policies, which had been condemned during the Cultural Revolution as "policies of national betrayal."[3] Zhou thus successfully resuscitated the industrial export sector, which helped guarantee financing of the Four Modernizations import substitution projects.

The Sino-American Rapprochement and the Oil Price Rise

The Beginning of the Tripolar Relationship

During the post–Cultural Revolution recovery and expansion period of the early 1970s, international factors continued to set policy parameters, but they were not the primary determinant. While the Sino-Soviet relationship had reached its nadir during the 1969 border clashes, China gained global legitimacy after reassuming its UN seat on 25 October 1971. With the Shanghai Communiqué of 28 February 1972, the partial lifting of the U.S. economic embargo, and the normalization of Sino-Japanese relations, the West no longer considered China as a dangerous pariah.

Although Nixon's 1972 visit profoundly affected the geopolitical balance,[4] bilateral trade remained low in comparison with China's European and Japanese trading partners. In 1974, Japan remained China's primary trading partner with

TABLE 5.1 SELECTED CHINESE FOREIGN TRADE STATISTICS, 1972–81
(U.S. $1 million)

	Japan		Britain		West Germany		USSR		United States	
	Imports	Exports	Imports	Exports	Imports	Exports	Imports	Exports	Imports	Exports
1972	627.4	411.8	185.9	134.0	183.5	90.4	116.8	133.5	3.3	9.6
1973	1,107.5	841.1	423.7	208.4	363.4	156.0	128.3	133.4	220.7	39.7
1974	1,982.7	1,142.6	443.8	282.1	493.9	205.2	145.0	155.0	372.9	102.9
1975	2,392.5	1,403.0	244.1	241.7	595.6	219.9	146.0	151.3	341.8	128.9
1976	1,816.6	1,222.9	169.9	266.7	721.0	224.9	246.4	168.4	160.6	156.0
1977	2,108.5	1,356.7	279.4	250.9	529.8	260.8	152.6	176.5	114.6	179.6
1978	3,105.2	1,718.7	296.3	370.4	1,030.1	329.5	206.9	229.7	721.1	270.7
1979	3,944.0	2,764.1	501.2	478.9	1,739.4	459.2	250.4	242.2	1,856.6	595.0
1980	5,168.9	4,032.2	540.0	563.7	1,332.8	710.5	264.1	228.3	3,830.2	981.1
1981	5,380.9	4,597.2	306.8	710.3	1,539.4	785.4	108.4	116.5	4,382.5	1,505.8

Source: Zhongguo Duiwai Jingii, *Zhongguo*, sect. 4, pp. 19, 58, 67, 68, 82.

TABLE 5.2 PETROLEUM EXPORTS, 1961–75
(10,000 metric tons)

Year	Crude oil exports	Refined oil exports
1961	———	0.05
1962	6.28	2.71
1963	7.47	0.66
1964	9.16	3.52
1965	19.64	10.22
1966	19.87	19.70
1967	16.07	13.60
1968	13.12	10.60
1969	10.70	14.21
1970	19.15	19.32
1971	26.25	37.35
1972	63.60	89.00
1973	183.41	116.17
1974	506.94	147.79
1975	987.79	210.06

Source: Zhongguo Duiwai Jingji, *Zhongguo,* sect. 4, p. 105.

total import/export volume about $3,125.26 million, followed by France, Britain, West Germany, and Canada. The United States was ranked sixth with a total import/export volume of $475.71 million (See table 5.1). Thus, the Sino-U.S. rapprochement and partial lifting of export controls did not significantly change the direction of trade.

The International Oil Price Rise

The international price of oil in 1973 did affect China's development strategy. The average official price for crude oil set by the Oil Producing and Exporting Countries (OPEC) group nearly quadrupled between the third quarter of 1973 ($3.02) and the first quarter of 1974 ($11.36).[5] The Chinese wanted to exploit the oil price rise to finance domestic development, even at the expense of domestic market supplies (table 5.2).

Yet the leadership approved the import substitution strategy more than a year and a half before the initial OAPEC (Organization of Arab Petroleum Exporting Countries) decision to raise the crude oil price to $5.12 a barrel. As early as

February 1972, the State Planning Commission began to formulate the $4.3 billion import substitution program, which received final State Council approval on 22 March 1973. The oil price rise thus did not influence the revival of a large-scale import substitution development strategy. However, increased oil export profits helped to finance and expand post-1973 import substitution projects, especially as global inflation increased China's import bill.[6]

The reemergence of a post–GLF style of development was neither a response to the 1972 Sino-U.S. rapprochement nor the 1973 rise in the oil price. Changes in the international environment played only a minor role. The catalyst was the restoration of the post–GLF coalition. Furthermore, the subsequent criticisms of the import substitution development strategy in 1974 and 1975 can only be attributed to the two-decade-long debate between import substitution and autarkic development advocates.

Domestic Environment: Political Chaos

The death of Marshal Lin Biao marked the end of the final "military" phase of the Cultural Revolution. Following the PLA's nationwide intervention in the Cultural Revolution on 23 January 1967, Mao bypassed Zhou Enlai, anointing Lin Biao as the chosen successor in September 1967.[7] Following the Soviet border clashes of 1969, Mao entrusted the safety and daily working of the state to Lin Biao. Formally appointed second in command during the Ninth Party Congress, Lin Biao was Mao's heir apparent.

Although worried about Lin Biao's ultimate ambitions in 1970,[8] Mao was physically and mentally unprepared for Lin Biao's failed military coup d'état. After 13 September 1971,[9] Mao again retreated to the second line to ponder his succession. He considered three surviving groups: the politics-in-command coalition led by Jiang Qing, the post–GLF coalition led by Zhou Enlai, and the remnants of the post–Lin Biao coalition.[10] Mao thus remained in his Zhongnanhai study and played an increasingly minor role in the state's everyday affairs, including foreign economic policy.[11] Li Zhisui reports that

> after Lin Biao's death, Mao's health took a turn for the worse. He never fully recovered from pneumonia in November 1970, when I was called back from Heilongjiang to treat him. But his physical decline after the Lin Biao affair was dramatic. When the immediate crisis was over, the arrests had been made, and Mao knew he was safe, he became depressed. He took to his bed and lay there all day, saying and doing little. When he did get up, he seemed to have aged. His shoulders stooped, and he moved slowly. He walked with a shuffle. He could not sleep. . . . After lying in bed for nearly two months, Mao was ready for reconciliation. He wanted the men he had purged to return.[12]

Mao thus agreed that Premier Zhou Enlai should regain government control. Following the death of Chen Yi, who had been disgraced during the Cultural Revolution, Mao approved Zhou Enlai's and the Political Bureau's initiative to rehabilitate other post–GLF leaders such as Chen Yun and Deng Xiaoping.[13] Furthermore, on 18 January 1972, just weeks before Richard Nixon's visit to the mainland, Li Zhisui reports that Mao made Zhou Enlai his successor, much to the consternation of Jiang Qing.[14]

Although Mao recovered somewhat and continued to intervene intermittently in the policy process, Zhou assumed greater responsibility over the affairs of state. With the aid of the rehabilitated post–GLF coalition, Zhou directed the readjustment of the Cultural Revolution's economic development strategy and readopted the large-scale import substitution strategy first implemented in the 1950s.

Readjustment of the Maoist Development Strategy

Domestic Economic Readjustment

Zhou Enlai's first task was to regain control of the civilian economy. On 21 August 1972, the CCP Central Committee and the Central Military Commission ordered military personnel participating in the PLA's Three Supports and Two Militaries Program to return to their units. Zhou eliminated the Military Control Commissions, the Mao Zedong Thought Propaganda Teams of the PLA, and the Leading Organizations Supporting the Broad Masses of the Left (Zhizuo Lingdao Jigou). Zhou furthermore relied on Marshal Ye Jianying to eradicate Lin Biao's influence within the military as well as to insulate the PLA from Jiang Qing's politics-in-command coalition.[15]

Second, the post–GLF coalition deemphasized the Third Front development approach. According to Naughton, the Third Front strategy fell apart with the demise of Lin Biao, the improvement in Sino-U.S. relations, and the high costs of the Third Front development projects. Thus,

> the proportion of national investment going to the key Third Front provinces Sichuan and Guizhou dropped sharply between 1971 and 1973. Construction of many projects was suspended or terminated in 1972–73; national construction teams were transferred to projects in eastern China, and many temporary laborers were returned to their villages. Within the Third Front, priorities were re-assessed and workers transferred to projects that were close to completion, while projects with little hope of immediate completion were suspended.[16]

The leadership no longer considered the industrial relocation as strategically crucial. In February 1973, Li Xiannian pointed out that "some things that the coastal areas lack have already been constructed in the interior." Recognizing that "some comrades" had criticized the overemphasis on military construction projects, Li now argued that the civilian economy should enjoy equal access to state investment capital.[17] Although Beijing continued to fund several large-scale Third Front projects, including several import substitution projects approved in 1973, the dream of the Third Front fundamentally died along with Lin Biao in 1971.

In addition to eradicating military influence, the post–GLF coalition readjusted the Maoist ideological tenets to formulate a new development strategy. While listening to the SPC's report on the 1973 plan, Zhou complained that ideologues had inhibited delegation reports on foreign medical and technological advances and thus had wasted state money.[18] Later, during the 1973 Conference on Strengthening Business Accounting and Reversing Industrial Losses (the title itself meaningful in light of the Cultural Revolution's attack on the accounting profession), several ministries and commissions openly criticized the previous development ideology. They were especially critical of the so-called Lin Biao ideas that "politics can assault all others" (*zhengzhi keyi chongji qita*) and "lips are the plan" (*zuiba jiu shi jihua*).[19]

This public attack spread simultaneously throughout the country,[20] culminating at the central work conference held 20–31 May 1973. While relaying Mao's general directives on economic work, Zhou emphasized the strengthening of economic planning and concentrating on "production only, and not the superstructure or if the line is not correct."[21] The new underlying ideology was summarized at a 1973 business conference: "Politics takes command in business and production; politics and economics should be combined in carrying out work."[22]

This gradual ideological readjustment resulted in Chen Yun's return from Jiangxi in April 1972 to assume a supervisory role over China's new import substitution development strategy.[23] Deng Xiaoping also returned from his garden exile in Jiangxi to regain his vice-premiership on 10 March 1973 and his seats on the Central Military Commission and the Political Bureau on 14 December 1973.[24] Yet, true to the non–zero sum game aspect of Chinese politics, Zhou was unable to rectify the Party completely. Jiang Qing's politics-in-command coalition remained a formidable opponent.[25]

Foreign Economic Policy Readjustment

In mid-1972, Zhou Enlai turned to Chen Yun to rebuild the foreign economic sector.[26] The China National Technical Import Corporation was reestablished to manage the importation of turnkey plants and technology.[27] Chen Yun reopened the People's Bank of China's (PBOC) Office of Financial Research to provide intelligent analysis of international currency transactions, which were key to financing China's development plans. Following David Rockefeller's discussions with Zhou Enlai on 29 June 1973, the Bank of China established financial ties with the Chase Manhattan Bank, including China's acceptance of traveler's checks.[28] To regain control over overseas Chinese funds and other forms of foreign exchange earned outside of trade, the Ministry of Finance also was given new powers to manage foreign exchange in September 1972.[29]

Perhaps most important, Chen Yun and the other members of the post–GLF coalition called for a change in the Cultural Revolution's interpretation of "self-reliance." On 11 September 1973, faced with the staggering cost of financing the proposed import substitution imports, Zhou Enlai approved the SPC's request to use foreign deposits. With access to $1 billion in Western loans,[30] Zhou approved Li Xiannian's suggestion to use such funds to finance the 1.7-meter steel rolling plant for the Wuhan Steel Works imported from West Germany.[31]

Chen Yun realized that the import substitution projects and the use of foreign loans contradicted Mao's dictum on self-sufficiency. He thus advised not to repeat the mistakes of the past when "old China procured old equipment."[32] Chen Yun also craftily suggested that foreign loans should be portrayed as a "very effective tool for domestic development" and thus totally separated from the idea of self-sufficiency.[33] Furthermore, Chen Yun argued that China also should take advantage of foreign commodity markets.[34]

Finally, Chen Yun sought to strengthen export processing. In analyzing China's potential to be a textile-exporting country on 12 October 1973, Chen Yun stated,

> We must make our calculations on a very large abacus. With a large Chinese population, we import fertilizer and equipment to produce fertilizer that in turn will increase grain production as well as our exports of rice and meat. This is export processing on a grand scale, and is the same as processing imported cotton for export. This logic makes perfect sense.[35]

By building a strong bureaucracy with clear administrative rules, the politics-in-command coalition could slowly be "educated" to accept the more flexible interpretation of self-reliance.

While rebuilding the foreign economic ministries and bureaucracies, the post–GLF coalition also strengthened the export manufacturing sector. On 15 December 1971, Zhou Enlai and Ye Jianying severely criticized the aircraft industry for shoddy production of aircraft for export. Of the forty new Jian-6 jet fighters destined for export, 17.5 percent (seven planes) failed the quality tests.[36] On 21 January 1972, Zhou also severely criticized the No. 1 (Changchun), No. 2 (Shiyan), Beijing, and Nanjing automobile factories for producing shoddy vehicles intended for the foreign military aid program. Zhou despairingly asked, "How can we provide foreign aid and prepare for war when quality drops the way it has?"[37]

Following Zhou's request, Li Xiannian carried out an inspection of the spring 1972 Guangzhou fair. "The premier wants me to discuss our desire to deal more effectively with the quality problem this year, and raise the issue as an understanding of the line (*tidao luxianshang lai renshi*). . . . Quality is also considered part of production."[38] Zhou concurrently issued directives to correct quality problems in exported canned goods, shirts, cameras, sample products exhibited at the trade fair, and certain industrial goods.[39]

Zhou personally visited Guangzhou in April 1972 to raise the quality problem to the Guangdong Party, government, and military leadership:

> How can Taiwan produce high-quality shirts, and we can't? We did it in the past, but we can't do it now? We are very troubled about this. We can't be boastful, just because foreign trade has had a bit of success. We are such a great country, a great people. Yet we export only one billion more shirts than Taiwan. This is nothing to brag about. . . . If there are any problems with these goods [dyed products], quickly get rid of them and don't try to sell the bad stuff. Don't think that everything is good! If twenty-nine provinces, municipalities, and special autonomous regions all carry out inspections, then they should simply get rid of the badly dyed textiles or poorly woven products. Just because you produce a good variety of products doesn't mean that you shouldn't pay attention to quality. If our dyed products are not good, then we need to import some and learn how to make them. We can only carry out a basic program of self-sufficiency. Who could ever say that we could become completely self-sufficient? If we need to import, then import. Our economy is backward. We come from a very poor background with nothing to offer and are thus in the midst of development. . . . Now we are in a period where nobody dares to carry out factory management, where anarchism is rampant and the leadership doesn't dare speak out. If you spoke out in 1967 during the high tide of ultraleftism, nobody listened. It has been five years since that time, and the situation has greatly changed.[40]

Despite Zhou's and Li's initiatives in the spring, problems continued to plague the fall 1972 trade fair. Following Nixon's February visit to the PRC, the fall fair was one of the largest and most important to date. Unfortunately, the Guangzhou organizers were unprepared to handle the large number of businesspeople and the increased export orders. Zhou immediately issued a three-point directive to

> (1) transfer temporarily vehicles and their drivers from Beijing, Tianjin, and Shanghai to Guangzhou. At the same time, you must temporarily requisition military vehicles, whose drivers must be good and accompany the vehicles. (2) Because there is not enough housing, we must borrow from other units and schools, especially those with decent kitchens. (3) Increase the number of restaurants, and transform the teahouses into restaurants.[41]

Zhou also issued several directives allowing foreign contract delivery dates to be extended to the spring 1973 fair. On 28 October the State Council subsequently issued an emergency circular ordering all localities and departments to guarantee export procurement schedules and product quality.[42] Li Xiannian promoted arts and handicrafts exports, which would "increase the number of exported material, somewhat resolve the domestic market demand, as well as absorb urban labor employment, and increase the income of communes, production brigades, teams, and commune members."[43] Zhou had already (in December 1971) ordered hotels to display traditional Chinese paintings in order to promote Chinese art exports.[44]

Although the fall 1972 fair achieved a record amount of more than $1 billion in transactions, Li acknowledged that Chinese units could not meet contractual quantity and quality requirements. Li called upon the Ministry of Foreign Trade to comply with Zhou Enlai's 1960 dictum to "take contracts seriously, and be as good as one's word."[45] Serious problems in military and industrial aid exports also continued unabated in 1973, forcing the State Council and Central Military Commission to adopt even more stringent measures aimed at the producers.[46]

For a longer-term solution, Chinese leaders turned to the post–GLF import substitution development strategies and the remunerative methods of the early 1960s.

Development Policy Innovation: The 4-3 Plan

Large-Scale Import Substitution

During a conference cosponsored by Ye Jianying in December 1971, Zhou Enlai argued, "We can't think that all things from capitalist countries are bad. Their goods have also been made by the working people. We can't think that we can build everything. Instead we must critically study foreign goods."[47] The post–GLF coalition thus revived the Four Modernizations development strategy originally proposed by Zhou during the fall of 1963 and superseded by the Third Front approach.

The Cultural Revolution was not as devastating to the national economy as the Great Leap, despite what mainland Chinese leaders and scholars say today.[48] While deep scars remained, especially in the industrial sector, the economy was healthy in comparison to the post–GLF economy.[49] Because the odious Soviet debt burden was no longer a factor, Zhou could formulate a development strategy with a large-scale import substitution component and again embark on his vision of long-term development interrupted by the Cultural Revolution.

While primarily responsible for the reintroduction of the import substitution strategy,[50] Zhou Enlai gained strong support from several key economic policy makers from the post–GLF period. They included the survivors of the Cultural

Revolution such as Li Xiannian and Yu Qiuli,[51] who had been protected by Zhou Enlai,[52] as well as victims such as Chen Yun (rehabilitated in 1972) and of course Deng Xiaoping (rehabilitated in 1973). As argued previously, Zhou, Yu Qiuli, and Li Xiannian had avoided a completely autarkic strategy during the Cultural Revolution by continuing small-scale import/export trade to provide needed raw materials and equipment for China's industrial infrastructure. In April 1971 before Lin Biao's death, they justified such imports as "better than importing complete turnkey plants."[53]

On 5 February 1972, Zhou took advantage of Lin Biao's demise and Mao's extremely weakened medical condition to alter the semiautarkic development course.[54] Zhou approved a SPC report submitted by Li Xiannian, Hua Guofeng, and Yu Qiuli that mandated the import of four chemical fiber and two chemical fertilizer turnkey plants worth $400 million that would be operational within five or six years. These technology imports were guided by the following Eight-Character Policy: study the technology, use it, reform your methods, and achieve your goal. Zhou subsequently "reported this to Mao Zedong for his approval."[55]

Later in November 1972, Zhou approved the import of fourteen additional chemical fiber and fertilizer turnkey plants worth $3.3 billion.[56] In addition, contracts were signed to import iron works from Japan's Hitachi Engineering, a small steel mill from Japan's Sumitomo Metal, and a steel-rolling plant from West Germany's Demag AG, as well as quite a few power plants from Japan (valued at $43 million), the USSR (valued at $24.5 million), France (valued at $10 million), the United Kingdom (valued at $8.4 million), Sweden (valued at $4 million), Italy (valued at $1.7 million), and Switzerland.[57] These contracts marked a revival for the first time since the early 1960s of the import substitution development program (see table 5.1).

Yu Qiuli complied with Zhou Enlai's directive to compose and submit to the State Council the 2 January 1973 "Report and Request for Instructions for Increasing Equipment Imports and Expanding Economic Exchange."[58] This *qingshi baogao* formally introduced China's new domestic development strategy—the 4-3 Plan (Sisan Fang'an) costing $4.3 billion.[59] Incorporating the import substitution projects approved in late 1971 and 1972, the plan included the importation of 43 coal mine facilities and three large electricity-generating plants as well as an assortment of turbines and jet engines, including the famous Spey engines from Britain.[60] The most publicized project was also its biggest—the $600 million 1.7-meter steel rolling plant for the Wuhan Steel Works (Wugang).[61] The *qingshi baogao* also approved an extra RMB 24 billion to construct supporting infrastructure projects. Eventually, the planned foreign exchange expenditures reached $5.14 billion, of which $3.96 billion was actually allocated by late 1977; by 1977 domestic costs reached RMB 26 billion.[62]

The scope of the 4-3 Plan far exceeded that of the post–GLF import substitution program, thus resembling the earlier, large-scale imports of Russian turnkey plants and equipment of the 1950s. Yet the leadership needed a more effective export strategy than those of the 1950s and early 1960s to finance the 1970s import substitution program.

Financing the Large-Scale Import Substitution Development Strategy

DEVELOPMENT OF TRADITIONAL AND NEW EXPORTS

The post–GLF coalition financed the import substitution program by developing both traditional and new sources of foreign exchange. Exports of Chinese arts and handicraft products had been a traditional source of foreign exchange. Yet the 1950s collectivization movement, especially the 1958 conversion of handicraft cooperatives to collectives and state-owned operations, and the Cultural Revolution had seriously affected production.[63] Following Li Xiannian's November 1972 call to improve arts and handicraft production, the State Council ordered the Ministries of Foreign Trade and Light Industry to increase arts and handicraft exports on 21 April 1973. Factory and workshop management was strengthened, schools and research institutes were reopened, and experienced craftsmen and new talent were encouraged. The post–GLF coalition expected foreign exchange earnings from arts and handicraft exports to increase from 400 million in 1973 to $800 million in 1975.[64]

The Chinese also began to promote foreign tourism. In the 1950s and early 1960s, the leadership permitted overseas Chinese to visit relatives and carry out limited sightseeing. This was justified for political (United Front activities) and economic reasons (increasing foreign exchange revenues, encouraging overseas Chinese investment in the mainland). By the early 1970s, the new leadership recognized that tourism could increase export demand and increase foreign exchange reserves. Such long-term benefits mitigated the high infrastructure cost. In spite of remnants of Cultural Revolution xenophobia, the leadership allowed more tour groups, including non-Chinese, to visit the mainland. To accommodate such tours, China International Travel Service (CITS) and local foreign affairs departments began to improve tourist facilities.[65]

To finance the import substitution program, China also was transformed into a nascent petroleum exporter. Foreign businesspeople had dreamed in the nineteenth century of supplying oil for the lamps of China. Starting with the February 1960 decision to develop the Daqing oil field, China began a crash program in becoming self-reliant in oil; it achieved this goal by 1965.[66] During the agricultural export procurement crisis of the early 1960s, Chinese leaders had initially exported their small supplies of crude and refined petroleum products between 1961 and 1962. Exports grew at a slow pace, but they nearly tripled between 1971 and 1972, and doubled again during the next few years (see table 5.2).

In the early 1970s, the leadership considered petroleum exports as a potentially important tool to finance the import substitution domestic development strategy.[67] While petroleum exports increased significantly before the global price increases of fall 1973, phenomenal growth occurred between 1973 and 1975. This was a response to the skyrocketing of the world price to more than $11 a barrel in 1974. Based on a Zhou Enlai directive, the SPC increased the 1974 unrefined petroleum export quota from 4 million tons to 6 million tons; the SPC increased exports of refined petroleum products from 1.5 million tons to 1.6 million tons.[68]

As in the case of edible oils during the 1959 GLF crisis (chapter 3), the leadership increased exports by reducing oil supplies to the domestic economy, which was urged to burn coal. Beijing thus reduced oil supplies to key industries by 2.34 million tons, to the fuel and chemical industry by 1.4 million tons, and to local medium- and small-scale industry by 660,000 tons. In July 1975, Li Xiannian argued that such conservation measures would allow China to substitute the export of foodstuffs for petroleum to finance Zhou's large-scale import substitution program.[69] The following month, Li admonished other members of the State Council "to criticize the fallacy, 'It is forbidden to burn our oil so that we can give it to foreigners.'" Li later blamed the Gang of Four for converting coal-fired plants to oil-fired plants, thus wasting petroleum reserves.[70]

Petroleum exports thus were a boon and a burden: a boon since oil exports were a major export revenue earner, a burden because exports were increased at the expense of the domestic market. As can be seen in Li Xiannian's comments to the State Council in August 1975, petroleum exports also became a sensitive political topic.

THE SPECIALIZED LOAN PROGRAM
FOR INDUSTRIAL EXPORT PRODUCTION

Besides exploiting traditional and new sources of export revenue, Zhou Enlai readopted the post–GLF export promotion policies. The policies undertaken under the Eight-Character Plan of the 1960s primarily addressed the agricultural export procurement problem. The policies undertaken to finance the 4-3 Plan primarily focused on the industrial export sector.

Besides criticizing "mistaken attitudes" in export production, Zhou also used positive incentives to correct industrial export problems. In 1972, the State Council approved a Ministry of Foreign Trade Plan to revive the Specialized Loan Program for Industrial Export Product Production.[71] Previously terminated during the Cultural Revolution, the State Council in 1972 admitted that "in the past, the results of the loans weren't bad and production was enlivened. In general, the loans were repaid." The State Council thus allocated RMB 200 million in 1972, which later increased to RMB 550 million in 1975. The loans were given to foreign trade industries, state-owned industrial or mining concerns, and collectives to "develop export industrial products, raise quality and variety, and improve packaging."[72]

THE SHORT-TERM FOREIGN EXCHANGE LOAN PROGRAM

The Specialized Loan Program, denominated in nonconvertible RMB, could not be used for importing advanced production equipment. Thus, a "new kind of work" was authorized by the Ministry of Foreign Trade and People's Bank of China June 1973 letter of instruction.[73] The Short-Term Foreign Exchange Loan Program was established under MFT's specialized foreign trade corporations (*waimao zhuanye gongsi*). The corporations distributed loans to production industries that would "import advanced technology, equipment, and materials; expand export commodity production capacity; raise product quality; increase variety; improve packaging and design; import raw and supplementary materials to be processed and exported; develop the transportation and tourism industries."[74]

In a fascinating example of the mainland's use of Hong Kong, the state accessed the Bank of China and its Hong Kong affiliates' foreign exchange deposits to make more than four thousand loans worth $634.82 million between 1973 and 1978.[75]

THE INVESTMENT FUND FOR EXPORT COMMODITY PRODUCTION

To strengthen the state's ability to guide foreign trade production, the leadership established an Investment Fund for Export Commodity Production (Chukou Chanpin Shengchan Cuoshi Touzi) in 1973. As a part of the Ministry of Foreign Trade's long-term investment strategy, the funds were invested in industrial, mineral, and agricultural sideline production and processing industries. Funds were given only to industries that could guarantee production input requirements (raw material, energy, labor), required little prior investment, and produced goods demanded on the world market. In 1973, RMB 94.85 million (rising to RMB 159.51 million in 1975) was invested in promising export industries to finance technological renovations and improve export quality and quantity.[76]

THE AGRICULTURAL SIDELINE BONUS SCHEME

The post–GLF coalition also revived its remunerative schemes promoting agricultural exports. On 19 March 1973, the State Council approved the State Planning Commission's plan to reinstate the agricultural sideline bonus scheme. The bonus schemes had become a major target during the Cultural Revolution and were vilified as an attempt to restore capitalism. According to the new bonus scheme, producers received bonuses for sixty-one items in short supply on the domestic market; the export bonus scheme included twenty-nine items. While the post–Cultural Revolution scheme was not as comprehensive as the post–

GLF bonus scheme, policy makers unified the bonus award system for both domestic and export market items.[77]

Case Study:
Export Commodity Processing Bases Policy Implementation

The post–GLF coalition also reestablished export processing zones. On 20 March 1973, ten days after Deng Xiaoping's resumption of his vice-premiership and one day after the reinstatement of the agricultural bonus system, the State Planning Commission approved the Trial Procedures for the Establishment of Export Agricultural and Sideline Commodity Production Bases and the Trial Procedures for the Establishment of Specialized Factories for the Production of Export Industrial Commodities.[78]

For the first time, the leadership regarded the ECPB idea as an important, practical tool for foreign export expansion. A few ECPBs had been established in the early 1960s, only to be vilified during the Cultural Revolution. Yet by the early 1970s, the Central Committee approved the reimplementation of the post–GLF export promotion schemes and codified methods of establishing and managing the export bases.

Export Production Bases for Individual Agricultural or Sideline Export Commodities

The Trial Procedures for the Establishment of Export Agricultural and Sideline Commodity Production Bases authorized the establishment of two types of bases. The first type was the export production base for individual agricultural or sideline export commodities (*danxiang chukou nongfu chanpin shengchan jidi*), hereafter called the single-item export base. It was the simplest of the five ECPB categories designated in the 30 June 1960 report (see chap. 3). Specializing in the production of a particular agricultural, sideline, local, specialty, animal, freshwater, or saltwater product, the single-item export base was probably the only type of ECPB operated on a large scale during the 1960s.

With the passage of the trial procedures, many prefectures, communes, production brigades, and state-run farms established single-item export bases in the 1970s. By 1982, twenty-four provinces, cities, or autonomous regions had constructed export bases for ninety-eight products; those bases produced RMB 1.75 billion in export goods.[79] They specialized in the production of local, indigenous products such as black tree fungus (*hei mu'er,* which is a popular ingredient for Chinese cooking) and dried hot peppers. Processing and packaging plants associated with the export base prepared the good for export, sometimes using imported materials and technology to enhance export product quality and quantity.[80]

An important example of the single-item export base was the Commodity

Production Base Specialized in Fresh Produce and Live Animals for Hong Kong and Macao (Zhuangong Gangao Xianhuo Shangpin Jidi). Established in 1974 to raise cattle for export to the Hong Kong and Macao markets, these bases imported high-quality breeding stock and artificial-insemination equipment. Within seven years, the export volume of live cattle had doubled, and foreign exchange receipts increased fivefold.[81] More than 98 percent of the cattle and 95 percent of the hogs exported to the Hong Kong and Macao markets originated from single-item export bases.[82]

The Comprehensive Bases for Export Commodity Production

The second type of ECPB authorized by the trial procedures was the comprehensive base for export commodity production (*chukou shangpin shengchan zonghe jidi*). The comprehensive base was a variation of the 1960 ECPB category that designated "a specific state-operated farm or prefecture to produce various types of export commodities" (appendix C). The new idea was designed "to place priority on three principles, namely giving priority to the production of agricultural and sideline products and their processing, to the production of fresh produce, and to the supply of the Hong Kong, Macao, and Japanese markets."[83]

Unlike the original 1960 idea, the comprehensive bases not only engaged in agricultural and sideline commodity production, but also in commodity processing and packaging; they also developed new export commodities including various light industrial export items. The bases thus increased the value-added content of Chinese exports, especially industrial export products. Foreshadowing the special economic zones established six years later in Guangdong and Fujian Provinces, these bases engaged in all aspects of agricultural and industrial export production.

In 1973, the first experimental comprehensive base for export commodity production was established in Foshan Prefecture, west of Guangzhou (Canton). The state allocated $2.75 million in foreign exchange for the project, which produced agricultural and industrial commodities for the Hong Kong and Macao markets.[84] The Foshan Comprehensive Base produced or processed high-quality rice, pigs, live fish, fresh vegetables, granulated sugar, silk and satin threads, clothing, ceramics, and rattan. It eventually produced electric fans, cotter pins, steel furniture, umbrellas, and plastic products and engaged in industrial ceramic research.

After two years, the experimental comprehensive base was considered a success. In 1972 Foshan produced 372 types of export goods worth RMB 248 million (procurement price), which were eventually exported or reexported to forty different countries. By 1981, the Foshan Comprehensive Base produced 791 types of export goods worth RMB 1.2 billion, which were eventually exported or reexported to eighty-one different countries.[85] Based on such success, the leadership approved comprehensive bases for Guangdong's Huiyang Prefecture

(1975), Zhanjiang Prefecture (1976); Hunan Province's Xiangtan Prefecture (1976); and Jiangsu Province's Suzhou and Yangzhou Prefectures (1976).[86]

The Specialized Factories

The Trial Procedures for the Establishment of Specialized Factories for the Production of Export Industrial Commodities was also approved on 20 March 1973. The trial procedures sanctioned the establishment of specialized factories, workshops, and mine operations (hereafter called specialized factories) dedicated to export production. First proposed by the 30 June 1960 report and revived to improve industrial exports, the leadership authorized specialized factories

> to promote more specialized production; to raise quantity and quality of export industrial products; to organize production according to the variety, specifications, color, style, packaging, design, and delivery time most suitable for sales abroad; to carry out production according to the dictates of sales; to conform production to suit the demands of sales; to deliver goods on time and according to the agreed-upon quality and volume; to develop gradually specialized factories as a key component of export commodity production.[87]

Theoretically, the specialized factories were not treated the same as their domestic brothers. They were granted procurement priority for production inputs, an idea first proposed in 1959 under the First Squeeze, Secondly Replace, Thirdly Exceed policy. Unlike their domestic counterparts, the factories were not judged according to the quantity produced and profit earned (*baxiang jingji kaohe zhibiao*). Success was judged upon the delivery of export goods that met contract obligations, were economically produced, and earned a satisfactory amount of foreign exchange.[88] Third, more than 70 percent of the factory's production had to be exported. Between 1973 and 1980, ninety-four factories, workshops, or mines were designated as "specialized"; the majority (fifty) were in Shanghai and produced various textile goods for export.[89] Besides producing profitable textile products,[90] they manufactured other light and industrial products including hot water vacuum bottles, cameras, security locks, and mercury.

Thus the export commodity production base policy, as embodied by the single-item export base, the comprehensive base, and the specialized factory, became a major component of Zhou Enlai's strategy to finance the 4-3 Plan import substitution development strategy. By augmenting the existing export production units under the Ministry of Foreign Trade with the various types of ECPBs, the country's export capacity was greatly expanded.[91]

To maintain this expansion, the state attempted to guarantee the inputs needed for MFT factories and ECPB export production. The new and revived export promotion programs offered such guarantees, which also included the technology needed to upgrade product quality and production efficiency and the investment capital needed to create new export opportunities.[92] Thus, the expansion of export capacity ensured a constant inflow of foreign exchange to finance the $4.3 billion import substitution development strategy.

Preliminary Studies to Establish a "Special Zone"

As early as 1973, Zhou Enlai explored the establishment of a special zone within China similar to the EPZ in Kaohsiung, Taiwan. During his June 1973 discussions with David Rockefeller, Zhou highly praised Taiwan's foreign economic policies. Zhou especially appreciated how Taiwanese leaders had analyzed Taiwan's comparative economic strengths to find their niche within the international division of labor. Zhou also praised their use of foreign capital, technology, and raw materials as well as their establishment of an EPZ or free port in Kaohsiung.[93]

During Australian prime minister Gough Whitlam's October–November 1973 visit to Beijing, Zhou again mentioned the Kaohsiung EPZ. Zhou apparently was well informed, describing Kaohsiung as "tax-free, attracts foreign capital that bring along raw materials to establish factories, which in turn utilizes Taiwan's cheap labor and fees to produce commodities that are sold abroad. In this way they have attracted a lot of capital to invest in Taiwan."[94]

According to Wang Jun from the Central Committee's Research Office on Documents, these were not random comments.[95] Zhou had authorized various government departments to begin preliminary studies on the establishment of a special zone in China based on the Kaohsiung EPZ. Not only did the PBOC investigate how to obtain foreign capital, it also raised $1 billion in foreign exchange to establish the EPZ.[96] During a State Council meeting, Zhou jocularly goaded Minister of Foreign Trade Li Qiang,

> Hey Mr. Foreign Trade Minister, you're not as good as Yen Chia-kan. He established an export processing zone in Kaohsiung, and has really developed their foreign trade. . . . In the past, China did not possess the right conditions. Now, the situation has changed. We must think a little bit more about how to do this.[97]

Unfortunately, Zhou did not have the time to "think a little bit more."

Conclusion

The post–GLF coalition, constantly learning and evaluating the effectiveness of their policies, changed China's inward orientation to reinitiate a large-scale import substitution development program. Yet the post–GLF coalition had perceived limitations to the import substitution path of inwardly oriented development and had begun to investigate the adoption of a more outwardly looking development regime, including the use of foreign investment and establishment of an EPZ.

This promising opening of the mid-1970s never occurred. While authorizing studies on outwardly oriented development, Zhou was being treated for bladder cancer. In the wings, the politics-in-command coalition was preparing its final assault. China's start along the East Asian path of outwardly oriented development would be delayed for another six years.

CHAPTER 6

The Abbreviated Leftist Response, 1974–1976

Not all of the policy elites were satisfied with the post–GLF coalition's remunerative approach to economic development. Opposition to Zhou Enlai's 4-3 Plan strategy was concentrated among members of the CCP Political Bureau who were the major theorists or activists of the Cultural Revolution, including Mao's wife, Jiang Qing; Wang Hongwen; Zhang Chunqiao; and Yao Wenyuan. This politics-in-command coalition—also known as the Gang of Four—rejected Zhou's use of the international marketplace and advocated the semiautarkic strategy of the Cultural Revolution.[1]

By the mid-1970s the politics-in-command coalition took advantage of Zhou's worsening medical condition to initiate the Anti-Lin, Anti-Confucius Campaign and an anti-rightist campaign. While ultimately failing, their actions had a direct, adverse effect upon the import-substitution domestic development strategy and ended any experiments with outwardly oriented development.[2]

Foreign Economic Policy and the Anti-Lin, Anti-Confucius Campaign, January 1974–October 1974

The Struggle for Succession

According to Li Zhisui, Mao designated Zhou Enlai as his successor in January 1972. Yet Mao was increasingly critical of Zhou's "revisionist" policies and his failure to consult the Chairman.[3] More significantly, Mao realized that Zhou was suffering from bladder cancer, which was discovered after a urinalysis on 18 May 1972.[4] After reporting to Mao on his medical condition in March 1973, Zhou sent a letter to Mao relating the Political Bureau's decision to reinstate Deng Xiaoping's Party status and his vice-premiership. Mao approved the decision, triggering the jockeying between the politics-in-command and the post–GLF coalitions for Mao's successor.[5] During the next two years, China's import substitution development strategy would be used as a major weapon to attack Zhou and Deng.

On 4 July 1973, Zhang Chunqiao and Wang Hongwen took advantage of

Zhou's sickness and Deng's relative weakness. On the very day that Zhou received cancer treatment at Jade Fountain Hill (Yuquanshan), the elites' sanitarium situated between the Summer Palace and the Fragrant Hills, Zhang and Wang attacked Zhou Enlai's management of the Ministry of Foreign Affairs during their conversation with Mao.[6] More ominously, the three discussed the Kuomintang (KMT) and Lin Biao's devotion to Confucianism.

Although realizing that he was again coming under indirect attack, Zhou did not express his concerns.[7] The following month, Jiang Qing revived this criticism, which was a veiled inference to Zhou Enlai's control of the state.[8] After nearly forty years of dealing with such criticism, Zhou avoided a major confrontation with Mao by submitting a self-criticism over the MFA incident; Zhou also suppressed Jiang Qing's attempts to expand the anti-Confucian campaign.[9]

But this was only the opening assault. Jiang Qing continued to control the propaganda organs, which published anti-Confucius tracts in the *Beijing ribao* and fomented demonstrations at Qinghua University.[10] Thus when Mao criticized Zhou Enlai on 17 November 1973 for making "wrong comments" to Henry Kissinger in regard to Sino-U.S. relations, Jiang Qing was ready to attack. During a Political Bureau meeting on that same day, Jiang Qing accused Zhou of being a "rightist capitulationist," who "is too impatient to wait to take Chairman Mao's place."

Zhou subsequently submitted two reports in which he apologized to Mao for "having not done enough" in his meeting with Kissinger. Over the next two weeks, the Political Bureau held a series of meetings to criticize Zhou and Ye Jianying.[11] Unfortunately for Jiang Qing, the meetings in November–December 1973 resulted in Mao's tempering his criticism of Zhou and preventing Jiang Qing's and Yao Wenyuan's attempts to join the Political Bureau's Standing Committee. Worst of all, Mao counterbalanced Jiang Qing's power by formalizing Deng Xiaoping's position on the Military Affairs Commission and the Political Bureau.[12]

Despite this apparent setback, Jiang Qing and the politics-in-command coalition rebounded by using their propaganda connections to republish the *Beijing ribao*'s anti-Confucius tract in the 28 December 1973 edition of the *Renmin ribao*. Two weeks later, Mao approved a letter from Jiang Qing and Wang Hongwen, who Mao felt were representative of a new leadership generation.[13] The letter ultimately resulted in the Anti-Lin, Anti-Confucius Campaign.[14]

The Glass Snail *and* Fengqing *Incidents*

As well as distorting Chinese history, literature, and arts to criticize Zhou Enlai during the first Anti-Lin, Anti-Confucius stage,[15] the politics-in-command coalition also resorted to xenophobia.[16] Following approval by Zhou Enlai and

Jiang Qing, China signed a contract with the Kodak Corporation in September 1973 to purchase a color kinescope production line.[17] While touring U.S. production facilities, the delegation from the Fourth Machine Ministry was presented with a glass snail as a token of remembrance in December 1973.

In February 1974, Xu Wenbin, a young cadre working in the ministry's No. 10 Design Department, complained to Jiang Qing about the glass snail. Jiang Qing personally delivered her response with a surprise visit to the ministry. While Xu did not come to work that particular day, Jiang Qing publicly condemned the gift as "profaning the Chinese, insulting, and implying that we crawl along the ground." She criticized the importation of a color kinescope production line as a "humiliation under imperialist pressure" and a symptom of "worshipping and having blind faith in foreign things." After confiscating the glass snail, she urged the ministry to complain to the U.S. representatives in Beijing; more ominously, she urged that China refuse to implement the import substitution project.[18]

Following several directives from Zhou Enlai, the MFA submitted a report on 21 February 1974 that contradicted Jiang Qing and absolved Kodak and the United States from wrongdoing.[19] The Political Bureau thus decided that "the speech given by Jiang Qing at the Fourth Machine Ministry should not be printed nor distributed. Copies already printed should be immediately returned."[20] Despite the retraction and her return of the glass snail to the ministry, Jiang Qing's action resulted in "the delay of importation of a color kinescope production line for several years and the cessation of other foreign advanced technology imports."[21] Thus, it is not surprising that anti-foreign protests sprang up concurrently in Shanghai, where dock workers protested against the importation of U.S. grain that apparently was infected with TCK smut (a fungus that causes disease in plants).[22]

The glass snail incident might seem incomprehensible. But to the Chinese elite, Jiang Qing's message was extremely clear. In 1958, Mao directly criticized Zhou Enlai, Chen Yun, Li Xiannian, and Bo Yibo as being against rash advance. A November editorial in *Renmin ribao* commented that such rightists "were like snails who slowly crawl along the ground." Consequently, these Chinese elites were forced to make several self-criticisms; Zhou was even forced to submit his resignation from the Political Bureau (see chapter 2). Mao had used the same verb "to crawl behind" (*gen zai bieren houmian yibuyibu de baxing*) to criticize China's development strategy in 1964 (see chapter 1). Jiang Qing was reminding Mao and the other elites that these elites had not learned their lesson in 1958 and were dangerous rightists who were betraying China to the foreigners.[23]

On 18 June 1974, Wang Hongwen initiated the second major attack on the post–GLF coalition's vision of development. As mentioned in chapter 3, the construction of oceangoing ships had been brought to a sudden halt in 1963 following the sinking of the *Great Leap,* which was a major international embarrassment. With Mao's and Zhou's approval in 1964, the Ministry of Communications endeavored to develop the domestic shipbuilding industry and buy foreign vessels to reduce the costs of leasing foreign vessels.

China continued to suffer from numerous problems in its indigenous shipbuilding industry during the next decade. Zhou Enlai criticized the overconfident officials in Shanghai and the Sixth Machine-Building Ministry in January 1970. "Some written materials claim that China's shipbuilding capabilities are just as good as Japan's. How could it be just as good? We are far below their capabilities."[24] Confronted with the increased Chinese demand for international cargo transport, Zhou Enlai in 1973 reauthorized the 1964 initiative. China would obtain foreign ships with loans from the Bank of China in order to reduce the cost of leasing foreign vessels by 1975.[25]

As China was obtaining ships on the international market in 1974, the Jiangnan Shipbuilding Factory in Shanghai was finishing the *Fengqing,* a 13,500-ton cargo vessel classified as a nonoceangoing vessel. Still concerned about the 1963 incident, the ministry feared that the *Fengqing*'s main engines, radar, and other major equipment were unreliable. To overcome bureaucratic myths of foreign goods, Shanghai shipbuilders erected a large-character poster stating, "We want the revolution; the *Fengqing* must be an oceangoing vessel." Hoping to avoid serious trouble during the initial stages of the Anti-Lin, Anti-Confucius Campaign, Zhou Enlai approved the *Fengqing*'s round-trip journey to Romania. Although its main engine broke down several times, the *Fengqing* successfully completed its long ocean voyage and returned to Shanghai in time for the 1974 Chinese New Year's celebration.[26]

Following the *Fengqing*'s successful return, Wang Hongwen charged in June 1974 that the Ministry of Communication had "taken the revisionist line" by promoting the acquisition of foreign vessels. Such policies were based on a "superstitious belief in the 'fake foreign devils' of the foreign bourgeoisie."[27] Such criticism was not out of character for Wang, who also was critical of the Ministry of Foreign Trade's preferential economic policy toward Hong Kong.[28] Wang Hongwen subsequently ordered the arrest, criticism, and denouncement of a vice–section chief from the Communications Ministry who was on board the *Fengqing* during the round-trip journey to Romania. Li Guotang apparently had complained about the ship's quality. Most perfidiously, Li had also objected to the repetitious screening of Jiang Qing's revolutionary model opera, *Azalea Mountain,* during the long nights on board ship.[29]

Mao had severely criticized Jiang Qing on 20 March and castigated the "four-person faction" of Jiang Qing, Zhang Chunqiao, Yao Wenyuan, and Wang Hongwen in 17 July 1974 for their factional activities.[30] However, Mao delayed his decisive blow to the Anti-Lin, Anti-Confucius Campaign until October 1974. Announcing the preparations for the Fourth NPC, the Central Committee issued a circular on 11 October 1974 that included Mao's opinion: "The Great Proletarian Cultural Revolution has already lasted eight years. Now it's best to settle down. The entire Party and army must unite."[31]

Mao was calling for conclusion of the campaign. By late summer 1974, Mao knew the seriousness of his own illness; Mao had also finally approved Zhou Enlai's exploratory surgery of 10 August 1974, which revealed Zhou's recurring bladder cancer to be terminal.[32] Mao thus had turned to Deng Xiaoping, his former close ally of the pre-GLF period, to be his anointed successor.

At the January 1975 Second Plenum Jiang Qing made one last assault on the post–GLF coalition to prevent the Party's formal approval of Deng's leadership positions.[33] She followed up on Wang Hongwen's June 1974 attack by approving an account of the *Fengqing* incident in the internal publication *Guonei dongtai qingyang* (Evidence of internal trends). She subsequently issued a letter on 13 October 1974 to the Political Bureau, stating that the *Fengqing* incident

> has aroused my full proletarian indignation. It must be asked whether the Ministry of Communications is a Ministry of the People's Republic of China that is led by Chairman Mao and the Central Party leadership. Although the State Council is a state organization under the dictatorship of the proletariat, there truly are a small number of people within the Ministry of Communications who worship and have blind faith in foreign things, [curry favors from foreigners,] as well as have a comprador bourgeoisie mentality. They are monopolizing power. . . . Can we afford not to struggle against such slavish mentality toward foreign things and this philosophy of crawling? . . . The Political Bureau must take a stand on this problem and adopt the necessary measures.[34]

The post–GLF coalition was repeating the same mistakes as the nineteenth-century Self-Strengthening proponents (such as Zeng Guofan, Li Hongzhang, Yuan Shikai), Chiang Kai-shek, Liu Shaoqi, and Lin Biao. They all had "adopted a slavish comprador philosophy of 'constructing ships is not as good as buying them; buying ships is not as good as renting them.'" All of these people were guilty of "promoting a political line of national betrayal."[35] Wang Hongwen, Zhang Chunqiao, and Yao Yilin thus suggested that the State Council, the Ministry of Communications, and other economic departments initiate an "education on political lines" (*luxian jiaoyu*).[36]

The politics-in-command coalition rejected Mao's 11 October call to "settle down" and instead called for renewed attacks. Jiang Qing engaged Deng Xiaoping in a protracted argument during a 17 October 1974 Political Bureau meeting. Subsequently, the politics-in-command coalition sent Wang Hongwen to Changsha to inform Mao, "Today, Beijing has the feeling of the Lushan conference [of 1959]." The ailing Zhou was described as plotting with Deng Xiaoping, Ye Jianying, and Li Xiannian.[37]

Mao's response no doubt was a shock to Wang Hongwen. Mao reportedly attacked Wang's alliance with Jiang Qing and advised Wang to ally with Deng Xiaoping.[38] After listening to Wang Hairong's and Tang Wensheng's (Nancy Tang's) account of the incident, Mao criticized Jiang Qing for exaggerating the importance of this "small issue." Mao advised Wang Hongwen, Zhang Chunqiao, and Yao Wenyuan not to follow Jiang Qing. Finally, Mao reasserted his belief that Deng should be confirmed as first vice-premier of the State Council and chief of the PLA General Staff. Mao thus thwarted the politics-in-command coalition, which was upbraided during the 1–3 November 1974 Political Bureau meeting.[39] It was during this time that Mao directed Li Xiannian to "enliven the national economy" (*ba guomin jingji gaoshangchu*),[40] bringing to an inglorious end to the campaign.

By 1974, Mao was in poor health. According to Li Zhisui, Mao had lost most of his eyesight. His arms and legs especially on his right side had atrophied. He could barely speak. By July, the Political Bureau was informed that Mao was suffering from Lou Gehrig's disease and was not expected to live beyond two years.[41] Although Mao had lost most of his physical capacities, he was still the preeminent leader. Competing policy makers such as Jiang Qing actively sought out Mao's gatekeepers—Mao's son Mao Yuanxin and his "nurse" Zhang Yufeng—to gain Mao's favor.[42]

The campaign of 1974 thus was only the first stage of the ultraleftist assault. The second stage commenced in November 1975 with the launching of an antirightist movement, the Repulse the Right-Deviationist Wind to Reverse the Verdicts Campaign (Fanji Youqing Fan'an Feng Yundong) (see below).

The Economic Cost of the Anti-Lin, Anti-Confucius Campaign

The 1974 campaign disrupted the entire economic structure. Production stoppages were frequent, various export quotas were unfulfilled, and the transportation sector was a mess. The transshipment of export goods previously had been an obstacle to complying with delivery schedules.[43] A State Council emergency circular had reduced the number of ships waiting to be loaded or unloaded from 210 ships in October 1973 to 180 ships in December 1973.[44] The campaign worsened the problem. Under the slogan "We must be master of the wharf and not the slaves to tonnage," dock workers slowed down their work; the result was a backup of 240–250 ships during the first quarter of 1974. More than forty ships waited more than a month to unload. The delay resulted in a $775,000 increase in vessel rental fees.[45]

Problems occurred not only at portage, but within the entire transportation and production system. At the April 1974 Conference on Grasping the Revolution and Promoting Production, ten State Council ministers reported serious problems in the production, energy, and transportation sectors. During the first quarter, steel production was estimated to be short by 830,000 tons; raw coal production by 2.45 million; washed coal by 930,000; chemical fertilizer by 830,000; and railroad transport tonnage by 8 million.[46] Such economic deterioration continued through the second quarter, and only moderated after August 1974.[47]

The Anti-Lin, Anti-Confucius Campaign directly caused the economic dislocation. According to the "Circular on Grasping the Revolution and Promoting Production" issued on 1 July 1974, worker and Party activists "struggled against" local industrial and Party cadre who maintained ideas of "Confucian production and Legalist rebellion" (*rujia shengchan, fajia zaofan*).[48] The activists promoted internal fighting and work stoppage to "go against the tide" (*fan chaoliu*) and "to refrain from the incorrect road of production." As a result, many cadre either were removed from office or "heard a boom and then fled away from their posts without being struggled against" (*buda zidao, yihong jiupao*).[49] To prevent further disruption and deterioration of the economic system, the circular thus forbade the "seizure of cadre. People are not to be attacked and arrested. All leading cadre and other personnel who are absent without leave are requested to return immediately to their posts. Economic and other disciplinary measures are not to be taken."[50]

The circular had the desired effect. By August, daily production of raw coal had risen 72,000 tons over July; daily steel production had risen 700 tons; the gross production value of machine goods rose 12 percent; and the number of unloaded trains was reduced to 112 trains.[51]

Zhou Enlai's Last Hurrah: The Four Modernizations Strategy

What effect did this campaign have on the import substitution development strategy? Although their criticism delayed several import substitution projects, the politics-in-command coalition lacked sufficient support to defeat the post–GLF's development strategy. The 4–3 Plan was not canceled. With the support of Zhou Enlai and Li Xiannian, Chen Yun directed on 12 October 1973 that the 4–3 Plan proceed, including the importation from the United States of $300 million in equipment and associated tools to produce rolled steel. Chen Yun argued that "if people criticize this as being a worshipper to everything foreign, then we'll for once be a worshipper."[52]

It is possible that the campaign delayed the improvement of international economic ties and indirectly affected the financing of the 4–3 Plan. According to a recently declassified Rand study on Sino-American diplomatic relations, Deng Xiaoping did not consider most-favored-nation status (MFN) as an important priority when he met with Henry Kissinger on 22 October 1974.[53] China could have financed imports of U.S. manufacturing technology by taking advantage of the reduced U.S. tariff to sell more Chinese goods on the U.S. market. Yet Deng Xiaoping perhaps was more concerned that the new designation might provoke conservative opposition; one week beforehand, on 13 October, Jiang Qing had indirectly accused Zhou and Deng of following a "comprador bourgeoisie ideology," and Wang Hongwen et al. were calling for a renewal of the Cultural Revolution.[54] While MFN became a very important bilateral issue by the end of the 1970s, supporters of the 4–3 Plan perhaps viewed MFN as an ideological booby trap in 1974.

The campaign created more direct problems for financing the import substitution strategy. According to the State Planning Commission's "Report on the Foreign Exchange Revenue and Expenditure Problem" submitted on 12 September 1974, the country incurred its first large foreign exchange deficit. During the first three quarters of 1974, the deficit reached $1.2–1.4 billion. At least one Western observer has attributed the deficit to "the world recession [that] dampened the demand for Chinese products."[55] The SPC's report paints a more complicated picture. The report cited five reasons for the foreign exchange deficit:

1. When arranging the import/export plan during the beginning of the year, there already was a planned $500 million deficit [that was hoped to have been resolved during the year].

2. Because of international market changes, most export product prices dropped; concurrently prices for imported steel, chemical fertilizers, chemical raw materials, etc. rose greatly.

3. Some large-volume export commodities weren't sold, while there were not enough supplies of export products.

4. There was an increase in exports outside the plan.

5. There was a rise in cost of vessel rental fees.[56]

While acknowledging the effect of the world recession, the report clearly stated that the major cause of the problems was the campaign. The report specifically cited the shortage in export commodity supplies and high foreign vessel rental fees resulting from port stoppages. Because of such disruptions, the State Council was unable to resolve an initially planned $500 million deficit in the import substitution program.

Promoting the "normalization" of economic life, policy makers allocated $120 million to the Ministry of Foreign Trade to "normalize" the foreign trade sectors. Li Xiannian suggested on 12 September 1974 an increase of certain exports—such as oil, tungsten, and sugar—as well as a postponement of certain imports—such as grains, cotton, and a portion of steel and chemical fertilizers. Li further called for the increased use of foreign trade loans, increased sales of Chinese gold reserves abroad, and a reduction in foreign vessel rental fees and other non–foreign exchange expenditures. By the end of 1974, "not only were foreign exchange receipts and expenditures balanced, but there was a slight foreign exchange surplus."[57]

Having recovered somewhat from the campaign's ideological foray, Zhou Enlai made his final push to enact his vision of China's future development path. In his last government work report before his death delivered to the Fourth NPC on 13 January 1975, Zhou revived the Four Modernizations Program that he had first presented to the September 1963 work conference (chapter 3). Zhou announced to the assembled NPC representatives,

> On Chairman Mao's instructions, it was suggested [by Zhou himself] in the Report on the Work of the Government to the Third National People's Congress that we might envisage the development of our national economy in two stages beginning from the Third Five-Year Plan: The first stage is to build an independent and relatively comprehensive industrial and economic system in fifteen years, that is, before 1980; the second stage is to accomplish the comprehensive modernization of agriculture, industry, national defense, and science and technology before the end of the century, so that our national economy will be advancing in the front ranks of the world.[58]

Always the tactician, Zhou emphasized that the Four Modernizations development strategy was based "on Chairman Mao's instructions." Zhou did not mention how the program had been supplanted in 1964 by the militaristic Third Front vision of development. Nor did he mention the autarkic cries of the Cultural Revolution that had so recently been echoed in the Anti-Lin, Anti-Confucius Campaign. Instead, Zhou called for an interim ten-year plan to be implemented between 1975 and 1985 that would "establish an independent and relatively comprehensive industrial structure and national economic system." Its completion would "forge ahead toward completion of the second stage of the magnificent goal [of the Four Modernizations]."[59]

By late 1975, Zhou was near death, and Deng was fighting for his political life. The ten-year import substitution development plan would be temporarily shelved, until Hua Guofeng could gain power.

Repulse the Right-Deviationist Wind to Reverse the Verdicts Campaign, November 1975–October 1976

Before we look at the second stage of assault on the import substitution domestic development strategy, which began in November 1975, it is first important to understand changes in the domestic political and economic situation during the interim period.

Dying of bladder, colon, and lung cancer,[60] Zhou Enlai with Mao's approval appointed Deng Xiaoping on 1 February 1975 to take charge of State Council work, including the issuance of important directives.[61] Deng continued Zhou's normalization policy by improving industrial management, production quality, and the status of technical specialists within the society.[62] He thus ensured that the national economy recovered from the Anti-Lin, Anti-Confucius Campaign. By 1975, the gross value of industrial output (GVIO) had increased 15.1 percent over the previous year; the gross value of agricultural output (GVAO) had increased 4.6 percent.[63]

While strengthening his position to counter the politics-in-command coalition, Deng began to implement Zhou's vision of development. During his discussions with U.S. Congressional leaders in April 1975, with French leaders in May, and American journalists in June, Deng reiterated the Four Modernizations' goals to achieve economic parity with the developed countries by the end of the century.[64] Echoing his April 1974 UN General Assembly speech, Deng told a U.S. Congressional delegation on 23 August 1975, "We firmly support self-reliance, but that doesn't mean autarky, and it doesn't mean a type of conservatism. We want to study and absorb world-class technology. As our economy develops, the prospects for our foreign trade will broaden."[65]

Still faced with financing import substitution imports, Deng suggested that China could expand its foreign trade. He improved export quality and quantity, especially concerning oil, chemicals, coal, and more traditional products.[66] While no new export promotion scheme was implemented in 1974, the Ministry of Foreign Trade's Circulating Funds to Promote Export Commodity Production (Waimao Fuchi Chukou Shangpin Shengchan Zhouzhuan Zijin) began to disburse funds in 1975. Funds for the Specialized Loan Program for Industrial Export Production and the Investment Fund for Export Commodity Production also were increased. In addition, the second comprehensive base for export commodity production was established in Guangdong's Huiyang Prefecture, east of Guangzhou and north of Hong Kong. Chinese exports thus rose to a record $7.26 billion (RMB 14.3 billion).[67] Interestingly, Deng also considered several innovative financing techniques, including using Chinese coal and oil to barter for foreign technology as well as using "deferred payment and installment payment" schemes.[68]

By 1975, Deng also realized that China could no longer implement a substantial foreign aid program. During the First and Second Five-Year Plans, China allocated more than 1.1 percent of its annual total fiscal expenditures to foreign aid (this figure apparently does not include Chinese expenditures during the Korean conflict). By 1970, China devoted 3.5 percent of its budget (RMB 2.25

billion) to its foreign aid program; this jumped to 5.1 percent (RMB 3.76 billion) in 1971 with the signing of the Economic and Military Materials Aid Agreement with Vietnam on 27 September 1971; it reached 6.7 percent in 1972, 7.2 percent in 1973, and 6.3 percent in 1974.

By 1974, the Vietnamese no longer needed military aid; some traditional Chinese aid recipients enjoyed an even higher standard of living than the Chinese did. Deng thus decided on 23 April 1975 to reduce the percentage of aid devoted to North Korea, Vietnam, Albania, Laos, and Kampuchea from 75 percent to below 50 percent, with the percentage devoted to African states increased. More important, he reduced total foreign aid outlays from their 1973 high of 7.2 percent of total fiscal expenditures to within 5 percent (RMB 5 billion).[69] The newly freed funds were diverted to China's own development program.

Deng also attempted to rectify Cultural Revolution ideology during the interim 1975 period with the publication of "The General Principles for Every Task of the Entire Party and Nation." Written by the newly rehabilitated director of the State Council's Office for Political Research, Deng Liqun, the "General Principles" directly attacked the anti-Zhou forces, who were described as "political swindlers who want to restore false Marxism." It strongly criticized "rebellion" (zao fan), "going against the tide" (fan chaoliu), and "the Four Bigs," which had been promoted during the Cultural Revolution and the Anti-Lin, Anti-Confucius Campaign. During a 27 April 1975 Political Bureau meeting, Deng Xiaoping and Ye Jianying directly countered the politics-in-command coalition's criticism about "empiricism" and directly criticized Jiang Qing's actions during the Anti-Lin, Anti-Confucius Campaign.[70] Though Zhou Enlai was slowly dying in a Beijing hospital, Deng continued to build consensus and expanded Zhou's post–Cultural Revolution domestic development strategy.

This return to normalization was, however, short-lived. Zhang Chunqiao and Yao Wenyuan in March 1975 borrowed Mao's criticisms at the 1959 Lushan conference to spark criticism of Deng Xiaoping and his "empiricism" (jingyan zhuiyi). Jiang Qing's propaganda machine spread this criticism nationwide by spring 1975.[71] Mao criticized the politics-in-command coalition's attack on empiricism during a 3 May 1975 Political Bureau meeting, and several Political Bureau meetings were held critical of Jiang Qing. While Jiang Qing submitted a self-criticism in 28 June, the politics-in-command coalition continued to fan the fire of rebellion, including publishing articles in August 1975 criticizing the use of foreign technology.[72]

Deng had forwarded to Mao an August 1975 letter critical of two Qinghua University Revolutionary Committee secretaries supportive of the politics-in-command coalition.[73] On 3 November 1975, a Great Debate on Education and Revolution was held at Qinghua, the premier Chinese university for science and technology and an important crucible for Cultural Revolution ideas.[74] Mao strongly supported the two secretaries, who were defending the legacies of the Cultural Revolution, especially an egalitarian educational system.[75] This letter was one of the first signals that Mao had switched his support from Deng to Jiang Qing's coalition. At its conclusion, the Central Committee sponsored a warning meeting (*dazhaohu hui*) of Party and military leaders in Beijing. The assembled cadre listened to a Mao Zedong–approved letter declaring that rightist-deviation was not unique to Qinghua. "This great debate must influence the entire country. [We] don't want old cadre to make new mistakes in this new movement."[76]

The second phase of the attack on the large-scale import substitution development strategy thus had begun. Now the primary target was no longer Zhou, but his appointed successor, Deng Xiaoping.

After Zhou Enlai's death on 8 January 1976, *Renmin ribao* (*People's daily*), *Hong qi* (*Red flag*), and *Jiefangjun bao* (Liberation Army daily) attacked rightist-deviation tendencies in the economic, educational, cultural, and health spheres. The rising political storm even forced a premature conclusion of the National Planning Conference on 23 January 1976. Conferees never discussed Deng's economic restructuring plans or the Twenty Points of Industry scheme.[77]

The new leftist attack again centered on the import substitution domestic development strategy. On 23 February 1976, the Central Committee sponsored another warning meeting for provincial, municipal, and regional military leaders. Zhang Chunqiao, a member of the Gang of Four, criticized Deng and "his" import/export policies. Calling Deng "a bourgeois comprador . . . more fierce than Chiang Kai-shek," Zhang criticized the importation of ethylene plants from abroad and the export of unrefined oil.[78]

On 2 March 1976, Jiang Qing called an unauthorized Conference of Twelve Provinces and Autonomous Regions. She continued Zhang's previous attack by disputing the veracity of Mao's statement to "enliven the national economy." She harshly criticized the domestic development program as "putting profits in command . . . taking the technologist road . . . [and] laying the material foundations for capitalism." She also denounced Deng's policy of exporting unrefined oil, coal, and cotton textiles to the capitalist market as "traitorous behavior."[79] Li Zhisui recalled Jiang Qing's criticisms, in which

> she began by comparing Deng Xiaoping to the Ming dynasty's Wu Sangui (1612–1678), who had turned China over to the control of the Manchus. Deng had also sold out to foreign countries, she said, citing the export of oil and textiles. Deng, it seemed, had allowed the sale of plain cotton cloth. Jiang Qing thought there was a lot more money to be made by selling textiles that had already been dyed.[80]

Zhang Chunqiao subsequently publicized the controversy at a 7 March 1976 meeting with a foreign delegation. Zhang compared the Chinese attempts at compensation trade with the trading practices carried out under Chiang Kai-shek.[81]

By April 1976, the stage was set for Deng's removal. Deng's major patron, Zhou Enlai, had died in January; Mao's directives supporting the Anti-Rightist Movement were published on 3 March;[82] and Deng was blamed for the violent 5 April Tiananmen incident.[83] On 7 April 1976, Mao Zedong reportedly stated, "The nature [of the problem] has changed. . . . Relieve Deng of all responsibilities."[84] Hua Guofeng was chosen to be the country's next premier and the Party's first vice-chairman.

During the spring and summer of 1976, the politics-in-command coalition continued to assault Zhou's import substitution development strategy. On April 26 and May 24, Yao Wenyuan claimed that financing the development strategy by exporting unrefined oil and coal "was shifting the world oil crisis [onto China]." Yao described the Zhou strategy as "a traitorous policy of capitulation toward imperialism and transforming China into a colony."[85]

The most virulent denunciation was voiced at the Political Bureau meetings of 13 March and 25 June. Chinese leaders who implemented Zhou's domestic development strategy were condemned as

> flunkies for the imperialists, selling out the country and being traitors. . . . The Ministry of Foreign Trade has a group of traitorous betrayers. . . . Within the Political Bureau itself there are members of the bourgeoisie and comprador bourgeoisie. . . . You worship foreign things, fawn on foreign powers, and have bought so much useless junk. Who knows how much money the Lockheed Corporation has given you.[86]

In June, Zhang Chunqiao and Yao Wenyuan described Chen Yun's oversight of the foreign economic system and the 4-3 Plan as "a serious problem. . . . His foreign trade work took a traitorous, capitulationist line."[87] At these Political Bureau meetings, the ECPB policy was also targeted. The establishment of a coal export base was decried as "giving foreign concessions to outside countries" (*zurang gei waiguo*).[88]

The attack on the domestic development strategy continued during the autumn of 1976. *Renmin ribao* published more than a hundred articles lambasting the "three poisonous weeds."[89] The *Renmin ribao* articles slandered Zhou's foreign trade policy as "selling out national sovereignty . . . inviting the wolf into the home . . . taking the old route of Li Hongzhang, Yuan Shikai, and Jiang Jieshi [Chiang Kai-shek]." Consequently, China's foreign imports and exports were severely affected (table 6.1).

TABLE 6.1 SELECTED CHINESE EXPORT/IMPORT FIGURES, 1972–81
(U.S. $100 million)

Year	Exports		Imports	
	Total	% change	Total	% change
1972	34.43	30.6	28.58	29.6
1973	58.19	69.0	51.57	80.4
1974	69.49	19.4	76.19	47.7
1975	72.64	4.5	74.86	−1.7
1976	68.55	−5.6	65.78	−12.1
1977	75.90	10.7	72.14	9.7
1978	97.45	28.4	108.93	51.0
1979	136.58	40.2	156.75	43.9
1980	182.72	33.8	195.50	24.7
1981	208.93	14.3	194.82	−0.3

Source: Zhongguo Duiwai Jingji, *Zhongguo,* sect. 4, pp. 3, 4.
Note: Percentage change is based on the change from the previous year.

Conclusion

By the mid-1950s, Chinese elites reevaluated the Soviet model of development, a move that resulted in China's adoption of a uniquely Chinese path toward self-reliance. Yet the Chinese elites disagreed over the correct path of inwardly oriented development. This lack of consensus subjected China to two decades of alternating phenomenal economic devastation and growth.

With Mao's death and the impending fall of the politics-in-command coalition in 1976, the two-decade-long development debate ended by default. The adherents to a more autarkic path were becoming a minority voice among the policy elites. It would no longer be considered traitorous to use the international marketplace to accelerate domestic economic growth.

This unanimity among the elites was short-lived. A new debate over the depth of involvement with the international economy was arising that would not be fully resolved until the early 1980s.

CHAPTER 7

The Great Leap Outward, 1977–1979

Following Mao's death on 9 September 1976 and Jiang Qing's downfall a month later, China began to exorcise the ghosts of Mao Zedong. Hua Guofeng joined the majority of policy elites to excoriate the gang's "ultraleftist" policies, which became convenient scapegoats for Cultural Revolution excesses, production shortfalls, and leaky faucets. Yet unlike his contemporaries, Hua did not desire to eradicate all ghosts of the past or to follow the East Asian path of outwardly oriented development.

Though faced with declining industrial productivity, Hua did not initiate major economic readjustments or formulate new innovative economic policies. Hua's Great Leap Outward in reality was a continuation of the inwardly oriented import substitution strategy first instituted in the 1950s and continued under Zhou Enlai's Four Modernizations Program. While approving the first experimental use of foreign capital for domestic investment since the Sino-Soviet joint ventures of the 1950s, Hua was reluctant to promote further radical change.

Deng Xiaoping, Chen Yun, and other members of the post–GLF coalition directly attacked the high economic costs of Hua Guofeng's Ten-Year Plan. After Hua's effective ouster in late 1978, the coalition not only readjusted Hua's grandiose schemes, but began the transformation from inwardly oriented to outwardly oriented development. This transitional phase—or proto-experiment with outwardly oriented development—resulted in the establishment of the special economic zones and other measures that reduced barriers to the international market.

Hua Guofeng's Ten-Year Plan

Political Chaos and the Readjustment of the Economy

Mao's death on 9 September 1976 cut short the politics-in-command coalition's bid for power. Hua Guofeng, Ye Jianying, Li Xiannian, and Wang Dongxing approved the arrest of Jiang Qing and company on the night of October 6, 1976.[1] Thus ended a purely Maoist emphasis on normative approaches to economic growth.

In view of the economic disruptions caused by the anti-rightist movement and the Tangshan earthquake of 1976, Premier Hua's most important task was national economic revival. During the first ten months of 1976, government expenditures exceeded receipts by RMB 2.37 billion. To prevent inflation, the Central Committee froze units' bank accounts from October 28 to December 31, 1976. In 1977 the State Council reduced fiscal spending,[2] including foreign aid;[3] sponsored various conferences investigating ways to rectify the general economic situation,[4] and ensured the supply of production inputs, especially raw materials, energy, and transportation.[5]

Although such measures aided economic recovery, the national economy still faced many difficult problems. As a result of poor management, production quality problems, industrial accidents, and inefficient labor and technology, more than 30 percent of Chinese industries were losing money. Such losses had not happened overnight. The State Council admitted in an 8 July 1977 circular that the number of unprofitable state-run industries between 1970 to 1976 rose from 28.9 percent to 37.2 percent; their losses increased from RMB 1.465 billion to RMB 7.247 billion. During the first five months of 1977, the amount of industrial plant losses increased 35 percent over the same period in 1976.[6] By the end of 1977, the situation had not greatly changed. Supplies of raw materials and energy and for heavy industry were in short supply, while the transportation and agricultural sectors remained problematic.[7]

According to an SPC and MFT report, the export sector also was endangered. During the first two quarters of 1977, the state failed to obtain sufficient rice, soybeans, hogs, unrefined and refined oil, coal, steel, concrete, and textiles for export. Raw materials, fuel, and electricity needed for export production were scarce. Coastal ports continued to be blocked. Consequently, "the fulfillment of export contracts and supplies to the Hong Kong/Macao market [was] affected."[8]

Li Xiannian was particularly concerned about the Hong Kong–mainland relationship. In the mid-1970s, Wang Hongwen had denounced the policy of "considering Hong Kong with a long-term perspective and fully utilizing it" (see chapter 6). During a speech to the National Foreign Trade Planning Conference of 27 January 1977, Li Xiannian reminded the conferees of Zhou Enlai's directive: "Every capable area must take some responsibility to supply Hong Kong. There cannot be any backtracking. This is an area of growing importance. Supplying Hong Kong is indeed a political responsibility." Li thus implored every province, city, and department to fulfill China's trade obligations to Hong Kong.[9] Eventually, the leadership established two ECPBs in the Hong Kong and Macao border regions in 1978; following the post–GLF's assumption to power, these ECPBs were transformed into SEZs.

Policy Innovation: The Contradictory Ten-Year Plan

On 26 October 1976, twenty days after Political Bureau members deposed Jiang Qing, Chairman Hua outlined his governing philosophy at a Central Propaganda Bureau meeting. Besides advocating intensified criticism of the Gang of Four and their "ultra-rightist line," Hua declared that "whatever policy Chairman Mao decided upon, we shall resolutely defend; whatever directives Chairman Mao decided upon, we shall steadfastly obey."[10]

This Two Whatevers approach encompassed policies that Mao either had strongly propounded (e.g., self-reliance) or had tacitly approved. Mao had been the preeminent leader: all policies needed "a nod" from the Chairman, even if they were not consistent with a Maoist vision. Thus, the former prefecture Party secretary of Mao Zedong's native village upheld Mao's strategy of accelerated industrial growth fueled by normative agrarian and industrial policies, yet supplemented it with Zhou's vision of large-scale import substitution development. The result was a contradictory economic strategy.[11]

On 18–23 February 1978, the Central Committee approved Hua Guofeng's Ten-Year Plan for Developing the National Economy.[12] Although never formally published, the Ten-Year Plan established priorities and goals until 1985 and reflected the ten-year development plans enunciated by Zhou Enlai in January 1975 (see chapter 5). The plan set the annual growth of the gross value of industrial output to exceed 10 percent as well as increased the annual steel output (60 million tons) and unrefined oil production (250 million tons). To achieve these goals, the total of capital construction funds used exceeded the amount for the previous twenty-eight years. Hua envisioned 120 large-scale industrial projects, including ten large iron and steel complexes, ten oil and gas fields, and thirty hydroelectric stations. Echoing Mao's dreams of the Great Leap two decades before, Hua desired to "surpass the British and catch up to the Americans" (*chao Ying gan Mei*).[13]

Agricultural and industrial renewal were conservatively promoted using a Maoist self-reliance philosophy. The agricultural sector would use the Dazhai model, which was a Shanxi production brigade sanctified in 1964 as the Maoist model of agricultural self-sufficiency. Chinese industry studied the self-reliant methods of Daqing, a Heilongjiang oil field established in 1960. Both models deemphasized the individual producer and innovative management reform.[14]

Import substitution projects also played an essential role in Hua's ten-year industrial expansion plan. In addition to accelerating the 4-3 Plan import substitution projects ordered in 1973, Yu Qiuli's State Planning Commission submitted on 17 July 1977 a more grandiose import substitution program rivaling the import substitution program of the 1950s. Yu planned to import energy, fuel, and raw material production plants—including a 600- or 900-megawatt nuclear power plant, four large-scale fertilizer plants and equipment, four agricultural insecticide plants, three large-scale petrochemical plants, and four synthetic textile plants or equipment.[15] The initial cost was $6.5 billion in foreign exchange and more than RMB 40 billion in domestic infrastructure investment. Additional projects substantially increased costs;[16] to establish the Baoshan steel complex outside Shanghai, the leadership needed an extra $4.8 billion in foreign exchange and RMB 21.4 billion from local sources.[17]

Planners had to divert a large percentage of government revenues to finance Hua's Ten-Year Plan. In 1975, approximately 14 percent of total national capital construction investment was devoted to the 4-3 Plan. By 1976, this percentage had grown to 21 percent, a figure that was to be maintained until 1985 under Hua's new Great Leap.[18] The large-scale import substitution strategy thus placed a heavy burden on the entire economy. In 1979 alone, the State Planning Commission estimated a 15 million ton shortage of fuel, 1 million ton shortage of concrete, and 75,000 square meter shortage of lumber. The central government planned to withhold RMB 2 billion from the localities and incur a $10 billion foreign exchange deficit.[19]

More ominously, the import substitution projects already in operation were not profitable. Approximately two-thirds of Zhou Enlai's 4-3 Plan import substitution projects were losing money; only one-third of the projects were "quickly put into operation, incurred low construction investment, enjoyed efficient operations, and quickly returned the initial investment."[20] These industrial losses in part were attributed to slow construction schedules caused by the 1974–76 political campaigns, the scarcity of building materials, and the delay of domestically supplied equipment. In addition, in certain cases the state lacked the appropriate technology, imported defective material, or duplicated existing capacity. In the case of thirteen chemical fertilizer turnkey plants, the SPC failed to import technology to manufacture spare parts. Subsequently, the state imported an additional $10 million in spare parts. Because projects lacked qualified personnel with management or technological expertise, imported equipment was misused, and productivity was low.[21]

The most publicized case of inefficiency was the Wuhan Steel Company's 1.7 million steel rolling mill project approved on 21 August 1972. China imported continuous-casting workshops and a hot-rolling steel plant from West Germany, a cold-rolling steel plant and a silicon steel plate plant from Japan. The Chinese themselves built a second steel mill. The total cost was RMB 3.89 billion; RMB 2.228 billion ($600 million) was for foreign equipment and technology imports. During its construction between June 1975 and December 1978, many problems were encountered, including the following:

1. A great amount of waste. Excluding the RMB 156 million resulting from construction slowdowns and stoppages, construction costs exceeded original estimates by RMB 190 million. High costs were incurred from low labor productivity, a low rate of machinery utilization, a high material consumption rate, and the costly extensions of foreign experts' contracts.

2. Inadequate preparatory research, discussion, and organization during the construction and production phases, all of which caused inefficient use of plant equipment.

3. Inadequate understanding of infrastructure requirements, especially the strict requirements regarding air, water, electricity, weather, and other resources. Originally dependent on the Hebei and Henan electrical grids, the plant sporadically was provided energy after a half-year delay. Raw material supplies were also inadequate, thus reducing production of various steel products. Projected production of hot-rolled steel was 29 percent of original estimates; of cold-rolled steel, 26 percent; of silicon steel, 18 percent; and of continuous-cast steel, 40 percent.[22]

Considering the overall costs and the low investment return, state expenditure devoted to the import substitution strategy was too high. Such costs planted the "seeds of change," enabling the post–GLF coalition to regain power by 1978.

Deng Xiaoping and the Great Leap Outward

Deng Xiaoping, Chen Yun, and others gradually realized the diminishing returns of China's previous import substitution programs. Convinced that Hua's Ten-Year Plan would create economic chaos, the post–GLF coalition engineered Hua's downfall. Having broken free from the shackles of Maoist self-reliance concepts and having learned the limitations of Zhou Enlai's Four Modernizations strategy, the post–GLF coalition experimented with outwardly oriented development under the rubric of "opening to the outside world" (*duiwai kaifang*).

Economic Chaos: Paying the Piper

During the State Council Ideological Discussion Conference held between July and September 1978, Hua accelerated the construction schedules of several major projects, including the Baoshan steel complex, the Pingguo aluminum mine, and the Three Gorges hydroelectric dam. The projected cost for each project exceeded RBM 20 billion.[23]

Deng Xiaoping, Chen Yun, and other veterans of the post–GLF leadership cadre opposed Hua's Ten-Year Plan. After receiving Deng's letter of 10 April 1977 requesting "his resumption of work," Hua and the Central Committee appointed Deng vice-premier during the Third Party Plenum in July 1977.[24]

Although Deng and others spent the following year rebuilding the post–GLF leadership coalition to counter Hua Guofeng,[25] they were unable to prevent the adoption of Hua's development program in 1978.[26]

Following its adoption, the post–GLF leadership argued that the strategy's "imbalance" and overreliance on foreign imports and capital would result in economic chaos.[27] Summarizing criticism voiced at the March 1979 meeting, Li Xiannian stated,

> Last year [1978] we created new inroads in [import work], and achieved great results. Yet, because we lacked experience and overall preparation, we became too rushed, and our priorities were not enunciated. Last year we signed $7.8 billion worth of import project contracts,[28] which will require payment in spot exchange. Most were steel and chemical projects; there were few coal, electrical generating, or petroleum projects, while even fewer required low investment, yielded quick returns, or earned significant foreign exchange. Most were turnkey projects, many of which lacked manufacturing technology or technology rights; many were located in similar areas. While we actually have signed only a few steel and chemical project contracts, we would need an additional $5 billion to finance all the proposed contracts. The imports have created many foreign exchange payments problems and difficulties for domestic auxiliary projects.[29]

Project financing was the major concern. Hua's strategy necessitated deficit financing: in 1979, the deficit totaled RMB 17.06 billion; in 1980, it totaled RMB 12.75 billion. Some $200–300 billion would be needed to finance the entire Ten-Year Plan.[30] Having grossly exaggerated fiscal revenue projections, Hua had also inaccurately calculated repayment projections.[31] In his 21 March 1979 speech to the Political Bureau, Chen Yun accused Hua and his allies as blinded by the desire to

> quicken [the development process] and catch up with other countries in eight to ten years. They only look at the situation of other countries and do not look at the realities of our country. Our industrial base and technological ability are not as good as theirs are. Some countries and areas developed fast and had the special help of the United States. [Hua Guofeng] only considered borrowing money and only looked at the fast development of other countries. This was wrong.[32]

As a result of the post–GLF coalition's actions, Hua's Two Whatevers philosophy was completely discredited. Hua made a self-criticism to 212 central and regional Party leaders attending the November–December 1978 Central Committee Work Conference.[33] Although "his ideas changed after the Third Plenum," Hua eventually resigned the chairmanship of the Party and the Central

Military Commission at the Political Bureau meeting of 10 November 1980.[34] Hua's coalition of supporters, such as Ji Dengkui, Wang Dongxing, Wu De, and Chen Xilian, eventually were ousted from the Political Bureau. In their place, the post–GLF leadership composed of Deng Xiaoping, Li Xiannian, Ye Jianying, Chen Yun, Wang Zhen, Bo Yibo, Yang Shangkun, and others took control. This old guard subsequently supported the elevation of younger reformers, such as Hu Yaobang and Zhao Ziyang.[35]

The post–GLF coalition shifted the Party's direction from political concerns "to socialist modernization construction."[36] Calling for a liberation in thinking, less fettered by the "Party directives," "Party interest," and "Party discipline,"[37] Deng proffered an alternate, pragmatic development approach based on the idea of "practice as the sole criterion of truth." This was an adaptive strategy allowing a more liberal interpretation of Maoist teachings, including the self-reliance principle.[38] No longer would leaders be obsessed to "catch up with other countries in eight to ten years."[39] This new leadership experimented with innovative ideas, including permitting foreign direct investment and establishing the special economic zones.

Readjustment of Domestic and Foreign Economic Policy

Inspired by Chen Yun's comments and impelled by a 6 January 1979 directive from Deng Xiaoping, the new leadership readjusted the import substitution domestic development strategy.[40] Formally proposed at the April 1979 work conference, the new strategy readjusted not only the 1979 plan, but the entire Ten-Year Plan.[41] At the April work conference, Li Xiannian declared,

> The Central Committee and State Council believe that we must focus on a period of three or more years to carry out readjustment of the national economy successfully. . . . Thus the current plan is: readjustment, reform, reorganization, and raising of standards. We will in part readjust the economy and in part continue forward. While carrying out readjustment, we will reform; while carrying out readjustment, we will reorganize and raise standards.[42]

Patterned on the post–GLF strategy of readjustment, consolidation, supplementation, and raising expectations of success (*tiaozheng, gunggu, chongshi, tigao*) of the early 1960s, the new Eight-Character Plan emphasized reform and reorganization. This emphasis underscored the leadership's perception that the post–Cultural Revolution domestic economic and political situation had changed significantly.[43]

THE CENTRAL WORK CONFERENCE OF 5–28 APRIL 1979

The Third Plenum had presented political solutions previously hammered out at the preceding Central Committee Work Conference of November–December

1978. The April 1979 work conference presented economic solutions previously hammered out at a series of preparatory meetings,[44] the most important of which was the 21–23 March 1979 Political Bureau meeting.

Li Xiannian's opening speech to the work conference reflected the collective decisions reached at the March meeting. According to the Central Committee circular, the speech was "an extremely important guiding document for successfully carrying out socialist economic construction at this time." It was the principal document issued by the new leadership outlining their intentions to readjust the domestic development strategy. The April work conference thus discussed the details and achieved consensus for the overall readjustment program.[45]

Readjustment of the 1979 Economic Plan Targets. At the March 1979 Political Bureau meeting, Deng directed, "The core duty at present is readjustment." Li Xiannian later added, "Of the four areas of readjustment, reform, reorganization, and raising of standards, the most crucial is readjustment. We say this because . . . it currently is the major obstacle to economic development."[46]

To overcome this "major obstacle," Li Xiannian and Chen Yun proposed on 14 March 1979 to establish the Finance and Economics Commission. The commission would "research and formulate financial and economic plans and policies and be the policy-making body in major matters in finance and economic work."[47] Approved by the Central Committee on 27 March 1979, the commission was led by Chen Yun, with Li Xiannian as vice-chairman and Yao Yilin as head of the Secretariat.[48]

The commission's first task was to readjust the 1979 economic plan. The planned agricultural growth rate was readjusted from 5–6 percent to over 4 percent (actual growth rate, 8.6 percent); the industrial growth rate was readjusted from 10–12 percent to 8 percent (8.5 percent); grain production was reduced from 639.5 billion *jin* to 625 billion (664.2 billion); coal from 658 million tons to 620 million; crude oil from 115 million to 110 million; steel from 34 million tons to 32 million; state-financed capital construction was reduced from RMB 45.7 billion to RMB 36 billion.[49]

Readjustment of "Proportional Imbalances." Second, the commission sought to readjust the "proportional imbalances" plaguing the national economy. Expanding upon Chen Yun's 21 March speech,[50] Li Xiannian specified five "proportional imbalances" in his work conference speech: (1) between agriculture and industry, (2) between light and heavy industry, (3) between the fuel and power industry and other industries, (4) between accumulation and consumption, and (5) between employment and the lack thereof.[51]

The reduction of the accumulation rate,[52] specifically the reduction of capital construction, was the quintessential problem encountered by the new leadership during the post–Ten-Year Plan readjustment period. Li Xiannian stated,

Last year [1978] the scale of construction again was too large. Investment has been repeatedly increased. Annual investment within the budget reached RMB 8.3 billion; independently financed investment also exceeded the plan and amounted to over RMB 3 billion. The more than 1,400 large and midsized projects under construction in 1977 increased to more than 1,700 [in 1978]. . . . Last year's fiscal revenue, calculated in terms of comparable items, increased RMB 20 million over the previous year: RMB 15 m was devoted to capital construction.[53]

To rectify the accumulation problem, whose 1978 rate had been exceeded only by the 1959 and 1960 rates,[54] Li sought to reduce all capital construction, including large turnkey projects and technology imports. Li also wanted to increase exports to pay for remaining technology imports as well as readjust prices for agricultural and industrial raw materials and finished products.[55] Although a substantial reduction did not occur until after 1980 (see following discussion on Yu Qiuli),[56] the initial readjustment initiative had a profound effect upon Hua's import substitution strategy.

READJUSTMENT OF THE IMPORT SUBSTITUTION PROGRAM

The End of the Petroleum Group. The new leadership's decision in March 1979 to readjust the scale of the import substitution program was not a rejection of the import substitution strategy, foreign technology, or foreign capital. Instead, it was a call for a more "rational," affordable strategy that reflected the Eight-Character Plan.[57] After economic readjustment was completed in "two or three years," the importation of complete plants and equipment would resume.[58] As Li announced during the April work conference,

Imports must progress at a proper order, with a correct beginning and end without being too hasty. After appropriate consideration, imports must be severely restricted until 1985. Approval of future imports will be based on future foreign exchange receipts earned from exports or available foreign loans. It also takes into consideration the domestic economy's ability to provide auxiliary items for import projects, but does not include compensation trade and equity joint ventures. Imports must focus on key areas, and on projects that require less coal, less electrical demand, less investment, have a quicker return on investment and a greater ability to earn foreign exchange.[59]

Implementation of this decision was not trouble-free. Chen Yun, Li Xiannian, and eventually Deng Xiaoping directly intervened to preserve certain large-scale import substitution projects, such as Baoshan.[60] More important, elites disagreed over the exact scale of readjustment: the State Planning Commission wanted to retain a large capital construction program, while the Ministry of Finance advocated retrenchment.[61] Yu Qiuli, a Political Bureau member and the head of the State Planning Commission, led the defense of previous policies.

Yu Qiuli had helped to design Zhao's 4-3 Plan and Hua's more grandiose version, of which Yu was appointed leader of the SPC's Small Group on Importation of New Technology (Yinjin Xinjishu Lingdao Xiaozu). After the post–GLF coalition readjusted Hua's development strategy, the State Council established the Small Leadership Group on Imports and Exports with Yu Qiuli as the Group Leader. Because of Yu's continued obstinacy,[62] Yu's two import groups were replaced by the Foreign Investment Control Commission (FICC) (Waiguo Touzi Guanli Weiyuanhui) and the State Import-Export Administrative Commission (SIEAC) (Jinchukou Guanli Weiyuanhui). On 26 August 1980, Yu Qiuli also lost his job as head of the SPC.[63]

The fall of Yu Qiuli signaled the end of the so-called Petroleum Group and the large-scale import substitution development strategy; a compromise was reached to scale back and refinance the major import projects of 1978 and 1979.[64] Future import projects would be smaller and strictly controlled by the central government.[65] To ensure the implementation of the new strategy, the State Council appointed Gu Mu, an important proponent of the readjustment policy, as the leader of the SIEAC and the FICC.[66]

Technology and Equipment Importation. After readjusting the scale of the import substitution program, the new leadership modified the import substitution strategy. Instead of the previous emphasis on importing complete plants, the new strategy emphasized importing technology and equipment. In April 1979, Li stated,

> We want to modernize and naturally must import advanced technology and equipment from foreign countries and utilize foreign capital. . . . Our goal is to increase our country's self-reliance. Thus we must import more manufacturing technology and technology patents, and gradually raise our own manufacturing ability.[67] We must support the plan of self-reliance as the primary goal and external assistance as a supplementary. We cannot rely on borrowing foreign capital.[68]

While self-reliance remained the country's major goal, the methods to achieve the goal were modified to reflect Chinese realities, in which

> capital is limited, we don't have enough technical personnel, and we have a large population. In carrying out modernization, we cannot but consider what is advanced and what is backward. We must distinguish the order of priority and urgency. There must be a logical arrangement. When we use advanced technology, we first must consider the urgent needs of projects that increase the country's power and strengthen national defense. As for new labor-saving

technology, we for now should reduce its application or not use it at all. . . .
In our country's long-term future, advanced and backward technology will
exist side by side in large, medium, and small enterprises and in the handicraft industry. Otherwise, we'll be unable to accommodate the large labor
force.[69]

The State Council thus approved fiscal measures "to encourage imports of
technology and reduce imports of equipment, especially the reduction or cessation of importing turnkey projects and equipment."[70] The first key regulation
was State Council document 79.197, "Circular on Domestic Pricing Methods
for Imported Technology," which exempted importers of licensed technology
from certain domestic price mark-ups and taxes.[71] Other measures passed in
1980 provided various RMB loans and accounting measures to reduce the cost
of importing manufacturing technology.[72] The State Council also encouraged
technology imports by taking initial steps to protect intellectual property rights
and strengthen trademark regulation.[73]

Policy Innovation: Financing the New Domestic Development Strategy

The cost of the small-scale import substitution development strategy was much
lower than Hua Guofeng's Ten-Year Plan. The new Chinese leadership still
needed to finance the existing turnkey projects and future technology imports,
however. Readjustment of the domestic development strategy increased exports
by ensuring the supply of production inputs, improving the quality of exports,
and increasing China's ability to absorb new ideas and technology.[74] Nevertheless,
new methods were needed to encourage export expansion.

In his 21 March speech, Chen Yun argued that past methods of expanding
agricultural exports would not succeed, "since we don't produce enough."[75] In
his April work conference speech, Li Xiannian thus stressed the importance of

meeting the demands of the international market, increasing our competitive
ability, soliciting help from potential backers, and increasing variety, quality,
and packaging. We must earnestly strengthen organization and leadership in
this task, enliven foreign trade, and fully bring into play the enthusiasm of the
localities and various departments. . . . We simultaneously must put great effort
into developing the tourist and related industries, actively attract overseas
Chinese foreign exchange, and increase non-trade foreign exchange receipts.[76]

The new leadership thus decided by the April work conference to strengthen
plan-oriented export promotion policies that had been implemented since the
late 1950s. They also decided to explore innovative ways to increase foreign
exchange revenues.

PLAN-ORIENTED EXPORT PROMOTION POLICIES:
STATE COUNCIL DOCUMENT 79.202

On 13 August 1979, the State Council issued document 79.202, "The Regulations Regarding Problems in Putting Great Effort in Developing Foreign Trade and Increasing Foreign Exchange Revenue." Document 79.202 was the principal document outlining the plan-oriented export promotion policies.[77] Citing the need to expand foreign exchange revenue to "accelerate socialist modernization construction," document 79.202 called on "every area and department [to] use all means available to increase export commodity production and energetically organize foreign exchange receipts obtained from nontrade activities." State Council document 79.202 was among the most important documents issued by the leadership in 1979.

Document 79.202 was composed of fifteen regulations. The second regulation implemented a contract system between the foreign trade unit and the export production enterprise. It also reaffirmed the Five-Priorities Policy first proposed in October 1959 (see chapter 3). Forgotten during the Cultural Revolution period, the policy guaranteed fulfillment of export contract obligations by assigning top priority to the production, procurement, and distribution of export commodities.

In a similar spirit, State Council document 79.206 altered the procurement price method for exports.[78] Several obstacles blocked the expansion of exports, including the following:

Industries were unwilling to expand exports that enjoyed a higher profit margin if sold on the domestic market.

Certain Chinese products were exported at a loss.

The cost of imported raw materials used to produce export goods was too expensive.

Document 79.206 thus manipulated production costs to encourage exports. For purely export commodities,[79] prices were divorced from the domestic sales price and calculated according to "normal" production costs and "reasonable" profit margins. As a result, the Wuxi No. 5 Radio Factory reduced production costs of its transistor radio by 43 percent, to RMB 14.40. The factory subsequently sold the radio to the state exporter for RMB 15, earning a profit of RMB .60 per radio.[80]

The sixth regulation of 79.202 revised export promotion policies of the 1960s and 1970s, especially for industrial and new product exports. These included the Foreign Trade Circulating Funds to Promote Export Commodity Production,[81] Investment Fund for Export Commodity Production,[82] and the Specialized Loan Program for Industrial Export Production.[83] Between 1972 and 1980, these three important export promotion measures financed more than 120,000 pieces of equipment for 7,000 projects at a cost of RMB 2.5 billion; they increased the value of production by RMB 11.6 billion.[84] The Short-Term Foreign Exchange Loan Program, initiated in 1973, also was revised in June 1979 and August 1980 (State Council document 80.222) to raise the quality of light textile exports. China could now make sleeves that did not shrink.[85]

In addition, the leadership approved new loan programs in 1979 and 1980 to encourage the export of local, industrial, and new products. The new Administrative Measures for Trial Production of New Export Commodities provided supplementary funds to revitalize traditional export commodities. The measures upgraded manufacturing technology; improved product quality, variety, and packaging; and financed product research and development.[86] On 11 October 1980, the Bank of China issued trial regulations for two new loans: the Medium- to Short-Term Specialized Loans for Export Commodity Production[87] and the Medium- to Long-Term Loans for Machinery and Equipment Exports.[88] The former provided low interest loans to older factories within the Ministry of Foreign Trade system and to collectives. Its purpose was to renovate existing plants producing equipment needed for export production. The latter provided sellers' credit to state industries exporting turnkey plants, equipment, or vessels.

The ninth regulation of 79.202 revised the foreign exchange retention scheme (*waihui liucheng*). Detailed supplementary guidelines were issued outlining retention procedures for foreign exchange earned through foreign trade[89] and non-commercial activities.[90] Previously, foreign exchange revenue was sold to the PBOC, which in turn distributed the foreign exchange according to the plan. By the early 1960s, localities were given a foreign exchange portion (*waihui fencheng*) to "bring the initiatives of the localities into full play." Although praised by Li Xiannian in 1965 as an effective tool to increase exports,[91] this economic incentive program was eliminated by May 1967. After more than a decade, enterprises and localities again were permitted to retain a larger percentage of foreign exchange earnings, which totaled nearly 10 percent of foreign exchange revenue.[92]

The tenth regulation of document 79.202 authorized preferential tax treatment to increase exports. Domestic taxes were primarily assessed through the commercial and industrial tax (*gongshangshui*), which had first been proposed on 13 September 1958.[93] The tax on twenty different categories of reprocessed materials for export, including cacao beans and man-made silk, was either reduced or eliminated.[94] This preferential treatment was expanded by the "Regulations concerning the Reduction or Elimination of the Commercial and Industrial Tax on Imported and Exported Commodities" of 30 December 1980.[95]

In addition, import and export customs duties were either eliminated or reduced. Since 1951, export taxes had restricted exports scarce on the domestic market. In 1980, the central government eliminated all export taxes.[96] Import customs duties were reduced or eliminated for many processing and assembly ventures, compensation trade, and other foreign exchange–earning endeavors.[97]

To encourage export expansion, regulation 11 not only called for a RMB devaluation (RMB 1.58=$1),[98] but also mandated a change in the internal settlement rate. The State Council thus approved document 80.196, Trial Procedures of the Domestic Settlement Rate for Foreign Exchange Earned from Trade. A more favorable internal exchange rate made exporting a more profitable endeavor for enterprises. It simultaneously protected domestic industry from international market competition.[99]

Preferential treatment also was accorded to the post–GLF program of using imports to develop exports. By 1980, the program had produced 31.6 percent of exports and earned $5.69 billion in foreign revenue.[100] Expanded in March 1979,[101] the program now allowed participating enterprises to be granted Five Priorities status (79.202, regulation 2).[102] Enterprises were assessed a lower RMB cost for imported materials under certain circumstances (State Council document 79.206, point 5);[103] they could retain 15 percent of their net foreign trade earnings (79.202, regulation 9). The enterprises also enjoyed a reduction or elimination of the industrial and commercial tax and various import duties (79.202, regulation 10).

Regulation 7 of 79.202 strengthened existing export processing zones. To run "well-managed" bases and establish "relatively advanced specialized factories and workshops and production bases," the SIEAC updated the 20 March 1973 regulations and issued trial procedures for both the ECPBs and the specialized factories.[104] New ECPBs were established in both the coastal areas and the interior;[105] their foreign exchange funding was increased[106] and guaranteed;[107] priority was accorded to them by all the export promotion schemes; and they enjoyed a selective reduction or elimination of import duties for production inputs. Finally, the Chinese Export Commodity Base Construction Corporation (Zhongguo Chukou Shangpin Jidi Jianshe Gongsi) was established in 1980. The corporation facilitated the import of needed production inputs and the establishment of joint ventures with domestic and foreign partners.[108]

THE "OPENING" POLICY:
THE DECISION TO USE FOREIGN CAPITAL MORE "ACTIVELY"

The new leadership also devised innovative measures to increase foreign exchange revenue outside the plan. They expanded traditional sources, such as overseas Chinese capital. They also opened the door to foreign direct investment, which as Deng Xiaoping stated in 1980, would "be supplementary to our developing socialist productive forces."[109] This opening policy thus was a tool to finance import substitution and to transfer technology and management techniques.

Ever since the Soviet repayment problems of the 1960s,[110] foreign capital had been a forbidden topic (*jinqu*).[111] Yet the Chinese had used deferred credit totaling $300 million between 1962 and 1968 and $1.2 billion between 1973 and 1977 to finance the import substitution program. For the most part, this was sellers' credit,[112] which was regarded as " 'standard commercial practice for deferred payment in international trade' and not as a form of foreign debt."[113]

With the announcement of the Ten-Year Plan in 1978, Hua Guofeng had adopted both traditional and relatively innovative measures to finance the large-scale import substitution strategy. As in the past, Hua expanded exports, used sellers' credit, and especially encouraged overseas Chinese remittances.[114] Strongly courted during the 1950s, overseas Chinese were legally allowed to establish schools and state-owned overseas investment enterprises.[115] Shunned during the Cultural Revolution, Hua Guofeng established or reestablished various Party, governmental, and nongovernmental bodies concerned with overseas Chinese affairs.[116]

Hua Guofeng must also be given credit for adopting innovative foreign economic policies, which formed the basis of the post–Third Plenum opening policy. For example, on 26 February 1978, Hua concluded a long-term trade agreement (LTTA) with Japan; the agreement "committed [Beijing] to the export of coal and oil in specified amounts of a period of time, marking an unmistakable break with the Gang's alleged objections to the sale of China's raw materials."[117] By the 1978 State Council Ideological Discussion Conference, Hua's Central Committee also had approved limited use of foreign capital to finance the accelerated import substitution projects.[118] The decision itself prompted the acceptance of officially supported credit (buyers' credit),[119] the adoption of State Council document 78.139 authorizing processing and assembly activities,[120] the undertaking of limited compensation trade,[121] and the introduction of foreign capital to construct luxury hotels for foreign tourists,[122] who were considered a major source of foreign exchange.[123]

Deng Xiaoping continued to argue for measures that were even more innovative. One week after the official close of the 1978 State Council Ideological Discussion Conference, Deng complained that conservative leaderships prevented a more "active" use of foreign capital. The Two Whatevers faction (including Hua Guofeng, Wang Dongxing, and Wu De) argued that Mao Zedong had not approved such measures; they thus prevented the inclusion of compensation trade and joint ventures in State Council document 78.139.[124] In the spirit of his 24 May 1977 attack on the Two Whatevers philosophy, Deng argued,

> There are many circumstances that didn't exist in Comrade Mao Zedong's life-time. . . . For instance, during Comrade Mao Zedong's lifetime, we also wanted to expand economic and technical exchange abroad. This included developing

economic and trade relations with some capitalist countries, even attracting for-. eign capital, carrying out equity joint ventures, etc. Yet the conditions weren't right and people blockaded us. . . . After a few years of hard work, the current international situation is much better than that of the past. . . . What is the point of holding high the banner of Mao Zedong Thought if we cannot make up our minds to do things just because Comrade Mao Zedong had not said them in the past?[125]

Deng Xiaoping argued for a more "active" use of foreign capital, including cooperative production, equity joint ventures, hundred-percent-foreign-owned ventures, compensation trade, and acceptance of capital from foreign governments and international organizations. Although unable in August 1975 to use foreign capital "actively," Deng now was politically strong. He most probably presented his formal proposals at the Central Committee Work Conference in November-December 1978.[126] By securing the direct support of the other post–GLF leadership group, especially Chen Yun and Li Xiannian, Deng succeeded in forming a winning coalition.[127] Deng built an even wider consensus during the Third Plenum and succeeded in emasculating the Two Whatevers faction.[128] After the Third Plenum, the post–GLF coalition stated, "Because capital is not enough, we can borrow from abroad."[129]

This decision signaled the finale to China's past policies of being closed to the outside world (*biguan zishou*).[130] It marked the beginning of the policy of opening to the outside world and invigorating the domestic economy (*duiwai kaifang, duinei gaohuo*).[131] According to Hu Yaobang, the new leadership adopted three methods of using foreign capital. The first method was

attracting direct investment, including equity joint ventures, cooperative ventures, joint development, compensation trade, processing and assembly, etc.; the second method [was] to obtain medium- and long-term loans from foreign governments and international financial organizations with low to average interest rates, and funds from the various development funds, relief funds, etc.; the third method [was] the common commercial loan.[132]

In contrast to Hua Guofeng, the new leadership considered foreign commercial borrowing (*ziyou waihui daikuan*) as the least desirable method of financing the development strategy. The LIBOR rate had jumped to 17 percent,[133] by August 1979, and the new leadership was unwilling to pay the high interest rates for the $9.82 billion commercial loans arranged by the Bank of China since March 1979.[134]

Chen Yun was especially critical of the reliance on commercial loans. Because China could not afford to borrow commercially the planned $5 billion for 1980, commercial loans were to be limited to small projects with quick returns on investment.[135] Chen Yun "warn[ed] those cadre who [were not] very clear-headed" that "foreign capitalists are capitalists."[136] Concurring with Chen Yun two years later in 1982, Hu Yaobang stated that international bankers were simply capitalists; so-called preferential loans were simply commercial loans with slightly lower interest rates.[137]

The new leadership thus sought alternative financing. Liberated from Maoist ideological constraints, the new leadership applied for official and officially supported credit and aid from international organizations. They readily accepted the ¥330 billion ($1.5 billion) loan issued at a 3 percent annual interest rate by the Japanese Overseas Economic Cooperation Fund. The initial loan provided funds for six major construction projects for harbor construction, railroad improvements, and hydroelectric dam construction.[138] The Chinese leadership also arranged more than $17 billion of officially supported credit (buyers' credit) from its trading partners.[139] Although buyers' credit was considered more economical than commercial loans,[140] domestic readjustment kept most of it from being used. Chen Yun again argued that equipment imports and use of buyers' credit should be reduced to reflect China's weak foreign exchange position.[141]

Finally, the Chinese sought to recover their seat within the various UN financial organizations, including the IMF and the World Bank.[142] While anxious to have access to low interest loans, the leadership was aware that the loans were limited in amount and subject to conditions. Chen Yun stated in September 1979 that "utilization of such loans could be to our benefit. Yet there will be conditions for their use, and their amount will not be large."[143]

In its greatest divergence from previous finance strategies, the post–GLF coalition sought "to seize the opportunity in using foreign capital as quickly as possible to import foreign technology and equipment and master advanced technology and management [techniques] from foreign countries."[144] Foreigners would provide the development capital, advanced technology, and management expertise, which were scarce on the domestic market. The Chinese would provide the labor and land, which were underutilized on the domestic market. With such an efficient supply of production inputs, the Chinese could compete effectively on the international market. They also could absorb the foreign technology necessary to become a major world trading power.

The new leadership thus formulated relatively innovative foreign investment regulations covering processing and assembly agreements, compensation trade, equity joint ventures, and other types of cooperative ventures. During the April work conference, the SPC reported the success of State Council document 78.139, adopted under Hua Guofeng, authorizing processing and assembling activities. During the six-month period following its promulgation, 661 processing and assembly agreements and 37 compensation agreements were signed (504 contracts signed with Hong Kong, 99 with Japan and 95 with the United States and

Europe). The agreements potentially meant the importation of $66 million of equipment and a net total of $123 million in foreign exchange revenue. The new leadership thus declared, "Experience has shown that developing such activities is very important to further bringing into play our country's labor potential and equipment capabilities; it develops production, raises the level of technology, expands trade, and increases foreign exchange revenue."[145]

These findings vindicated Deng Xiaoping's policy of actively using foreign capital first proposed in 1975 and argued throughout 1978. The State Import-Export Administrative Commission, the State Economic Commission, the State Commission for the Control of Import and Export Affairs, and the Ministry of Foreign Trade submitted the 4 August 1979 report to revise State Council document 78.139.[146] The State Council subsequently approved document 79.220 on 3 September 1979.[147]

Document 79.220 included more detailed regulations regarding processing and assembly activities. More significantly, it also included regulations for compensation trade, which Deng had proposed during his January 1979 visit to the United States.[148] Document 79.220 provided incentives to renovate existing plant facilities, granted greater access to domestic and foreign exchange funds, and encouraged the use of domestic production inputs. Local economic growth was encouraged by decentralizing certain decision-making powers, developing exports important to the local economy, and encouraging greater cooperation between domestic production units.[149]

Second, the Chinese improved cooperative arrangements with foreign petroleum companies to develop China's offshore petroleum resources. In March 1979, Chen Yun stated, "America's prospecting technology is very advanced; thus let's use American technology to carry out oil prospecting. We can see quick results if we develop our petroleum [resources]."[150] Chen Yun considered cooperation agreements, coupled with compensation trade, co-production, and assembling and processing an excellent method to increase foreign exchange earnings.

Third, the Chinese established the China International Trust and Investment Corporation (CITIC). In February 1979, Deng Xiaoping and several other top leaders directed Rong Yiren, a prominent Shanghai industrialist before 1949, to propose a plan to attract foreign capital. In collaboration with Vice-Premier Gu Mu, Rong Yiren proposed in March 1979 to establish CITIC "in order to attract foreign capital, import advanced technology, and serve the Four Modernizations. CITIC would concentrate and uniformly attract foreign capital; in accordance with the state plan and the wishes of the investor, investment would be made in state construction."[151]

Rong's proposal was approved on 25 March 1979 by the Central Committee after the important 21–23 March Political Bureau meeting. On 2 June 1979, the

State Council issued a Circular approving the establishment of CITIC as a "social-ist state enterprise" directly under the State Council.[152]

Finally, the Chinese leadership's most daring initiative was adopting the joint venture law at the Fifth National People's Congress in 1979. For the first time since the 1950s, foreigners were allowed to establish joint ventures in China. Priority was given to

> projects that need little investment and yield quick returns and in addition are advanced by world standards; enterprises that can increase the competitive capa-bility of exports and products on the international market; projects that will carry out technological renovation and expansion by tapping the potential and renewing existing domestic enterprises; projects that provide scarce products, etc.[153]

In a letter to the Central Committee, Li Xiannian and Peng Zhen urged that the joint ventures adopt a board of directors system; establish a general manager responsibility system; not expropriate the capital belonging to either the Chinese or the foreign joint venture partners; give the joint venture operators the right to hire and fire staff and workers; impose a preferential tax rate of 35 percent; and calculate the salaries of the staff and workers according to the highest domes-tic rate.[154] Various regulations were issued during the following months, includ-ing regulations concerning the use of labor,[155] land usage,[156] registration procedures,[157] and taxation.[158]

Case Study: The Establishment of the Special Economic Zones

In July 1979, the Central Committee of the Chinese Communist Party approved document 79.50, granting Guangdong and Fujian Provinces extraordinary pow-ers in economic and foreign trade activities. Document 79.50 also established special economic zones in Shenzhen (previously Baoan County) and Zhuhai municipalities in Guangdong Province.[159] Two additional zones were author-ized on 16 May 1980 with the issuance of Central Committee document 80.41; these were established in Guangdong's northeast port of Shantou (Swatow) and in Fujian Province's major port city, Xiamen (Amoy).

The early SEZ policies were an important experiment in China's tentative reach toward outwardly oriented development. The resulting coastal development strat-egy yielded several variations of the SEZ idea, including the fourteen open coastal cities, economic and technological development zones (ETDZs), and economic development areas that were established along the Chinese coast in the 1980s.

Yet China's initial opening policy was not based on outwardly oriented devel-opment. The foreign economic policy formulated in the late 1970s and early 1980s continued the import substitution strategies implemented since the 1950s.

Domestic factors thus determined Chinese foreign economic policy during China's initial opening period.

PROBLEMS OF THE INTERNATIONAL ENVIRONMENT ARGUMENT

Current Western studies, often relying on historical precedent, suggest that the zones are the twentieth-century variation of the treaty port idea.[160] Others argue that the zones are part of an international trend toward establishing export processing zones, which were popular in the developing world during the 1960s and 1970s.[161] Both explanations are parsimonious, yet lack explanatory power.

The historical approach is based on the centuries-old desire to isolate Western influence to the coastal treaty ports. Two special economic zones (Shantou and Xiamen) and many of the fourteen open cities established in 1984 (including Shanghai, Tianjin, and Dalian) are in cities that were nineteenth-century treaty ports. Such historical arguments help to explain the establishment of the SEZs in remote areas of China, as policy makers continued a policy to isolate foreign bourgeois capitalist influences; they also explain the neocolonialist critique of the early 1980s. Most of all, they complement the romantic notion of history repeating itself. Yet the argument explains neither the vast difference between nineteenth-century imperialism and twentieth-century nationalism, nor the adoption and implementation of the SEZ policy.

The international environment argument has some validity. The post–GLF coalition seriously studied the development experiences of other developing countries.[162] As vice-chairman of the SIEAC, Jiang Zemin—the current CCP general secretary—led a delegation to study nine EPZs in Sri Lanka, Malaysia, Singapore, the Philippines, Mexico, and Ireland in September and October 1980. While in Geneva, the delegation held two days of talks with UN researchers concerning the establishment of such zones.[163] Chinese researchers also conducted extensive research on the development of world EPZs, with special attention to those in Taiwan, South Korea, the Philippines, Malaysia, Thailand, India, and Sri Lanka.[164]

Second, the Chinese rationale for setting up the zones was similar to that of other foreign countries. In general, countries establish such zones to strengthen comparative advantage by maximizing "the use of production factors and other domestic resources, in particular the labor force; [to stabilize] the balance of payments–capital movements and current payments in accordance with export flows; [and to facilitate] the acquisition of skills and know-how and, more generally, technology transfer."[165]

During a 25 November 1985 speech, Shenzhen's vice-mayor Zou Erkang revealed that initially Chinese policy makers used the experiences of foreign zones as a reference "to increase employment, earn foreign exchange, and absorb foreign technology and management [techniques]."[166]

Lastly, an international environment argument explains the formulation of the SEZ regulations. Several Chinese delegations went abroad during the late 1970s to investigate other zones.[167] SEZ regulations were "formulated based on actual conditions in China, and used the beneficial experiences of some foreign export processing zones and free trade areas."[168]

The international environment explanation is attractive because it conforms with the Nye's and Keohane's view of an increasingly interdependent world.[169] Yet the international environment explanation suffers from three major problems. The initial idea for the zones no doubt originated from abroad, yet the international environment explanation fails to explain the decision to experiment with the zone idea in July 1979. The timing also was not propitious. The explosive growth of the EPZs beginning in the 1960s had been greatly curtailed by the late 1970s.[170] Chinese scholars argue that this was the result of global protectionism and stagflation following the 1978 oil crisis, a decline in international investments, and a rise in competition among existing EPZs.[171]

Like their global counterparts, the Chinese leadership hoped to improve the employment situation and increase access to foreign capital, technology, and management techniques. Yet unlike most of their counterparts, the Chinese retained their import substitution strategy. The leaders of the smaller NIES—such as South Korea, Singapore, and Taiwan—had discovered in the 1960s the diminishing return of an import substitution strategy. They thus adopted types of outwardly oriented strategies that allowed import substitution for certain industries while using their comparative advantage to expand exports in other sectors. Some economies adopted a more extreme export-oriented development strategy, which viewed exports as the engine for domestic development; they adopted positive administrative incentives to promote the export sector (chapter 1).

Following the 1971 UN International Development Office report "Industrial Free Zones as Incentives to Promote Export-Oriented Industries," export-oriented development became the rationale for establishing EPZs around the world.[172] Most Asian economies adopting an export-oriented strategy established EPZs, including South Korea (Mashan and Iri) and Taiwan (Kaohsiung, Nantze, and Taichung).[173] Yet, after readjusting its import substitution domestic development strategy in 1979 and 1980, China continued its inward-looking development strategy. Only after 1982 did China initiate a more outwardly oriented strategy.[174]

Finally, while initially modeled after other foreign EPZs, the Chinese concept was unique. The SEZ's assigned mission was far more complex than that of any other EPZ in the world economy. Consequently, the Chinese SEZs have been the largest in the world in terms of area, population, and economic infrastructure. Although other command economies have established various types of economic zones, the Chinese SEZS are the most comprehensive and ambitious. As Vice-Mayor Zou Erkang stated in 1985,

> In the past, there had never been an idea such as the special economic zone. The task has never been undertaken and is thus a new idea. I remember a few foreign delegations, some from capitalist countries and some Party delegations, asking the same question about the theoretical foundation for establishing the SEZS. A ready-made theoretical foundation truly cannot be found in books. Beginning with *Das Kapital* to Stalin's *Socialist Economic Problems* and Chairman Mao's *On the Ten Great Relationships,* no one has written about delineating an area of a socialist country to attract foreign capital. The theory came from practice.[175]

It is only by analyzing such "practice" that an understanding of the timing, the context, and the uniqueness of Central Committee document 79.50 will be achieved.

READJUSTMENT AND CENTRAL COMMITTEE DOCUMENT 79.50

The Adoption of Document 79.50. The readjustment of the import substitution development strategy and the search for alternative financing directly determined Guangdong's and Fujian's future prosperity. The Guangdong and Fujian economies were in terrible disarray as a result of central government development and defense strategies of the 1950s and 1960s. Strategically situated on the opposite sides of the Pearl River estuary, Guangdong Province's Baoan and Zhuhai Counties share contiguous borders with Hong Kong and Macao respectively; Fujian lies 130 kilometers from Taiwan at the narrowest point of the Taiwan Strait. Beginning in the 1960s (chapter 3), these areas as well as other coastal and border regions were intentionally kept underdeveloped to establish a "political frontier defense."[176]

Consequently, the economic situation in the two provinces was critical by the late 1970s. According to document 79.50, economic growth rates for Guangdong had been lower than the national average during the 1960s and 1970s. Food production in Guangdong between 1966 and 1978 had an "average annual growth rate of . . . only 1.6 percent, which could not keep up with the 2.2 percent annual provincial population growth rate." Food production in Fujian was also low; "the average amount of food per person in 1978 [was only] 594 *jin* (297 kilos), which [was] lower than the national average." In addition, the provinces faced serious fuel, energy, and commodity shortages as well as transportation bottlenecks.

Unemployment and private debt were particularly high. According to document 79.50, more than three hundred thousand Fukienese were euphemistically "waiting for work." The number of economic refugees "escaping abroad [was] growing year by year." From 1949 to 1979, the Chinese estimated that ninety thousand people escaped to Hong Kong from Shenzhen. During the last half of 1979, more than thirty thousand escaped.[177] After the establishment of the Shekou Industrial Zone in the Shenzhen SEZ in 1979, the first priority was to dispose of hundreds of rotting corpses that had washed along the beaches as a result of unsuccessful attempts to escape to Hong Kong.[178]

Initial attempts to improve the economy were concentrated in the Pearl River Delta region bordering Hong Kong. This area includes only 18 percent of the total Guangdong land mass, yet produces more than half of Guangdong's agricultural and manufactured goods.[179] In 1973, the provincial government established the first comprehensive ECPB in Foshan, which is west of the provincial capital of Guangzhou. In 1975, an export commodity processing base was established in Huiyang Prefecture on the Hong Kong border, while in 1976 a third comprehensive ECPB was established south of the Pearl River Delta in Zhanjiang Prefecture (see chapter 5).

Guangdong provincial leaders hoped that these comprehensive bases would promote regional economic development, guarantee exports to the Hong Kong and Macao markets, and reduce economic migration.[180] Unfortunately, these comprehensive ECPBs failed. By 1977, China encountered production and transportation difficulties in supplying the Hong Kong and Macao markets with agricultural and semiprocessed goods.[181] Once in January 1977 and again in October, Li Xiannian reminded conferees to the National Foreign Trade Planning Conference, "The first priority of China's exports is still the Hong Kong–Macao market."[182]

Guangdong's second initiative to improve the border economy resulted in State Council document 79.38. On 14 February 1979, the State Council approved Guangdong's "Tentative Plans for Constructing Foreign Trade Bases and Establishing Municipal Governments in Baoan and Zhuhai Counties."[183] Modifying the export commodity production base policy, the State Council agreed that the two municipalities

> within a few years . . . would develop into very substantial export commodity production [bases] that [combine] both the industrial and agricultural sectors, into . . . tourist [areas] that will attract Hong Kong and Macao tourists and into . . . a new type of border city. This would simply be called the "three construction projects" (*sange jiancheng*).[184]

In addition, the State Council promised RMB 150 million to construct the new border cities (*bianjie chengshi*).[185] Guangdong leaders organized a work team composed of representatives of various provincial departments to plan the two cities' development.[186]

The third attempt was made by a new Guangdong leadership, which endorsed a more ambitious strategy. The Third Plenum of December 1978 approved Xi

Zhongxun as first Party secretary of the Guangdong Communist Party; Yang Shangkun was appointed second secretary.[187] Strong supporters of Deng Xiaoping, Xi and Yang were searching for innovative ways to improve the Guangdong economy. The top leadership had already approved in late 1978 or early 1979 the active use of foreign capital from overseas Chinese and foreign sources. In January 1979, Li Xiannian approved the request of the Guangdong Revolutionary Committee and the Ministry of Communications to establish the Shekou Industrial Zone. In February 1979, Deng Xiaoping and other senior members of the Central Committee and State Council directed Rong Yiren to consider methods to attract foreign capital.

Thus during a March 1979 meeting of the Central Committee, Xi Zhongxun and Yang Shangkun proposed that the central government "positively bring into play the superior conditions of Guangdong Province, expand foreign economic trade, reform the economic management structure, and accelerate its economic development."[188] They suggested that the southeast coastal region would be an excellent area to experiment with new development strategies. Guangdong and Fujian provincial leaders believed that the provinces enjoyed certain "superior conditions": namely, their proximity to Hong Kong, Macao, and Taiwan and the approximately 8.2 million Cantonese and 5 million Fukienese compatriots (*tongbao*) living abroad. In 1978, Cantonese living abroad had sent more than $450 million in remittances to their mainland relatives; in 1978, Fukienese relatives remitted more than $100 million. According to 79.50, these overseas Chinese, many of whom were "scientific and technical specialists, industrialists, or businessmen with considerable capital," also requested "to return to the province and to invest in the operating factories and start up other industrial activities."

In analyzing the Guangdong proposal during the spring of 1979, the post–GLF coalition no doubt realized that Shanghai and Tianjin possessed similar if not superior conditions.[189] Shanghai was the primary producer of export goods and had received substantial state investment to improve export production.[190] These areas eventually were granted greater decision-making rights, but not as extensive as those granted by document 79.50. The members of the Political Bureau also must have realized that only innovative measures could improve the economic situation in the southeast coastal region, that improvement of the local economy would staunch the flow of illegal immigration to Hong Kong and encourage foreign investment from compatriots living overseas, and that experimentation in the relatively unimportant southeast coastal region would not harm the overall national economy.

This last point would seem particularly persuasive; it explains the limited experimentation in more advanced areas such as Shanghai. The new leadership did not experiment in vital economic regions: thus experiments in agricultural reforms were first implemented in the poor and relatively remote area of Anhui Province;

comprehensive urban reforms were first carried out in Shashi in Hubei Province in 1981 and Changzhou in Jiangsu Province in 1982. Unlike Shanghai, Guangdong and Fujian Provinces also were geographically and economically isolated from China proper. Experimentation could be conducted without harming the overall national economy.

In addition, many Political Bureau members were very familiar with the southeast coastal region or shared a common Kejia (Hakka) heritage. Although Deng Xiaoping was born in Sichuan, his father's ancestors were Kejia who had immigrated from Guangdong;[191] Ye Jianying was also Kejia, born in Meixian County, Guangdong.[192] Zhao Ziyang, an alternate member of the Political Bureau, had held high Party and government posts in Guangdong since the 1950s. Political Bureau members with strong Fujian connections included Fang Yi (born in Xiamen) and Peng Chong (born in Zhangzhou, just east of Xiamen).

Familiarity with the region probably influenced the Political Bureau's adoption of the Guangdong proposal in March 1979; consensus politics also is a credible explanation for the incorporation of Fujian into the original Guangdong proposal, which was submitted as a report to the Central Committee (the Fujian proposal was a report and a request for instructions, implying a different status between the two documents). After five months of discussions and investigation, the CCP Central Committee and the State Council issued Central Committee document 79.50 on 15 July 1979. The document approved the Two Reports of Guangdong and Fujian Provincial Committees concerning the Carrying Out of Special Policies and Flexible Measures in Foreign Trade Activities.[193]

Document 79.50 authorized the Guangdong and Fujian leaderships to use "special policies and flexible measures" to implement an experimental development strategy. Basically, this strategy would promote an opening to the outside world, a relaxation of domestic economic policy, and a decentralization of decision-making powers. It enabled the two provinces to assume responsibility for provincial planning in the domestic and foreign trade sectors, retain fiscal control over both domestic and foreign trade revenue under a contract system, introduce the market mechanism to regulate material supplies and commercial ventures, expand provincial powers over material pricing, and implement banking and labor salary reforms.[194]

The new leadership also encouraged the two provinces to increase foreign exchange revenue. According to document 79.50, Beijing granted the two provinces "special policies and flexible measures in the foreign trade activities." Guangdong and Fujian were to recover and expand their traditional export trade to Hong Kong, Macao, and other foreign markets. Goods should be exported that were "high foreign currency earners" whose production would "expand employment." The provinces were to "develop high-grade precision products" that would be "competitive on the international market." They were also to increase "middle- and small-scale processing of goods with materials imported from abroad."

Besides increasing foreign trade revenue, the provincial leaders were to cultivate traditional and nontraditional sources of foreign capital. Document 79.50 mandated the two provinces to "seek assistance from abroad as a supplement" by targeting the 8.2 million Cantonese and 5 million Fukienese living abroad, especially in Hong Kong and Macao. Although admitting a "lack [of] experience" and "very little [understanding]" about foreign economic activities, the two provinces could expand nontraditional foreign capital sources. Both provinces were to seek to "develop the tourist industry" and expand processing and assembly activities. They also were to expend "great efforts" in developing compensation trade, initiating equity joint ventures, and exploring other cooperative ventures.

According to 79.50, Guangdong would double its foreign exchange earnings by 1985 ($5 billion); by 1990, the leadership hoped the province would quadruple the figure to reach $10 billion. As a poorer province reliant on government subsidies, Fujian would quadruple its foreign exchange receipts to $1.4 billion by 1985 and would seek to earn $3.5 billion by 1990. This was a tenfold increase over its 1978 rate. Although profits would be reinvested in the local economy, a set percentage would be remitted to the state to finance China's smaller-scale import substitution strategy.

Document 79.50 and the Establishment of the Special Economic Zones. The origins of the zone concept can be traced to different initiatives undertaken in late 1978 and early 1979. Following a foreign trip in autumn 1978, the Chinese minister of communications, Ye Fei, proposed a zone initiative, resulting in the establishment of the Shekou industrial zone in January 1979.[195] Later, Shekou was incorporated within the Shenzhen SEZ proposal, but it maintained its autonomous identity as a Ministry of Communications and CMSN fiefdom.

Before the Third Plenum of 1978, the Guangdong provincial leadership proposed an expanded version of the ECPB concept (State Council document 79.38). Provincial authorities hoped to transform Shenzhen and Zhuhai into urban export centers focusing on industrial, agricultural, and tourist sectors. Hong Kong businessmen suggested the actual name and operating parameters of the Shenzhen SEZ;[196] Singapore industrialist Luo Xinquan and Hong Kong industrialist Tang Bingda later played key roles in establishing the Shantou SEZ.[197]

Yu Guangyuan, a famous economist from the Chinese Academy of Social Sciences, claims to have inspired the Shenzhen SEZ's housing sector and border structures. During the November 1978 Central Work Conference, Yu approached the Guangdong Party chairman, Xi Zhongxun, with a plan to allow Hong Kong residents desiring to escape Hong Kong's high cost of living to rent apartments in Shenzhen. According to Yu,

I thought that this piece of land (at that time I did not call it an SEZ) would have a border with both Hong Kong and the interior; the [Hong Kong] border would be liberally enforced; the border with the interior would be strictly enforced. There would be a road constructed between this land and Hong Kong with freedom of movement. A person could work in Hong Kong/Kowloon and his family live in this area; at night the person would return to Shenzhen. In the morning, the person again would take a boat or car to work in Hong Kong/Kowloon.[198]

Yu again approached the Guangdong leadership at the December Third Plenum with a more detailed plan to make China a "Red landlord" (*hongse de dizhu*).[199] Similar concepts were incorporated in the Guangdong proposal to the March Central Committee meeting.

No doubt these and other proposals were discussed at the 21–23 March Political Bureau meeting.[200] Final approval was achieved after Deng Xiaoping directed, "Then let's have a special zone!"[201] Deng formally proposed their establishment during the April 1979 work conference, stating, "We can delimit an area called a special zone. Was Shaanxi-Gansu-Ningxia not a special zone? Since the central authorities lack funds, we call on [the two provinces] to find a way out."[202]

On 15 July 1979, document 79.50 formally approved the construction of the two Guangdong zones. Afterward, Deng assumed direct responsibility, stating in 1984 that "the running of the SEZs was my initiative and the CCP Central Committee approved it."[203] In the 1980s, he continued to supervise various stages of SEZ development.

The zones became one of the crucial initial experiments with outwardly oriented development. Motivated by economic exigency, the post–GLF coalition set aside traditional ideas of "closing the country from international intercourse" (*biguan zishou*) and "natural economy." They clarified the Maoist tenet of "primarily relying on self-reliance, while using foreign assistance as a supplement" and implemented a policy of "using foreign things for China's benefit" (*yang wei Zhong yong*).[204]

Guangdong and Fujian Provinces initially were assigned to manage the experiment. Like the leaders of the Shaanxi-Gansu-Ningxia border area in the 1930s and 1940s, leaders of the two provinces would experiment with various economic and political reforms, but for the first time, reforms included foreign investment and the SEZs.[205] As chairman of the Shaanxi-Gansu-Ningxia People's Committee during the 1930s, Xi Zhongxun had gained experience in such experimentation; in 1979, he applied this experience as the first Party secretary of Guangdong Province.

The special economic zone idea, like the export commodity processing base idea of 1960, was another way to guarantee export supplies to pay for an import substitution program. By 1979, the basic ECPB idea, as expressed in State Council

document 79.38, was expanded in light of the new policy on foreign capital investment. According to State Council document 79.202, the Chinese would implement two versions of the export base idea: the original ECPB version, which would
remain within the state command economy structure (79.202, regulation 8); and
the zone idea, which in theory would be financed with foreign capital investment and more responsive to the international market (79.202, regulation 14).

According to document 79.50, overseas Chinese—especially Hong Kong and
Macao businessmen—and foreigners could invest directly in the zones by establishing factories or setting up joint ventures. Such ventures enjoyed preferential tax treatment and could repatriate legal profits. In addition, the provinces
and the national government would finance infrastructure needed for foreign
trade development (customs, commodity inspection, quarantine border inspection, banking, post and communication facilities). Unlike their interior counterparts, the zones would enjoy a more liberalized banking system, simplified
procedures for border crossings, and a higher wage structure. The zones would
enjoy far greater autonomy than the more traditional ECPBs. In certain cases,
they enjoyed decision-making powers equal to if not greater than those enjoyed
by Beijing, Tianjin, and Shanghai.

Chen Yun, who had strongly supported the ECPB idea in May 1961, underscored the importance of the SEZ during his 18 September 1979 speech. He rea-
soned that the only "reliable" foreign exchange sources to finance the large-scale
import projects were foreign exchange revenue from increasing petroleum and
coal exports; net foreign exchange revenue derived from tourism; increased payments of foreign exchange turned in to the central government from special areas
built in Guangdong and Fujian; and an increase of foreign exchange turned over
to the central government earned from the export of textiles, light and heavy
industrial products, arts and handicraft objects, and the like.[206] Yet Chen Yun
was also aware that the development of zones into reliable foreign exchange
"machines" would take time. He warned, "It is estimated that it will take ten
years before the first three of these categories . . . can annually render several
billions of foreign exchange to the central government. This is not something
that can be easily accomplished in one or two years."[207]

These were prophetic words. The Zones were originally designed to both generate foreign exchange revenue to fuel China's scaled-down import substitution
strategy and transfer technology to the interior. It would take a long time before
either of these assigned roles could be fulfilled.

Conclusion

While the cycling of import substitution and autarky strategies ended in 1976,
by the late 1970s a new debate had arisen within the Chinese elites over whether

China should continue the same inwardly oriented development regime. Hua Guofeng, content to expand upon Zhou Enlai's Four Modernizations program, which had been based on large-scale import substitution development strategy, proposed his Ten-Year Plan. Yet based on their two-decade experience, the post–GLF coalition had learned the pitfalls of the large-scale import substitution strategy. After overcoming Hua's opposition, these elites drastically altered not only the 1979 plan, but the entire Ten-Year Plan—including Hua Guofeng's accelerated import substitution program. Canceling or renegotiating many of the major turnkey plant projects of 1978 and 1979, the leadership adopted a new import substitution strategy emphasizing technology and equipment importation. As a result of incremental learning, the Chinese leadership never again adopted a large-scale import substitution strategy.

This learning galvanized the post–GLF elite to begin experimenting with outwardly oriented development as symbolized by the special economic zones.

CHAPTER 8

Conclusion

Changes in the International Environment

Changes in the international environment initially determined China's development strategy. Yet by the mid-1950s, although the international environment determined the parameters within which Chinese policy makers could maneuver, domestic debates over the proper pathway of Chinese development became the primary determinant of foreign economic policy. Deng Xiaoping commented during his Jilin work-conference speech of 16 September 1978[1] and his Four Basic Principles speech of 30 March 1979 that the international environment had become favorable to China. Proof was found in the international community's reaction to the February–March 1979 Chinese invasion of Vietnam. Deng remarked in his 30 March 1979 speech that "looking at the international reaction to the recent counterattack in self-defense, most people are sympathetic to us."[2]

Such an optimistic view of the international environment was the result of China's normalization of relations with many Western countries by the late 1970s, especially with Japan and the United States. Japan had established diplomatic relations with the PRC following the "Nixon shock" of July 1971. With the conclusion of the Sino-Japanese Peace and Friendship Treaty in 1978, China officially exorcised its profound feelings of enmity toward Japan (though China will never forget nor forgive Japan for World War II, especially in light of Japan's failure to sign a more complete apology in 1998).

The normalization of relations with the United States in 1979 was even more profound. During his visit to the United States in January 1979, Deng Xiaoping set aside the Taiwan problem[3] and encouraged an increase in political and economic cooperation. For instance, Deng encouraged an increase of U.S.-China trade, including the use of compensation trade. China would permit trade in coal, mineral ores, and light textiles in exchange for capital or technology. In return, Deng sought MFN status for China. In addition, a process of clearing unresolved claims and assets was undertaken.[4] As a result, the United States removed its objections to China's participation in the International Monetary Fund and the World Bank.

Accompanying this normalization of diplomatic and economic relations, government officials and businessmen on three continents again contracted "China fever." The Japanese, who had begun trading with the Chinese as early as 1954 with the tacit approval of the United States, signed a long-term trade agreement with the Chinese on 26 February 1978. The agreement guaranteed the sale of $7–8 billion of Japanese plants and technology and $2–3 billion in Japanese machinery and construction materials; China would finance the acquisitions by exporting $10 billion worth of crude oil and coal.[5]

After breaking the UN embargo after 1957 and expanding trade with the Chinese in the early 1960s and early 1970s, the Europeans were next to sign long-term trade agreements with China in 1978 and subsequently extended MFN status to China in 1980.[6] The French signed a $13.6 billion agreement in December 1978, and the British signed a $14 billion agreement in March 1979.[7] Characteristic of its foreign trade policy, the United States never concluded such an agreement and was one of the last major trading partners to provide export financing (in April 1980).[8] While the U.S. government was immune to China fever, American businesspeople and their counterparts in Japan and Europe swarmed into Beijing with unrealistic visions of inflated profit margins.

Normalization of relations with the major Western countries allowed China to discard many remaining shreds of its "pariah" status. The Chinese leadership thus operated within newly expanded political and economic parameters without many of the Cold War restrictions. Yet restrictions remained, especially in the technology transfer area, China's relationship with the Soviet Union and its allies, and China's relationship with anti-Communist regimes such as Taiwan and South Korea. Such restrictions would require a longer period to resolve.

Comparatively unfettered by international constraints, the Chinese leadership was now free to trade with whomever it pleased, including the United States, and to follow the other East Asian economies' example of adopting an outwardly oriented development regime that regarded the international environment as a potential partner.

Changes in the Domestic Development Regime

With the accession of the post–GLF elite coalition in late 1978, the basic contradiction in inwardly oriented development strategies was resolved. As Lowenthal had predicted in 1970, Mao's emphasis on normative approach to development strategy was discredited and forgotten—except by the likes of Deng Liqun. Free of ideological constraints imposed by the Maoist xenophobes and the international constraints imposed by the United States, the new post–GLF coalition redefined the term "self-reliance." Retaining its polemical value to strengthen nationalism and justify its legitimacy, the post–GLF coalition championed the goal of self-reliance achieved through limited cooperation with the outside world.

This did not imply that the new leadership coalition suddenly adopted an outwardly oriented development regime. The initial opening strategy championed by the new elite was in reality a more flexible approach to the import substitution strategy implemented since the 1950s. To finance the remaining large-scale import substitution projects such as Baoshan and to expand the importation of foreign advanced technology, the State Council strengthened many of the export promotion strategies of the 1950s and 1960s, including the Five-Priorities Policy, various export loan programs, and a new foreign exchange retention scheme; the council also legalized the *yijin yangchu* idea, which was first proposed in 1957 and implemented in earnest in 1961. Finally, the State Council expanded the number of export commodity processing bases, which had first been approved by Premier Zhou Enlai in 1960.

These programs were all included within the state plan. The Chinese export sector continued to be managed by the state behind a highly protectionist wall of high tariffs, an overvalued exchange rate, and other administrative barriers to free economic exchange. The new elite's opening strategy as perceived in 1979 thus did not require China's economic policies to be responsive to the international market. Insulated from such international pressures, the domestic political and economic situation continued to be the primary variable affecting the domestic development strategy and its foreign economic policy component, which included the SEZ policy.

Yet the opening policy did diverge from past strategies by legalizing limited forms of foreign direct investment, with which Hua Guofeng had first experimented in 1978. The expansion of the processing and assembly agreements (*san-lai yibu*), the establishment of the special economic zones, and the joint ventures with foreign investors heralded an initial step to adopting an outwardly oriented strategy. By the mid-1980s, this proto-experiment with an outwardly oriented regime would be considered a success, although problems encountered during the experimentation period contributed to Chen Yun's break with the post–GLF coalition starting in 1982.[9]

Despite certain setbacks, Deng and others realized that an outwardly oriented strategy could fuel a dramatic growth in domestic economic development with minimal political costs. Thus during the thirty-fifth anniversary of the PRC in October 1984, one of the most talked about floats in the Tiananmen parade came from within the Shenzhen Special Economic Zone with the capitalistic slogan "Time is money, efficiency is life." Seventeen years before, millions of Red Guards and the PLA had deliriously chanted Mao's Little Red Book parading in front of the Chairman; in 1984, Peking University students joyously ran past Mao's picture chanting Deng Xiaoping's name. Emboldened by the success of the initial outwardly oriented experiments, Deng and the remaining elite coalition embarked upon a coastal development strategy. The coastal areas would gradually be integrated with the international economy, while the less-developed interior areas would be shielded behind various administrative barriers.

Whereas many of the East Asian economies had made the decision to start experimenting with outwardly oriented development by the late 1950s, it took the Chinese twenty years to resolve their internal debate over the role the international market should play in domestic development. During these two decades, the outwardly oriented development strategies implemented by the East Asian economies accelerated growth in the domestic economy and the foreign trade sector, improved economic efficiency, and fostered technical transfer.[10] While the Chinese dragon continued to chase its tail in search of the elusive goal of self-reliance, the mini-dragons became international economic powerhouses. Not until the mid-1980s did the Chinese leadership begin to mirror the policy actions of the East Asian economies by promoting limited integration with the international market while promoting protection of specific industrial sectors.

As a result of the Chinese attempt to become full-fledged members of the international economic community in the 1990s, the Chinese bureaucracies and state-owned enterprises are paying the high costs involved with global economic integration. They have not enjoyed the moratorium on certain transaction costs previously enjoyed by the Asian economies during the Cold War. For decades, the Asian economies discriminated against foreign goods and services and engaged in a high degree of counterfeiting to build up their domestic economies. In the past, the United States tolerated such behavior to build a strong Asian bulwark against communism. In the post–Cold War world, China will not enjoy the luxury of such a long free ride. The member countries of the World Trade Organization have demanded that China adhere to the international economic norms of a developed economy; this demand will adversely affect the weakest components of the Chinese juggernaut—the state sector.[11]

Implications of the Study

This study has argued that Chinese elite politics in general cannot be considered as a zero-sum game, but as a non–zero sum game. Individual elites might lose an argument because of the apparent failure of their preferred policy pathway. Such failure often is followed by a closing of the elite ranks, or, in Goldstein's systemic view, bandwagoning. Yet such bandwagoning was a strategic, short-term ploy. Despite their self-criticisms and mea culpas, elites did not abandon their particular Weltanshauungs. They waited for the most opportune time to discredit current policy and to reimplement their own solutions. Policy analysts can observe the results of such interrelated, non–zero sum games as a repetition or cycling of policy initiatives throughout the late 1950s, 1960s, and 1970s. Empowered by the perception of crisis, dominant policy elites readjusted the former strategy and introduced their own preferred pathway of development.

This cycling of policies—which has been described as Chinese crisis cycles— is a tempting heuristic device to explain changes in Chinese development strategy before 1979. A cycle approach does not need to treat the antinomy of policies as contributing to a "static" policy environment as Nathan earlier posited. Concerned that Western theories continued to impose this dialectic view of the policy development process, Nathan argued for a learning model in which policy options were "so multiform and complex that the choices are really more than two, and might best be regarded as infinite."[12] In other words, Chinese elites have the ability to learn from their experiences; they are not caught in an unchanging looping of history.

Yet there need not be an artificial separation between cyclic and linear views of the Chinese policy process.[13] The repetition of certain patterns and phases of the policy process does not preclude the evolutionary development of policy initiatives. While Chinese elites can learn from past policy successes and failures, their ability to implement progressive change can be interrupted by recurring policy patterns initiated by a change in the ruling elite coalition. A victorious elite coalition not only reintroduces policies that have been criticized by the previous leadership coalitions, but improves and expands the concepts. Under such conditions, policy learning can occur over time, but at an incremental pace.[14]

Although further research must be done on the elites' actual process of learning,[15] experimentation appears to be a key tool of the Chinese policy maker. Policy makers learn from earlier experimentation and use this knowledge to improve new policy initiatives. Although the learning process was irregular because elites were often in conflict, learning did take place. During the proto-experiment with autarky during the Great Leap Forward, Mao experimented with a purely domestic development strategy that relied on indigenous technology, including backyard steel furnaces to replace certain imported steels. Although the proto-experiment ended in disaster, Mao learned that he needed to rely less on administrative tools and to emphasize normative tools to tap the underlying potential of the Chinese workforce. The perception of international threat in 1964 was thus an important opportunity for Mao to tap the unbridled energies of Chinese nationalism and mobilize the people to promote self-reliance.

Documenting Mao's learning curve in regard to foreign economic policy is difficult because of the lack of direct documentation. However, one can infer from Mao's associated writings and by the actual foreign economic policy adopted that a learning process took place. Mao rejected the large-scale import substitution strategy of the 1950s as being too Soviet-centric and hobbling China's independence. During the Cultural Revolution Mao learned that he could not rely solely on indigenous technology and raw materials and thereafter implemented only a semiautarkic strategy. Discovering that China needed to depend more heavily on the Western marketplace for modernization, Mao acquiesced to Zhou Enlai's call to resurrect China's import substitution development strategy in the early 1970s. Assuming such a two-decade-long learning process took place, it thus could be argued that Mao eventually returned to his pre-1949 ideas about foreign trade. Yet there is little evidence that Jiang Qing's coalition supporting Mao agreed to follow Mao's path. Instead, they unsuccessfully attempted to implement a far more orthodox version of autarky than implemented during the Cultural Revolution.

The learning process in foreign economic policy is far easier to document for those elites supporting the remunerative-administrative approach to Chinese development. In the case of the export processing zones policy, Zhou Enlai and others were faced with a dwindling supply of production inputs used in export production during the Great Leap. Zhou initially solved the problem in the early 1960s by establishing a simple processing zone. After Zhou regained control of the state in 1971, the new economic leadership reviewed the experiences of the 1960s and determined to expand the EPZ concept to include comprehensive export production bases by the 1970s. Joseph Nye would define the incremental learning of the pre-1978 period as "simple learning," which "uses new information merely to adapt the means, without altering any deeper goals in the ends-mean chain. The actor simply uses a different instrument to attain the same goal."[16]

In a certain perverse fashion, one could also argue that Deng Xiaoping and the other members of the post–GLF coalition learned a lesson or two from the Cultural Revolution. While the post–GLF had recentralized foreign economic policy in the early 1960s, Mao had completely reversed the process by the mid- to late 1960s. Such decentralization allowed the localities to rely on their own initiatives to establish a self-sufficient economy. Deng Xiaoping followed a similar policy when he decentralized certain domestic and foreign economic powers to Guangdong and Fujian Provinces in 1979. Because Beijing did not have the money to develop the southeast coastal areas, the two provinces would have to become self-sufficient. And they did—spectacularly!

Yet after 1978 the post–GLF coalition also was involved in a more profound learning process. The leaders had discovered the limitations of inwardly oriented development and would never again adopt a large-scale import substitution strategy. Instead, after 1978 they began to experiment with outwardly oriented development. This "simple learning" process was now replaced by "complex learning," which "involves recognition of conflicts among means and goals in causally complicated situations, and leads to new priorities and trade-offs."[17]

For instance, after gaining experience from running the EPZs for nearly twenty years, Chinese leaders decided to transform the concept into the special economic zones, which became the key component of the proto-experiment with an outwardly oriented development regime. It was within the zones that the Chinese experimented with many of the Western-style management techniques and other "capitalist" forms that were gradually integrated into the mainstream Chinese economy.

Nathan's other criticism concerning policy interdependence, however, is applicable to this study, which has primarily focused on the changes in foreign economic policy during the pre-1979 period. To prove that policy elite coalitions held conflicting views of development strategy, further studies must investigate other policy areas such as agriculture or commercial policy. While this study briefly touched on other policy areas,[18] further investigation must demonstrate some semblance of policy interdependence or synchronism to prove the suitability of the opinion-group/crisis-cycle approach.

Finally, this study is based on two basic assumptions. It has assumed that the pre-1979 policy elites enjoyed autonomy when formulating foreign economic policy. Second, though lacking more concrete evidence of the existence of coherent coalitions coalescing around shared visions of the development process, this study has analyzed the policies actually adopted to determine whether policies share similar characteristics—such as remunerative or normative qualities. Such assumptions have been made because the China field continues to be plagued by a lack of primary sources. Until the Walls of Jericho—or the Great Wall—come tumbling down, China specialists will continue to grope for reliable measures—as well as endure the barbs of self-deluding positivists who allege that "area studies have failed to generate scientific knowledge."[19]

China is no longer the reluctant dragon. After several centuries of relative dormancy, China is once again making its presence felt on the world stage—both politically and economically. A detailed knowledge of China's past behavior must be the foundation of any future policy to persuade the Chinese dragon to accept international norms of behavior, whether they are in human rights, nuclear proliferation, or economic exchange.

Appendix A

Michel Oksenberg has already detailed the various problems facing China scholars while conducting research on mainland China.[1] Since the publication of his essay in 1987, the increased information exchange between Chinese bureaucracies and the desire of aging economic policy elites to secure their place in China's history have accelerated the publication of primary and secondary sources of high academic quality. Yet this explosion of information cannot be compared to the treasure trove of materials that has poured out of the Kremlin. Chinese editors of the central leadership speech and policy collections as well the authors of personal memoirs and policy studies continue to adhere to the Party line as dictated by the Sixth Plenum of the Eleventh Party Congress and to promote the "moderate" policies of Deng Xiaoping and the "opening."[2] Thus, various collections covering the Cultural Revolution and the politics-in-command coalitions are virtually nonexistent. The more sensitive materials are either published on a restricted basis (*neibu*) and so are generally not available in China or in the West, or they are heavily edited to promote the Party line. Until the barriers to true information exchange crumble, any analysis of Chinese policy decisions will continue to be problematic.[3]

One case in point: the initial idea for the study is based on the work of Tan Qingfeng, Yao Xuecong, and Li Shusen, who in 1984 published a Chinese study titled *Waimao fuchi shengchan shijian* (The Practice of supporting foreign trade production). Unlike many of the repetitive and general foreign economic policy studies published in the 1980s, this is an excellent comprehensive analysis of Chinese foreign trade promotion strategies from the 1950s to the early 1980s. Unfortunately, the study is *neibu,* and not generally available.

Although it has recently become fashionable for Chinese policy elites to publish their autobiographies,[4] relatively few memoirs are publicly available from China's top economic policy elite active during the pre-1978 period. Luckily, Bo Yibo published *Ruogan zhongda juece yu shijian de huigu* (Looking back on certain important decisions and events). Bo's autobiography is the only substantial memoir from a Political Bureau member dealing with economic policy during the pre–Cultural Revolution period. Bo reveals the problems with which the policy elites grappled from his perspective as minister of finance (1949–53), vice-chairman of the State Planning Commission (1954–56), Political Bureau member, vice-premier, and chairman of the State Economic Commission (1956–66). The two-volume work is obviously biased and self-serving. Yet the work is extremely interesting and insightful. This study relies on Bo's work to reflect the thinking of a key member of the post–GLF elite coalition, which supported a more remunerative, less normative approach to economic development.

To make up for this lack of personal memoirs, this study must rely on the collected writings of the policy elites. This study relies on several published collections, including the following:

Jianguo yilai Mao Zedong wengao (The post-1949 manuscripts of Mao Zedong). From this, together with *Mao Zedong sixiang wansui* (translated in *Miscellany of Mao Tse-tung Thought*) and other translations, one can begin to piece together Mao's writings. Although quite extensive, the *Jianguo* series continues to frustrate scholars because it lacks speeches from key periods.

Zhou Enlai jingji wenxuan (A selection of Zhou Enlai's economic works). This is an excellent collection on Premier Zhou's economic policy speeches.

Chen Yun tongzhi wengao xuanbian (Selections of Comrade Chen Yun's manuscripts [1956–1962]); *Chen Yun wenxuan, 1956–1985* (Chen Yun's selected works, 1956–85); *Chen Yun wenxuan* (Chen Yun's selected works), vol. 3.

Li Xiannian lun caizheng jinrong maoyi, 1950–1991 (Li Xiannian's discussions on finance and trade, 1950–91). Li Xiannian was one of the few economic policy elites to survive the Great Leap, the Cultural Revolution, the struggle for Mao's successor, and the post-1979 period. Although missing a large portion of his Cultural Revolution writings, the collection is a valuable source of Li's economic thinking and proof that he was a consummate political player akin to Zhou Enlai.

With these works and Bo Yibo's autobiography, one can begin to piece together the Weltanshauung of key members of the economic policy elite (for a further discussion of decoding elites' views, see chapter 1).

The study compensates for the lack of personal accounts by using restricted and open collections of internal policy documents and policy summaries issued by the Central Committee, the State Council, and various ministries since 1949.

Not surprisingly, most of the newly issued documents and speeches on Chinese foreign trade discovered thus far have focused on the post-1978 period; documents from before this period remain relatively scarce.[5] These collections are edited—sometimes heavily—and certain sections and statistics are plainly omitted. Despite such limitations, the collections—especially the restricted ones—are indispensable sources to trace the policy process.

This study relied on two other major Chinese sources to trace the policy process: elite chronicles and studies emanating from the Central Committee's Office of Documentary Research (Zhonggong Zhongyang Wenxian Yanjiushi). Some of the elite chronicles were amazingly invaluable, such as the newly issued, three-volume chronicle on Zhou Enlai by Zhonggong Zhongyang Wenxian Yanjiushi, *Zhou Enlai nianpu (1949–1976)* (A chronicle of Zhou Enlai's life [1949–76]). Along with Bo Yibo's memoirs, Zhou's *Chronicle* provides an unparalleled and invaluable insight into the Chinese political process. A less systematized but equally important source of pre-1979 foreign policy documentation and analysis can also be found in internal journals, such as the Party Document Office's *Dang de wenxian,* which began bimonthly publication in 1988.

To understand the importance of these documents, it is useful to refer to Michel Oksenberg's categorization of the seven channels of communication used in the Chinese policy-making process: formal and informal meetings, formal written communications, internal publications, mass media, informal written communications, telephone calls, and inspection and investigation visits.[6] Because access to much of this documentation is restricted, only documents in the first, second, fourth, and seventh categories have been used in this study; it has been difficult to document more informal channels of communication.

FORMAL AND INFORMAL MEETINGS

The first category of communication channels, formal and informal Central Committee meetings, has been extensively catalogued by Kenneth Lieberthal and Bruce Dickson.[7] For texts of internal leadership speeches and correspondence, the study primarily relies on different collections of materials from Mao Zedong, Deng Xiaoping, Chen Yun, and Li Xiannian.[8] For the post-1978 period, this study primarily relies on the *Sanzhong quanhui yilai zhongyao wenxian xuanbian* (Selected important documents issued since the Third Plenum), issued by the Research Office on Central Documents of the Chinese Communist Party (Zhonggong Zhongyang Wenxian Yanjiushi) in August 1982. This important collection includes many of the major speeches of the central leadership ranging from Chen Yun's 12 November 1978 speech to the northeast group at the Central Committee Work Conference to Hu Yaobang's closing remarks at the

Party's Twelfth Plenum on 6 August 1982. All of these collections remain incomplete; references from Bo Yibo or other secondary accounts have supplemented the primary sources.

FORMAL WRITTEN COMMUNICATIONS

Kenneth Lieberthal has written about Oksenberg's second category, formal written communications, in his *Central Documents and Politburo Politics in China.*[9] However, Lieberthal's insightful analysis of *zhongfa* documents might give the impression that the Central Committee is the only organization issuing key documents. Although *zhongfa* documents are the highest form of "official documents"—a term perhaps more appropriate than "central documents"—they are not the only powerful documents that can transform the bureaucratic system. Other organizations, such as the State Council, issued extremely important documents (*guofa*) independently or in conjunction with the Central Committee. Myriad other formal written communications are also issued by the various central government commissions, ministries, bureaus, and offices; similar provincial government organizations also issue formal documents.

The official documents cited in this study were excerpted from restricted policy collections from various sources including the Ministries of Foreign Economic Relations and Trade, Commerce, Finance, the Bank of China, and the State Council Office on the Special Economic Zones. These official document collections cover only certain time periods and thus are incomplete, especially for the pre-1979 period. I thus have augmented the collections with internal and openly published summaries of policies and speeches, especially *Zhonghua Renmin Gongheguo jingji guanli dashiji* (A document collection of Chinese economic and management laws and regulations), which is an excellent "reader's digest" of Chinese policies and speeches from 1949 to 1985; and *Zhonghua Renmin Gongheguo jingji dashiji, 1949–1980* (A chronology of major events in the PRC's economy [1949–80]), in which the editors extensively comment on particular policies. Analysis of particular policies has also been greatly facilitated by various Chinese policy chronologies, yearbooks, and studies.

Undoubtedly, formal written communications is the largest channel of communications and deserves a separate, more in-depth treatment. For the sake of brevity, here I will simply describe the ten basic types of Chinese official documents as determined by the Office of the State Council.[10] The first type includes two forms of orders: *mingling* and *zhiling*. *Mingling* are simple and concise orders issued by the top leadership and top leadership bodies to announce important laws, administrative measures, or appointments or dismissals that must be carried out immediately. An excellent example is the "Order Establishing the Ministries of Foreign Trade and Commerce and Eliminating the Ministry of

Trade," issued by the Government Administrative Council on 15 August 1952 (chapter 2). A *zhiling* is a combination of directives and regulations issued to lower-level organs by state organizations; there is no *zhiling* in this study.

The second type is composed of decisions (*jueding*) and resolutions (*jueyi*). Decisions are issued by the major governing bodies, such as the Central Committee, the State Council, and the NPC; they announce decisions on important policies, laws, or other measures. One of the Party's most significant *jueding* was "the Decision to Agree to Comrade Mao Zedong's Proposal That He Not Continue as the Next Candidate for the Chairmanship of the PRC," which was approved by the Sixth Plenum of the Eighth Party Congress on 10 December 1958 (chapter 1). *Jueyi* are formulated and adopted at government or Party conferences to convey the Party's plans and policies. Rewriting Party history according to the victorious post–GLF coalition's viewpoint, the sixth Plenum of the eleventh Central Committee approved "The Resolution on Certain Historical Problems since the Founding of the PRC" on 27 June 1981 (see Introduction).

Unlike orders, the third type of official documents, directives (*zhishi*), can be issued by any upper-level organization to subordinate organs. Although not as authoritative as orders, directives can be effective policy tools to outline the basic principles and methods necessary to complete a specific task or to solve a certain problem. For the most urgent problems, emergency directives (*teji* or *jinji zhishi*) are issued. For example, this study cites a series of emergency agriculture measures adopted during the summer of 1959 to overcome the agricultural crisis created by the Great Leap Forward (Introduction; chapter 3). A cursory review of collected official documents indicates that directives were seldom issued in the 1980s.

The fourth type of official documents—bulletins (*bugao*), proclamations (*gonggao*), and notices (*tonggao*)—are used to communicate with large groups of people. Bulletins are issued by government organizations, industries, or schools to announce important decisions or measures. State or Party organizations issue proclamations in newspapers, television or radio to announce important events or regulations. Notices are posted within particular units and provide information on regular matters of concern. Examples are not included within this study.

The circular (*tongzhi*) is the fifth type of official document. The circular is the most common channel of communication and the most widely cited official document in the study. Since the 1970s, the leadership has preferred to issue circulars instead of the more serious orders directives, and comments on reports (*pishi*). Circulars are used to notify subordinate organs of the views and directives of the leadership or to inform subordinates or counterparts of the approval of certain laws and regulations and other pertinent information. This study includes the "Circular concerning the Publication of 'The Trial Procedures for Specialized Factories for Industrial Product Exports' and 'The Trial Procedures for Export Commodity Production Bases for Agricultural Sideline Products,'" approved by the State Council and issued by the SIEAC on 10 August 1980 (chapter 7). Emergency circulars (*jinji tongzhi*), which demand a higher level of compliance, can also be issued. For instance, on 30 November 1980 the State Council issued the "Emergency Circular on Reducing Capital Construction Expenditures" to make all departments comply with the Political Bureau's decision to readjust China's development strategy (chapter 7).

A sixth type of official documents, notification (*tongbao*), is devoted to mass reeducation and propaganda. Notifications can relate the activities of a model citizen, such as a Lei Feng, but also the resignation of leaders, such as the "Notification of the Political Bureau Meeting of the CCP Central Committee," which was issued 10 November 1980 when Hua Guofeng resigned his chairmanship of the Party and the Central Military Commission (chapter 7). Notifications can also be issued in praise of a unit's success, such as the "Notification of Successfully Carrying Out the 1968 Spring Guangzhou Export Production Trade Fair," issued by the CCP Central Committee, the State Council, the Central Military Commission, and the Central Cultural Revolution Group on 8 March 1968 (chapter 4).

The seventh type is the important avenue for lower-level bureaucracy to effect change in the system: the report (*baogao*) and the request for instructions (*qingshi*). One type of report, the work report (*gongzuo baogao*) describes particular circumstances, problems, and solutions encountered in a specific task during a specific period; the situation report (*qingkuang baogao*) describes major problems or unforeseen circumstances or disasters and suggests solutions; an inquiry report (*dafu baogao*) is a direct written response to upper-level inquiries; an accompanying report (*baosong*) is a simple document attached to written materials or materials sent to higher authorities.

A more formal method for garnering leadership approval for lower-level initiatives is for an organization to combine a request for instructions with a report (*qingshi baogao*). These combined documents argue a case for policy change and ask for approval from the higher authority. Thus in the case of Central Committee document 79.50, which established the SEZ concept, Guangdong Province submitted a report to the Central Committee outlining how it would apply the April work conference decision to allow the province to "bring into play Guangdong's favorable conditions." Fujian provincial authorities petitioned for a status similar to Guangdong's by submitting both a report and a request for instructions; Central Committee document 79.50 approved the Fujian request, but with reservations (see chapter 7).

The written reply (*pifu*) is the eighth type and is a direct response from upper-level bureaucracy to a particular unit's request for instructions; the request can be rejected, approved, basically approved (*jiben tongyi*), or approved in principle (*yuanze tongyi*). The State Council issued document 38 in 1978 as a written reply approving Guangdong's request to construct an export commodity production base and to establish municipal governments in Baoan and Zhuhai Counties, which were converted into special economic zones in 1979 (chapter 7). Written comments (*piyu*) can be comments written by the top elite remarking on a published report, such as Li Xiannian's *piyu* of a Xinhua news report of 19 February 1974 (chapter 6).

Previously, whenever a report or a request for instructions involved outside units, a comment (*pishi*) was issued. For instance, a comment was issued accompanying the proposal to establish urban people's communes in March 1960 (chapter 3), while Zhou Enlai issued a comment concerning the problems encountered during the fall 1973 Guangzhou Trade Fair (chapter 5). During the 1980s, units preferred to issue circulars.

The ninth type of official document is the letter (*han*). Like circulars, letters can be sent by both subordinate and governing bodies or to counterparts. Letters informally discuss particular problems; replies (*dafu, fuhan*) are also informally written. For instance, on 30 July 1961 Li Xiannian wrote a letter to Mao Zedong and the Central Committee concerning the importing of grain to relieve starvation in China's large urban cities; the letter in turn was approved and transmitted as an official document on 2 August 1961 (chapter 3). On 10 April 1977, Deng Xiaoping sent a letter to Hua Guofeng requesting reinstatement; this document eventually was designated Central Committee document 77.15 (chapter 7). To expand the scope of foreign investment in China, Li Xiannian and Peng Zhen authored a letter, which eventually was attached to Central Committee document 80.14 (chapter 7).

The final type of official document is the conference summary (*huiyi jiyao, zuotanhui jiyao*). Certain summaries, extracted from conference minutes (*jilu*), are considered important documents conveying specific policies; these are approved by the top-level organization and issued as official documents. For example, Hua Guofeng called a series of conferences in April 1977 to discuss capital construction, the metallurgical industry, energy conservation, and the railroads reports (chapter 7). Summaries of all the major SEZ conferences held from 1979 to 1982 were submitted to the Party Central Committee, the State Council, or both; they subsequently were approved and transmitted (*pizhuan*) as Central Committee documents, with additional comments added by the leadership (chapter 7).

There is an additional type of official document not included in the Office of the State Council classification: the opinion (*yijian*). Opinions, similar to reports, are submitted by subordinates or colleagues to represent the views of an individual or office on a particular matter. Once approved, they act as a frame-work for action. This study includes opinions issued by the top leadership, such as the opinion submitted by Li Fuchun, Li Xiannian, and Bo Yibo to the Central Committee just before the second Zhengzhou conference of February–March 1959 criticizing the Great Leap Forward (chapter 3). They can be issued by one or more bureaucratic organizations, such as the Ministry of Foreign Trade's 1972 opinion on the Specialized Export Loan Program (chapter 5); they can also be submitted by "civilians," such as Wang Renzhong, who in April 1966 believed that politics should be in command (chapter 4).

The opinion, like the report, is an important initial step in the policy for-mulation process. In early 1978 the State Council approved an opinion that urged the greater use of overseas Chinese capital (chapter 6). In the case of estab-lishing the China International Trust and Investment Corporation, Deng Xiaoping directed Rong Yiren to propose innovative methods to use foreign capital in February 1979. Rong subsequently submitted "A Few Initial Opinions on Recommending the Establishment of an International Trust and Investment Corporation" to the Central Committee in March 1979; it was subsequently used as the basis for the CITIC regulations approved by the State Council (see chapter 7).

Of the sixteen types of official documents, the majority (orders, directives, deci-sions, resolutions, bulletins, proclamations, notices, circulars, notifications, writ-ten replies, and opinions) are issued by supervising organizations (*xiaxing wen*). Reports and requests for instructions are submitted by subordinate organs to higher-level offices (*shangxing wen*). Circulars and letters can be sent to higher and lower bureaucratic levels, as well as to bureaucratic colleagues (*pingxing wen*).

Most official documents are assigned identification labels (*fawen zihao*) not-ing the year (*niandu*), issuing unit (*bianzi*), and document sequence number (*xuhao*). For uniformity and clarity, this study first cites the Chinese title and the English translation of the official document, followed by the Chinese acronym of the issuing unit (Jinchuyinzi), the year ([19]81), the document sequence num-ber (046), a more complete title of the issuing unit if necessary, and the date of approval or issue. Subsequent reference to the document is simplified to include the issuing unit, the year, and the document sequence number.

MASS MEDIA AND INFORMAL WRITTEN COMMUNICATIONS

The mass media was Oksenberg's fourth category of communication channel. Newspapers and journals cited in the study are national-level publications, such as *Renmin ribao* (People's daily) and *Guangming ribao*. In addition, translations of Chinese newspaper and journal articles printed in Foreign Broadcast Information Service, Daily Report, and Joint Publications Research Service are used.

The study relies on an informal letter supposedly written by Mao Zedong to Jiang Qing on 8 July 1966 that supports Lin Biao's concepts of a cycling of chaos (chapter 1). The letter was first published in English by the Taiwanese publication *Issues and Studies* in 1973. Although they have provided the West with a variety of interesting source materials and insights, Taiwan's intelligence sources can also be self-serving.

Whether it is Mao's letter printed in a Taiwan publication or his collected writings published in the 1990s, all materials must be treated with caution. Mao Zedong aptly described the problem as

> looking at problems statically: it does not regard problems from their development, failing to see the contents through the forms, or the essence through the superficial. The "Internal Reference" [*sic*] of the New China News Agency must be read, but it isn't good to read it too much either. The report on the Peking University problem in 1957, for example, indicated that the rightists were making a reckless attack and creating a terrible situation. Ch'en Po-ta went there to see for himself, and found that it wasn't that bad at all. Or, take the speech of Lin Hsi-ling: the first day it was marvelous, the second day the number of people refuting him increased, and by the third day, he was rebutted [*trans. note:* original translator mistook Lin for a man]. What is written in the "Internal Reference" is history. It must be read, but it must not be over-read. If one believes everything in books, it is better not to read books at all. When King Wu chastised Chou, blood flew so profusely that it floated pestles. Mencius refused to believe it. Now when we say books we mean newspapers and periodicals, and "Internal Reference" is one of them. We cannot believe everything in them. When we listen, we must listen to both sides.[11]

The deluge of new Chinese materials can be exhilarating. However, one must always keep in mind that old axiom that history is written by the victors.

Appendix B

1. As of 15 October, only 66.4 percent of this year's RMB 10 billion Export Commodity Procurement Plan has been completed; only 65 percent of the 7.9 billion Commodity Export Plan has been completed.[1] Because of this, the Central Committee believes that the completion of foreign trade responsibilities is a major problem influencing the speed of China's socialist construction. We must adopt the First Squeeze, Secondly Replace, Thirdly Exceed policy. Following the principle of considering both foreign and domestic needs, we must put all our efforts into squeezing from the domestic economy all commodities that have not met the export plan and whose domestic consumption can be reduced or eliminated (*shaochi buchi, shaoyong buyong*) to meet export requirements. As for commodities in which we absolutely have no means to produce, we must replace them with other exportable commodities. As for commodities in which we not only can meet but exceed production plans, we must work hard to exceed those planned export amounts. While exporting those goods that are in large volume, are important, and are valuable and easy to sell abroad, we must not forget the smaller-volume commodities. All export commodities must fully comply with the principles of the Five Priorities, specifically priority to all export commodities, in production/processing, priority in access to raw materials and to packaging supplies, priority in procurement, and priority in transportation.

2. The Central Committee and the State Council have decided to establish temporarily an Export Office to supervise and speed up this work. Yao Yilin is appointed to head the office.

Appendix C

CCP CENTRAL COMMITTEE APPROVAL OF EXPORT COMMODITY
PRODUCTION BASE ESTABLISHMENT, 30 JUNE 1960

The report stated that to comply fully with the Central Committee directive to establish export commodity production bases, the Ministry of Foreign Trade convened a National Work Conference on Foreign Trade on 4–20 April.[1] The conference relayed and discussed the Central Committee directive, caused a common understanding [of the directive's meaning], clarified principles, exchanged experiences, and researched the plan.

1. The guiding principles for establishing the export commodity production bases are to arrange and unify a plan; to rely on the localities and strengthen cooperation;[2] to promote self-sufficiency and increase production and encourage economy of resources;[3] to vigorously develop and have a keen grasp on the essentials; to combine current needs with long-term intentions; to establish processing bases in areas of raw material production.

2. The export commodity production bases are divided into five general types: (1) specific state-operated farms or prefectures that produce various types of export commodities (for instance, a Hainan Island Production Base for tropical Asian products and tropical crops; production bases in the Mishan, Hejiang, and Xinjiang large reclamation areas);[4] (2) specific areas for the production of a certain commodity (for instance, the apples of Liaoning); (3) specialized factories (or workshops) or specialized mines; (4) agricultural sideline commodity processing bases; (5) export commodity packaging materials production bases.

3. According to the policy to establish export commodity production bases, the Ministry of Foreign Trade will draw up the initial 1960–62 planning for the export commodity production zone. It is estimated that after the implementation of this plan, our country's sources for export goods will be somewhat reliably guaranteed; the variety of export commodities will increase greatly; and their quality will more suit the demands of the outside, foreign market. The Ministry of Foreign Trade has decided that to carry out well the concrete plan, it will immediately set about cooperating with the appropriate areas and depart-

ments in establishing key export commodity production bases. It will pay close attention to develop the base [construction] work in the key areas of the Hainan Island district, the Pearl River Delta, and the three reclamation areas of Mishan, Hejiang, and Xinjiang. Close attention will also be given to bases producing such key commodities as cotton yarn and cloth, pork, flue-cured tobacco, apples, tea, sericulture, [and mercury] etc.

[The Ministry of Foreign Trade advocated that in establishing the export commodity production bases, the measures taken should reflect the local conditions and the variety (of commodities to be produced). Many different types of bases should be established. . . . According to the then current projections of the Ministry of Foreign Trade, within a few years, the production of the most important export commodities would be "basified" (*jidihua*) and the specifications and quality of export commodities would be standardized.][5]

Appendix D

1. Since July 1960, the completion of the foreign trade procurement and export plan has not been successful; the import plan has been completed quickly; a major deficit has been created in the state's foreign exchange receipts.[1] According to the report of the Ministry of Foreign Trade, as of July 25, only 43.3 percent of the original quota for the annual export commodity procurement plan had been met; only 38 percent of the original annual export quota had been met. Yet the original annual import quota had already been fulfilled by 52.7 percent. According to this rate, it is estimated that by the year's end, the deficit toward the socialist countries could reach RMB 1.7–2 billion; debts owed to the Soviet Union could reach RMB 1.4–1.6 billion; debts owed to our brotherly countries in Eastern Europe could reach RMB .3–.4 billion. This is a serious political problem confronting the whole Party.

2. The Central Committee seriously discussed the foreign trade problem at the Beidaihe Central Work Conference. All the Central Committee, local, and ministerial officials attending believed that during the three years proceeding 1960, a foreign trade policy that proportions income according to export potential and subordinates domestic consumption to foreign sales [*liangshou weiru, neixiao yiban fucong waixiao*] should firmly be carried out. Imports for 1960 must be strictly controlled; the 1961 import plan must be firmly reduced; we must exceed the 1960 and 1961 export [quotas]; we must be sure in the same years to reduce the outstanding bills of trade toward the Soviet Union and Eastern European brother countries, and in the next year pay them back in full. This is not only a problem related to our country's socialist construction. It is a problem related to the international reputation of our country. It influences our implementation of our struggle against imperialism, various countries' reactionary forces, and contemporary revisionism and its followers. The Central Committee asks that the entire Party urgently motivate its membership with a firm resolve to succeed and with a vigor greater than the last half of 1959 to stress increased

production and practice of economy, procurement, export, allocation, and transportation and a comprehensive launching of a mighty procurement, export allocation, and transportation campaign, and to fulfill the foreign trade procurement and export goals set by the Beidaihe Central Work Conference.

3. The Central Committee has decided to establish a three-man foreign trade command post composed of Zhou Enlai, Li Fuchun, and Li Xiannian with Zhou Enlai as the leader. It will have full authority to direct the national procurement, export, allocations, and transportation campaign and will strictly control imports. There will not be any increase of new imports in 1960, unless approved by the three-man group. The group also will be responsible for formulating the 1961 foreign trade plan. The first Party secretary of each province, city, and autonomous region Party Committee will personally take charge of setting up a foreign trade command post for the local area and speedily carrying out the work with the pertinent specialized secretaries taking specific responsibility.

Abbreviations

CYNP	Liu Shufa, *Chen Yi nianpu*
DJFZH	Zhejiangsheng Sifating, Zhejiangsheng Duiwai Jingji Maoyiting, ed., *Duiwai jingji falü zhengce huibian*
LSQLXJJ	Liu Shaoqi, *Lun xin Zhongguo jingji jianshe*
LSQNP	Zhonggong Zhongyang Wenxian Yanjiushi, *Liu Shaoqi nianpu*
MZDWW	Mao Zedong, *Mao Zedong waijiao wenxuan*
RZJSH	Bo Yibo, *Ruogan zhongda juece yu shijian de huigu*
SQYZWX	Zhonggong Zhongyang Wenxian Yanjiushi, ed., *Sanzhong quanhui yilai zhongyao wenxian xuanbian*
WFSS	Tan Qingfeng, Yao Xuecong, and Li Shusen, ed., *Waimao fuchi shengchan shijian*
YCKTGWX	Guowuyuan Tequ Bangongshi, Bangongting Mishuju, ed., *Yanhai chengshi kaifang he tequ gongzuo wenjian xuanbian*
ZDNP	Zhonggong Zhongyang Wenxian Yanjiushi, *Zhu De nianpu*
ZDZ	Zhonggong Zhongyang Wenxian Yanjiushi, *Zhu De zhuan*
ZELJJWX	Zhonggong Zhongyang Wenxian Yanjiushi, *Zhou Enlai jingji wenxuan*
ZELNP	Zhonggong Zhongyang Wenxian Yanjiushi, *Zhou Enlai nianpu (1949–1976)*
ZRGJD	Fang Weizhong, ed., *Zhonghua Renmin Gongheguo jingji dashiji (1949–1980)*
ZRGJFX	Zhongguo Shehui Kexueyuan, Faxue Yanjiusuo, ed., *Zhonghua Renmin Gongheguo jingji fagui xuanbian, 1979.10–1981.12*
ZRGJGD	Dangdai Zhongguo De Jingji Guanli Bianjibu, ed., *Zhonghua Renmin Gongheguo jingji guanli dashiji*

Notes

PREFACE

1. Oksenberg, "Politics Takes Command," 543–90.

2. For instance, Gao Yu, the former deputy editor of *Jingjixue zhoubao* and later a reporter for the Hong Kong monthly *Ching pao*, was sentenced to six years in prison for "'illegally providing state secrets to people outside the borders'" in November 1994. For more information, see *Hsin pao*, 27 March 1995, trans. in FBIS, *China*, 27 March 1995.

3. Reardon, "Learning," 479–511.

4. R. Bernstein, *Beyond Objectivism*, 140.

5. According to Gadamer,

The horizon is the range of vision that includes everything that can be seen from a particular vantage point. . . . The horizon is, rather, something into which we move and that moves with us. Horizons change for a person who is moving. Thus the horizon of the past, out of which all human life lives and which exists in the form of tradition, is always in motion. It is not historical consciousness that first sets the surrounding horizon in motion. But in it this motion becomes aware of itself.

Quoted in R. Bernstein, *Beyond Objectivism*, 142–44.

6. Gadamer, "The Problem of Historical Consciousness," 152.

7. R. Bernstein, *Beyond Objectivism*, 173.

INTRODUCTION

1. National Bureau on Statistics, *China Statistical Yearbook*, 537; idem, *China Foreign Economic Statistical Yearbook, 1998*, 23. All dollar figures are U.S. dollars unless otherwise noted.

2. Based on purchasing-power parity, the International Monetary Fund concluded in May 1993 that the Chinese economy was the third-largest in the world, following the United States and Japan. Using a slightly different measurement technique, the World Bank determined that China was the world's second-largest economy in 1990. For a general description, see the *New York Times*, 20 May 1993 and the *Washington Post*, 4 July 1993.

3. *Wall Street Journal*, 9 June 1997.

4. For a detailed analysis, see Jacobson and Oksenberg, *China's Participation;* Zhang Tianyu, ed., *Shiji zhijiao de zhongxing zhanlüe*, 38–58; *Washington Post*, 16 November 1999; Prybyla, "On the PRC and the WTO."

5. English-language publications generally have translated the phrase "*duiwai kai-*

fang" as the "open door" policy. Many Chinese scholars hold that this translation has a nineteenth-century imperialist overtone, with connotations of foreign trade concessions and a loss of Chinese sovereignty. The Chinese consider translations such as "opening to the outside" or "opening" as more appropriate.

6. Toffler, *Third Wave; Wall Street Journal,* 23 June 1995; Rozman, "China's Quest," 383–402; Huntington, "Lonely Superpower," 35–49.

7. *New York Times,* 19 November 1996. On China's potential power, see Kim, "China as a Great Power," 245–51; Segal, "Does China matter?" 24–36.

8. For instance, see the *Wall Street Journal,* 27 December 1994, 30 December 1994; and the *Washington Post,* 1 January 1994, 5 January 1994.

9. For instance, see Barnett, *China's Economy;* Crane, *Political Economy;* Harwit, *China's Automobile Industry,* 15–42; Howell, *China Opens Its Doors;* Hsu, *China's Foreign Trade Reforms,* 2–22; Jacobson and Oksenberg, *China's Participation;* Kleinberg, *China's "Opening,"* 7–12; Lardy, *Foreign Trade,* 16–36; Lieberthal and Oksenberg, *Policy Making;* Pearson, *Joint Ventures;* Riskin, *China's Political Economy;* Shirk, *How China Opened Its Door,* 8–11; World Bank, *China: External Trade,* 95–100; Woetzel, *China's Economic Opening,* 26–37.

10. On the effect of the embargo on Chinese trade during the 1960s, see Lardy, "Economic Development," 187; on foreign trade's contribution to domestic development, see Riskin, *China's Political Economy,* 317; on the impression that China previously pursued autarky, see *The Economist,* 28 June 1997.

11. Perkins, "China's Economic Policy," 488–90.

12. Yahuda, *Towards the End of Isolationism,* 52.

13. Reardon, "Bird."

14. See Zhonggong Zhongyang, Guowuyuan Pizhuan Guangdong Shengwei, Fujian Shengwei, "Guanyu duiwai jingji huodong shixing texu zhengce he linghuo cuoshi de liangge baogao" [Two reports concerning the implementation of special policies and flexible measures in foreign trade activities], Central Committee/State Council document 79.50, approved and transmitted on 15 July 1979, trans. in Reardon, ed., "China's Coastal Development Strategy, 1979–1984, I," 19–44.

15. *WFSS,* 164.

16. Crane, *Political Economy;* Oborne, *China's Special Economic Zones.*

17. Reardon, "Rise," 301.

18. Zhou Xiaoquan and Ma Jianqun, *Zouxiang kaifangxing jingji,* 1–2.

19. For instance, see Liu Xiangdong, "Jicheng Mao Zedong."

20. Perkins, "Central Features," 130–33; idem, "Reforming China's Economic System," 627–82; Eckstein, *Communist China's Economic Growth,* 117–30.

21. Lardy, *Foreign Trade,* chap. 2.

22. Ibid., 31; idem, "Economic Development," 180–97.

23. World Bank, *China: External Trade;* idem, *China, Socialist Economic Development,* 2:411–17.

24. For instance, see Ahn, *Chinese Politics;* Bachman, *Bureaucracy;* idem, *Chen Yun;* MacFarquhar, *Origins,* vols. 1–3; Teiwes, *Politics.*

25. Yahuda, *Towards the End of Isolationism,* chap. 2.

26. Whiting, *Chinese Domestic Politics,* 53–85.

27. Barnett, *China's Economy,* 12–13, chap. 2.

28. Bachman, *Bureaucracy,* 96–132; Lieberthal and Oksenberg, *Policy Making,* 169–268.

29. Harwit, *China's Automobile Industry,* 41.

30. Van Ness, "Three Lines," 113–42.

31. Solinger, *From Lathes to Looms.*

32. This study considers three separate levels of analysis: the international environment (systemic), domestic determinants, and decision-making levels (subsystemic). For a basic discussion of the "levels of analysis" issue, see Jervis, *Perception,* chap. 1; Singer, "Level-of-Analysis Problem"; Waltz, *Man;* and Allison, "Conceptual Models."

33. Lowenthal, "Development," 33–116.

34. For instance, see "Guanyu nongye de wu tiao jinji zhishi" [Five emergency directives on agriculture], issued by the CCP Central Committee on 7 May 1959, in ZRGJGD, 126.

35. For policies related to the bonus schemes, see "Guanyu yijiuliuba niandu shougou nongfu chanpin jiangshou biaozhun de tongzhi" [Circular on 1968 bonus standards in agricultural sideline production procurement], issued by the State Council on 16 June 1968, ibid., 248; for elimination of the foreign exchange retention schemes, see "Guanyu quxiao feimaoyi waihui fencheng banfa de tongzhi" [Circular on abolishing the method of apportioning foreign exchange for nontrade channels], issued by the State Council on 9 May 1967, ibid., 240.

36. See *Renmin ribao,* 14 October 1972; and ZRGJD, 499–500.

37. "Guanyu zengjia shebei jinkou, kuoda jingji jiaoliu de qingshi baogao" [Report and request for instructions concerning the increase of equipment imports and the expansion of economic exchange], submitted by the State Planning Commission to the State Council and approved in principle on 22 March 1973, in ZRGJGD, 272, 275.

38. ZRGJD, 496–98; ZRGJGD, 270.

39. ZRGJD, 492–93.

40. "Jianli chukou nongfu shengchan jidi shixing banfa" [Trial procedures for establishing export production bases for agricultural or sideline export commodities], issued by the State Planning Commission on 20 March 1973, in WFSS 123–27.

41. "Guanyu shixing nongfu chanpin tongyi jiangshou banfa de qingshi baogao" [Report and request for instructions for implementing a unified bonus scheme for agricultural or sideline products], submitted by the State Planning Commission and approved and transmitted by the State Council on 19 March 1973, in, ZRGJGD, 275.

42. The coalition name's derived from the Opinion on Putting Politics in Command submitted by Wang Renzhong to the CCP Central Committee, which subsequently approved and transmitted it on 10 April 1966. See chap. 4.

43. Quoted from Jiang Qing's 2 March 1976 speech to the Conference of Twelve Provinces and Self-Autonomous Regions, cited in, ZRGJD 561, and, ZRGJGD, 295.

44. Zhang Zerong, ed., *Zhongguo jingji tizhi gaige jishi,* 139; Hua Guofeng, "Report on the Work of the Government," 7–41.

45. Li Xiannian, "Zai zhongyang gongzuo huiyishang de jianghua," in SQYZWX, 117.

46. "Lizheng wancheng dangnian duiwai maoyi de shougou he chukou renwu de jinji zhishi" [Emergency directive to exert utmost effort to meet foreign trade procurement and export responsibilities], issued by the CCP Central Committee and the State Council, 26 October 1959, in ZRGJGD, 131.

47. Waimao fuchi chukou shangpin shengchan zhouzhuan zijin was first implemented in 1975. See WFSS 83; Duiwai Jingji Maoyibu Renshi, *Chukou huoyuan gailun,* 87.

48. Chukou chanpin shengchan cuoshi touzi originated in 1973. See WFSS, 111; Duiwai Jingji Maoyibu Renshi, *Chukou huoyuan gailun,* 91.

49. Chukou gongyepin shengchan zhuanxiang daikuan was instituted in 1964 to increase industrial export quality and variety and to improve packaging. See *WFSS*, 69; Duiwai Jingji Maoyibu Renshi, *Chukou huoyuan gailun* 86.

50. "Duanqi waihui daikuan shixing banfa" [Trial procedures for short-term foreign exchange loans], Jishengzi 73.196, approved by the State Revolutionary Planning Committee on 28 May 1973, as cited in "Guanyu zhuanfa 'Duanqi waihui daikuan shi-xing banfa' xi zunzhao zhixing" [Hoping that one complies with the 'implementation of the trial procedures for short-term foreign exchange loans'], Maochudaierzi 73.99/Yinwazi 73.135, issued by the Ministry of Foreign Trade and the People's Bank of China on 16 June 1973, in Zhongguo Renmin Yinhang Jihuasi, *Lilü,* 378–79.

51. See *WFSS*, 67.

52. See "Guanyu fangzhi gongye fazhan fangzhen de qingshi baogao" [Report and request for instructions on the textile industry development plans], issued by the Ministry of Textile Industry and approved and transmitted by the CCP Central Committee on 1 September 1960, in *ZRGJGD*, 146.

53. "Guanyu jianli chukou shangpin shengchan jidi de qingshi baogao" [Report and request for instructions on establishing an export commodity production base], submit-ted by the Ministry of Foreign Trade and approved by the CCP Central Committee on 30 June 1960, in *ZRGJGD*, 143.

54. For translations of these documents, see Reardon, "China's Coastal Development Strategy," 1979–1984, II," 79–82, 39–42; idem, "China's Coastal Development Strategy, 1979–1982, I," 9–18, 19–44.

1. The Domestic Determinants of Chinese Foreign Economic Policy

1. Krueger, "Why Trade Liberalization Is Good," 1514–17.

2. Gillis, Perkins, Roemer, and Snodgrass, *Economics of Development,* chap. 15; Krueger, *Trade Policy and Developing Nations,* 6; Luedde-Neurath, *Import Controls,* as cited in Grabowski, "Import Substitution," 535.

3. Robert Keohane defines regimes as agreed-upon principles, rules, and norms that govern policy behavior. See Keohane, *After Hegemony,* 59–60.

4. For an interesting, contrasting view, see Grabowski, "Import Substitution," 541.

5. Weisskopf, "Patterns," 61–63.

6. Yahuda, *Towards the End of Isolationism,* 63; Nai-Ruenn Chen, "China's Foreign Trade in Global Perspective," 124.

7. Balassa, *Process,* 5–11.

8. The "infant industry" argument is part of the larger debate between the mercan-tilist approach of state intervention in the marketplace (List and Hamilton) and the neo-classical economic approach of nonmarket intervention (Smith, Ricardo). For more information, see Roll, *History of Economic Thought,* 63, 149, 228–30.

9. Myint, *Exports,* 105.

10. World Bank, *China: External Trade,* 5.

11. Balassa, *Process,* 5–18. For Balassa's discussion on the role of the market in deter-mining inwardly versus outwardly oriented development, see 18–22.

12. Krueger, "Trade Policy and Economic Development," 3–5, 11–12.

13. Fei, Ohkawa, and Ranis, "Economic Development," 35–64; for the similar "flying geese" explanation, see Bernard and Ravenhill, "Beyond Product Cycles and Flying Geese," 171–209.

14. Grabowski, "Import Substitution," 544.

15. Prebisch, *Economic Development;* H. Singer, "Distribution," 473–85. For the neo-classical critique of the deterioration of terms of trade for primary product exporters, see Balassa, "Comment," 304–11.

16. Waltz, *Theories of International Relations,* 18–37.

17. Baldwin, "Neoliberalism," 1–25. Wallerstein's world systems theory could be considered a third contending paradigm, but Ruggie argues that in reality it is a subsystemic approach. See Ruggie, "Continuity," 261–75.

18. Keohane, *After Hegemony;* Keohane, ed., *Neorealism;* Keohane and Nye, *Power.*

19. Moore, "China as a Latecomer," 187–208; Krasner, *Structural Conflict,* 58; Lardy, *Foreign Trade,* chap. 2; Reynolds, "China in the International Economy," 73; Eckstein, "The Chinese Development Model," 106–7.

20. Waltz, *Man,* 167–71.

21. Waltz, *Theories of International Relations,* 11, 104–7, 118, 177, 199; Conybeare, *Trade Wars,* 233–61.

22. Ward, "The Chinese Approach to Economic Development," 93.

23. Sutton, *Western Technology,* 9, 250–52, 260–63, 342. For a detailed list of the companies and technologies transferred, see 329–32, 336–39.

24. Ground, "Genesis," 179–203.

25. Myint, *Exports.*

26. Myint, "'Classical Theory,'" 317–37.

27. Although not as directly involved in the bipolar conflict, Malaysia, Indonesia, and Singapore also followed import substitution development following decolonization in the 1950s and 1960s. Thailand, which remained an independent state, experimented with import substitution development from 1971 to 1980, which coincided with the U.S. withdrawal of sixteen thousand troops from Thailand (Nixon Doctrine, 1969). See World Bank, *East Asian Miracle,* 123–56. For an overview of List's views, see Roll, *History,* 227–31.

28. Gerschenkron, *Economic Backwardness.*

29. Myint, "Infant Industry."

30. Herschman, "Political Economy," 1–32; Balassa, *Process,* 4–6.

31. Eckstein, *Communist China's Economic Growth,* 183–241; idem, *China's Economic Revolution,* 50–58, 233–76.

32. World Bank, *East Asian Miracle,* 105–56.

33. Ibid., 59, 124; Balassa, *Process,* 12–18; Lardy, *Foreign Trade,* 37–82; World Bank, *China, Socialist Economic Development,* 2: 411–63; Reardon, "Rise," 293–94.

34. Gillis, Perkins, Roemer, and Snodgrass, *Economics of Development,* 440–51. The Foreign Trade Regimes and Economic Development Series analyzes import substitution and the development paths of ten developing states. For instance, see Díaz-Alejandro, *Foreign Trade Regimes,* chaps. 3, 4, 5.

35. Lardy, *Foreign Trade,* 18; also see Yahuda, *Towards the End of Isolationism,* 64.

36. Lardy, *Foreign Trade,* 29.

37. Ibid., chap. 2; World Bank, *China: External Trade,* 95–99; Reynolds, "China in the International Economy," 83–90; Zhang Peiji, "Guanyu woguo duiwai maoyi fazhan zhanlüe de tantao," 26–36.

38. While also recognizing the duality of self-reliance, Yahuda argued that "it bespeaks more of an attitude of mind than a specific set of policies" (*Towards the End of Isolationism,* 52–53). This study modifies Yahuda's definition by arguing that the different perceptions of self-reliance are an attitude of mind that are manifested in specific sets of policies.

39. Eckstein, *China's Economic Revolution,* 37–65; Skinner and Winckler, "Compliance Succession," 412. In a critique of an early draft, Thomas Bernstein disagreed with Skinner and Winckler's disaggregation of coercive techniques and normative compliance. He argued that the two "went hand-in-hand, as I think is very visible from the GLF. If you opposed the normative goals of the GLF, you were a rightist and got purged. . . . there is [a] great German saying that illustrates the point: 'Un willst Du nicht mein Bruder sein, so schlag Ich Dir den Schaedel ein (If you don't want to be my brother, I will beat your brains in).'" Coercive and remunerative compliance also go hand in hand. During the pre–GLF, pre–Cultural Revolution, and post–Cultural Revolution periods, coercive techniques remained the basis for export commodity procurement; remunerative methods supplemented coercive techniques, especially during the pre–Cultural Revolution period to increase producers' motivation.

40. Zhong Jifu, "Methods," 3–11.

41. Lardy, *Agriculture,* 30–36. For an interesting discussion of the Chinese planners' realization of their differences with their Soviet counterparts during the mid-1950s, see Lardy's Introduction in Lardy, *Chinese Economic Planning,* vii–xii.

42. Eckstein, *Revolution,* 58–63. When analyzing agricultural policy, Lardy instead uses an economic term, indirect planning (*jianjie jihua*), to describe this study's remunerative-administrative approach. The timing and definition of indirect planning mirrors the remunerative-administrative approach adopted by this study, with the exception of the post–Cultural Revolution period of 1971–74. See Lardy, *Agriculture,* 18–19. For a contrasting neoinstitutional interpretation, see Bachman, *Bureaucracy,* chap. 3.

43. Lardy, *Agriculture,* 37–41.

44. Mao Zedong, "Speech on the Book 'Economic Problems of Socialism,'" in *Miscellany,* 129.

45. Mao Zedong, "Critique of Stalin's 'Economic Problems of Socialism in the Soviet Union'" (1959?), ibid., 191.

46. Mao Zedong, "Reading Notes on the Soviet Union's 'Political Economy,'" ibid., 299.

47. Mao Zedong, "Reading Notes on the Soviet Union's 'Political Economics,'" ibid., 293, 279, 283.

48. Mao Zedong, "Speech at the Sixth Plenum of the Eighth Central Committee," presented on 19 December 1958, ibid., 143.

49. Mao Zedong, "Reading Notes," ibid., 291.

50. Eckstein, *Revolution,* 32–37; also see Gurley, *China's Economy,* 1–19. When analyzing agricultural policy, Lardy uses an economic term, direct planning (*zhijie jihua*), to describe this study's normative-administrative approach. The definitions of direct and indirect planning mirror the normative-administrative and remunerative-administrative approach adopted by this study. See Lardy, *Agriculture,* 19–21.

51. Yahuda, *Towards the End of Isolationism,* 39.

52. This simplified periodization roughly corresponds to Lardy's analysis of agricultural policies, except for the 1971–74 period. See Lardy, *Agriculture,* 19. It also corresponds with Hans Heymann's view of China's five development phases between 1952 and 1974. See Heymann, "Acquisition and Diffusion." The import substitution development period roughly coincides with the World Bank's description of the "four waves" of imports: 1956–60, 1964–66, 1973–77, 1978. See World Bank, *China: External Trade,* 95–96.

53. Harding, "Competing Models," 62–63.

54. David Bachman's 1991 neoinstitutionalist approach challenges this broad statement. For a cogent critique of the factional and bureaucratic models, see Yan Sun, *Chinese Reassessment*, 13–15; Chan, "Leaders," 57–78; and Bachman's rebuttal, "Chinese Bureaucratic Politics," 35–55. For the seminal discussion on Soviet autonomy, see F. Griffiths, "Tendency Analysis," 335–78, esp. 341.

55. R. Inman, "Markets"; D. Little, "Rational Choice Models," 35–52.

56. See the various contributors to Buchanan, Tollison, and Tullock, eds., *Toward a Theory*.

57. Meier, "Policy Lessons," 6; Olson, *Rise and Decline*, chap. 4.

58. Green and Shapiro, *Pathologies;* Walt, "Rigor or Rigor Mortis," 5–48; Mansbridge, "Rise and Fall"; Sen, "Rational Fools"; Jachtenfuchs, *International Policy-Making*, 5–17; Johnson and Keehn, "Disaster in the Making," 14–22; Johnson, "Preconception," 170–74.

59. Grindle, "New Political Economy"; Grindle and Thomas, *Public Choices*.

60. Mansbridge, "Rise and Fall," 71–143.

61. Zhou Enlai was the best practitioner of such strategic behavior. Although outwardly supporting Mao during the Seven Thousand Cadre Conference in 1962, Zhou continued to promote the Liu-Deng program to repeal the GLF approach and institute a more remunerative-administrative approach. See Lieberthal, "Great Leap Forward," 326–27.

62. The author would like to thank Hiroyuki Imai for suggesting the convergence of public- and self-interest.

63. For a basic discussion on game theory, including interrated games, see Oye, "Explaining Cooperation," 1–24.

64. Teiwes, *Leadership*, 11–23. Teiwes does not directly address the cycling of development strategies, but he does explain "shifting of CCP policies" as a result of Mao's dialectical view of the world.

65. Mao Zedong, "Talks at the Nan-ning Conference," 13 January 1958, in *Miscellany*, 80–84. Although revealing that Mao made a similar comment in Hangzhou a few days beforehand, Teiwes ignores Mao's comments at Nanning. See Teiwes, *China's Road*, 73, 31–34.

66. Teiwes, *Politics*, 301.

67. ZELNP, 2:195.

68. Ibid., 1:340–41.

69. MacFarquhar, *Origins*, 2:32–33, 173; idem, 1:105–7, 152–56.

70. Mao Zedong, "Gongzuo fangfa liushitiao (caoan)" [Sixty articles on work methods], in *Jianguo*, 7:64.

71. Teiwes, *China's Road*, 119–25; ZELNP, 2:189, 190; Lardy, "Chinese Economy under Stress," 378–80; Yang Dali, *Calamity*, 44.

72. RZJSH, 2:813. Bo's account was quoted selectively from the original text. There are similarities with the more extensive version of Mao's 21 November talk at the expanded Political Bureau meeting in Wuchang published in Mao Zedong, *Secret Speeches*, 481–517. The sources for the translation come from *Mao Zedong sixiang wansui* and *Xuexi ziliao, xuyi*, which were both issued during the Cultural Revolution. It thus is not surprising that the Cultural Revolution sources would not include Mao's self-criticism, although they do mention Mao's use of high-yield statistics to "prove there is no opportunism and no danger [of my] losing my Party membership" (504); "If with a death toll of 50 million [Mao is talking about the dismissal of the Guangxi Party secretary held responsible for famine deaths in 1957], you didn't lose your jobs, I at least should lose

mine; [whether I would lose my] head would also be open to question" (494–95). For a basic outline of the speech, see Zhonggong Zhongyang Wenxian Yanjiushi, ed., *Jianguo,* 7:553–54; also see Lieberthal and Dickson, *Research Guide,* 77–78.

73. Tong Xiaopeng, *Fengyu sishinian,* 2:363; also see Mao Zedong, "Yige jiaoxun," 17; Yan Wen, "Jiu 'zuo' de qibu," 28–32. For Mao's inability to take full responsibility for failure, see Teiwes, *China's Road,* 183–84.

74. Mao Zedong, "Speech at the Lushan Plenum," 23 July 1959, in *Chairman Mao,* 143. According to Schram's footnotes, Mao's allusion to burial puppets "has come to designate the author of any diabolical invention, or more generally the bringer of misfortune." "Descendants" refers to his first son, killed in 1950, and his second, who "was so mistreated, according to Red Guard sources, that his mind was affected." The xx probably stood for Chen Yun.

75. "Tongyi Mao Zedong tongzhi tichu de guanyu ta buzuo xiajie Zhonghua Renmin Gongheguo zhuxi houxuanren de jianyi de jueding" [The decision to agree to Comrade Mao Zedong's proposal that he not continue as the next candidate for the chairmanship of the PRC], approved by the Sixth Plenum of the Eighth Party Congress on 10 December 1958, in Liao Gailong, ed., *Zhongguo Gongchandang lishi dacidian* 202. For lists of the various texts available, see Lieberthal and Dickson, *Research Guide,* 78.

76. ZELNP, 2:192. For a detailed discussion of "compressing air" (*yasuo kongqi*), see Teiwes, *China's Road,* 134.

77. Joseph, *Critique,* 67–68.

78. See an interesting account of Zhou's drinking during the plenum's closing banquet in Li Zhisui, *Private Life,* 281–82; also see MacFarquhar, *Origins,* 2:173. Zhou also got drunk following the criticism of Peng Dehuai at Lushan in 1959; see MacFarquhar, *Origins,* 3:548, n. 206.

79. Mao Zedong, "Zai di'erci Zhengzhou huiyishang de jianghua," 17–22; idem, *Mao Zedong sixiang wansui* (1969), 279–88. Also see MacFarquhar, *Origins,* 2:chap. 8. Teiwes credits Mao's evolving understanding of provincial conditions for his "anti-left" posture. See Teiwes, *China's Road,* 143–46.

80. RZJSH, 2:832; *Mao Zedong sixiang wansui* (1967), 51–53, 58–62; *Miscellany,* 175–81. For a general outline of Mao's speech, see Mao Zedong, *Jianguo,* 8:196–97.

81. Mao Zedong, "Dui zhongyang guanyu ziliudi deng wenti de zhishi de piyu xiugai he daini de buchong zhishigao" [A supplementary directive to the written comments that were revised and drafted by others concerning the Central Committee's directive on private plots and other problems], in Mao Zedong, *Jianguo,* 8:305–8; for a listing of various emergency measures adopted during the May–June period, see chap. 3.

82. Li Zhisui, *Private Life,* 301–5; Tong Xiaopeng, *Fengyu sishinian,* 2:367–68. Li interprets Mao's visit as an attempt to understand the problems of the GLF by returning to an area he knew well. It also can be interpreted as attempt to return "home" to recover from the problems of the two plenums. Also see MacFarquhar, *Origins,* 2:187–90.

83. "Criticism of Documents Issued in the Name of the Center by Liu Shaoqi and Yang Shangkun," issued on 19 May 1953, in Mao Zedong, *Writings,* 1:344–64; Li Zhisui, *Private Life,* 174–75; Lieberthal and Dickson, *Research Guide,* 94–95.

84. Teiwes, *Leadership,* 49.

85. Ibid., 28.

86. Stuart R. Schram, "Mao Tse-tung's Thought," in MacFarquhar and Fairbank, *Cambridge History,* 15:72.

87. Zhou Enlai, "Di'erge wunian jihua de liangge zhongyao wenti" [Two major problems of the Second Five-Year Plan], presented on 15 November 1963 to the Supreme State Conference, in *ZELJJW*, 525.

88. MacFarquhar, *Origins* 3:66.

89. Lieberthal, "Great Leap Forward," 319. For more information on the unraveling of the Yan'an coalition, see 316–35; also MacFarquhar, *Origins*, 2:173.

90. MacFarquhar, *Origins*, 3:11–16; Lieberthal, "Great Leap Forward," 325.

91. MacFarquhar, *Origins*, 3:168–72.

92. Ibid., 276.

93. For instance, see Lardy, *Agriculture*, 43–45.

94. Teiwes, *Leadership*, 38–42.

95. Ibid., 40; Teiwes similarly argues that Mao suffered from "intellectual incoherence" during the 1956–57 period. See Teiwes, *China's Road*, 183.

96. Mao Zedong, "Speech to a Symposium of Delegates to the First Meeting of the Second National Committee of the ACFIC," 8 December 1956, in *Writings*, 2:200.

97. Mao Zedong, "Speech at the Lushan Plenum," 23 July 1959, in *Chairman Mao*, 142; also see Mao Zedong, "Talk at an Enlarged Central Work Conference," 30 January 1962, ibid., 175–76, in which Mao states, "I have paid rather more attention to problems relating to the system, to the productive relationships. As for productive forces, I know very little." For further discussion of Mao's political approach to China's economic development, see Dwight H. Perkins, "China's Economic Policy and Performance," in MacFarquhar and Fairbanks, *Cambridge History*, 15:475–80.

98. *Jiefang ribao*, 5 June 1967, as quoted in *RZJSH*, 2:978.

99. Mao Zedong, "Talk at an Enlarged Central Work Conference," 30 January 1962, in *Chairman Mao*, 177; italics added. For the Chinese version, *Mao Zedong wenji*, 8:304.

100. Lieberthal, "Great Leap Forward," 354. MacFarquhar hints that Mao possibly transferred power to Liu Shaoqi at the Seven Thousand Cadre Conference; this transfer would explain Liu's more assertive behavior in 1962. See MacFarquhar, *Origins*, 3:172, 262–74. For more on the dissolution of the Yan'an coalition and Mao's search for political allies, see Ahn, *Chinese Politics;* MacFarquhar, *Origins*, 2; Harding, "Chinese State."

101. Mao Zedong, "Guanyu renzhen diaocha gongshe neibu liangge pingjun zhuyi wenti de xin" [Letter on resolutely investigating the problem of two egalitarianisms within the communes], in *Jianguo*, 9:440–42.

102. *RZJSH*, 2: chap. 32; Ruan Ming, *Deng Xiaoping*, 70–71.

103. *RZJSH*, 2: chap. 33. Proponents of a Mao-in-command interpretation focus on Mao's actions in the agricultural front, where he was very effective after mid-1962 at stopping the remunerative trend. They do not address other sectors of the economy, such as industrial and foreign economic policy, where remunerative policies continued to be implemented.

104. Harding, *Organizing China*, 231.

105. Lieberthal, "Great Leap Forward," 335–48.

106. MacFarquhar, "Succession," 335–36.

107. Ibid., 340–42.

108. For the bandwagon effect following the Lushan conference, see Yang Dali, *Calamity*, 67.

109. Goldstein, *Bandwagon;* for a similar critique, see Richard Baum's review in *American Political Science Review*, 237–39.

110. "Opinion group" is the most appropriate term. Franklyn Griffiths used the term

"tendency" to emphasize the potential of informal groupings to become organized. Griffiths uses Truman's concept of a "potential group or interest" "characterized as 'a becoming stage' of group activity based on 'widely held attitudes that are not expressed in interaction,' but which may become the basis of interaction." See Griffiths, "Tendency Analysis," 347. Such arguments support the idea of proto-interest groups, which are more detectable in Soviet and Chinese politics than actual interest groups are. The term "opinion group" also is more reflective of the similarities and differences of individual perceptions and more appropriately emphasizes the decision-making level of analysis.

III. Robert Bates has suggested a synthesis of rational choice and cultural approaches. See Bates, de Figueredo, and Weingast, "Politics of Interpretation," 603–42.

112. Grindle and Thomas, *Public Choices,* 41.

113. Ibid., 8.

114. F. Griffiths, "Tendency Analysis," 362.

115. Ibid., 342.

116. Joseph, *Critique;* also see Ahn, *Chinese Politics;* Eckstein, *China's Economic Revolution;* Schurmann, *Ideology.*

117. Harding, *China's Second Revolution;* Jacobson and Oksenberg, *China's Participation;* Van Ness and Raichur, "Dilemmas"; Solinger, *Chinese Business;* and Yan Sun, *Chinese Reassessment.* For a succinct analysis of the various tendency/opinion-group models in the China field, see Harding, "Competing Models," 66–69; for the "two-line-struggle" model, see Solinger, *Chinese Business,* 61, n. 1.

118. Lowenthal, "Development," 54; also see Lowenthal, "Postrevolutionary Phase," 1–14.

119. Oksenberg, "Politics Takes Command," 590.

120. Cumings, "Political Economy," 425–26.

121. Oksenberg and Goldstein separate those elites holding more "extreme" opinions into "militant fundamentalists" and "Westernized Chinese." They furthermore argue that "the Chinese hierarchy at any given moment is dominated by a coalition of two or more of the four opinion groups." See Oksenberg and Goldstein, "Chinese Political Spectrum," 11. This study incorporates these "extreme" opinions with the more "mainstream" groupings of "radical conservatives" and "eclectic modernizers," with whom they share many basic opinions.

122. Xin, *Mao Zedong's World View,* 13.

123. Mao Zedong, "Instructions at a Discussion Meeting Attended by Some of the Delegates to the Second Session of the First Committee of the All-China Federation of Industry and Commerce," presented 8 December 1956, in *Miscellany,* 38. Also see Yahuda, *Towards the End of Isolationism,* 50–52.

124. Sun Yeli, "Wenge houqi Chen Yun guanyu dui ziben zhuyi guojia maoyi wenti de jidian sikao," 1084; Lieberthal, "Great Leap Forward," 304; Schram, "Mao Tse-tung's Thought," 36.

125. Lieberthal, "Great Leap Forward," 303–4. For more insight on Mao's views on self-reliance, see Jin Chongji, "Mao Zedong de duli zizhu sixiang," 21–24.

126. Lewis and Xue, *China Builds the Bomb,* 221.

127. Mao Zedong, "Yao xia juexin gao jianrui jishu," 10; for the Nie Rongzhen and Zhou Enlai citations, see chap. 3.

128. Mao Zedong, "Ba woguo jianshe chengwei shehui zhuyi de xiandaihua de qiangguo," 34.

129. Whiting, *Chinese Domestic Politics,* 54–55.

130. Ibid., 56.

131. For a discussion of Chinese neomercantilism, see Kleinberg, *China's "Opening."*

132. For instance, see Chen Dacai, "Zhou Enlai," 62–66.

133. M. Levine, *Found Generation;* Chae-Jin Lee, *Zhou Enlai;* Nora Wang, "Deng Xiaoping," 698–705.

134. M. Levine, *Found Generation,* 11.

135. For an overall view of Zhou Enlai's view on China's foreign economic policy, see Cao Yingwang, "Zhou Enlai," 47–53.

136. Li Ruizhen and Yao Yuanyang, "Chen Yun," 977–87; Chen Yun, "Yao yanjiu dangdai ziben zhuyi" [We must research contemporary capitalism], in *Wenxuan,* 3:217–18.

137. Zhang Guotao, Introduction, ii. For more information on Liu Shaoqi, see Dittmer, *Liu Shaoqi.*

138. Oksenberg and Goldstein, "Chinese Political Spectrum," 9–10; Harding, "Competing Models," 68–69.

139. P. Chang, *Power and Policy.* Chang published a second edition in 1978.

140. Teiwes, *China's Road,* 7–8.

141. Ibid., xi.

142. Chen Boda, "Wuchan jieji wenhua dageming de liangtiao luxian" [The two lines in the Great Proletarian Cultural Revolution], delivered at a central work conference, October 9–28, 1966, in ZELNP, 3:75–76.

143. Lieberthal, "Great Leap Forward," 328.

144. Linda Chelan Li applies this same approach to understand the political relationship between Beijing and the provinces. See Li, *Centre and Provinces.*

145. Bachman, *Bureaucracy,* 181; Teiwes, *China's Road,* 183.

146. While Zhou Enlai, Bo Yibo, and Li Xiannian changed their positions when faced with Mao's opposition, Peng Dehuai, Deng Zihui, and Peng Zhen stood their ground; Chen Yun made self-criticisms and subsequently retreated out of harm's way. For a fascinating comparison of Zhou's and Chen's survival strategies, see MacFarquhar, *Origins,* 3:434–35.

147. Grindle and Thomas, *Public Choices,* 41.

148. For instance, Li Zhisui, *Private Life;* Zhu Jiamu, "Chen Yun"; Tong Xiaopeng, *Fengyu sishinian,* vol. 2; Chae-jin Lee, *Zhou Enlai;* Dittmer, *Liu Shaoqi;* Bachman, *Chen Yun;* Witke, *Comrade Chiang Ch'ing.*

149. For instance, ZELNP, LSNP; ZDN; Liu Shufa, ed., *Chen Yi nianpu.*

150. For example, Bo Yibo states that Chen Yun strongly supported the backyard furnace approach of the GLF that had been decided at the Beidaihe expanded Political Bureau conference of August 1958. This evidence has not been included in *Chen Yun wenxian, 1956–1985* or *Chen Yun tongzhi wengao xuanbian.* Following Chen Yun's death, his 21 October 1958 discussion supporting backyard furnaces was published. See Chen Yun, "Guanyu xibei xiezuoqu jiben jianshe gongzuo de jige wenti," 8–13. Chen Yun, who had originally opposed "rash advance," and the other members of the post–GLF elite coalition obviously have much to hide about their complicity in the GLF strategy of 1958.

151. Li Zhisui, *Private Life,* viii.

152. Ruan Ming, *Deng Xiaoping.*

153. Teiwes, *China's Road,* 17, 258–59.

154. For an interesting review of cycles in the economics literature, see Berry, *Longwave Rhythms.*

155. Modelski, "Long Cycle"; Vernon, *Sovereignty at Bay;* Kurth, "Political Conse-quences," 1–34; Krasner, "State Power," 317–47; Kindleberger, *World in Depression;* Gilpin, *War and Change;* McKeown, "Tariffs."

156. For a general description, see Fairbank, Reischauer, and Craig, *East Asia,* 70–82; Pye, *China,* 57–59; Fairbank, *United States and China,* 90–95. For a detailed description and analysis of Chinese and Western cyclical interpretations of Chinese impe-rial history, see Meskill, ed., *Pattern.*

157. "Great chaos will lead to great order. The cycle appears every seven or eight years. The demons and monsters will come out by themselves. Their class character dictates it." Mao Zedong, "Letter to Jiang Qing," 94. Translated in Li Zhisui, *Private Life,* 461–62. There is a discrepancy between these two English translations.

158. Spence, *Search,* 649–50.

159. Fieldwork, Beijing, Shanghai, and Guangzhou, July 1994.

160. Skinner and Winckler, "Compliance Succession," 410–38; also see Winckler, "Policy Oscillations," 734–50.

161. Eckstein, "Economic Fluctuations," 693.

162. Imai, "Explaining China's Business Cycles," 154–85; also see idem, "China's Endogenous Investment Cycle," 188–216.

163. Dittmer, "Patterns of Elite Strife and Succession in Chinese Politics," 405–30; Crane, *Political Economy,* 146; Shirk, "Political Price of Reform Cycles" as cited in Baum, *Burying Mao,* 6–7.

164. Baum, "Road to Tiananmen," 340–471; Pye, *Dynamics,* 6, 21–22. Also see Goldman, "Party Policies."

165. Lowenthal, "Development," 54.

166. Harwit, *China's Automobile Industry,* 41; Harding, *Second Revolution,* 83–84; Howell, 32–35; 252–59.

167. Solinger, *Chinese Business,* 298.

168. Solinger, "Commerce," 97.

169. Ibid., 98.

170. Ibid., 104.

171. Hung Yu, "History Develops in Spirals," as cited in Nathan, "Policy Oscillations," 731.

172. Nathan, "Policy Oscillations," 728; also see idem, "Factionalism Model."

173. Winckler, "Policy Oscillations," 734–50.

174. Zhou Enlai, "Guomin jingji fazhan de fangzhen he mubiao" [The plans and goals of national economic development], delivered during the discussion of the "Guanyu gongye fazhan wenti (chugao)" [Industrial development problems (initial draft)] on 23 August 1963, in ZELJJWX, 516–17.

175. Pye, *Dynamics,* 54–59; Solomon, *Mao's Revolution.*

176. For a neo-Marxist view on crisis, see Carnoy, *The State and Political Theory,* 130–40; Mattick, *Economic Crisis;* Castells, *Economic Crisis.* For the statist view, see Skocpol, "Bringing the State Back In," 9–11; Rueschemeyer and Evans, "The State," 64–65; Nelson, *Economic Crisis;* Singh and Tabatabai, *Economic Crisis;* Binder et al., *Crisis and Sequences.*

177. Grindle and Thomas, *Public Choices,* chap. 4.

178. Calder, *Crisis and Compensation,* 20, 40.

179. Tsou Tang, *Cultural Revolution,* xxxii.

180. Solinger, *From Lathes to Looms,* 27, 30.

181. Li Xiannian, "Zuohao wuzi tongyi guanli gongzuo" [Do a good job in unifying management over goods and materials], speech delivered on 6 June 1962 to the National Work Conference on Material, in *Li Xiannian*, 2:27–28.

182. Jiang Siyi, ed., *Zhongguo renmin*, 592.

183. On the role of economic crisis as the catalyst of economic readjustment, see Naughton, *Growing*, chap. 2.

184. Solinger, *From Lathes to Looms*, 9–16.

185. Prybyla, *Reform in China*, 120.

186. "Zhongguo Jingji Tizhi Gaige Shiyong Cidian" Bianxiezu, *Zhongguo*, 4; Zhang Tianrong et al., *Zhongguo gaige dacidian*, 848–49.

187. According to Pye, the term "readjustment" promoted in 1962 and 1979 "explains more about power relationships than [about] policy choices," in that "the 1962 slogan was advanced to mobilize support for an emerging faction—the typical way that symbols are used in Chinese politics—while the 1979 slogan was floated in a spirit of revenge against the remnants of a declining faction." See Pye, *Dynamics*, 163.

188. Bennett, *Yundong*.

189. Although supporting a factional analysis, Pye's analysis of the Chinese need for consensus is particularly enlightening. See Pye, *Dynamics*, chap. 2; also see Lieberthal and Oksenberg, *Policy Making*, 23–24.

190. Tsou Tang, *Cultural Revolution*, 17.

191. Joseph, *Critique*, 77–79; for an interesting discussion during the Seven Thousand Cadre Conference of January 1962 among the Party elites concerning Mao's responsibility, see *RZJSH*, 2:1026–29.

192. Joseph, *Critique*, 140–50, 179–82.

193. Lieberthal, *Governing China*, 66–67.

194. Li Xiannian, "Duiwaimao gongzuo de jidian yijian" [Several opinions on foreign trade work], a portion of the summary speech to the National Party Secretary Conference on Finance and Trade, 12 May 1959, in *Li Xiannian*, 1:345.

195. Reardon, "Bird," chaps. 6 and 7; idem, "China's Coastal Development Strategy, 1979–1982, II," Introduction.

196. For an interesting analysis of this bottom-up approach to policy implementation as applied to the agricultural sector, see Yang Dali, *Calamity*, chap. 6.

197. Lieberthal and Oksenberg, *Policy Making*, 35–62; Harding, 66–67.

2. Antinomies of Chinese Development, 1949–1958

1. S. Levine, *Anvil of Victory*, 68–72, 175–96, 240–41.

2. Dongbei Maoyi Zonggongsi, "Diyi jidu duiwai maoyi gongzuo zongjie yu di'er jidu duiwai maoyi yijian" [A summary of the first quarter's foreign trade work and opinions concerning the second quarter's foreign trade], Liaoning Danganguan Dongcaiwei Dangan, 5065 *juan*, 1–4, 15, as cited in Meng Xianzhang, ed., *Zhongsu maoyishi ziliao*, 531–34; also see Goncharov, Lewis, and Xue, *Uncertain Partners*, 13.

3. Liu Shaoqi, "Liji jinxing duiwai maoyi" [Immediately carry out foreign trade], draft of an internal Party directive submitted on 16 February 1949, in *LSQLXJJ*, 64–68; Mao Zedong, "Zhongguo renmin yuanyi tong shijie geguo renmin youhao hezuo" [The Chinese people wish to have friendly cooperation with every country in the world], 15 June 1949, in *MZDWW* 89–91. For a more complete collection of foreign commercial, industrial, and finance policies during this period, see Zhongguo Shehui Kexueyuan,

ed., *Gongye juan,* 751–93; idem, *Jinrong juan,* 753–904; idem, *Gongshang tizhi juan,* 765–804.

4. Liu Shaoqi, "Guanyu xin zhongguo de jingji jianshe fangzhen" [Plans for the economic construction of the new China], June 1949, in *LSQLXJJ,* 148. This was originally an outline prepared for Liu's June–July 1949 trip to Moscow. For Liu Shaoqi's important contribution to establishing China's foreign trade structure, see Zhang Feihong, "Liu Shaoqi yu xin Zhongguo de duiwai maoyi gongzuo," 69–72.

5. *LSQNP,* 2:217–20; Meng Xianzhang, *Zhongsu maoyishi ziliao,* 536. For more in-depth information, see Zhu Yuanshi, "Liu Shaoqi 1949 nian mimi fangsu," 74–89.

6. Meng Xianzhang, *Zhongsu maoyishi ziliao,* 598.

7. For various policies relating to Soviet aid in the industrial, coal, electricity, petroleum, heavy and light industries, see Zhongguo Shehui Kexueyuan, ed., *Gongye juan* 751–78. For detailed summary of the meeting and the agreements signed, see Shi Zhe, "'Zhongsu youhao tongmeng huzhu tiaoyue' qianding shimo," 52–57.

8. "Guanyu daikuan gei Zhonghua Renmin Gongheguo de xieding" [Agreement on a loan for the People's Republic of China], signed by the PRC and the Soviet Union on 24 February 1950, in Zhonggong Zhongyang Wenxian Yanjiushi, ed., *Jianguo,* 1:123–24; *ZELNP,* 1:24–25.

9. *RZJSH,* 1: 300.

10. "Zhongsu liangguo guanyu dijie youhao tongmeng huzhu tiaoyue ji xieding de gonggao" [The Sino-Soviet announcement concerning the conclusion of the Sino-Soviet Treaty of Friendship, Alliance, and Mutual Assistance and Agreements], announced in Moscow on 14 February 1950, in Zhonggong Zhongyang Wenxian Yanjiushi, ed., *Jianguo,* 1:117–25.

11. *Renmin ribao,* 12 April 1950.

12. Reardon-Anderson, *Yenan,* 73–78.

13. Liu Shaoqi, "Zhongsu liangguo zai Xinjiang sheli jinshu he shiyou gongsi wenti" [The problem of establishing Sino-Soviet metal and oil joint venture companies in Xinjiang], report submitted to Mao Zedong on 2 January 1950, in *LSQXZJJ,* 150–51; for the agreements establishing the various business ventures, see Zhongguo Shehui Kexueyuan, ed., *Gongshang juan,* 780–804; idem, *Gongye juan,* 792–93.

14. Nakajima, "Foreign Relations," 269; *Renmin ribao,* 5 April 1950; Goncharov, Lewis, and Xue, *Uncertain Partners,* 7. For more details on these agreements, see Meng Xianzhang, *Zhongsu maoyishi ziliao,* 551–60.

15. *LSQNP,* 2:246.

16. Mastanduno, "Management," 244–45; Hughes and Luard, *Economic Development,* 156; O. Lee, "U.S. Trade Policy toward China," 42–46.

17. Kaufman, "Eisenhower's Foreign Economic Policy," 105.

18. Qing Simei, "Eisenhower Administration," 126.

19. Comments made by Zhou Enlai at the forty-fourth session of the Government Administration Council held on 4 August 1950, in *ZELNP* 1:62.

20. Meetings between Zhou Enlai and Bo Yibo, Ye Jizhuang, etc., held on 31 August 1950, ibid., 1:73.

21. "Duiwai maoyi guanli zanxing tiaoli" [Temporary regulations on foreign trade management], issued by the Government Administrative Council on 9 December 1950, in *ZRGJGD,* 15. The Ministry of Trade would be divided in 1952 to form the Ministry of Foreign Trade and the Ministry of Commerce. See "Guanyu chengli duiwai maoyi bu, shangye bu, chexiao maoyi bu de mingling" [Order establishing the Ministries of

Foreign Trade and Commerce and eliminating the Ministry of Trade], issued by the Government Administrative Council on 15 August 1952, in ZRGJGD, 33. For Zhou's 1950 discussion on establishing new customs procedures and Zhou's 1952 order (*mingling*) to place customs under the MFT, see ZELNP, 1:66, 274–75.

22. "Guanyu jinzhi guoying, gongying qiye ji jungong bumen zai shichang caigou jinkou wuzi de zhishi" [Directive of forbidding the purchase of imported goods in the marketplace by state-owned and publicly owned enterprises as well as military industrial departments], issued by the Central Finance and Economy Commission, 22 December 1950, in ZRGJGD, 15.

23. Y. Wu, *Economic Survey,* 458–59. American government and business properties were seized and American public and private financial accounts were frozen in December 1950. See "Guanyu guanzhi Meiguo zai Hua caichan, dongjie Meiguo zai Hua cunkuan de mingling" [Orders on putting controls on American property and freezing American deposits in China] issued by the Governmental Administrative Council on 28 December 1950, in ZRGJGD, 16; on 12 January 1951, Zhou Enlai exempted assets of American-subsidized schools, churches, and hospitals. See ZELNP, 1:116–7, 119. In 1952, Zhou Enlai approved the closure of foreign commercial banks and businesses. See Zhou Enlai's citation of a July 1952 directive from the Governmental Administrative Council on closure of foreign businesses, ibid., 278; "Guanyu dui waishang yinhang tingye qingli" [Clearing up the suspension of business of foreign banks], approved on 22 August 1952, in ZRGJGD, 33.

24. Hughes and Luard, *Economic Development,* 129.

25. ZELNP, 1:189; for the complete text, see *Current Background,* no. 134 (Hong Kong: U.S. Hong Kong Consulate General, 5 November 1951).

26. Zhou Enlai's cable to Li Fuchun et al. on 19 March 1950, in ZELNP, 1:29; Zhou Enlai's cable to the chairman of the Soviet Council of Ministers of 13 May 1950, ibid., 39.

27. Meng Xianzhang, *Zhongsu maoyishi ziliao,* 553. For problems related to the increased military expenditures in 1950–51, see ZELNP, 1:115–6; for information on the arming of sixty Chinese divisions, see Mao Zedong's cable to Stalin as drafted by Zhou Enlai issued on 28 March 1952, ibid., 228–29; on the 1 February 1951 loan, see Zhou Enlai's cable to Li Qiang on 31 January 1954, ibid., 349–50.

28. Zhou Enlai's remarks (*piyu*) appended to "Guanyu binggong wenti de jueding" [Decision on the munitions problem], signed on 21 May 1952, ibid., 239. The leadership estimated that it would take three to five years before China could be self-sufficient in military munitions and army weaponry. See "Guanyu binggong gongye jianshe wenti de baogao" [Report on constructing the munitions industry], submitted by Zhou Enlai on 26 July 1952 and later approved by the Central Committee, ibid., 251.

29. "Guanyu Sulian pai sheji xiaozu lai woguo yuanzhu wenti de baogao" [Report on the Soviet Union's sending a small design team to China for assistance], submitted by Wu Xiuquan, with a comment by Zhou Enlai issued on 26 July 1950, ibid. 59.

30. On 28 January 1953, Zhou Enlai sent a telegram to Li Fuchun and Ye Jizhuang concerning the formulation of five-year plans for both industrial production and armament industry construction. See ibid., 1, 282.

31. Lewis and Xue, *China Builds the Bomb;* idem, *China's Strategic Seapower.*

32. Harwit, *China's Automobile Industry,* 16–20.

33. Zhou Enlai's statement to the National Defense Industry Conference, delivered on 19 May 1952, in ZELNP, 1:238; also Zhou's statement to the 162nd meeting of the

Government Administration Council on 12 December 1952, ibid., 272–73. For Zhou's definition of constructing both the economy and culture, see his talk to the 146th meeting of the Government Administration Council on 25 July 1952, ibid., 250–51.

34. Mao Zedong, "Lun shida guanxi" [On the Ten Great Relationships], in *Xuanji,* 5: 271–72.

35. See Zhou Enlai's comment to a 23 November 1957 meeting of the State Council. At the time, the state had a shortfall in foreign exchange, and the leadership needed to prioritize its imports. See ZELNP, 2:100.

36. Citing a Chinese study, Lewis and Xue counter this view by arguing that "Mao's formula favoring civilian construction had been ignored." See Lewis and Xue, *China's Strategic Seapower,* 76–77. To resolve this problem, a detailed analysis of accurate Chinese military budget figures is necessary.

37. Directive drafted by Liu Shaoqi for the Central Committee on 30 March 1950, in *LSQNP,* 2:246. For other elites on the Soviet experience, see Zhou Enlai, "Report on the Proposals for the Second Five-Year Plan for Development of the National Economy," in *Eighth National Congress,* 1:281; Bachman, *Bureaucracy,* 176.

38. Discussion held between Mao Zedong, Zhou Enlai, and Gao Gang on 3 March 1950 and the cable sent to Li Fuchun et al. on 19 March 1950, in ZELNP, 1:26–27, 29. The leadership was especially concerned about full Soviet disclosure and again insisted upon complete information when formulating the FFYP. See ibid., 258. This might explain a 1960s comment by Mao Zedong that the Soviets always held something back.

39. Zhou Enlai Letter to Chen Yun, Bo Yibo, and various Central Bureaus dated 14 February 1952, ibid., 216. The exact distribution of military and economic projects is unclear. According to Zhou Enlai's revision of a cable to Xu Xiangqian dated 12 July 1951, China signed agreements with the Soviets for "the production of seven types of weapons and their associated armaments and the establishment of four new factories." See ibid., 157. "Guanyu Sulian zhengfu yuanzhu Zhongguo zhengfu fazhan Zhongguo guomin jingji de xieding" [Agreement of the Soviet Union's government to aid China's government in developing the Chinese national economy], signed on 15 May 1953, states that fifty projects were involved during the previous three years. See ibid., 297–98. According to Yahuda, the plants "turned out to be the rehabilitation of the Japanese heavy industry plants which the Russian armies had stripped from Manchuria in 1945." See Yahuda, *Towards the End of Isolationism,* 70.

40. Letter from Zhou Enlai to Chen Yun dated 4 June 1950, in ZELNP, 1:45. By 1952, there were 252 Soviet experts. See Zhou Enlai letter to Molotov dated 21 September 1952, ibid., 260.

41. Cable from Zhou Enlai to Wang Zhen and Saifuding dated 7 January 1951, ibid., 113–14. Zhou continued to emphasize domestic content during the formulation of the FFYP. See ibid., 259.

42. *LSQNP,* 2:273.

43. Zhou Enlai discussion of 4 February 1952 that resulted in "Guanyu 1952 nian xuanpai fusu liuxuesheng gongzuo de baogao" [Report on sending Chinese students to the Soviet Union for study in 1952), in ZELNP, 1:214; for a detailed listing of the occupations and requirements for the pre-1953 period, see Zhongguo Shehui Kexueyuan, ed., *Gongye juan,* 787–91.

44. Xin, *Mao Zedong's World View,* 19.

45. Liu Shaoqi's 28 July 1952 talk to Chinese students traveling to Moscow to study, in *LSQNP,* 2:301.

46. Ibid., 340.

47. In February 1950, Mao and Zhou agreed to the Soviet request to provide tungsten, antimony, and tin; they rejected the Soviet request for lead. During the subsequent negotiations of the Sino-Russian trade agreement, Zhou Enlai complained that some of the prices of export goods were set at too low a level, while prices for Soviet imports were sometimes too high. He warned that China in the future needed to avoid similar problems. See Zhou Enlai and Mao Zedong's joint cable sent on 2 February 1950, and Zhou Enlai's cable to Li Fuchun, et al., sent on 9 April 1950, in ZELNP, 1:23, 31.

48. Ibid., 259; "Pizhuan Hainandao wenti zuotanhui jiyao" [The approval and transmittal of the Summary of the Conference on the Hainan Island Problem], State Council document 80.202, issued on 24 July 1980, trans. in Reardon, "China's Coastal Development Strategy, 1979–1982, I," 67–82; N. Khrushchev, Khrushchev Remembers, 465.

49. "Baogao liangnianlai Sulian bangzhu gaijian gongchang de sheji qingkuang" [Report on the planning status of the factories that the Soviet Union has helped to rebuild during the past two years], submitted to the Central Committee by the Central Finance and Economy Commission on 9 February 1952, in ZRGJGD, 29; ZRGJD, 64–65.

50. Zhu Jiamu, "Chen Yun yu Zhongguo gongyehua de qibu," in Chen Yun, 1:287; Zhou Enlai, "Diyige wunian de jiben renwu" [The basic task for the FFYP], a political report presented on 29 September 1953 to the Second National Organization Work Conference, in ZELJJWX, 158–59.

51. Li Fuchun, "Diyige wunian jihua de fangzhen he renwu" [Direction and mission of the FFYP], presented to the second session of the First NPC on 5 July 1955, in Li Fuchun, Li Fuchun xuanji, 133–48. For a more general description of the model, see Bachman, Bureaucracy, 98–99.

52. Yeh, "Soviet and Communist Chinese Industrialization Strategies," 328–40.

53. Yahuda, Towards the End of Isolationism, 69–70.

54. ZELNP, 1:130–31.

55. Ibid., 257–58.

56. RZJSH, 1:288; the cable drafted by Zhou Enlai on behalf of the Central Committee on 14 February 1953 and Zhou's views expressed on 17 and 23 February 1953, in ZELNP, 1:284–85; also see Zhou's comments to Song Shaowen on 8 April 1953, ibid., 293.

57. Rawski, "Choice," 194–95.

58. Li Fuchun and Mikoyan signed eight agreements in Moscow, including "Guanyu Suweiai Shehuizhuyi Gongheguo Lianmeng Zhengfu yuanzhu Zhonghua Renmin Gongheguo Zhongyang Renmin Zhengfu fazhan Zhongguo guomin jingji de xieding" [Agreement with the USSR to help the central people's government of the PRC develop the Chinese national economy], cited in ZRGJGD, 41; also see ZELNP, 1:297–98.

59. RZJSH, 1:540.

60. Mao Zedong, "Telegram to the USSR," issued 15 September 1953, in Writings, 1:394–96.

61. ZELNP, 1:416.

62. RZJSH, 1:296–79. In the original 1957 report written by Li Fuchun, "Guanyu xiugai zai diyi wunian jihua qijian qianding de Sulian yuanzhu wuoguo jianshe xiangmu liangguo xieding de baogao" [Report on revisions of the signed bilateral agreements of the Soviet Union's help to China's construction projects during the First Five-Year Plan], Li states that the Soviets originally agreed to participate in 255 projects during the FFYP. However, "due to various reasons" the number was reduced to 181 military and economic construction projects. See ZELNP, 2:73.

63. *RZJSH*, 1:297. The Chinese also concluded 116 import agreements with the six. See Long Chucai, *Liyong waizi gailun,* 222–26.

64. Cable to Ambassador Ceng Yongquan from Zhou Enlai, 16 January 1955, in *ZELNP*, 1:441–24; also see Zhou Enlai's 10 March 1957 statement to a visiting Czechoslovakian delegation, ibid., 2:25.

65. Long Chucai, *Liyong waizi gailun,* 222; *ZELNP*, 1:563, 2:205; also see *Renmin ribao,* 12 October 1954, 8 April 1956.

66. *RZJSH*, 1:297.

67. Lewis and Xue, *China's Strategic Seapower,* 76. Lewis and Xue also provide slightly different numbers for the number of military projects constructed during the FFYP.

68. *Ta Kung Pao,* 14 February 1960. At least three different agreements were negotiated concerning Soviet experts: on 15 May 1953, 7 April 1956, and again in 1957. See *ZELNP*, 2:71. For Chinese measures to accommodate the Russian experts, including the establishment of the Office on Foreign Experts, see ibid. 1:308. Riskin states that approximately eleven thousand Russians and fifteen hundred Eastern European technical specialists went to China during this period. Riskin, *China's Political Economy,* 74. For an interesting discussion of bilateral educational and technical exchanges, see Ray, "Chinese Perceptions," 48–51.

69. Naughton, "Pattern," 232.

70. *Ta Kung Pao,* 1 January 1958.

71. During the last two quarters of 1957, the Ministries of Commerce of the Soviet Union and China began direct exchange of daily consumer items; the exchange was conducted as barter trade. The Chinese also began negotiations with the Eastern European socialist countries in 1958 to expand the barter trade in consumer goods. See *Renmin ribao,* 7 March 1958.

72. Rawski argues that the FFYP was a "balanced-growth strategy of development . . . which was a genuine effort to create a program that, when extended into the 1960s, would endow China with an integrated industrial sector capable of sustaining growth and structural change." He describes the Soviet industrial projects as "the core of the plan." See Rawski, "Choice," 200.

73. *Ta Kung Pao,* 1 January 1958; Perkins, "Central Features," 133.

74. Rawski, "Choice," 202.

75. "Zhongguo zhengfu dui Sulian zhengfu beiwanglu he Sulian guojia jiwei guanyu Zhongguo wunian jihua renwu de yijianshu de huiwen" [Memorandum of the Chinese government to the government of the Soviet Union and the reply to views of the Soviet government's planning committee on China's Five-Year Plan], composed by Zhou Enlai and approved at the expanded meeting of the Party's Secretariat on 19 May 1953, in *ZELNP*, 1:301–2.

76. For an overall view, see Riskin, *China's Political Economy,* 74–77.

77. Naughton, "Pattern," 234.

78. See Chen Yun, "Speech by Chen Yun," in *Eighth National Congress,* 2:167–68.

79. The seventy-fifth meeting of the Government Administration Council held on 9 March 1951, cited in *ZELNP*, 1:138.

80. Y. Wu, *Economic Survey,* 459.

81. *WFSS*, 60.

82. Shang Pingshun and Yan Caijun, eds., *Zhongguo waihui tizhi gaige,* 61.

83. *ZRGJD*, 79; also see the initial discussion of manipulating foreign exchange rates that took place on 31 August 1950, in *ZELNP*, 1:73.

84. Riskin argues that although the Soviet aid was not extortion, the Soviets did impose a shorter repayment schedule on long-term loans than the World Bank did. See Riskin, *China's Political Economy,* 74–76.

85. For an extensive collection of documents concerning the problems of remittances and investment in China by overseas Chinese during the 1949–52 period, see Zhongguo Shehui Kexueyuan, ed., *Gongshangjuan,* 767–74; idem, *Jinrongjuan,* 799–844; for an overall analysis of foreign exchange during the 1950–52 period, see ibid., 896–904.

86. "Guanyu qiaohui wenti de baogao," issued by the Central Committee on 10 February 1955, in *ZRGJD,* 138. For more detailed estimates see Lin Jinzhi, ed., *Huaqiao huaren,* 267–73; Wu Chun Hsi, *Dollars Dependents,* 142. For a comprehensive discussion of remittances and the role of overseas Chinese in China's economic development, see Bolt, "China's Development and the Chinese Overseas."

87. Y. Wu, *Economic Survey,* 469; *ZRGJD,* 194.

88. "Guowuyuan guanyu guanche baohu qiaohui zhengce de mingling" [Order issued by the State Council concerning fully implementing the policy of conserving overseas Chinese remittances], signed by Zhou Enlai on 23 February 1955, in *ZELNP,* 1:453.

89. According to a 6 September 1952 letter from Zhou Enlai to Molotov, the Chinese initially estimated that the cost of Soviet imports under the FFYP would be 18.43 billion rubles (old). China would repay the Soviets by exporting 13.81 billion rubles of goods, providing 620 million rubles of foreign currency, and asking for a Soviet loan of 4 billion rubles; ibid., 258.

90. *Renmin ribao,* 12 October 1954; *RZJSH,* 1:300; *ZELNP,* 1:416.

91. Dangdai Zhongguo Congshu Bianjibu, *Dangdai Zhongguo waijiao,* 29; *Renmin ribao,* 7 April 1956; Riskin, *China's Political Economy,* 103; *RZJSH,* 1:300; Zhou Enlai's cable to Ambassador Liu Xiao for Vice-Minister of Foreign Trade Li Zheren, 9 February 1955, in *ZELNP,* 1:449. For additional information, see Gurley, *China's Economy,* 163–64; Riskin, *China's Political Economy,* 76.

92. Eckstein, *Communist China's Economic Growth,* 263–64.

93. For a similar approach, see Gourevitch, *Politics,* 911, and Hawes, *Philippine State,* 163.

94. For instance, see Liu Shaoqi, "The Political Report of the Central Committee of the Communist Party of China to the Eighth National Congress of the Party," in *Eighth National Congress,* 1:47–49; Zhu Jiamu, "Chen Yun yu Zhongguo gongyehua de qibu," 300–301; "Speech by Comrade Po I-po," in *Eighth National Congress,* 2:45–62; Mao Zedong, *Miscellany,* 77–84, as cited in Bachman, *Bureaucracy,* 84, n. 63. This does not imply that these elites were always in complete agreement on other issues of economic development. For instance, Bachman argues that Chen Yun and Li Xiannian differed with Li Fuchun and Bo Yibo over the roles of the plan and the marketplace. Bachman sees Zhou as a balancer of the planning and financial coalitions; this study interprets Zhou's actions as more assertive and very Machiavellian. See Bachman, *Bureaucracy,* chap. 4 and 5.

95. Teiwes argues that the Third Plenum "began an important shift of policy, although in key respects initially it was more rhetorical and philosophical than substantive." See Teiwes, *China's Road,* 71.

96. Mao marked his change of thinking at the time of the Ten Great Relationships speech. See MacFarquhar, *Origins,* 2:39.

97. *RZJSH,* 1:472. On 6 December 1955, Mao gave his "Talk on Opposing Right-Deviation and Conservatism," in which he stated that "we should not always compare ourselves with

the Soviet Union. After three five-year plans we shall be able to produce twenty-four million tons of steel. This is faster than the Soviet Union." Mao Zedong, *Writings,* 1:682.

98. Mao Zedong, "Summing-up Speech at Sixth Expanded Plenum of Seventh Central Committee," September 1955, in *Miscellany,* 17; for Mao's objections to projected growth targets, see Teiwes, *China's Road,* 21.

99. *RZJSH,* 1:522. Italicized section is from *LSQNP,* 2:347. Also see *ZELNP,* 1:524; MacFarquhar, *Origins,* 1:30–32; *RZJSH,* 1:466–76. The 5 and 6 December 1955 talks appear to be different talks on the same theme.

100. Tong Xiaopeng, *Fengyu sishinian,* 2:349–50.

101. Mao Zedong, "Talk Opposing Right-Deviation and Conservatism," presented on 6 December 1955, in *Miscellany,* 28; for an alternate translation, see *Writings,* 1:679–84. *Miscellany* uses an alternate translation—"bold advance—for *maojin.* This does not incorporate the "risky" connotations of the term (i.e., *mao* comes from *maoxian,* 'to take a risk or a chance'). This study adopts the translation used by Teiwes and Sun. See Teiwes, *China's Road,* xi.

102. Zhou Enlai, "Guanyu muqian xingshi de baogao" [Report on current conditions], presented on 29 December 1955 to the National Conference of Factory and Mining Managers, in *ZELNP,* 1:531–52; *RZJSH,* 1:527–28.

103. *RZJSH,* 1:526.

104. Ibid., 544.

105. Zhou Enlai's discussion with Chen Yun at the twenty-first full session of the State Council on 21 December 1955, in *ZELNP,* 1:529; *RZJSH,* 1:526. For a contrasting interpretation, see Teiwes, *China's Road,* 22–23, 23, n. 10.

106. Zhou Enlai, "Guanyu muqian xingshi de baogao" [Report on current conditions], presented on 29 December 1955 to the National Conference of Factory and Mining Managers, in *ZELNP,* 1:532.

107. During his discussion with Chen Yun at the thirtieth full session of the State Council on 12 June 1956, Zhou Enlai stated the following:

> Since last December, rash advance has cropped up. Thus, the situation of today is different from last December's. No longer can we just try to prevent rash advance, but must oppose it! If rash advance continues, we will lose contact with reality, the masses, and our current needs and possibilities. We don't want to throw cold water on the masses, but we also cannot let the demands of a minority of activists become the needs of the masses.

See *ZELNP,* 1:587. Also see MacFarquhar, *Origins,* 1:86–91; Teiwes, *China's Road,* 25–32.

108. Zhou Enlai's letter to Mao Zedong, 26 May 1958, in *ZELNP,* 2:145, 147.

109. For a much more detailed account of the socialist "high tide" period, see MacFarquhar, *Origins,* 1:15–32; Bachman, *Chen Yun,* 59–65; idem, *Bureaucracy;* Lardy, "Economic Recovery," 180–84; Riskin, *China's Political Economy,* 81–100; Lin, Fan, and Zhang, *Kaige xingjin de shiqi,* 611–67; Teiwes, *China's Road,* chaps. 1 and 2.

110. They included (1) Mao Zedong's "Yijiuwuliunian dao 1967 nian quanguo nongye fazhan gangyao" [Outline of national agricultural development from 1956 to 1967]; see *ZELNP,* 1:537; MacFarquhar, *Origins,* 1:27–9; (2) the Twelve-Year Long-term Plan for Scientific and Technical Development; see *RZJSH,* 1:509–17; and (3) the State Planning Commission's "Zhonghua Renmin Gongheguo fazhan guomin jingji de shiwunian yuanjing jihua gangyao (caoan)" [Outline of the Fifteen-Year Long-Range Plan for Developing

the PRC's National Economy (draft)]; see ZELNP, 1:550. For a more detailed account of this plan, see, RZJSH, 1:523–25.

111. ZELNP, 1:534–35, 552–53.

112. Ibid., 576. Originally, Zhou had directed Li Fuchun to put forward 197 projects. See Zhou Enlai's cable to Mao Zedong, 2 January 1956, and his discussions with Li Fuchun January 3–4, 1956, in ZELNP, 1:534–35. For Zhou's position on industrial and scientific parity, see Zhou Enlai's "Guanyu zhishi fenzi wenti de baogao" [Report on the problem concerning intellectuals], fourth section, presented to the Central Committee's Conference on Intellectuals on 14 January 1956, in ZELJJWX, 235.

113. Zhu De's discussion with Li Qiang on 5 February 1956, in Zhu De riji, as quoted in Wang Xiangli, "Zhu De," 48, n. 6.; ZDNP, 398–99.

114. Zhu De, "Waichu shicha de baogao" [Report on my investigations around the country], submitted on 18 April 1957 to the Central Committee, in Zhu De, Zhu De xuanji, 351. For a general description of the trips, see ZDZ, 671–74.

115. ZDZ, 52–53.

116. Ibid., 669–70; see also Zhu De, "Zai quanguo caizheng huiyishang de jianghua," 32; Li Hongcai, "Zhu De," 31–32.

117. ZELNP, 1:544: also see Xiong Huayuan, "Lun Zhou Enlai zai fan maojin zhong de tansuo," 10–11.

118. ZELNP, 1:543.

119. Mao Zedong, "Talk on Opposing Right-Deviation and Conservatism," presented on 6 December 1955, in Writings, 1:682–83; also in Miscellany, 29; for a slightly different translation, see Writings, 1:681.

120. Li Zhisui, Private Life, 578; Teiwes, China's Road, 48. In his Preface to Li Zhisui's biography, Andrew Nathan points out that Li Zhisui's views of the internal political dynamics were heavily influenced by Li's patron, Wang Dongxing (Li Zhisui, Private Life, viii). Wang apparently felt that "Zhou Enlai was a coward." This was perhaps the result of Zhou's succumbing to Jiang Qing and Kang Sheng's opposition to elevating Wang Dongxing to the Political Bureau before the Ninth Party Congress. According to Li Zhisui, Wang stated, "He did precisely what Jiang Qing and Kang Sheng asked him to do . . . . The man has no sense of personal loyalty" (Li Zhisui, Private Life, 511–12).

121. RZJSH, 1:531.

122. Zhou Enlai, "Jingji gongzuo yao shishi qiushi" [Economic work must seek truth from facts], comments to the twenty-fourth meeting of the State Council on 8 February 1956, in ZELJJWX, 251–52. For a fairly comprehensive account of Zhou's opposition to rash advance during early to mid-1956, see RZJSH, 1: chap. 21; for Mao's point of view, see Mao Zedong, "Talks at the Nan-ning Conference," presented on 13 January 1958, in Miscellany, 80. For an alternate interpretation, see Teiwes, China's Road, 24.

123. For a detailed description of this marathon reporting session, see RZJSH, 1: chap. 19; Mao Zedong, "Dui zhongyang suoni gedi jingji gongzuo huibao tigang de piyu he xiugai" [Approval and revision of the economic work report outline drafted by the Central Committee], in Jianguo, 6:54–56; LSQNP, 2:358–63. Also see Lardy, "Economic Recovery," 180–81.

124. MacFarquhar, Origins, 1:332, n. 4.

125. RZJSH, 1:472.

126. ZELNP, 1:548.

127. Ibid., 554.

128. This can explain Chen Yun's cryptic comments to the Eighth Party Congress, where he was supporting Zhou's idea to expand trade with the West. See Bachman, *Bureaucracy,* 67.

129. Zhou Enlai, "Xiang yiqie guojia de changchu xuexi" [Study the strong points of every country], presented on 3 May 1956, in ZELJJWX, 256; also see Zhou's cable to Mao Zedong and the Central Committee on 24 January 1957, in which he summarizes his visit to the Soviet Union and counsels patience in maintaining the relationship, in ZELNP, 2:15. For the Chinese Political Bureau's decision to label Khrushchev's speech a "mistake," see ibid., 1:551.

130. ZDNP, 402.

131. Mao Zedong, "Zuo geming de zujinpai" [Be activists in promoting the revolution], delivered to the Third (enlarged) Plenum of the Eighth Party Congress on 9 October 1957, in *Xuanji,* 5:473–74.

132. Zhou Enlai's discussion with Kádár on 4 October 1957, in ZELNP, 2:83.

133. Ibid., 1:563.

134. Zhu De, "Fayan tigang" [Speech outline], 27 April 1956, as quoted by Wang Xiangli, "Zhu De," 48, n.4.

135. ZELNP, 1: 574–75.

136. Ibid., 574, 578, 579, 598.

137. Bachman, *Bureaucracy,* 67, n.15. Zhang's outspoken views as head of the China Democratic League eventually led to his downfall during the Anti-Rightist Campaign of 1957. See Goldman, "The Party and the Intellectuals," 251, 254; MacFarquhar, *Origins,* 1:275–78.

138. RZJSH, 1:544.

139. Zhou Enlai's comments to the State Council's Standing Committee meeting on 11 October 1956, in ZELNP, 1:626.

140. For an interesting Chinese discussion of Mao's desire to study foreign countries, see Zhang Wenru, *Mao Zedong,* 236–40. Zhang attempts to show that Deng Xiaoping's "opening" policy is following Mao's views; unfortunately, Zhang can only quote the Ten Great Relationships as evidence of Mao's openness to the outside world: he totally ignores Mao's views during the 1960s.

141. Mao made a similar comment in 1920, when he argued that

comrades should be scattered all over the world to conduct investigations. Some of us should go to every corner of the globe; we should not all be in one place. The best way is to have one or several comrades open up a certain area. We should open up all "fronts." We should send people to act as our vanguard in all directions.

See Xin, *Mao Zedong's World View,* 18–19.

142. See Teiwes, "Establishment and Consolidation," 127.

143. RZJSH, 1:484. The exact dating of Mao's comment is problematic. Bo states that Mao made it during the heavy industry reporting sessions, which apparently took place 14–27 February. See ZELNP, 1:548. Thus, it is unclear whether Mao or Zhou initiated the suggestion to study capitalist countries at this juncture. In January 1957, Mao Zedong stated,

We still should learn from the Soviet Union. We can learn a lot of things from them. But we should learn selectively. We should learn progressive and useful things and should study their blunders critically. In three five-year plans we should be able to learn their basic things. We should also learn from other countries than the Soviet Union. Chou's slogans abroad are to seek peace, friendship, and knowledge. Knowledge should be sought everywhere. It is too monotonous to seek it only in one place.

See Mao Zedong, "Summary of Conference of Provincial and Municipal Committee Secretaries," in *Miscellany,* 57.

144. Mao Zedong, "Speech to a Symposium of Delegates to the First Meeting of the Second National Committee of the ACFIC (All-China Federation of Industry and Commerce), in *Writings,* 2:204; Mao Zedong, "Zili gengsheng weizhu, zhengqu waiyuan weibu" [Rely mainly on one's own efforts, while striving to make external assistance supplementary], delivered on 17 June 1958, in *MZDWW,* 318.

145. Yahuda, *Towards the End of Isolationism,* 65. Liu Xiangdong quotes Mao as stating in September 1956 that even when China became a fully industrialized socialist country, it could never afford to close its door to the global economic, technological, or cultural spheres. See Liu Xiangdong, "Jicheng Mao Zedong," 28.

146. Mao Zedong, "Reading Notes on the Soviet Union's 'Political Economics,'" in *Miscellany,* 296. Yahuda argues that China did not join COMECON (Council for Mutual Economic Assistance) because of the Soviets' emphasis on comparative advantage. See Yahuda, *Towards the End of Isolationism,* 69; E. Friedman, "Maoist Conceptualizations," 197–205.

147. Mao Zedong, "Speech at the Conference of Heads of Delegations to the Second Session of the Eighth Party Congress," delivered on 18 May 1958, in *Miscellany,* 120; Yahuda, *Towards the End of Isolationism,* 49–52. For Mao's views on the teacher-student metaphor, see Mao Zedong, "Speeches at the Second Session of the Eighth Party Congress," 17 May 1958, in *Miscellany,* 101.

148. Eckstein, *China's Economic Revolution,* 58. For more analysis on the GLF's distinct nature, see Meisner, *Mao's China,* 223–25. Also see Mao Zedong, "On the Correct Handling of Contradictions among the People," delivered on 27 February 1957, in *Secret Speeches,* 185–89.

149. *RZJSH,* 1:485–90. Kau and Leung do not mention the first version, which was more critical of the Stalinist model. Mao Zedong, *Writings,* 2:43–45.

150. Teiwes, "Establishment and Consolidation," 125–29. Also see Mao Zedong, "Lun shida guanxi," in *Xuanji,* 267–77; MacFarquhar, *Origins,* 1: chap. 5.

151. Teiwes, *China's Road,* 54–66.

152. Mao Zedong, *Writings,* 2:185.

153. Mao Zedong, "Instructions at a Discussion Meeting Attended by some of the Delegates to the Second Session of the First Committee of the All-China Federation of Industry and Commerce," delivered on 8 December 1956, in *Miscellany,* 40.

154. *RZJSH,* 1:492.

155. Mao Zedong, *Writings,* 2:186.

156. Mao Zedong, "Zuo geming de zujinpai" [Be activists in promoting the revolution], in *Mao Zedong xuanji,* 5:473.

157. Mao Zedong, "Yi zili gengsheng weizhu tongshi bu fangsong zhengqu waiyuan" [While primarily following the policy of self-reliance, we cannot be lax in searching for foreign aid], October 1938, in *MZDWW,* 16; also see Mao Zedong, "Kangzhan yu waiyuan de guanxi" [The relationship between the anti-Japanese war and foreign aid), 20 January

1939, ibid., 18–20; Yang Ruiguang, "Zongguan Mao Zedong de duiwai jingji jiaowang sixiang," 73–74.

158. "Report to the Second Plenary Session of the Seventh Central Committee of the Communist Party of China," translated in Mao Zedong, *Selected Writings,* 4:379.

159. Mao Zedong, "On Coalition Government," in *Mao Zedong xuanji* (N.p.: Northeast Publishing House, 1948), 336, as reprinted in U.S., Department of State, Bureau of Intelligence and Research, *Chinese Communist World Outlook,* 45. For cogent discussion on the pre-1949 attitudes toward self-reliance and foreign trade, see Yahuda, *Towards the End of Isolationism,* 53–59.

160. Mao Zedong, *Selected Works,* 4:299, 3:252–54. Yahuda points out that Mao's admiration for England and the United States was also eliminated. See Yahuda, *Towards the End of Isolationism,* 54.

161. Mao Zedong, "On Correctly Handling Contradictions among the People," in *Writings,* 2:340.

162. Li Xiannian, "Jinyibu zuohao waimao gongzuo" [Further improve foreign trade work], in *Li Xiannian,* 1:308.

163. For instance, see Teiwes's discussion of Chen Yun's January 1957 speech, in Teiwes, *China's Road,* 63–64.

164. Yang Ruiguang, "Zhongguan Mao Zedong de duiwai jingji jiaowang sixiang," 78.

165. Mao Zedong, "Talk on the Third Five-Year Plan," presented on 6 June 1964, in *Miscellany,* 355.

166. Mao Zedong, "Speech at the Sixth Plenum of the Eighth Central Committee," presented on 19 December 1958, in *Miscellany,* 143–44.

167. Mao Zedong, "Interjections at Conference of Provincial and Municipal Committee Secretaries (Collected)," January 1957, in *Miscellany,* 51.

168. Mao Zedong, "Reading Notes on the Soviet Union's 'Political Economics,'" in *Miscellany,* 287.

169. Ibid., 287–88 (italics added).

170. Ibid., 296.

171. Li Xiannian, "Jinyibu," in *Li Xiannian,* 1:308; Wang Xiangli, "Zhu De," 44–46.

172. Wang Xiangli, "Zhu De," 44.

173. For more information on the reaffirmation of Zhou's economic approach, see MacFarquhar, *Origins,* 1: chap. 10; Lardy, "Economic Recovery," 180–84. While admitting that the congress "was less of a personal triumph," Teiwes still maintains a Mao-in-command interpretation. See Teiwes, "Establishment and Consolidation," 129–33.

174. See ZELJJW, 278–328; for the official English translation, see *Eighth National Congress,* 1:261–328. Mao not only approved Zhou's report, but sent a letter to Zhou requesting a reduction in projected grain and cotton production targets for 1962. Faced with the elites' decision not to pursue rash advance, Mao realized that for now, he had to cooperate. For more on the effect of Mao's revisions, see ZELNP, 1:615–16; for an interesting defense of the Mao-in-command interpretation, see Teiwes, *China's Road,* 33–48.

175. Zhou Enlai, "Diyige wunian de jiben renwu," in ZELJJWX, 158–59.

176. *Eighth National Congress,* 1:288, 289.

177. Ibid., 282.

178. Bachman, *Bureaucracy,* 72.

179. Mao Zedong, *Secret Speeches,* 482, esp. n.7; for Mao's changing views on *ti-yong* (Chinese learning for substance [*ti*] and Western learning for practical application [*yong*]), see Yahuda, *Towards the End of Isolationism,* 78–79.

180. This passage is omitted in the 1969 translation of *Selected Works*. See 4:369.

181. Deng Xiaoping argued that Mao had always been for developing foreign economic relations, but was stymied by the Gang of Four. Deng would obviously want to state that the opening had Mao's backing. See Liu Xiangdong, "Jicheng," 29.

182. van Eekelen, *Indian Foreign Policy*, 38–63.

183. *RZJSH*, 1:485.

184. Ibid., 2:575–79.

185. MacFarquhar, *Origins*, 1:175–76; *ZELNP*, 1:639–51, 2:1–18. The trip included official visits to North Vietnam, Cambodia, India, Pakistan, Nepal, Afghanistan, India, the Soviet Union, Poland, Hungary, and Ceylon.

186. E. Friedman, "Maoist Conceptualizations," 193–95.

187. Zhang Zhi'an, "Lüelun Chen Yun duiwai kaifang de jingji sixiang," 526–27.

188. "The Barter Trade Control Regulations of 14 March 1951," as cited in Y. Wu, *Economic Survey*, 459; also see 463–64. For an overall view of China's response, see Dong Zhikai, "Wushi niandai fan 'fengsuo, jinyun' de douzheng ji qi qishi," 85–87.

189. Hughes and Luard, *Economic Development*, 133; Epstein, 192, 196–200. Also see Zhou Enlai's discussion with the Indian ambassador on 14 June 1956, in *ZELNP*, 1:588–89; Tsang, *Hong Kong*, 72–80.

190. Hughes and Luard, *Economic Development*, 130.

191. Ibid.

192. Ibid., 133.

193. Tucker, "House Divided," 35–62.

194. C. Lee, *Japan Faces China*, 137; *ZELNP*, 1:240.

195. White House cabinet meeting minutes, 6 August 1954, as cited in Qing Simei, "Eisenhower Administration," 140, n.16.

196. Trade with Japan dropped precipitously in 1958, in part because of the Great Leap Forward, but also because of Chinese displeasure concerning a 2 May 1958 incident in which a PRC flag was torn down from a Nagasaki department store exhibit on Chinese stamps. Trade relations recovered in the 1960s, and trade was even relatively strong during the Cultural Revolution. For an interesting analysis of Sino-Japanese trade relations, see C. Lee, *Japan Faces China*, chap. 4.

197. Foot, "Search," 143–63; Mastanduno, "Management," 245; *ZELNP*, 2: 59; O. Lee, "U.S. Trade Policy toward China," 46–49.

198. Zhou Enlai's report to a Conference of Leading Party Cadres from Yunnan on 6 February 1957, in *ZELNP*, 2:19. This apparent improvement in Sino-U.S. relations led Zhou to direct Chongqing cadre in February 1957 to preserve local sites where the United States gave support to China during World War II. See *ZELNP*, 2:20.

199. Qing Simei, "Eisenhower Administration," 131–36; Hughes and Luard, *Economic Development*, 136.

200. NSC 5429/5, paragraph 4.d, as cited in U.S., Department of State, *Foreign Relations of the United States, 1955–1957, vol. 3: China*, 668.

201. Eckstein, *Communist*, 273; O. Lee, "U.S. Trade Policy toward China," 49–51.

202. See discussion concerning "Guanyu Xianggang gedanwei maoyi jigou tongyi fangan" [Plan to unify the Hong Kong trade organizations], proposed by the Ministry of Trade and approved by the Central Committee on 31 August 1950, in *ZELNP*, 1:72–73.

203. "Guanyu Meidi caozong lianheguo dahui feitongguo dui women shixing jinyun'an hou dui gexiang gongzuo de zhishi" [Directive on various tasks following the American imperialists manipulating the UN General Assembly's illegally adopting the embargo

action against China], issued by the Central Finance and Economy Commission on 28 June 1951, in ZRGJD, 50.

204. Szczepanik, *Economic Growth,* 45–57.

205. A November 1949 meeting between Zhou Enlai and Xu Guomao, the general director of Hong Kong's Jincheng Bank, in ZELNP, 1:15.

206. Szczepanik, *Economic Growth,* 154.

207. Zhou Enlai, "Guanyu Xianggang wenti" [Concerning the Hong Kong problem], delivered on 28 April 1957 to a Conference of Shanghai People Involved in Industry and Commerce, in ZELJJWX, 352–54.

208. Szczepanik, *Economic Growth,* 26–31, 91–105.

209. For instance, see "Guanyu nongcun juxing shehui zhuyi dabianlun zhong qiaoqu yingdang zhuyi de jixiang wenti de baogao" [Report on several problems that must be addressed in carrying out socialist mass debates in the agricultural areas inhabited by overseas Chinese], discussed by the State Council on 7 September 1957, in ZELNP, 2:75. Zhou supported the report submitted by the Party Office on Overseas Chinese Affairs that attempted to reduce the more violent aspects of the Anti-Rightist Campaign.

210. For instance, see ZELNP, 2:96, 111–12.

211. For an analytical argument on the effect of foreign direct investment (FDI) on China's development, see Hou, *Foreign Investment,* 154–64.

212. Third meeting between Zhou and Polish authorities held on 12 January 1957, in ZELNP, 2:9.

213. Wang Xiangli, "Zhu De," 46; Zhu De, "Zengjia chukou chanpin, fazhan Hainan jingji," 34–35.

214. ZELNP, 2:31.

215. Zhou Enlai, "Zai shehui zhuyi jianshe zhong, huo yidianr you haochu" [There are benefits to being more flexible while carrying out socialist construction], speech to the forty-fourth meeting of the full meeting of the State Council on 6 April 1957, in ZELJJWX, 350–51; ZELNP, 2:31. Also see Zhou's comments made at the forty-sixth meeting of the State Council on 12 April 1957, in ZELNP, 2:33.

216. "Huaqiao touzi xingban xuexiao banfa" [Procedures for overseas Chinese to invest in establishing schools] and "Huaqiao touzi yu guoying huaqiao touzi gongsi de youdai banfa" [Preferential measures for overseas Chinese investment in state-owned overseas Chinese investment enterprises], submitted by the State Council and approved by the Eighth Meeting of the NPC Standing Committee on 1 August 1957, in ZRGJD, 194.

217. Lin Jinzhi, ed., *Huaqiao huaren,* 478–84. By 1956, twenty-one OCIEs had been established in Guangdong, producing 130 different types of goods worth RMB 71 million between 1955 and 1956; fourteen OCIEs were established in Fujian, producing RMB 44 million worth of goods between 1955 and 1956. See Liu Hua, "Jianguo chuqi qiaowu gongzuo shuping," 19.

218. Lin Jinzhi, *Huaqiao huaren,* 484.

219. ZRGJD, 463–64, 495.

220. Zhongguo Duiwai Maoyi, *Zhongguo duiwai maoyi gailun,* 127.

221. Guangdong Nianjian Bianji, *Guangdong,* 225.

222. Zhu De, "Waichu shicha de baogao," in *Zhu De xuanji,* 350.

223. Discussion with Luo Fanqun and others on 8 February 1957, in *Zhu De riji* [Zhu De's diary], as cited in Wang Xiangli, "Zhu De," 45.

224. WFSS, 43; Zhongguo Duiwai Maoyi, *Zhongguo duiwai maoyi gailun,* 143.

225. WFSS, 43.

226. Gongheguo Lingxiu Dacidian Bianweihui, ed., *Gongheguo lingxiu dacidian—Zhu De*.

227. Comments made by Zhou Enlai in a State Council Standing Committee meeting of 8 June 1956 while discussing "Yijiuwuliunian duiwai maoyi jihua zhong zhuyao qingkuang ji wenti de baogao." [Report on the main conditions and problems of the 1956 foreign trade plan], in ZELNP, 1:586.

228. Eckstein, *Communist China's Economic Growth*, 188.

229. Teiwes recounts Mao's criticisms of the Hangzhou meeting of January 1958, during which when Mao

> set fire (*fang huo*) to Enlai, I had Old Ke [Qingshi] to back me up. In Hangzhou I really couldn't hold it back any longer [and] let off several years of anger at Bo Yibo [saying] I won't listen to your stuff, what are you talking about? I haven't read the budgets for the past few years, it's just been you pressing me to sign my name to them.

See Teiwes, *China's Road*, 73. During his 13 January 1958 talk at Nanning, Mao stated that

> like the United Nations of Dulles the Political Bureau has become a voting machine. You give it a perfect document and it has to be passed. Like the opera, you have to go on stage and perform since the show has been announced. The document itself does not go into textual research and essence, and it also has foreign words. I do have a method, and that is passive resistance. I will not read it. For two years I have not read your documents and I do not expect to read them this year either.

See Mao Zedong, "Talks at the Nan-ning Conference," 13 January 1958, in *Miscellany*, 80; for not reading NPC reports see "Talks at the Nan-ning Conference," 11 January 1958, in *Miscellany*, 77.

230. Lewis and Xue, *China's Strategic Seapower*, 11–12; idem, *China Builds the Bomb*, 62–63.

231. Dangdai Zhongguo Congshu, *Dangdai Zhongguo waijiao*, 30–32, 111–16.

232. Mao Zedong, "Speech at the Tenth Plenum of the Eighth Central Committee," 24 September 1962, in *Chairman Mao*, 190; Zhang Wenru, *Mao Zedong*, 234; Lewis and Xue, *China's Strategic Seapower*, 14–18.

233. Ellison, ed., *Sino-Soviet Conflict*, 113; Eckstein, *Communist China's Economic Growth*, 140.

234. RZJSH, 2:1138–44.

235. Pang Xianzhi, "Chongwen Mao Zedong guanyu fangzhi heping yanbian de jiaodao," 12; Li Jie, "Dui Mao Zedong fangzhi heping yanbian sixiang de huigu he sikao," 39–45. Li Jie argues that after pointing out the dangers of "peaceful evolution" in 1959, Mao reemphasized its threat in 1962, and it became a core idea in his fight against the revisionists within the Party.

236. RZJSH, 2:1144.

237. Dangdai Zhongguo Congshu, *Dangdai Zhongguo waijiao*, 31. For an interesting Soviet account of this period, see Klochko, *Soviet Scientist*.

238. For the speech outline, see Mao Zedong, *Jianguo*, 8:121. Also see Dangdai Zhongguo Congshu, *Dangdai Zhongguo waijiao*, 106; Mao Zedong, "Du Sidalin 'Sulian shehui zhuyi jingji wenti' pizhu" [Commentary and annotations on Stalin's *Economic*

Problems of Socialism in the USSR] in *Jianguo,* 7:667–76. For an interesting discussion of the influence of Stalin's *Economic Problems,* see Fewsmith, *Dilemmas of Reform,* 64. For a complete listing of Mao's comments on the need to change the Soviet model, see *RZJSH,* 1:470–1.

239. Goldman, "The Party and the Intellectuals," 14:257; MacFarquhar, *Origins,* 1:297–98.

240. Yahuda, *Towards the End of Isolationism,* 77.

241. Lieberthal, "The Great Leap Forward," 14:299–305.

242. Riskin, *China's Political Economy,* 114–31; Eckstein, *China's Economic Revolution,* 54–59.

243. Mao Zedong, "Yijiuwuqinian xiaji de xingshi" [The situation as of summer 1957] in *ZELNP,* 2:62.

244. "Comrade Khrushchev told us that the Soviet Union could exceed Great Britain's [steel production] within fifteen years. I can also state that China possibly will meet and exceed Great Britain. I have spoken twice with Comrades Bolite [Harry Pollit] and Gao Lan [John Gollan], and asked them about the conditions of their country. They stated that currently Great Britain produces 20 million tons of steel annually, which might rise to 30 million within 15 years. As for China, after fifteen years we possibly will produce 40 million tons. Wouldn't that surpass Great Britain?" See *RZJSH,* 2:691–92; Mao Zedong, *Writings,* 2:787. For more information on the British Communist Party, see Thompson, *Good Old Cause.*

245. *RZJSH,* 2:699.

246. Mao apparently made this decision around 16 August 1958 before an expanded meeting of the Political Bureau at Beidaihe. See ibid., 702.

247. Mao Zedong speech to the 18 February 1958 expanded meeting of the Political Bureau. See ibid., 653. For Teiwes's interpretation, see Teiwes, *China's Road,* 76–82.

248. Lieberthal, "Great Leap Forward," 307; also see MacFarquhar, *Origins,* 2:51–54. For Deng's views on the usefulness of the mass line in political and economic work, see Teng Hsiao-ping, "Report on the Revision of the Constitution of the Communist Party of China," in *Eighth National Congress,* 1:175–87.

249. In his speech "On the Cooperatization of Agriculture," delivered on 31 July 1955, Mao stated that "some comrades disapprove of the Party Center's policy of keeping the steps taken toward our country's agricultural cooperativization at pace with those taken toward the country's socialist industrialization, even though this policy has been proven to be a correct one in the Soviet Union." See Mao Zedong, *Writings,* 1:600–602, especially 601, n. 23. Mao publicly criticized Deng's "right deviation and empiricism" in "The Debate over Agricultural Cooperativization and the Present Class Struggle," delivered on 11 October 1955 at the Sixth Plenum of the Seventh Party Congress. See ibid., 640–42.

250. MacFarquhar, *Origins,* 1:19.

251. *ZELNP,* 1:316–17.

252. MacFarquhar, *Origins,* 2:58.

253. Ibid., 59:63.

254. Tong Xiaopeng, *Fengyu sishinian,* 2:356; Teiwes, *China's Road,* 245, 246, 250–51. For an interesting explanation of Li Fuchun's exemption from Mao's wrath, see Teiwes, *China's Road,* 49–51.

255. MacFarquhar, *Origins,* 1:19; *RZJSH,* 1: chap. 15. David Bachman argues that the GLF was originally championed by Li Fuchun, Bo Yibo, and others representing plan-

ning and heavy industrial sectors and was opposed by Chen Yun, Li Xiannian, and Deng Zihui and others in the financial, agricultural, commercial, and light industrial sectors. See Bachman, *Bureaucracy,* chaps. 4 and 5. Bo Yibo's, Tong Xiaopeng's and MacFarquhar's accounts suggest that while many within the elite initially "opposed rash advance," these elites—specifically Chen Yun, Li Xiannian, and Bo Yibo—underwent self-criticism at the 18 February 1958 Political Bureau meeting to avoid the fate of Deng Zihui.

256. Bo Yibo, "Respect and Remembrance—Marking the Sixtieth Anniversary of the Founding of the CCP," in FBIS, *China,* 29 July 1981, K33, as cited in Bachman, *Chen Yun,* 69; ZELNP, 2:120.

257. Chen Yun, "Shehui zhuyi gaizao jiben wancheng, yihou de xin wenti" [New problems following the basic completion of socialist transformation], *Chen Yun wenxuan, 1956–1985,* 1–27. For an interesting discussion of this period, see Lardy and Lieberthal, *Chen Yun's Strategy,* xiv–xxi, and Bachman, *Chen Yun,* 62–68.

258. Bachman, *Chen Yun,* 65–70; Teiwes, *Politics,* 268–71. For Chen Yun's influential role in economic policy formulation, see Teiwes, *China's Road,* 49. Teiwes argues that Mao "regarded Chen Yun [as] the principal culprit"; see *China's Road,* 73–74.

259. MacFarquhar, *Origins,* 2:60–61.

260. Tong Xiaopeng, *Fengyu sishinian,* 2:357–58.

261. On 25 August 1958, Chen Yun spoke at the Conference for Industrial Sector Party Secretaries that was presided over by Mao. According to Bo,

> Seeing that solely relying on "foreign steel mills" will not achieve the steel quotas for the next two years, Comrade Chen Yun suggested in his speech that they must rely on the Party committees to mobilize the masses to set up the "backyard furnaces," and stated that the "backyard furnaces" still have a role to play in China's fate. (RZJSH, 2:705)

For similar comments from Chen Yun directly on 21 October 1958, see Chen Yun, "Guanyu xibei xiezuoqu jiben jianshe gongzuo de jige wenti," 8–13.

262. Teiwes, *China's Road,* 73.

263. Tong Xiaopeng, *Fengyu sishinian,* 2:357. Also see Mao Zedong, "Talks at the Nan-ning Conference," 11, 12 January 1958, in *Miscellany,* 77–84.

264. MacFarquhar, *Origins,* 1:8. During this period, Zhou Enlai rebuked one of his secretaries, Fan Ruoyu, for lacking appreciation of Zhou's previous conflicts with Mao. See Teiwes, *China's Road,* 98.

265. ZELNP, 2:116, 120; Tong Xiaopeng, *Fengyu sishinian,* 2:357; Teiwes, *China's Road,* 74–75.

266. Liu Shufa emphasizes Mao's role in relieving Zhou "according to the decision of the fifth session of the First NPC" on 11 February 1958. See Liu Shufa, ed., *Chen Yi nianpu,* 732. Also see ZELNP, 2:124; MacFarquhar, *Origins,* 2:73–74.

267. ZELNP, 2:133, 134.

268. Mao Zedong, "Speech at the Hankow Conference," 6 April 1958, in *Miscellany,* 88.

269. ZELNP, 2:143–44.

270. Tong Xiaopeng, *Fengyu sishinian,* 2: 358; for a translation of their self-criticisms during winter–spring 1958, see Teiwes, *China's Road,* 245–57.

271. Tong Xiaopeng, *Fengyu sishinian,* 2:360; ZELNP, 2: 145.

272. Tong Xiaopeng, *Fengyu sishinian,* 2: 359–60.

273. Ibid., 392; MacFarquhar, *Origins,* 3:175–79.

274. Teiwes, *China's Road,* 92–99.

275. *RZJSH,* 2:698. Also see Deng Xiaoping's account of Mao's impassioned behavior, in Deng Xiaoping, *Wenxuan,* 260.

276. Tong Xiaopeng, *Fengyu sishinian,* 2:358–59.

277. Lieberthal, "Great Leap Forward," 316.

278. According to MacFarquhar, the Zunyi incident

illustrates one of Chou's salient characteristics—his unwillingness to elevate policy into principle and go to the wall when a confession of error could allow him to continue in office. Doubtless this attitude explains why he has been able to serve in the Politburo under every leader of the CCP, another unique record, and one which has laid him open to charges of opportunism. But it seems more likely that service as much as survival has been the mainspring of Chou's conduct; he has dedicated his life to the revolution and he has not allowed considerations of "face" to prevent him from continuing to contribute to the cause.

MacFarquhar, *Origins,* 1: 8; also see Tong Xiaopeng, *Fengyu sishinian,* 2, 363.

279. On 15 January 1956, Li Fuchun, the head of the State Planning Commission, submitted China's Second Five-Year Plan and a Fifteen-Year Long-term Plan to the Soviet Central Committee. On 17 August 1956, the chairman of the Soviet Planning Commission met in person with Li to relate the astounded reaction of the Soviet planners to the Chinese plan, which the Soviets considered far too ambitious. See *RZJSH,* 1:527, 544.

280. Mao Zedong made specific comments on 14 February 1956 during the reports of the thirty-four ministries and commissions on the Chinese economy. See ibid., 528.

281. Mao related that during his visit to China between 31 July and 3 August 1958, "Khrushchev didn't really believe. . . . He didn't ask what the real situation was and was very skeptical." Bo Yibo told Ivan Arkhipov, who had been the general advisor to the Soviet foreign experts in the PRC during the 1950s, that "China takes the mass line, and has put on line the backyard furnaces. The plan will definitely be realized. Arkhipov smirked a bit and retorted that even if more backyard furnaces were brought on line, there wouldn't be any change." Ibid., 2:704–5. In December 1984, Arkhipov became the first high-ranking (first deputy premier) Soviet official to visit China since 1969; the visit resulted in four economic, scientific, and technical accords. See *Washington Post,* 24 December 1984; "Zhong-Su maoyi," *Guojimaoyi* 10 (1985): 13–18.

282. Mao Zedong, "Talk at an Enlarged Central Work Conference," 30 January 1962, in *Chairman Mao,* 178.

283. *RZJSH,* 2:636; Teiwes, *China's Road,* 71. MacFarquhar describes the plenum as

the longest session held by the 8th CC prior to the Cultural Revolution, and indication presumably of the importance of the topics discussed. It was also the largest pre–cultural revolution plenum, which suggests that, having restored unity, the top leadership were anxious to demonstrate it to the widest possible audience.

See MacFarquhar, *Origins,* 1:307.

284. Mao Zedong, "Zuo geming de zujinpai" [Be activists in promoting the revolution], in *Xuanji,* 5: 473.

285. Teiwes, *China's Road,* 67–68.

286. *ZELNP,* 2:90.

287. Teiwes, *China's Road,* 71. Teiwes does not mention Zhou's conference.

288. *ZELNP,* 2:91.

289. Wang Xiangli, "Zhu De," 45.

290. Li Xiannian, "Jinyibu," in *Li Xiannian*, 1:308.

291. Notes from Zhu De's written comments of 9 October 1957, as cited in Wang Xiangli, "Zhu De," 48, n. 11.

292. Ibid., 44.

293. Ibid.

294. Li Xiannian, "Yinianlai caimao gongzuo de chubu jingyan" [My initial experience after one year of conducting finance and trade work], speech to the National Conference of Party Secretaries in Finance and Trade Work, 27 April 1959, in *Li Xiannian*, 1:334; also see idem, "Jinyibu zuohao waimao gongzuo," ibid., 308.

295. Zhou Enlai, "Waimao gongzuo shisi tiao" [Fourteen points in foreign trade work], delivered to a meeting of provincial, municipal, and SAR financial and trade secretaries and leaders of seventeen state council ministries on 11 May 1959, in ZELJJWX, 395–402.

296. MacFarquhar, *Origins*, 3:142; also see 193, where it is stated that Mao reluctantly accepted the appointment of Chen Yun to lead the Finance and Economics Small Group and Chen Yun's economic recovery plans in 1962 because "he felt he had no other option at this point."

297. Ibid., 179.

298. Zhou Enlai, "Waimao gongzuo shisi tiao," in ZELJJWX, 395.

299. Hughes and Luard, *Economic Development*, 131–38.

3. Neomercantilism versus Self-Sufficiency, 1959–1966

1. Anecdote taken from a fall 1985 lecture given by Professor Li Debin, Economics College, Peking University.

2. "Jiejue dangqian shiyou gongying wenti de jinji zhishi" [Emergency directive to resolve the supply problems of edible oils], issued by the CCP Central Committee, 26 May 1959, in ZRGJGD, 126. One *jin* is equivalent to 0.5 kilograms.

3. ZRGJD, 262. Grain production includes rice, wheat, corn, soybeans, and other assorted grains. Oil-bearing crops includes plants such as peanut, rape, and sesame. For an overall view of the problem, see Lardy, "Chinese Economy under Stress," 369–78.

4. Bernstein, "Stalinism," 339–77. For a further discussion of mortality estimates, see Yang Dali, *Calamity*, 37–39; MacFarquhar, *Origins*, 3:1–8.

5. "Guanyu kaizhan yi baoliang, baogang wei zhongxin de zengchan jieyue yundong de zhishi" [A directive on launching a campaign to increase production and austerity primarily in grain and steel], issued by the CCP Central Committee on 14 August 1960, in ZRGJGD, 145; ZRGJD, 277; Chen Yun, *Chen Yun tongzhi*, 116–19. For recent Western interpretations of the "Great Crisis," see Yang Dali, *Calamity*, 54–66.

6. "Guanyu jiejue shichang qinggongyepin gongying wenti de yijian" [An opinion on resolving problems in light industrial commodity supplies], approved and transmitted by the CCP Central Committee on 24 February 1959; in ZRGJGD, 123. At this time, Li Fuchun and Li Xiannian were members of the CCP Secretariat; Bo Yibo was head of the State Economic Commission (SEC).

7. For a discussion of the first and second fronts, see MacFarquhar, *Origins*, 1:152–56.

8. RZJSH, 2:838. "Chairman Mao stated that he wanted to leave [the quotas] alone, and even went as far as to say that [he] still must observe the situation to determine whether the entire line is or is not correct." Bo states that a minority of the Party elites held this

position at Wuchang, but fails to identify those elites (887). Teiwes argues that Mao was "ambiguous" in his attempts to "cool down" the GLF during this period. See Teiwes, *China's Road,* 125–35.

9. See "Guanyu dali jinsuo shehui goumaili de jinji zhishi" [Emergency directive on shrinking social buying power], issued by the CCP Central Committee, 1 June 1959, in *ZRGJGD,* 127; "Guanyu 1959 nian shehui shangpin goumaili he shangpin gongyingliang zhijian de pingheng qingkuang de baogao" [Situation report on the equilibrium between social commodity buying power and the amount of commodity supplies in 1959], submitted by Li Xiannian and transmitted by the CCP Central Committee on 24 June 1959, ibid., 128; "Guanyu shichang wujia he huobi liutong wenti de baogao" [Report on the problem of market prices and money circulation], submitted by Li Xiannian and transmitted by the CCP Central Committee, 16 September 1961, ibid., 169–70.

10. Yan Wen, "Jiu 'zuo' de qibu," 34–37; "Guanyu nongye de wu tiao jinji zhishi" [Five emergency directives concerning agriculture] issued by the CCP Central Committee on 7 May 1959, in *ZRGJGD,* 126; "Guanyu sheyuan siyang jiachu jiaqin, fenpei ziliudi he chongfen liyong lingxing xiansan tudi deng sige wenti de zhishi" [Directives on four problems concerning commune members privately raising livestock and poultry, the allotment of private plots and full utilization of scattered, nonutilized plots, etc.], issued by the CCP Central Committee on 11 June 1959, in *ZRGJD,* 248.

11. Zheng Derong, *Zhongguo jingji tizhi,* 77–78; *RZJSH,* 2:887–88. The steel quota was further reduced to 12 million tons one month later at the Lushan conference. See *Renmin ribao,* 14 July 1981.

12. *ZELNP,* 2:236, 237, 238–39; Tong Xiaopeng, *Fengyu sishinian,* 2:366–67.

13. Dangdai Zhongguo Congshu, *Dangdai Zhongguo de jingji,* 83.

14. Mao Zedong, "Several Important Instructions," in *Miscellany,* 183; "Mao Zedong Discusses Economic Work with Other Leading Comrades at Lushan," in *ZRGJD,* 253. Chen Yun continued as head of the State Commission for Capital Construction but was granted a three-month leave by Mao to recuperate from an illness. See Mao Zedong, "Tongyi Chen Yun yinbing xiuyang de pifu" [Approval of Chen Yun's rest and rehabilitation from sickness], in *Jianguo,* 8:294–95.

15. *RZJSH,* 2:888.

16. *ZELNP,* 2:243.

17. Ibid., 248.

18. MacFarquhar, *Origins,* 2:306–7.

19. Mao Zedong, "A Criticism Disseminated by the CCPCC on 'Anshan Municipal Party Committee's Report on the Developing Situation of Technical Innovation and the Technical Revolutionary Movement on the Industrial Front' " presented March 1960, in *Miscellany,* 230; MacFarquhar, *Origins,* 2:306–9.

20. Joseph, *Critique,* 77–81. For more on the second Great Leap, see Lieberthal, "Great Leap Forward," 318–19. For an excellent example of this delay in policy retrenchment, see MacFarquhar, Origins, 3:102; for Anshan, see ibid., 149.

21. Yang Dali, *Calamity,* 62.

22. Tong Xiaopeng, *Fengyu sishinian,* 2:389; *ZELNP,* 2:356–57; also see Zhou's comments to the State Council Standing Committee meeting held 12–14 December 1960 that was also attended by several vice-premiers, in *ZELNP,* 2:379.

23. MacFarquhar, *Origins,* 3:100–120; Lewis and Xue, *China's Strategic Seapower,* 34; Goldman, "Party Policies," 268–74.

24. *ZELNP,* 2:193.

25. Speech to the Ministry of Foreign Trade Conference on 23 December 1958, in ZELNP, 2: 196; also see ZELJJWX, 677, n. 175. Teiwes argues, "While it is easy to believe that these actions corresponded to Zhou's own beliefs, it was only with Mao's authority that he began to speak out." There is no evidence that Mao in December 1958 approved Zhou's forceful comments forbidding "a Great Leap Forward in exports." See Teiwes, *China's Road,* 139.

26. ZELNP, 2: 202, 205, 208, 209. From December 1958 to May 1959, Zhou also discussed foreign economic policy with Liao Zhengzhi and Lei Renmin.

27. Li Xiannian, "Jinyibu," in *Li Xiannian,* 1: 308; Zhou Enlai, "Waimao gongzuo shisi tiao," in ZELJJWX, 396; ZELJJWX, 677, n. 176.

28. ZELJJWX, 677, n. 176.

29. Li Xiannian, "Jinyibu," in *Li Xiannian,* 1:309.

30. ZELNP, 2:202.

31. "Guanyu shangpin fenji guanli banfa de baogao" [Report on the division of management over commodities], submitted by the Ministry of Commerce, the Ministry of Grains, the Ministry of Foreign Trade, the Ministry of Health, the Ministry of Aquatic Products, and the Ministry of Light Industry, and approved by the State Council on 12 February 1959, in ZRGJGD, 122.

32. "Guanyu zhixing duiwai maoyi jihuazhong cunzai wenti de qingshi baogao" [The report and request of instructions concerning existing problems in carrying out the foreign trade plan], submitted by the Party Committee of the Ministry of Foreign Trade and approved by the Central Committee on 18 March 1959, in ZELJJWX, 677, n. 176.

33. Li Xiannian, "Yinianlai caimao gongzuo de chubu jingyan" [Initial experience in finance and trade work during the past year], in *Li Xiannian,* 1:335.

34. Ibid. Li is referring to "Guanyu jiaqiang shichang guanli he gaizao siying shangye de zhishi" [Directive on strengthening management of the market and transforming the private commercial sector], approved by the Central Committee on 13 July 1954, in ZRGJGD, 57–58; also see Zhongguo Duiwai Maoyi, *Zhongguo duiwai maoyi gailun,* 146.

35. ZELNP, 2:205; Long Chucai, *Liyong waizi gailun,* 222. For an early Western interpretation of the 1959 technology agreement, see Cheng Chu-yuan, *Economic Relations,* 5, 18–19, 102.

36. Zhou Enlai, "Muqian shehui zhuyi jianshe de sixiang renwu" [Four Tasks of the current socialist construction], report delivered to the Conference for Cadres above Office and Bureau Levels organized by the Party Committee of Heilongjiang Province on 24 December 1959, in ZELJJWX, 404.

37. Zhou Enlai, "Waimao gongzuo shisitiao," in ZELJJWX, 395–402; Chen Yun, "Luoshi gangtie zhibiao wenti" [The problem of making practicable the steel target), in *Wenxuan,* 120–29. For an English translation, see Lardy and Lieberthal, *Chen Yun's Strategy,* 117 26.

38. "Jiejue dangqian shiyou gongying wenti de jinji zhishi" [Emergency directive on resolving the current problem in oil supplies], issued by the CCP Central Committee and the State Council, 26 May 1959, in ZRGJGD, 126.

39. Yang Dali, *Calamity,* 65–66.

40. "Guanyu zai dazhong chengshi jiaoqu fazhan fushipin shengchan de zhishi" [Directive to develop the production of agricultural sideline products in the suburban areas of large- and medium-sized cities], issued by the Central Committee on 4 July 1959, in ZELNP, 2:241. For Li Xiannian's discussion of the problem, see Li Xiannian, "Jiajin fazhan dazhong chengshi jiaoqu de fushipin shengchan" [Step up the production of agri-

cultural sideline products in the suburban areas of large- and medium-sized cities], 4 July 1959, in *Li Xiannian,* 1: 359–66.

41. "Lizheng wancheng dangnian duiwai maoyi de shougou he chukou renwu de jinji zhishi" [Emergency directive to exert utmost effort to meet foreign trade procurement and export responsibilities], issued by the CCP Central Committee and the State Council, 26 October 1959, in ZRGJGD, 131.

42. Li Xiannian, "Duiwai maoyi gongzuo de jidian yijian," in *Li Xiannian,* 1:344.

43. "Lizheng wancheng dangnian duiwai maoyi de shougou he chukou renwu de jinji zhishi" [Emergency directive to exert utmost effort to meet foreign trade procurement and export responsibilities], issued by the CCP Central Committee and the State Council, 26 October 1959, in ZRGJGD, 131.

44. Li Xiannian, 28 February 1960, National Conference of Financial and Trade Party Secretaries, approved by the CCP Central Committee on 3 March 1960, in ZRGJGD, 138.

45. "Guanyu 1959 nian duiwai maoyi shougou renwu he chukou renwu chao'e wancheng de baogao" [Report on exceeding the 1959 foreign trade procurement and export targets], issued by the State Council's Office for Finance and Trade and approved and transmitted by the CCP Central Committee on 13 February 1960, in ZRGJGD, 136–73.

46. Anastas Mikoyan, deputy premier of the Soviet Union, told Adlai Stevenson during a 1958 interview that "under existing agreements . . . [China] would be allowed to incur a deficit payment balance of up to three hundred million rubles." See Adlai E. Stevenson, "Stevenson Notes Red China's Rise," *New York Times,* 2 October 1958, as cited in Mayer, *Sino-Soviet Relations,* 159.

47. Long Chucai, *Liyong waizi gailun,* 223; W. Griffith, *Sino-Soviet Relations,* 182. For the initial estimates of the money owed on the nine Soviet loans, see ZELNP, 1:457–58.

48. Long Chucai, *Liyong waizi gailun,* 222.

49. Ibid.; *Renmin ribao,* 11 May 1969. For more background on the final amount, see ZELNP, 1:349–50; Zhou Enlai, "Kefu muqian kunnan de zhuyao banfa" [The chief methods to overcome the current problems], speech delivered to the Central Committee's enlarged work conference on 7 February 1962; in ZELJJWX, 452.

50. "Guanyu quandang dagao duiwai maoyi shougou he chukou yundong de jinji zhishi" [Emergency directive for the whole party to make great efforts in the campaign for foreign trade procurement and export], issued by the CCP Central Committee on 10 August 1960, in ZRGJGD, 144–45. For full translation of the text, see appendix D.

51. W. Griffith, *Sino-Soviet Relations,* 185; also see idem, *Rift,* 295.

52. Li Xiannian, "Liangnian yilai guomin jingji tiaozheng gongzuo qude juda chengjiu" [The two years of readjustment work pays off with tremendous achievements], presented to the NPC et al. on 5 August 1963 and approved and transmitted by the Central Committee on 11 August 1963; in *Li Xiannian,* 2:134; Cheng Chu-yuan, *Economic Relations,* 132, 162. This apparently was a Sino-Russian agreement to repay the 1960 trade debt within five years on an interest-free basis. See MacFarquhar, *Origins,* 3:529, n. 6.

53. ZELNP, 2: 355–56, 500.

54. Ibid., 337.

55. Ibid., 446.

56. Zhou Enlai, "Kefu muqian kunnan," in ZELJJWX, 452.

57. Zhou Enlai, "Zai disanjie quanguo renmin daibiao dahui diyicishang de *Zhengfu gongzuo baogao,*" 18. In the 1964 government work report, Zhou reports that RMB 6.67 billion would be spent by the end of 1964.

58. Zhou Enlai, "Guomin jingji de tiaozheng gongzuo he dangqian renwu" [The readjustment of the national economy and current tasks], from Zhou's work report delivered to the NPC on 28 March 1962, in *ZELJJWX*, 477.

59. *ZELNP*, 2:336.

60. "Letter of the Central Committee of the CCP of February 29, 1964, to the Central Committee of the CPSU," in W. Griffith, *Sino-Soviet Relations*, 183.

61. For instance, see Guojia Jihua Weiyuanhui Dangzu, "Shi shengchan he jianshe zai fazhanzhong dedao tiaozheng, gonggu, chongshi he tigao," 3–4; Wu Qungan, "Guanyu Zhou Enlai 1960 nian shending tiaozheng jingji fangzhen de kaozheng," 15–16.

62. *RZJSH*, 2:893–99; *ZRGJD*, 279; MacFarquhar, *Origins*, 3:81–83; Tong Xiaopeng, *Fengyu sishinian*, 2:389.

63. *ZRGJD*, 279. The original State Planning Commission report discussed in August–September 1960 by the State Council proposed a six-character plan: *zhengdun, gonggu, tigao* (reorganizing, consolidating, and having higher expectations of success). See Tong Xiaopeng, *Fengyu sishinian*, 2: 389. On 30 August 1960, Zhou Enlai suggested the addition of *chongshi* (supplementation), and then changed "reorganizing" to "readjusting" on 5 September 1960. The Central Committee legitimized the phraseology when it approved the State Planning Commission's "Yijiuliuyi nian guomin jingji jihua kongzhi shuzi de baogao" [Report on controlling the amounts of the 1961 national economic plan) on 30 September 1960. See *ZELNP*, 2:346.

64. "Guanyu 1961 nian guomin jingji jihua kongzhi shuzi de baogao" [Report on controlling the 1961 state economic plan figures], submitted by the Party Committee of the State Planning Commission (SPC) and approved by the CCP Central Committee on 30 September 1960, in *ZRGJGD*, 147–48.

65. For an exhaustive analysis of the Seven-Thousand Cadre Conference of January–February 1962, see MacFarquhar, *Origins*, 3: chap. 7. MacFarquhar adds,

> Despite his "self-criticisms," Mao did not hint publicly at formally handing over power to his more sober colleagues. Could he have done so in private? . . . The behaviour of Mao's colleagues after the Seven Thousand Cadres Conference certainly suggests that they considered a new era had begun even if a formal rite of passage had not yet been celebrated. But however they interpreted Mao, they would find that he had only beat a temporary retreat after the conference was over. (172)

66. *Liangshou weiru* literally is "to proportion income (*ru*) in light of one's receipts (*shou*)." It is a variant of *liangru weichu*, which is translated as "to proportion expenditures in light of one's income (*chu*)."

67. Chen Yun, *Tongzhi*, 118.

68. "Guanyu quandang dongshou, daban nongye, daban liangshi de zhishi" [A directive for the whole Party to make great efforts in promoting agriculture and grain production], issued by the Central Committee on 10 August 1960, in *ZRGJGD*, 144.

69. Li Xiannian, "Liangnian yilai," in *Li Xiannian*, 2:114.

70. Zhou Enlai made the decision after meeting with Chen Yun and Ye Jizhuang just before he boarded a plane for Burma. See *ZELNP*, 2:382. Lardy reports that the first wheat import contracts were signed in October 1960. See Lardy, "Chinese Economy under Stress," 382. Citing Tao Zhu, MacFarquhar dates the Standing Committee's decision as December 1960. See MacFarquhar, *Origins*, 3:488, n. 6. Also see "Guanyu 1961 nian duiwai maoyi ruogan wenti de qingshi baogao" [The report and request of instructions concerning various foreign trade problems in 1961], submitted by the State Council Office

of Finance and Trade on 18 January 1961 and approved by the CCP Central Committee on 7 February 1961, in *ZRGJGD*, 156; *ZRGJD*, 296–97; Li Xiannian, "Zuohao jinkou liangshi de jiexie, zhuanyun gongzuo" [Do a good job at accepting, unloading, and transshipment of grain imports], 27 January 1961, in *Li Xiannian*, 1:441–42.

71. *ZELNP*, 2:388–89.

72. "Guanyu zuohao jiexie, zhuanyun jinkou liangshi gongzuo de jinji tongzhi" [Emergency circular on doing a good job at receiving, unloading, and transshipment of grain imports], issued by the Central Committee on 30 January 1961, in Dangdai Zhongguo Shangye, 214. For a detailed description of the Central Work Group's composition, see MacFarquhar, *Origins,* 3:488, n. 16.

73. Li Xiannian, "Guanyu liangshi wenti de yifeng xin" [A letter on the grain problem], sent on 30 July 1961 to Mao Zedong and the Central Committee, which approved and transmitted the letter on 2 August 1961, in Li Xiannian, 1:469–70; idem, "Zhengque chuli neiwaimao de guanxi," ibid., 455.

74. Li Xiannian, "Kefu dangqian jingji kunnan de jige wenti" [Several problems in overcoming the current economic problems], 20 March 1961, in *Li Xiannian,* 1:448–49; idem, "Guanyu 1961 nian duiwai maoyi ruogan wenti de qingshi baogao," ibid., 455; *ZRGJD*, 296–97; *ZELNP*, 2:385. Zhou Enlai initially approved 1.5 million tons on 30 December 1960; the amount was then increased to 4 million tons and again to 5 million tons on 22 February 1961. See *ZELNP*, 2:393. The 1961 amount was later increased to 10 billion *jin* by September to "make up for the domestic market grain deficit." See "Guanyu shichang wujia he huobi liutong wenti de baogao" [Report on market prices and monetary circulation problems], submitted by Li Xiannian and approved by the CCP Central Committee on 16 September 1961, in *ZRGJGD*, 165–66. For an overall view of the problem, see Perkins, "Central Features," 133.

75. Sun Yeli, "Wenge houqi Chen Yun," 1085. This is perhaps why the grain imports were described as *zhuankou liang* (entrepôt grain). See MacFarquhar, *Origins,* 3:24.

76. *RZJSH*, v. 2, 1064; Li Xiannian, "Shichang qingkuang haozhuanhou xuyao jixu jiejue de wenti" [Problems that must continue to be resolved following the turnaround in market conditions], an outline of a report on finance, monetary, and trade work submitted to Liu Shaoqi on 6 December 1963, in *Li Xiannian,* 2:170–71.

77. Li Xiannian, "Liangnian yilai," in *Li Xiannian,* 2:133.

78. Li Xiannian, "Liangshi gongzuo de zhongyao jingyan" [The important experience gained in dealing with grain], an outline of a report delivered to the Secretariat of the Central Committee on 22 February 1965, in *Li Xiannian,* 2:235.

79. Li Xiannian, "Shichang qingkuang haozhuanhou xuyao jixu jiejue de wenti," in *Li Xiannian,* 2:171.

80. This is not to argue that China earned foreign exchange by increasing its export of rice. Mah Feng-hwa argues that the value of wheat imports between 1960 and 1967 was greater than the value of rice exports by $1.8 billion. See Mah, *Foreign Trade.*

81. Li Xiannian, "Liangnian yilai," in Li Xiannian, 2:124; Chen Yun, "Speed up Development of the Nitrogenous Chemical Fertilizer Industry" (May 1961), as translated in Lardy and Lieberthal, *Chen Yun's Strategy,* 129–38.

82. "Introduction," in Lardy and Lieberthal, *Chen Yun's Strategy,* xxviii.

83. Li Xiannian, "Shichang qingkuang haozhuanhou xuyao jixu jiejue de wenti," in *Li Xiannian,* 2:170.

84. Li Xiannian, "Shichang xingshi haozhuan" [The marketplace turns for the better], a report delivered to Mao Zedong on 23 June 1963, in *Li Xiannian,* 2: 105–10.

85. Li Fuchun, "March On!"

86. Nie Rongzhen, "Guanyu lizu guonei fazhan keji deng wenti xiang zhonggong bing Mao Zedong de baogao," 8–9; Zhou Enlai, "Zai Nie Rongzhen," 10; ZELNP, 2:330–31.

87. "Letter," in W. Griffith, *Sino-Soviet Relations,* 183. Also see "Source Material: Several Important Problems Concerning the Current International Situation," *Bulletin of Activities* 17 (25 April 1961), in C. J. Cheng, *Politics of the Chinese Red Army,* 481–83.

88. ZELNP, 2:351–52; also see Zhou's remarks to an ambassadorial reception for socialist country representatives on 9 March 1961, in ZELNP, 2:396–97.

89. MacFarquhar, *Origins,* 3:121; ZELNP, 2:389–90; ZELNP, 2:394. Although thanking the Soviet ambassador for the grain loan in March 1961, Zhou Enlai stated that China's needs were dependent on the 1961 fall and winter harvests and the fall 1961 purchases on the international market. China would accept the loan of Cuban sugar. See ZELNP, 2:397, 400.

90. "Guanyu 1962 nian duiwai maoyi jihua de baogao" (Report on the 1962 foreign trade plan], submitted by the MFT and approved by the CCP Central Committee on 28 February 1962, in ZRGJGD, 171; MacFarquhar, *Origins,* 2:126–29.

91. Zhongguo Duiwai Jingji, *Zhongguo,* sect. 4, pp. 55, 57, 59, 64.

92. Li Xiannian, "Liangnian yilai," in *Li Xiannian,* 2: 125.

93. For instance, on 1 October 1963, Zhou intervened to stop demonstrations against the Soviet Union in Beijing and on 18 September 1965 attempted to restrain rash actions by Chinese sailors whenever they saw Russians. See ZELNP, 2:583, 756.

94. Li Xiannian, "Liangnian yilai," in *Li Xiannian,* 2:115; ZRGJGD, 144. There is some discrepancy in these numbers. Long Chucai states that by mid-1960, 184 complete plant and equipment projects still were under various stages of completion. See Long Chucai, *Liyong waizi gailun,* 223.

95. Lewis and Xue, *China Builds the Bomb,* 70–72.

96. "Guanyu chengli jiaqiang dui yuanzineng gongye lingdao de zhongyang shiwuren weiyuanhui de jianyi" [Suggestion for the establishment of a fifteen-member central commission to strengthen leadership over the nuclear industry), submitted by Luo Ruiqing on 30 October 1962 and approved by Mao Zedong on 3 November 1962, in ZELNP, 2:510, 512–13. For a detailed analysis, see Lewis and Xue, *China Builds the Bomb,* 131–34.

97. ZELNP, 2:516. For instance, China imported an East German reaction chamber sometime after summer 1961. See Lewis and Xue, *China Builds the Bomb,* 164.

98. ZELNP, 2:143; C. Lee, *Japan,* 37–39.

99. CYNP, 2:741.

100. "Guanyu zujin Zhongri guanxi de zhengzhi san yuanze he maoyi san yuanze" [The three principles in politics and trade to promote Sino-Japanese relations], talk to the Sino-Japanese Trade Promotion Committee of Japan, on 27 August 1960, in ZELJJWX, 410–11; C. Lee, *Japan,* 141–42.

101. C. Lee, *Japan,* 42–48, 143–58; Eckstein, *Communist China's Economic Growth,* 202–12.

102. Zhou Enlai, "Zhongri jingji hezuo yingdang ba yanguang fang de gengyuan xie" [We must look further down the road in promoting Sino-Japanese economic cooperation], speech to a visiting Japanese delegation on 23 April 1964, in ZELJJWX, 539.

103. Zhou Enlai held discussions between 29 July and 3 August 1963 with Li Xiannian, Bo Yibo, Tan Zhenlin, Deng Xihui, and others concerning the 1964 economic plan; see ZELNP, 2:569. Chen Boda, whom MacFarquhar describes as one of Mao's

"trusties" along with Lin Biao and Kang Sheng, wrote a report in 1963 summarizing China's industrialization experience. Chen highly praised the GLF and did not mention the need to readjust the strategy after 1961. See Zhou Enlai, "Guomin jingji fazhan de fangzhen he mubiao," in *ZELJJWX*, 517–18; MacFarquhar, *Origins*, 1:142–43, 3:439.

104. Cao Yingwang, "Ye Jianying," 87.

105. Zhou Enlai, "Ba woguo jianshe chengwei qiangda de shehui zhuyi de xiandai-hua de gongye guojia" [Using construction to transform China into a formidable social-ist modernized industrial country], 23 September 1954, in *ZELJJWX*, 176.

106. MacFarquhar, *Origins*, 1:53–56; Cao Yingwang, "Ye Jianying," 87.

107. Zhou Enlai, "Muqian shehui zhuyi jianshe de sixiang renwu" [Four tasks in con-temporary socialist construction], a report presented to a cadre conference organized by the Heilongjiang Party Committee on 24 December 1959, in *ZELJJWX*, 408; Cao Yingwang, "Ye Jianying," 88.

108. Cao Yingwang, "Ye Jianying," 87; *ZELNP*, 2:277.

109. Zhou Enlai, "Dangqian jianshezhong de jixiang renwu" [Several tasks in our current construction efforts], presented to the thirty-seventh expanded meeting of the NPC's Standing Committee on 3 April 1961, in *ZELJJWX*, 425.

110. Lewis and Xue, *China Builds the Bomb*, 51.

111. Zhou Enlai, "Yao zhongshi jishu liliang" [We must highly value technological capabilities], 24 December 1962, in *ZELJJWX*, 501.

112. Zhou Enlai, "Guanyu guofang jungong shengchan de jige wenti" [Several prob-lems with national defense production], presented to a conference of cadre from mili-tary industries in the northeast on 8 June 1962, in *ZELJJWX*, 193.

113. *ZELNP*, 2:547.

114. Ibid., 528. Originally, the Third FYP was to be implemented between 1963 and 1967. Following the economic disaster of the GLF, the Central Committee delayed imple-mentation until 1966, and a transitional period was declared for the interim.

115. Ibid. Note the inversion of agriculture and industry following the GLF disaster and the change from the general phrase "scientific culture" to a more specific phrase, "science and technology."

116. *ZELJJWX*, 690.

117. Zhou Enlai, "Jiancheng shehui zhuyi qiangguo, guanjian zaiyu shixian kexue jishu xiandaihua" [The key to building a strong socialist country is in realizing scientific and technological modernization], delivered on 29 January 1963, in *ZELJJWX*, 503–4.

118. MacFarquhar, *Origins*, 3:622, n. 27.

119. *ZELNP*, 2:551–55. Apparently Chinese sonar devices in the 1970s were substan-dard; it is unclear if the *Great Leap* built in the early 1960s was even equipped with such devices. See Lewis and Xue, *China's Strategic Seapower*, 290, n.75. Even in 1974, the Chinese Ministry of Communications worried that the main engines, radar, and other major equipment of domestically produced ships were unreliable; see chap. 4.

120. Zhou Enlai, "Di'erge wunian jihua de liangge zhongyao wenti," in *ZELJJWX*, 526–27.

121. *ZELNP*, 2:599.

122. The strategy was based partly on a 23 June 1963 report submitted by Li Fuchun. See Li Fuchun, "Guanyu gongye fazhan guihua wenti gei Zhou Enlai de baogao" [Report submitted to Zhou Enlai on the problem of industrial development plan], in *Xuanji*, 314–19.

123. *ZELNP*, 2:577; Zhou Enlai, "Guodu jihua he changyuan guihua" [The transitional plan and long-range program], presented to the fourth session of the Second NPC on 2 December 1963, in *ZELJJWX*, 692, n. 258.

124. In August 1963, Zhou initially proposed a ten-year development plan whose goal was to establish by 1975 an independent national economic system "that not only included industry, but also agriculture, commerce, science and technology culture, and education and national defense." See Zhou Enlai, "Guomin jingji fazhan de fangzhen he mubiao," in ZELJJWX, 519.

125. ZELNP, 2:577–78. Previous Western dating of Zhou's plan was set one year later in December 1964. See Barnett, *China's Economy*, 13.

126. ZELNP, 2:586.

127. Naughton takes another approach. He argues that the Four Modernizations strategy called for "an expansion of a self-sufficient industrial system" based on the "gamble that it had imported sufficient Soviet technology to permit the expansion of a 'basic' industrial sector." According to this view, the Four Modernizations did not call for an increase in import substitution projects. See Naughton, "Pattern," 242.

128. Lieberthal and Oksenberg, *Policy Making*, 195.

129. Zhou Enlai, "Guodu jihua he changyuan guihua," in ZELJJWX, 530–31.

130. Li Xiannian, "Yiju xinqingkuang zuohao waimao gongzuo" [Do a good job in foreign trade work according to the new situation], speech to the National Foreign Trade Planning Conference, delivered on 26 September 1963, in *Li Xiannian*, 2:148–49.

131. ZELNP, 2:473;550.

132. Ibid., 564.

133. Sun Yeli, "Wenge houqi Chen Yun," 1085; C. Lee, *Japan*, 47, 145.

134. Long Chucai, *Liyong waizi gailun*, 230; for a listing of turnkey projects and equipment imports, see Price, "International Trade," 603; Heymann, "Acquisition," 712–21.

135. Sun Yeli, "Wenge houqi Chen Yun," 1085.

136. Alexander Eckstein argues that there was a tacit agreement among COCOM members to impose a five-year limit on trade credits on all Communist countries; the lack of "sizable long-term credits" delayed China's post–GLF recovery. See Eckstein, *Communist China's Economic Growth*, 265–67; Long Chucai, *Liyong waizi gailun*, 230.

137. Lieberthal and Oksenberg, *Policy Making*, 175–81; Heymann, "Acquisition," 719–25.

138. Li Xiannian, "Zhengque chuli neiwaimao de guanxi" [Correctly resolve the relationship between domestic and foreign trade], 30 May 1961, in *Li Xiannian*, 1:456.

139. "Guanyu zhuajin wancheng jinnian de chukou renwu zuzhi mingnian de chukou huoyuan de tongzhi" [Circular on completing export obligations for this year and organizing next year's export sourcing], issued by the CCP Central Committee on 30 November 1962; in ZRGJGD, 183. Chinese exports to Hong Kong in 1960 totaled $191.6 million; in 1962, $216.7 million; in 1964, $390.89 million; in 1966, $561.88 million. See Zhongguo Duiwai Jingji, *Zhongguo*, sect. A, p. 12.

140. "Guanyu zhuajin duiwai maoyi shougou he chukou gongzuo, banhao Guangzhou chukuo shangpin jiaoyihui de tongzhi" [Circular on paying close attention to this year's foreign trade procurement and export work and successfully operating the Guangzhou export commodity trade fair] issued by the CCP Central Committee on 23 February 1963; in ZRGJGD, 187.

141. "Guanyu 1963 nian qiuji Zhongguo chukou shangpin jiaoyihui de zongbaogao" [Overall report on China's fall 1963 export commodity trade fair], issued by the MFT and approved by the CCP Central Committee on 13 December 1963; in ZRGJGD, 200.

142. Li Xiannian, "Zhengque chuli neiwaimao de guanxi," in *Li Xiannian*, 1:457; Chen

Yun, "Manage Foreign Trade Work Well," May 1961, as translated in Lardy, Lieberthal and *Chen Yun's Strategy*, 141–43.

143. *ZRGJD*, 366.

144. "Guanyu quandang dagao duiwai maoyi shougou he chukou yundong de jinji zhishi" [Emergency directive directing the entire Party to initiate a large-scale campaign in foreign trade procurement and exports], issued by the Central Committee on 10 August 1960, in *ZELNP*, 2:339; *ZRGJGD*, 135.

145. Li Xiannian, "Duiwaimao gongzuo de jidian yijian," in *Li Xiannian*, 1:347–48.

146. Ibid., 348.

147. According to the Chinese Marxist definition, this would include "land, forests, rivers, mineral resources, machines, equipment, factory buildings, materials for production and construction (*shengchan jianzhu wu*), means of transportation, raw materials, subsidiary materials (*fuzhu wuliao*)." Labor, however, would have not been included, since it would have been translated as means of labor (*laodong ziliao*). According to classical Marxist theory, labor is not a factor of production but the primary productive force. See Xu Dixin, *Zhengzhi jingjixue cidian*, 1:86–88; Shanghai Shehui Kexueyuan Bumen Jingjisuo, *Jingji dacidian*, 159; and Scruton, *Dictionary*, 250–51, 378–79.

148. Li Xiannian, "Zuohao wuzi tongyi guanli gongzuo," in *Li Xiannian*, 2:22.

149. "Guanyu jiaqiang wuzi gongying gongzuo he jianli wuzi guanli jigou de qingshi baogao" [Report and request for instructions on strengthening material supplies and establishing a material management structure], submitted by the SEC and approved and transmitted by the CCP Central Committee on 18 May 1960, in *ZRGJGD*, 142.

150. Li Xiannian, "Zuohao wuzi tongyi guanli gongzuo," in *Li Xiannian*, 2:23.

151. Ibid., 22.

152. Li Xiannian, "Zuohao wuzi tongyi guanli gongzuo," in *Li Xiannian*, 2:25–28.

153. "Guanyu shengchan difang chukou gongkuang chanpin suoxu yuanliao wenti de dianbao" [Cable on the problem of raw materials needed for local production of industrial and mineral export products], issued jointly by the SPC and SEC on 1 June 1961, in *ZRGJGD*, 160.

154. "Guanyu zai caimao xitong jianli cailiao guanli jigou de qingshi baogao" [Report and request for instructions on establishing a materials management organization within the financial and trade system], submitted by the MFT and approved in principle and transmitted by the State Council, 30 June 1961, in *ZRGJGD*, 162–63.

155. Li Xiannian, "Yiju xinqingkuang," in *Li Xiannian*, 1:152.

156. Li Xiannian, "Duiwaimao gongzuo de jidian yijian," in Li Xiannian, 1:345.

157. Li Xiannian, "Caimao bumen yao jianjue guanche 'tiaozheng, gonggu, chongshi, tigao' de fangzhen" [Finance and trade departments must resolutely carry out the guiding principles of "adjustment, consolidation, augmentation and raising expectations"], speech to the National Conference of Finance Bureau and Department Heads, 22 January 1961, in *Li Xiannian*, 1:437.

158. Li Xiannian, "Yiju xinqingkuang," in *Li Xiannian*, 1:152.

159. Li Xiannian, "Shangye he waimao ruogan gongzuo wenti" [Certain problems in commercial and foreign trade work], delivered at an office conference of the State Council Office of Finance and Trade, on 25 August 1965, in *Li Xiannian*, 2:254.

160. "Guanyu shengchan difang chukou gongkuang chanpin," in *ZRGJGD*, 160. The text of the original Zhou directive has yet to be located, but was probably issued in spring 1961.

161. "Guanyu 1961 nian duiwai maoyi ruogan wenti de qingshi baogao," in *ZRGJGD*,

160; also see the discussions of "Dui liangshi gongzuo de jidian yijian" [Some views on grain work], which was discussed in November 1961, in *ZELNP*, 2:441–42.

162. Professional Conference on Problems of Gold Production called by the SEC on 20 June 1961, in *ZRGJGD*, 161.

163. Li Xiannian, "Yiju xinqingkuang" in *Li Xiannian*, 1:151. Also see "Guanyu fangzhi gongye fazhan fangzhen de qingshi baogao" [Report and request for instructions on the textile industry development plans], issued by the Ministry of Textile Industry and approved and transmitted by the CCP Central Committee on 1 September 1960, in *ZRGJGD*, 146; Zhongguo Duiwai Maoyi, *Zhongguo duiwai maoyi gailun*, 146–47; *WFSS* 44–50; He Xinhao, "Yijin yangchu," 119–26.

164. "Yijin yangchu shixing banfa" [Trial procedures for the importation of materials to develop exports] was submitted by the SPC et al. and approved by the State Council on 26 March 1979.

165. "Guanyu nongcun laodongli anpai de zhishi" [Directive on arranging the agricultural labor force], issued by the CCP Central Committee on 15 May 1960, in *ZRGJGD*, 142.

166. "Guanyu nongcun renmin gongshe dangqian zhengce wenti de jinji zhishixin" [An emergency directive letter on current policy problems in agricultural people's communes], in *ZRGJGD*, 148. Mao Zedong approved a Zhou Enlai report that criticized communal kitchens, the egalitarianism of the supply system, and the calculation of work points. See "Guanyu nongcun zhengce wenti de diaocha baogao" [An investigative report on problems of agricultural policy], approved by Mao Zedong on 7 May 1961, in *ZRGJGD*, 158.

167. The conference also approved RMB 2.5 billion to compensate commune members whose means of production were "transferred arbitrarily." *ZRGJD*, 287–89.

168. Li Xiannian, " 'Fazhan jingji, baozhang gongji' shi banhao shehui zhuyi shangye de jiben chufadian" [The basic starting point for successfully conducting socialist commerce is to "develop the economy and guarantee supplies"], speech to the Tenth Plenum of the Eighth Communist Party Congress, delivered on 25 September 1962, in *Li Xiannian*, 2:38; also see Li Xiannian, "Shaogou shaoxiao shi kefu liangshi kunnan de jiji fangzhen" [Less state procurement and sales is an activist policy to overcome the grain problem], delivered to the National Conference of Grain Bureau and Department Heads, on 9 January 1963, in *Li Xiannian*, 2:91–96.

169. Li Xiannian, "Guanyu dangqian caimao gongzuo de jige wenti" [Several current problems facing finance and trade work], in a letter submitted to the Central Work Conference on 4 June 1964 and approved and transmitted by the CCP Central Committee on 15 June 1964, in *ZRGJGD*, 207; *Li Xiannian*, 2:207–18.

170. Chen Yun, "Manage Foreign Trade Work Well," May 1961, as translated in Lardy and Lieberthal, *Chen Yun's Strategy*, 139, 140.

171. "Guanyu tigao liangshi shougou jiage wenti de baogao" [Report on the problem of raising the grain procurement price], issued by the Small Group on Food Price Problems and approved by the CCP Central Committee on 15 January 1961, in *ZRGJGD*, 154.

172. "Guanyu liangshi jiangli banfa he youliao jiage wenti" [Methods for the grain bonus and problems in the oil crop price], issued by the State Council Office of Finance and Trade and approved and transmitted by the CCP Central Committee on 8 November 1960, in *ZRGJGD*, 148–149.

173. Ibid., 148.

174. *WFSS*, 19; *ZRGJGD*, 207.

175. "Guanyu shougou zhongyao jingji zuowu shixing liangshi jiangli de zhishi"

[Directive on carrying out the grain bonus in procuring important cash crops], issued by the CCP Central Committee on 3 April 1961, in *ZRGJGD,* 157.

176. "Guanyu gongying chukou shangpin tongyi zuojia de zhanxing guiding" [Provisional regulations on a unified price fixing for supplied export commodities], approved by the State Council in November 1965, *WFSS,* 52–56.

177. For a complete account of the export procurement bonus schedule, see *WFSS,* 16–43.

178. Li Xiannian, "Kefu dangqian jingji kunnan," in *Li Xiannian,* 1:448–49.

179. Ibid., 449–50.

180. *WFSS,* 69. The exact method of loan disbursal was first codified in 1964 and recodified in 1972, 1975, and 1982. See ibid., 70; "Chukou Gongyepin Shengchan Zhuanxiang Daikuan banfa" [Procedures for the Specialized Loan Program for Industrial Export Production], Maojizongzi 82.35, issued by the Ministry of Foreign Economics and Trade et al. on 13 May 1982, in Zhongguo Renmin Yinhang Jihuasi, *Lilü,* 803–6.

181. *WFSS,* 60.

182. Duiwai Jingji Maoyibu Renshi Jiaoyuju, *Chukou huoyuan gailun,* 49; Zhongguo Duiwai Maoyi, *Zhongguo duiwai maoyi gailun,* 140; Li Xiaoxian, ed., *Duiwai maoyi yuanli,* 53.

183. See "Guanyu jianli chukou shangpin shengchan jidi de qingshi baogao" [Report and request for instructions on establishing an export commodity production base], submitted by the MFT and approved by the CCP Central Committee on 30 June 1960, in *WFSS,* 143. Summary of the report is translated in appendix C.

184. Chen Yun, "Manage Foreign Trade Work Well," May 1961, as translated in Lardy and Lieberthal, *Chen Yun's Strategy,* 141, 142.

185. Li Xiannian, "Shouhui xiafang nongcun de jiceng caimao jigou" [Recentralize the basic finance and trade organizations from the countryside], 22 June 1959, in *Li Xiannian,* 1:356–58.

186. "Guanyu zai dazhong chengshi jiaoqu fazhan fushipin shengchan de zhishi," [Directive to establish agricultural sideline production bases in the suburban areas surrounding the medium and large cities], issued by the Central Committee on 4 July 1959, in *ZELNP,* 2:241, n. 1. Li Xiannian, "Jiajin, fazhan dazhong chengshi jiaoqu de fushipin shengchan," in *Li Xiannian,* 1:361.

187. *ZRGJD,* 252–53.

188. "Guanyu dachengshi fushipin shengchan qingkuang he jinhou yijian de baogao" [A report on the current and future agricultural sideline production in large urban areas], issued by the State Council's Financial and Trade Office, approved and transmitted by the CCP Central Committee on 15 November 1960, in *ZRGJGD,* 150.

189. Cheng Chu-yuan, *China's Economic Development,* 155–58.

190. *ZELNP,* 2:298.

191. "Guanyu chengshi renmin gongshe wenti de pishi" [A comment on urban people's communes], issued by the CCP Central Committee on 9 March 1960, in *ZRGJGD,* 138; *ZRGJD,* 266–67.

192. Tan Qingfeng, "Jianli chukou shangpin shengchan tixi chutan," 4.

193. For more information, see *WFSS,* 14; Li Xiaoxian, *Duiwai maoyi yuanli,* 53; Wang Jun, " 'Wenge' houqi Zhou Enlai," 73–74.

194. Chen Yun, "Manage Foreign Trade Work Well," May 1961, as translated in Lardy and Lieberthal, *Chen Yun's Strategy,* 142.

195. In 1973, the State Council issued "Jianli chukou nongfu chanpin shengchan jidi

shixing banfa" [Trial procedures for export commodity production bases for agricultural sideline products] and "Jianli chukou gongyepin shengchan zhuanchang shixing banfa" [Trial procedures for specialized factories for industrial product exports]. See *WFSS*, 123–27; *ZRGJD*, 123.

196. Wang Shouchun, *Zhongguo duiwai*, 39; Zhongguo Duiwai Maoyi, *Zhongguo duiwai maoyi gailun*, 140; Li Xiaoxian, *Duiwai maoyi yuanli*, 53.

197. Li Xiannian, "Yi ju xinqingkuang," in *Li Xiannian*, 1:151.

4. Chaos and the Cultural Revolution, 1966–1971

1. Spero, *Politics*, 82, 196. The Kennedy Round did not reach an agreement on tariff reduction on agricultural goods and manufactured goods from the "South." There is no evidence to suggest that this lack of agreement had an adverse effect on world market demand for Chinese exports.

2. For instance, see "Guanyu gongye jiaotong he jiben jianshe danwei ruhe kaizhan wenhua dageming yundong de tongzhi" [Circular on how industrial, transport, and capital construction units should carry out the Cultural Revolution movement], issued by the CCP Central Committee and State Council on 2 July 1966; "Guanyu dangqian gongye shengchan qingkuang de baogao" [Report on the present industrial production conditions], issued by the Shanghai Party Committee and approved and transmitted by the CCP Central Committee on 19 July 1966, in *ZRGJGD*, 234. For an overall analysis, see State Statistical Bureau, "Concerning the Speed of Economic Development during the Ten Years of Domestic Turmoil," in Schoenhals, ed., *China's Cultural Revolution*, 262–66.

3. *ZRGJD*, 426–27.

4. Zhongguo Duiwai Jingji, *Zhongguo*, sect. 4, p. 8.

5. Guojia Tongjiju, ed., *Zhongguo tongji nianjian, 1983*, 158–62. Yang Dali argues that the agricultural sector was insulated from the violence of the Cultural Revolution largely through the efforts of Zhou Enlai and Tan Zhenlin. See Yang Dali, *Calamity*, 102–4.

6. *ZRGJD*, 426–27.

7. For instance, see Li Fuchun, "Woguo guomin jingji yijing kaishi quanmian haozhuan," 8; Zhou Enlai, "Zai disanjie," 18.

8. *RZJSH*, 2:1144. In 1953, Secretary of State John Foster Dulles described the strategy of "peaceful evolution," in which domestic pressures within the Communist state would cause socialist states to "evolve" to capitalism.

9. "Zhongguo Gongchandang zhongyang weiyuanhui tongzhi" [Circular of the Central Committee of the Chinese Communist Party], issued on 16 May 1966, in Union Research Institute, ed., *CCP Documents*, 20–28.

10. For an excellent collection of translated primary documents on the attacks, see Schoenhals, *China's Cultural Revolution*, pt. 2, sect. C.

11. "Guanyu fandui jingjizhuyi de tongzhi" [Circular on opposition to economism], issued by the CCP Central Committee on 11 January 1967, in Union Research Institute, *CCP Documents*, 166.

12. *Far Eastern Economic Review*, 8 September 1966, 443–54, as reprinted in Schoenhals, *China's Cultural Revolution*, 141–46; also see ibid., pt. 2, sect. E.

13. Petri, "Chinese Molestation of Diplomats," reprinted in Schoenhals, *China's Cultural Revolution*, 169–73.

14. *RZJSH*, 2: chap. 40.

15. *WFSS*, 14.

16. "Guanyu 1968 niandu shougou nongfu chanpin jiangshou biaozhun de tongzhi" [Circular on 1968 bonus standards in agricultural sideline production procurement], issued by the State Council on 16 June 1968, in ZRGJGD, 248. Also see the circular issued by the CCP Central Committee, the Central Cultural Revolution Committee, the State Council, and the Central Military Commission, "1969 nian chengxiang jumin mianbu fenpei wenti" [Problem of distributing cotton cloth to inhabitants of cities and suburbs in 1969], issued on 4 March 1969, in ZRGJGD, 252.

17. "Guanyu zhengzhi guashuai wenti de yijian" [Opinion on putting politics in command], submitted by Wang Renzhong, and approved and transmitted by the CCP Central Committee on 10 April 1966, in ZRGJGD, 231.

18. Ibid., 252.

19. WFSS, 70.

20. "Guanyu quxiao feimaoyi waihui fencheng banfa de tongzhi" [Circular on abolishing the method of apportioning foreign exchange for nontrade channels], issued by the State Council on 9 May 1967, in ZRGJGD, 240.

21. WFSS, 49.

22. For instance, see "Huaqiao dingqi chuxu cunkuan zhangcheng" [Regulations regarding overseas Chinese fixed savings deposits], issued by the People's Bank of China in January 1958 and revised April 1960 and July 1960, in Zhonghua Renmin Yinhang Jihuasi, *Lilü,* 273–74; "Guanyu xiugai huaqiao chuxu cunkuan lilü he zengjia cunqi zhonglei de tongzhi" [Circular on revising the interest and deposit schedules of overseas Chinese fixed savings accounts], Yinguoqingcaozi 60.154, issued by the People's Bank of China on 19 June 1960, ibid., 277–78; and "Guanyu chuxu ruhe jisuan lixi deng wenti de zhonghe jieda" [A comprehensive response to calculating interest rates on savings deposits and other such problems], ibid., 349–52.

23. "Guanyu caizheng maoyi he shougongye fangmian ruogan wenti de baogao" [Report on several policy problems in finance, trade, and the handicraft industries], submitted by the State Council's Office of Finance and Trade and the SPC and approved by the CCP Central Committee on 24 September 1966, in ZRGJGD, 236.

24. ZRGJD, 463–464.

25. "Guanyu chexiao huaqiao touzi gongsi de baogao" [Report on closing the Overseas Chinese Investment Company], submitted by the military representative of the People's Bank of China and approved by the State Council on 22 May 1970, in ZRGJGD, 258.

26. ZRGJD, 495; "Guanyu huaqiao touzi jige wenti de dafu" [Response to several problems in overseas Chinese investment], Yinjunmiyezi 70.154, issued by the People's Bank of China on 29 May 1970, in Zhongguo Renmin Yinhang Jihuasi, *Lilü,* 362–63. It is interesting that many of the export promotion measures were formally ended in the early 1970s when Zhou Enlai had regained power. One possible explanation is that these measures had been moribund during the Cultural Revolution, but not officially eliminated. When Zhou regained power after 1971, he administered an administrative coup de grace and proceeded to build China's foreign economic policy anew.

27. For an interesting analysis of this problem drawn from interviews with overseas Chinese, see Pepper, *Radicalism,* 540–43, 545–47.

28. WFSS, 14.

29. ZRGJGD, 261.

30. Other ministries also reverted control to local authorities. For instance, the Ministry of Rural Reclamation (Nongkenbu) in 4 January 1970 surrendered control of

rubber reclamation areas (*xiangjiao kenqu*) in Yunnan, Fujian, Guangxi, and Shantou (Guangdong Province). On the same date, Guangzhou Military District's Production and Construction Corps was ordered to surrender control over the Hainan Island and Zhejiang Rubber Reclamation Areas, the South China Tropical Products Institute, and all industries associated with the corps to the local authorities. See the State Council/State Military Commission circular issued on 4 January 1970 in *ZRGJGD*, 256.

31. See Mao Zedong's 6 June 1964 speech to the central work conference, in *RZJSH* 2:1199.

32. Zhonggong Zhongyang Wenxian Yanjiushi, ed., *"Guanyu jianguo yilai dang de ruogan lishi wenti de jueyi" zhushiben*, 551, as quoted in Zheng Derong et al., *Zhongguo jingji tizhi*, 222.

33. Riskin, "Neither Plan nor Market," 135.

34. According to Bo Yibo,

> The First, Second, and Third Fronts are delineated according to China's geography. The coastal areas are the First Front, the intermediate areas are the Second Front, and rear areas are the Third Front. The Third Front is divided into two large sections: the Southwest Third Front includes the entire or a large portion of Yunnan, Guizhou, and Sichuan Provinces as well as the western parts of Hunan and Hubei Provinces; the Northwest Third Front includes the entire or a large portion of Shaanxi, Gansu, Ningxia, and Qinghai Provinces as well as the western parts of Henan and Shanxi Provinces. There is also a Large and Small Third Front: the Southwest and Northwest are the Large Third Front; the provincial hinterlands of the intermediate and coastal areas are the Small Third Front.

See *RZJSH*, 2:1200.

35. Ibid., 1216.

36. For a similar approach and a detailed chronology of events, see Sun Dongsheng, "Woguo jingji jianshe," 42–48.

37. Riskin, "Neither Plan nor Market," 137–48; also see Barry Naughton, "Industrial Policy," 164–67.

38. Mao Zedong, "Reading Notes on the Soviet Union's 'Political Economics,'" in *Miscellany*, 296.

39. Gurley, *China's Economy*, 5.

40. Mao Zedong, *Chairman Mao*, 65. For an analysis of this policy, see Liu Guoguang, ed., *Zhongguo jingji fazhan zhanlüe wenti yanjiu*, 264–87.

41. *RZJSH*, 1:483–84; MacFarquhar, *Origins*, 3:370.

42. *ZELNP*, 1:571. For Zhou's initial reaction to Mao's views, see 567.

43. John Holdridge, telephone interview, 13 January 1997; Holdridge, *Crossing the Divide*, 21–22. Holdridge was in charge of the mainland analysis unit attached to the U.S. consulate in Hong Kong between 1962 and 1966. Also see MacFarquhar, *Origins*, 3:376.

44. Naughton, "Third Front," 352; *RZJSH*, 2:1019–20.

45. Bo Yibo, "Guanyu yijiuliusinian jihua," 5–7; *RZJSH*, 2:1194.

46. Li Xiannian, "Shichang qingkuang haozhuanhou xuyao jixu jiejue de wenti," in *Li Xiannian*, 2:170, 180–218.

47. "Guanyu lizheng 1964 nian chao'e wancheng yiyierqianwan meiyuan qiaohui renwu de qingshi baogao" [Report and request for instructions on working hard to meet and exceed the overseas Chinese U.S. dollar remittances for 1964 of U.S. $120 million,

submitted by the Small Group on Overseas Chinese Remittances and approved by the Central Committee and the State Council on 21 May 1964, in ZRGJGD, 207.

48. *RZJSH,* 2:1194; Li Fuchun, "Nuli jiejue renmin chi chuan yong" [Work hard to resolve the problem of eating, wearing, and using], delivered on 20 March 1963 to a Small SPC Leadership Conference, in *Xuanji,* 305–8; Sun Dongsheng, "Woguo jingji jianshe," 42–43.

49. *Renmin Daxue fuyin baokan ziliao: guomin jingji yu jihua* [People's University reprints: National economy and plan], 4 (1981): 57, as cited in Naughton, "Third Front," 352, n. 4.

50. For more information, see the collection of documents concerning the Third FYP draft in *Dang de wenxian* 51 (1996): 10–25.

51. MacFarquhar, *Origins,* 3:364.

52. Li Zhisui, *Private Life,* 413–14.

53. Mao Zedong, "Remarks at a Briefing," March 1964, in *Miscellany,* 343.

54. MacFarquhar, *Origins,* 3:622, n. 27.

55. Teiwes, *Politics,* 452.

56. MacFarquhar, *Origins,* 3:143–72.

57. Jiang Siyi, *Zhongguo Renmin,* 1533.

58. Li Zhisui, *Private Life,* 412.

59. Lieberthal, "Great Leap Forward," 337–40; "Guanyu cong jundui choudiao 5,300 ming ganbu dao difang zhengzhi jigou gongzuo de tongzhi" [Circular on transferring 5,300 military cadre to work in local government organizations," issued by the CCP Central Organization Bureau and the PLA's General Political Department on 12 May 1964, in Jiang Siyi, *Zhongguo Renmin,* 1534. For more on *xitong,* see Lieberthal, *Governing China,* 194–207.

60. "Guanyu zuzhi junshi yeying huodong de lianhe tongzhi" [Joint circular on organizing military camps], issued by the Commission on Physical Education, the Headquarters of the General Staff, the General Political Department of the PLA, the Ministry of Education, the All-China Federation of Trade Unions, the Central Committee of the Communist Youth League, and the All-China Women's Federation on 2 June 1964, in Jiang Siyi, *Zhongguo Renmin,* 1534–35. The military camps were designed to teach the masses common military skills such as how to fire weapons, and also to provide them with the "political" weapon of Mao Zedong Thought. For more on militarizing the economy, see Naughton, "Patterns," 239–40.

61. Zongcanmoubu Zuozhanbu, "Zongcan zuozhanbu de baogao," 34–35; *RZJSH,* 2:1198; Sun Dongsheng, "Woguo jingji jianshe," 44.

62. Jiang Siyi, *Zhongguo Renmin,* 1533.

63. "Guanyu zai guofang gongye xitong jianli geji zhengzhi gongzuo jiguan de ruogan wenti de jianyi" [An opinion on the various problems of establishing political affair organizations within various levels of the defense industry bureaucracy," submitted by Luo Ruiqing, chief of the General Staff, and approved by the Central Committee on 6 June 1964, in Jiang Siyi, *Zhongguo Renmin,* 1535.

64. *ZELNP,* 2:643; Sun Dongsheng, "Woguo jingji jianshe," 44; for a different translation, see Mao Zedong, "Talk on the Third Five-Year Plan," 6 June 1964, in *Miscellany,* 354. For a similar quote, see Mao Zedong, "Interjections at a Briefing of the State Planning Commission Leading Group," 11 May 1964, in *Miscellany,* 349. For Mao Zedong's analysis of Stalin's experience during the war and its contribution to the Third Front idea, see Sun Dongsheng, "Woguo jingji jianshe," 43.

65. Mao Zedong, "Talk on the Third Five-Year Plan," in *Miscellany,* 353.

66. Ibid., 354; *RZJSH,* 2:1200 (The *Wansui* and Bo accounts overlap with the phrase "As long as imperialism exists . . . " Because of the lack of further evidence, the sequencing of the rest of the quote is unclear). Mao Zedong, *Jianguo,* vol. 11, does not contain this speech. For a description of the Panzhihua steel complex, see *RZJSH,* 2:1203–05; Naughton, "Third Front," 356–58.

67. *RZJSH,* 2:1194–96.

68. Ibid., 1200.

69. Whiting, "Sino-Soviet Split," 536–37; for Soviet troops massing along the Sino-Soviet border, see Sun Dongsheng, "Woguo jingji jianshe," 43.

70. MacFarquhar, *Origins,* 3:360–64.

71. John Holdridge, telephone interview, 13 January 1997.

72. *ZELNP,* 2:662–63; Manchester, *Glory,* 1016–18.

73. This slightly alters the argument put forward by Barry Naughton, who was the first Western economist to describe in detail the enormous cost of the Third Front program. Naughton has persuasively argued that "the entire Chinese leadership—led by Mao—took the strategic threat from the United States very seriously beginning in 1964." Based on the newly issued primary documents, this study argues that the threat was not perceived by the elites until summer 1964 and that the primary threat was from the Soviet Union; following the Gulf of Tonkin incident, the United States and the Soviet Union were deemed to be the primary threats. However, the new evidence substantiates Naughton's argument that Mao "called for drastic acceleration of the pace of inland construction" two weeks after the Gulf of Tonkin incident of 4 August 1964. See Naughton, "Third Front," 371; idem, "Industrial Policy," 157; Lieberthal and Oksenberg, *Policy Making,* 187–88.

74. *RZJSH,* 2:1197–98.

75. Sun Dongsheng, "Woguo jingji jianshe," 46–47; *ZELNP,* 2:659, n. 1.

76. Li Fuchun, Bo Yibo, and Luo Ruiqing, "Guanyu guojia jingji jianshe ruhe fangbei diren turan xiji wenti de baogao," 33–34; *RZJSH,* 2:1200.

77. Zhonggong Zhongyong, "Guanyu jiaqiang yierxian de houfang jianshe he beizhan gongzuo de zhishi," submitted by Zhou Enlai and Luo Ruiqing on 29 October 1964, and approved by the Central Committee on 29 October 1964; *ZELNP,* 2:645, 654, 655.

78. Zhou Enlai, "Fazhan guomin jingji de zhuyao renwu" [The primary task in developing the national economy], delivered to the NPC on 21 December 1964, in *ZELJJWX,* 563–66.

79. Zhou Enlai, "Guanyu jiben jianshe de jige wenti," 39; *ZELNP,* 2:724.

80. "Guanyu yinjin xinjishu gongzuo jige zhuyao wenti de baogao" [Report on several important problems with importing new technology], submitted by the Small Group on New Technology Imports and approved by the Central Committee on 13 April 1965, in *ZRGJGD,* 215. Italics added.

81. Ibid.; "Guanyu bixu yange kongzhi cong zibenzhuyi guojia jinkou de tongzhi" [Circular on strictly controlling imports from Western countries], a report submitted by the Central Committee's Office of the Three-Man Small Group on Foreign Trade and approved by the Central Committee and the State Council on 13 April 1965, in *ZRGJGD,* 215; *ZELNP,* 2:729–30.

82. Jiang Siyi, *Zhongguo Renmin,* 1560.

83. *ZELNP,* 2:729, 763.

84. Yu's key associates included Kang Shien, Tang Ke, and Song Zhenming. For an

excellent account of the Petroleum Group, see Lieberthal and Oksenberg, *Policy Making*, chap. 5.

85. *RZJSH*, 2:1205–07; *ZELNP*, 2:745, n. 1; also see the interesting exchange between Zhou and Yu concerning the priority given to agriculture and national defense on 13 November 1958, in *ZELNP*, 2:763–64.

86. Lieberthal and Oksenberg, *Policy Making*, 192, 196.

87. *RZJSH*, 2:1216–17.

88. Naughton, "Third Front," 379; for a Chinese accounting of the Third Front's achievements and cost, see Sun Dongsheng, "Woguo jingji jianshe," 47–48.

89. Guangdong Nianjian Bianji, *Guangdong*, 209, 519; Guojia Tongjiju, *Zhongguo tongji nianjian, 1984*, 326–28; Vogel, *One Step Ahead*, 35–40.

90. Perkins, "China's Economic Policy," 515; Cheng Chu-yuan, "China's Industry," 155.

91. *ZELNP*, 3:336, 398–99, 404.

92. Ibid., 272.

93. Wang Jun, "'Wenge' houqi Zhou Enlai," 72.

94. *ZELNP*, 3:280–81.

95. In 1966, Demag of West Germany led a Western European consortium into negotiations over a large steel plant; the negotiations failed. See Stahnke, "Political context," 149–53. In 1967, Lowey Engineering of Britain and Mannesman of West Germany signed a $6 million contract to export a steel tube plant to China; Mannesman delivered the plant and equipment to China in 1968. See Heymann, "Acquisition," 714. Lieberthal and Oksenberg report that "in 1966–67, the Chinese purchased equipment from France for geophysical surveys which it used in the Bohai. By 1969, it had successfully and secretly bought an $11 million drill ship from Japan." Lieberthal and Oksenberg, *Policy Making*, 195.

96. For instance, see Zhou's 21 June 1970 criticism of cadre engaged in Sino-Japanese fishery talks who knew nothing about the global fishery industry, in *ZELNP*, 3:374–75; Zhou's promotion of foreign trade in October 1970, ibid., 398.

97. Ibid., 76.

98. Stahnke, "Political Context," 155.

99. Price, "International Trade," 602.

100. Zhongguo Duiwai Jingji, *Zhongguo*, 108–20; *ZELNP*, 3:294.

101. Mao Zedong, "Reading Notes on the Soviet Union's 'Political Economics,'" in *Miscellany*, 296.

102. For further discussion, see Perkins, "China's Economic Policy," 486–90.

103. "Guowuyuan pizhuan 'Zhongguo Renmin Yinhang guanyu hongweibing chachao de waibi piaoju he waibi youjia zhengjian chuli wenti de baogao,'" State Council document 68.23, issued on 17 January 1968, as translated (under the title "On how to handle foreign currency, foreign currency receipts, and foreign currency securities confiscated by Red Guards") in Schoenhals, *China's Cultural Revolution*, 245–64.

104. Peng Jianxin, "Zhou Enlai," 31.

105. "Guanyu kaihao chunji Guangzhou chukou shangpin jiaoyihui de tongzhi" [Circular on successfully carrying out the spring Guangzhou Export Production Trade Fair], jointly issued by the CCP Central Committee, the State Council, the Central Military Commission, and the Central Cultural Revolution Group on 13 April 1967, in *ZRGJGD*, 240. Zhou describes this as a directive approved by Mao. See *ZELNP*, 3:144.

106. Peng Jianxin, "Zhou Enlai," 31.

107. *ZELNP*, 3:145–46; Peng Jianxin, "Zhou Enlai," 31.

108. C. Lee, *Japan*, 151.

109. Whiting, *Chinese Domestic Politics*, 58; for problems encountered by West German technicians, see Stahnke, *"Political Context,"* 155–57.

110. *ZELNP*, 3:180–82, 438–40.

111. Vogel, *Canton*, 334; *ZELNP*, 3:188–89.

112. Harding, "Chinese State," 182–85.

113. MacFarquhar, "Succession," 306–11.

114. Peng Jianxin, "Zhou Enlai," 31; Vogel, *Canton*, 336.

115. "Guanyu kaihao 1968 nian chunji chukou shangpin jiaoyihui de tongzhi" [Circular on successfully carrying out the 1968 spring Guangzhou Export Production Trade Fair], jointly issued by the CCP Central Committee et al. on 8 March 1968, in *ZRGJGD*, 247–48.

116. Peng Jianxin, "Zhou Enlai," 29.

117. C. Lee, *Japan*, 155.

118. Ibid., 158. For a very useful chart detailing particular fairs and the corresponding numbers of participants, see 164.

119. Theroux, "Legal and Practical Problems," 548.

120. Peng Jianxin, "Zhou Enlai," 31.

121. *ZELNP*, 3:161.

122. Ibid., 185–86.

123. Ibid., 193.

124. Ibid., 260.

125. Ibid., 400.

126. Ibid., 266, 268, 398.

127. For an analysis of the period, see Lupton, "Hong Kong's Role," 184–87.

128. *ZELNP*, 3:169.

129. Ibid., 211.

130. Ibid., 339.

131. C. Lee, *Japan*, 158; Zhongguo Duiwai Jingji, *Zhongguo*, sect. 1; p. 104.

132. Batsavage and Davie, "China's International Trade and Finance," 712.

133. *WFSS*, 49. Similar shortages faced the domestic economy by 1970. See Cheng Chu-yuan, "China's Industry," 159.

134. Wang Jun, "'Wenge' houqi Zhou Enlai," 73.

5. Resurrecting the Four Modernizations, 1971–1974

1. *ZRGJGD*, 267; *ZRGJD*, 483. According to Zhou's *Chronicle*, Zhou increasingly gained power in various sectors after the Ninth Party Congress in 1969. Perhaps Zhou's revival was in part due to his developing a successful working relationship with Lin Biao. See Li Zhisui, *Private Life*, 538–39. One simple indicator: for five years during the Cultural Revolution, Zhou intentionally never issued autographs. In July 1970, Zhou decided to give the daughter of the Ceylonese ambassador an autograph. See *ZELNP*, 3:379.

2. *ZELNP*, 3:350.

3. Provincial foreign trade bureaus (*sheng duiwai maoyi ju*) were reestablished only in 1973. For example, see Zhejiangsheng Jingji, *Zhejiang shengqing gaiyao*, 413. Foreign trade corporations were also revitalized; the Technical Import/Export Corporation was reopened in late 1972. See Cheng Chu-yuan, *China's Economic Development*, 450.

4. For the exact measures adopted by the United States to relax its economic embargo, see O. Lee, "U.S. Trade Policy," 57–61.

5. Spero, *Politics,* 264.

6. Zhongguo Duiwai Jingji, *Zhongguo,* sect. 4, p. 105; Barnett, *China's Economy,* 425; Lieberthal and Oksenberg, *Policy Making,* 199; Whiting, *Chinese Domestic Politics,* 60.

7. Union Research Service, *CCP Documents,* 193–197; ZELNP, 3:191.

8. ZELNP, 3:361, 364.

9. For a concise account of the 9.13 incident, see MacFarquhar, "Succession," 311–34; for the PLA version, see Jiang Siyi, *Zhongguo Renmin,* 1622–26; also see Tong Xiaopeng, *Fengyu sishinian,* 2:457–66; Li Zhisui, *Private Life,* 536–41.

10. MacFarquhar, "Succession," 336–40.

11. Yahuda, *Towards the End of Isolationism,* 66–67. Yahuda does state that Mao "had in effect at least tacitly approved" foreign economic policy initiatives of the early to mid-1970s.

12. Li Zhisui, *Private Life,* 542–43.

13. MacFarquhar, "Succession," 347–51; ZELNP, 3:509, 583; Tong Xiaopeng, *Fengyu sishinian,* 2:470–74; Li Zhisui, *Private Life,* 544–46.

14. Li Zhisui, *Private Life,* 547–52.

15. ZRGJGD, 270; ZRGJD, 496–98; MacFarquhar, "Succession," 334.

16. Naughton, "Third Front," 362.

17. Li Xiannian, "Jiben jianshe yao jizhong liliang da jianmiezhan" [Capital construction must concentrate its powers to fight a war of annihilation], delivered to an expanded meeting of the Small Leading Group of the National Planning Conference, on 21 February 1973, in *Li Xiannian,* 2:270–72.

18. Zhou Enlai, "Yao xue waiguo de changchu" [We must study the strengths of foreign countries], comments made on 26 February 1973, in ZELJJWX, 641; Wang Jun, "'Wenge' houqi Zhou Enlai," 71.

19. ZRGJD, 499–500.

20. For instance, see "Wuzhengfu zhuyi shi jiamakesi zhuyi pianzi de fangeming gongju," *Renmin ribao,* 14 October 1972.

21. "Zhi zhuyi shengchan, bu zhuyi shangceng jianzhu, luxian budui," in ZRGJGD, 276. For an excellent analysis of the attempt to criticize the "ultraleftism" of the Cultural Revolution, see Joseph, *Critique,* 120–50.

22. ZRGJD, 499–500.

23. Chen Donglin, "Chen Yun," 1092; Sun Yeli, "Women zuo gongzuo," 29–32.

24. ZELNP, 3:583, 636–37. For more on Deng during the 1973–75 period, see Chi Hsin, *Teng Hsiao-ping.*

25. MacFarquhar, "Succession," 340–42.

26. Sun Yeli, "Women zuo gongzuo," 29–30.

27. Theroux, "Legal and Practical Problems," 541; Batsavage and Davie, "China's International Trade," 712. For the strengthening of the Foreign Experts Bureau, see ZELNP, 3:581–82.

28. Zhou Enlai, "Xunqiu butong zhengzhi zhiduxia youliyu shuangfang fazhan maoyi de banfa" [Searching for methods to be used by two different political systems that are mutually beneficial to develop trade], 29 June 1973, in ZELJJWX, 642–47; Wang Jun, "'Wenge' houqi Zhou Enlai," 71.

29. "Guanyu shixing feimaoyi waihui guanli banfa de tongzhi" [Circular on the imple-

mentation of methods to manage foreign exchange earned in noncommercial transactions], Caiyuzi 72.39, issued by the SPC and MOF on 30 September 1972, in Caizhengbu, ed., *Feimaoyi waihui zhidu huibian,* 3–6.

30. "Guanyu yinhang liyong guowai cunkuan chengdan yibufen chengtao shebei jinkou waihui zhifu renwu de qingshi baogao" [Report and request for instructions concerning the bank's use of foreign deposits to assume a portion of the foreign exchange payments for the turnkey plants and equipment imports], submitted to Li Xiannian by the SPC and approved by Zhou Enlai on 11 September 1973, in *ZELNP,* 3:620–21; Chen Yun, *Wenxuan,* 3:217–18.

31. *ZELNP,* 3: 621, n. 1.

32. Ibid., n. 2

33. Chen Yun, *Wenxuan,* 3:217–18; Sun Yeli, "Women zuo gongzuo," 30–31.

34. Chen Yun, "Jinkou gongzuo zhong liyong shangpin jiaoyisuo de wenti" [Problem of using commodity exchanges in import work], in Chen Yun, *Wenxuan,* 3:221–22.

35. Chen Yun, "Liyong guonei fengfu laodongli shengchan chengpin chukou" [Use China's abundant labor to produce finished products for export], ibid., 224. For an interesting discussion on this period, see Sun Yeli, "Wenge houqi Chen Yun," 1088–89.

36. *ZELNP,* 3:499–501. Ye Jianying had assumed responsibility for the daily workings of the Central Military Commission. See *ZRGJD,* 483.

37. "Zhiliang zheiyang xiajiang, ruhe yuanwai, ruhe beizhan?" See *ZRGJGD,* 269; Harwit, *China's Automobile Industry,* 20–26.

38. Peng Jianxin, "Zhou Enlai," 29.

39. *ZRGJD,* 492–93. Zhou received similar reports during the spring of 1971, when certain foreign businesspeople complained that their Chinese counterparts did not deliver goods according to the contractually stipulated time. See *ZELNP,* 3:457.

40. *ZELNP,* 3:518–19.

41. "Zhou zongli pishi" [Directive issued by Premier Zhou], issued on 2 November 1972, cited in Peng Jianxin, "Zhou Enlai," 30.

42. "Guanyu zuzhihao qiuji Guangzhou jiaoyihui chukou huoyuan de jinji tongzhi" [Emergency circular on correctly organizing export commodity procurement for the fall Guangzhou trade fair], issued by the State Council on 28 October 1972, ibid., 29.

43. Li Xiannian, "Zhuajin shougongyipin he tute chanpin de shengchan yu shougou" [Pay close attention to the production and procurement of arts and handicrafts], a letter sent to the State Planning Commission and the Ministries of Foreign Trade, Light Industry, Agriculture and Forestry, and Commerce on 4 November 1972, in *Li Xiannian,* 2:263.

44. *ZELNP,* 3:503.

45. Li Xiannian, "Waimao gongzuo yao zhong hetong, shou xinyong" [Our foreign trade work must take contracts seriously and be as good as one's word], a letter sent to Yu Qiuli, Yuan Baohua, and the Ministry of Foreign Trade on 17 May 1973, in *Li Xiannian,* 2:283.

46. "Guanyu zai yuanwai junshi zhuangbei zhong suo faxian de zhiliang wenti de baogao" [Report on quality problems discovered in military aid equipment], issued by the General Logistical Department and approved and transmitted by the State Council and Central Military Commission on 18 June 1973, in *ZRGJD,* 513–14.

47. *ZELNP,* 3:501–502.

48. According to current Chinese statistics, the rate of decrease in the gross value of social product (includes agricultural, industrial, construction, transportation, and commercial indicators) between its high in 1960 (RMB 267.9 billion) and its low in 1962 (RMB

180 billion) was greater than the drop between its high in 1966 (RMB 306.2 billion) and its low in 1968 (RMB 264.8 billion). Somewhat more detailed statistical comparisons can be made by consulting Guojia Tongjiju, *Zhongguo tongji nianjian, 1983.*

49. For a general review on industrial economic reforms during the post–Cultural Revolution period, see Dangdai Zhongguo Congshu, *Dangdai Zhongguo waijiao,* 148–51.

50. Lieberthal and Oksenberg, *Policy Making,* 200.

51. Lieberthal and Oksenberg argue that Yu Qiuli, who formally took control of the State Planning Commission in 1970, and his Petroleum Group were especially supportive of the reintroduction of the import substitution strategy and its strong emphasis on modernizing China's petrochemical industries. See ibid., 196–98.

52. Ibid., *Policy Making,* 192; Harding, "Chinese State," 179.

53. ZELNP, 3:449.

54. Mao had become seriously ill in mid-January 1972. See ZELNP, 3:509–13; Li Zhisui, *Private Life,* 547–62.

55. The report was titled "Guanyu jinkou chengtao huaxian, huafei jishu shebei de baogao" [Report on importing chemical fiber plants and fertilizer turnkey plants, equipment, and technology], in ZELNP, 3:511; Chen Donglin, "Chen Yun," 1093, 1095; Heymann, "Acquisition," 719–20. Wang Jun argues that the Eight-Character Policy remains China's guiding policy today. See Wang Jun, "'Wenge' houqi Zhou Enlai," 72–73.

56. ZELNP, v. 3, 565.

57. Heymann, "Acquisition," 714–17.

58. "Guanyu zengjia shebei jinkou, kuoda jingji jiaoliu de qingshi baogao" [Report and request for instructions concerning the increase of equipment imports and the expansion of economic exchange] was submitted to the State Council by the SPC on 2 January 1973 and approved in principle on 22 March 1973, in ZRGJGD, 272, 275; ZRGJD, 505–6.

59. The SPC also submitted "Guanyu chengtao shebei jinkou wenti de qingshi baogao" [Report and request for instructions concerning the importation of complete plants and equipment imports] on 13 March; it was approved in principle by the State Council on 22 March 1973. See ZELNP, 3:571.

60. Zhou Enlai first approved the Spey engine imports in July and December 1971. See ibid., 472, 543.

61. The Central Committee and State Council had already approved the project on 21 August 1972. For more detail, see ZRGJGD, 270; ZRGJD, 496–98; ZELNP, 3:571.

62. ZRGJGD, 270; ZRGJD, 496–98.

63. "Guanyu banhao shougongye shengchan hezuoshe, genghao de wei nongye shengchan wei shichang fuwu de baogao" [Report on running well the handicraft industry production cooperatives and improving production for the agricultural industry and service for the market], issued by the General Office of the State Handicraft Cooperatives and approved by the State Council on 9 March 1963, in ZRGJGD, 188–89; Shanghai Shehui Kexueyuan, *Shanghai jingji,* 244–46.

64. "Guanyu fazhan gongyi meishu shengchan wenti de baogao" [Report on the problem of developing arts and handicraft production], issued by the MFT and the Ministry of Light Industry and approved and transmitted by the State Council on 21 April 1973, in ZRGJGD, 276; ZRGJD, 511. Also see Chen Yun, "Gongyipin chukou wenti" [Export problems of arts and handicrafts], in *Wenxuan,* 3:225–27.

65. "Guanyu jiaqiang difang lüyou jigou de qingshi baogao" [Report and request for instructions on strengthening the local tourist organizations], issued by the Ministry of

Foreign Affairs and agreed and transmitted by the State Council on 30 May 1973, in ZRGJGD, 276.

66. Zhonggong Zhongyang Wenxian Yanjiushi, ed., *Guanyu jianguo yilai,* 264, as cited in Zhang Wenru, *Mao Zedong,* 222.

67. Lieberthal and Oksenberg, *Policy Making,* 198–99.

68. "Guanyu jieyue ranliaoyou de anpai qingkuang baogao" [Situation report on arrangements to conserve fuel oil], issued by the SPC and approved and transmitted by the State Council on 1 March 1974, in ZRGJGD, 282–83.

69. Li Xiannian, "Jieyue ranliao, shaoshao yuanyou" [Conserve fuels and burn less oil], speech to the leaders of the State Planning Commission, the Ministry of Foreign Trade, the Ministry of Petrochemicals, the Ministry of Coal Industry, and other departments on 25 July 1975, in *Li Xiannian,* 2:305; for more information on the problems of foodstuffs procurement to finance the import substitution program, see *Li Xiannian,* "Fazhan yangzhu shi jian dashi" [The development of the pork industry is a very important matter], speech given on 7 September 1975 to the Conference on Live Pig Production, convened by the State Council, in *Li Xiannian,* 2:293.

70. Li Xiannian, "Yao guiding jieyue yongyou de banfa" [We must formulate regulations on petroleum conservation], a speech to the first meeting of the State Council on 23 August 1975, in *Li Xiannian,* 2:306; "Chongfen liyong dizhi ranliao" [We must fully use lower-quality fuels], 29 January 1977 letter to Yu Qiuli, ibid., 307.

71. "Chukou gongyepin shengchan zhuanxiang daikuan de yijian" [An opinion on the specialized loan program for industrial export product production], issued by the MFT and approved by the State Council in 1972, in WFSS, 70.

72. For an analysis of the loans and their post-1972 result, see WFSS, 70–83; Wu Wutong, *Duiwai maoyi jichu zhishi gailun,* 30–32.

73. "Guanyu zhuanfa 'duanqi waihui daikuan shixing banfa' xi zunzhao zhixing (fu: duanqi waihui daikuan shixing banfa)" [The letter of instructions concerning the issuance of "The Provisional Measures for Short-Term Foreign Exchange Loans" (attached: The Provisional Measures for Short-Term Foreign Exchange Loans)], Maochudaierzi 73.99/Yinwaizi 73.135, issued by the MFT and the People's Bank of China on 16 June 1973, in Zhongguo Renmin Yinhang Jihuasi, *Lilü,* 378–79.

74. Duiwai Jingji Maoyibu Renshi, *Chukuo huoyuan gailun,* 89.

75. Between 1973 and 1979, 2,010 projects received loans totaling $247.37 million. See WFSS, 93–94, 104; Duiwai Jingji Maoyibu Renshi, *Chukuo huoyuan gailun,* 90; Li Xiaoxian, *Duiwai maoyi yuanli,* 60–61; Wu Wutong, *Duiwai maoyi jichu zhishi gailun,* 33–34.

76. WFSS, 111–15; Duiwai Jingji Maoyibu Renshi, *Chukou huoyuan gailun,* 91–92; Li Xiaoxian, *Duiwai maoyi yuanli,* 61; Wu Wutong, *Duiwai maoyi jichu zhishi gailun,* 34–35.

77. "Guanyu shixing nongfu chanpin tongyi jiangshou banfa de qingshi baogao" [Report and request for instructions on implementing a unified bonus scheme on agricultural sideline products], submitted by the SPC and approved and transmitted by the State Council on 19 March 1973, in ZRGJGD, 275; WFSS, 21, 38–41.

78. "Jianli chukou nongfu chanpin shengchan jidi shixing banfa" [Trial procedures for export commodity production bases for agricultural sideline products]; "Jianli chukou gongyepin shengchan jidi shixing banfa" [Trial procedures for specialized factories for industrial product exports], approved by the State Council and issued by the SPC. A detailed description of the texts is provided in WFSS, 123–27; ZRGJD, 123. The trial

procedures were updated in 1979 and issued by the Import/Export Management Committee on 10 August 1980; see chap. 6.

79. *WFSS*, 161. For a complete listing of single-item export bases as of 1982, see Duiwai Jingji Maoyibu Renshi, *Chukou huoyuan gailun,* 69–78.

80. *WFSS*, 163. Forty-two single-item bases were dedicated to the production of grain, edible oil, and food products; fifty-one produced local products and livestock. See Duiwai Jingji Maoyibu Renshi, *Chukou huoyuan gailun,* 58.

81. *WFSS*, 162 (for more information see 160–64); Duiwai Jingji Maoyibu Renshi, *Chukou huoyuan gailun,* 57–59; Zhongguo Duiwai Maoyi, *Zhongguo duiwai maoyi gailun,* 141; Wu Wutong, *Duiwai maoyi jichu zhishi gailun,* 49–50.

82. Duiwai Jingji Maoyibu Renshi, *Chukou huoyuan gailun,* 58.

83. Zhongguo Duiwai Maoyi, *Zhongguo duiwai maoyi gailun,* 140–41.

84. *WFSS*, 118.

85. For more complete information, see ibid., 127–36; Vogel, *One Step Ahead,* 181–89, 343–46.

86. Others include Hubei Province's Jingzhou Prefecture (1976); Jiangsu Province's Nantong Prefecture (1980) and Xuzhou Prefectures (1980); Zhejiang Province's Jiaxing Prefecture (1978) and Taizhou Prefecture (1980); Henan Province's Nanyang Prefecture (1978); Shandong Province's Yantai Prefecture (1976), Weifang Prefecture (1976), Linyi Prefecture (1978), Heze Prefecture (1980), and Qingdao City (1979); Hebei Province's Zhangjiakou Prefecture (1976) and Shijiazhuang Prefecture (1981); Shanxi Province's Yanbei Prefecture (1977); Xinjiang Province's Tulufan Prefecture (1979); Liaoning Province's Lüda City (1979), and Yingkou City (1981); and Heilongjiang Province's Suibei Prefecture (1980). For more detail, see *WFSS*, 136–54; Zhongguo Duiwai Maoyi, *Zhongguo duiwai maoyi gailun,* 140–41; Duiwai Jingji Maoyibu Renshi, *Chukou huoyuan gailun,* 55–7, 65–68; Wu Wutong, *Duiwai maoyi jichu zhishi gailun,* 47–49.

87. *WFSS*, 165. Article I of the 1979 provisional measures outlines similar responsibilities of the specialized factory.

88. For a detailed analysis of the eight-item assessment index (*baxiang kaohe zhibiao*), see *WFSS*, 166.

89. The specialized factories were in Shanghai (fifty), Jiangsu (twenty-five), Beijing (eight), Guangdong and Guizhou (three each), Hunan (two), and Henan, Hubei, and Shanxi (one each). Seventy-seven specialized factories produced textile goods, three produced light industrial goods, three produced handicrafts, two produced local and animal products, five processed metallic ore products, one made pharmaceuticals, and three were packaging plants. See *WFSS*, 164.

90. Forty-eight of the Shanghai specialized factories producing textiles earned $198 million in 1978, $310 million in 1980, and $334 million in 1982. See ibid., 165.

91. Wu Wutong, *Duiwai maoyi jichu zhishi gailun,* 54.

92. These included the Specialized Loan Program for Industrial Export Production, the Investment Fund for Export Product Production, the Short-Term Foreign Exchange Loan to MFT industries, and the annual state allocation of foreign exchange to the ECPBS. See *WFSS*, 71, 92, 112, 118. Another major source of funds included the Circulating Fund to Promote Export Commodity Production (Fuchi Chukou Shangpin Shengchan Zhouzhuan Zijin), which was established in 1975. See ibid., 83–90; Duiwai Jingji Maoyibu Renshi, *Chukou huoyuan gailun,* 87–88. The MFT also used a portion of Foreign Trade Circulating Funds (Waimao Zhouzhuan Zijin) to aid construction of export bases. See the example of investment in the Zhejiang Eel Production Base, ibid., 90–91.

93. Zhou Enlai, "Xunqiu," in *ZELJJWJ*, 645.

94. *ZELNP*, 3:630–31.

95. Wang Jun, "'Wenge' houqi Zhou Enlai," 71–72.

96. Ibid., 71. Chen Yun mentions this same amount, but as mentioned above it is directed to finance the import substitution program. See Chen Yun, *Wenxuan*, 3:217–18.

97. Li Qi, *Zai Zhou Enlai shenbian de rizi*, 702, as cited in Wang Jun, "'Wenge' houqi Zhou Enlai," 72. Yen Chia-kan was a technocrat appointed premier of the Executive Yuan in Taiwan beginning in 1963 and was responsible in large part for the Taiwanese economic miracle. In 1972, Yen was appointed vice-president of the Republic of China.

6. The Abbreviated Leftist Response, 1974–1976

1. Li Zhisui states that on 17 July 1974, Mao criticized Jiang Qing during a Political Bureau meeting, "separating himself from her politically and warning her, Zhang Chunqiao, Wang Hongwen, and Yao Wenyuan against forming a Shanghai faction of four. From warnings such as this came the later epithet Gang of Four." Li Zhisui, *Private Life*, 583–84; Zhonggong Zhongyang Dangshi, *Zhonggong dangshi dashi*, 389.

2. For a detailed analysis of the polemic debates within China's external publications, see Whiting, *Chinese Domestic Politics*, 61–70.

3. Li Zhisui, *Private Life*, 576.

4. *ZELNP*, 3:526; Li Zhisui, *Private Life*, 572–73; Tong Xiaopeng, *Fengyu sishinian*, 2:519. Li Zhisui reports that Mao refused to allow Zhou to undergo treatment in May 1972. Ye Jianying appealed to Mao on 2 March 1973 to allow immediate treatment, to which Mao acceded. See *ZELNP*, 3:581. For a detailed discussion of Zhou's sickness, the effect on his work schedule, and its connection with the Anti-Lin, Anti-Confucius Campaign, see Tong Xiaopeng, *Fengyu sishinian*, 2:545.

5. *ZELNP*, 3:583; Yu Shicheng, *Deng Xiaoping yu Mao Zedong*, 269–75.

6. This concerns the analysis of the SALT I agreement in the MFA's internal publication, *Xin qingkuang* [New situations]. For a detailed explanation, see *ZELNP*, 3:603–604; Zhonggong Zhongyang Dangshi, *Zhonggong dangshi dashi*, 385; Tong Xiaopeng, *Fengyu sishinian*, 2:520–21.

7. Tong Xiaopeng, *Fengyu sishinian*, 2:521.

8. For instance, in June 1974, Jiang Qing spoke at several factories and communes in the Tianjin area, claiming that the "campaign against Confucianists continues up to today" and implying that Zhou was the head of them. See *ZELNP*, 3:671.

9. Ibid., 604, 610.

10. Ibid., 609–10, 618, 631, 639.

11. Ibid., 634–35; Tong Xiaopeng, *Fengyu sishinian*, 2:521–22.

12. Zhou's protégé and apparent successor, Deng Xiaoping, was allowed to take his seat on the Central Military Commission and the Political Bureau in December 1973. See *ZELNP*, 3:636–38.

13. Ibid., 614–15.

14. Ibid., 642–43; Tong Xiaopeng, *Fengyu sishinian*, 2:523; *ZRGJD*, 521–22; Zhonggong Renminglu, ed., *Zhonggong*, 9A; MacFarquhar, "Succession," 343–47.

15. For an interesting study tracing the historical background of the campaign, see Tien-wei Wu, *Lin Biao;* for an analysis of other cultural attacks on Zhou Enlai, see Tong Xiaopeng, *Fengyu sishinian*, 2:532–33.

16. According to Lieberthal and Oksenberg, Zhou and his development strategy were

directly criticized in large-character posters plastered on the walls of the Ministry of Fuels and Chemical Industry. See Lieberthal and Oksenberg, *Policy Making,* 200.

17. Tong Xiaopeng, *Fengyu sishinian,* 2:533.

18. Ibid.; ZELNP, 3:650.

19. Apparently, the MFA determined that "snails made from glass and from chocolate are gifts cherished by Americans." For more details on this and the entire incident, see Shi Shi, "'Woniu shijian' shimo," 52–53.

20. ZELNP, 3:650.

21. ZRGJD, 523; also see Chen Donglin, "Chen Yun," 1095–96; Tong Xiaopeng, *Fengyu sishinian,* 3:534.

22. Li Xiannian, "Renzhen zuohao jinkou liangshi de jianyi gongzuo" [Conscientiously do a good job in quarantining imported grains], a comment (*piyu*) written by Li Xiannian on a Xinhua news report, issued on 19 February 1974, in *Li Xiannian,* 2:286.

23. *Renmin ribao,* 13 November 1957; RZJSH, 2:636; ZELNP, 2:145.

24. ZELNP, 3:345, 671.

25. Ibid., 581.

26. Tong Xiaopeng, *Fengyu sishinian,* 2:534; ZELNP, 3:678, n. 1.

27. ZRGJD, 531.

28. According to Li Xiannian, Wang Hongwen rejected close economic connections with Hong Kong and questioned the policy and those who supported it. Li quotes Wang as asking, "Why must we guarantee supplies to Hong Kong's market? Why must we be occupied by the Hong Kong market? If we have the goods we'll export; if we don't, we won't export." Li states that the Hong Kong policy was formulated by Mao. See Li Xiannian, "Jiji zengjia chukou" [Actively increase exports], in a speech to representatives of the National Foreign Trade Planning Conference, delivered on 27 January 1977, in *Li Xiannian,* 2:311.

29. ZELNP, 3:678, n. 1; Tong Xiaopeng, *Fengyu sishinian,* 2:534–35.

30. ZELNP, 3:657, 673; Tong Xiaopeng, *Fengyu sishinian,* 2:530–31. For Mao's coining the term "Gang of Four," see ZELNP, 3:686–87.

31. This was an opinion from Mao, transmitted to the Fourth Plenum of the National People's Congress and contained in a CCP Central Committee circular. ZELNP, 3:678; ZRGJD, 534.

32. ZELNP, 3:674; Li Zhisui, *Private Life,* 585.

33. The approval of Deng's political power occurred during the Second Plenum of the Tenth Party Congress meeting on 8–10 January 1975; his position was formalized during the Fourth NPC meeting held 13–17 January 1975.

34. ZELNP, 3:678.

35. Ibid., 671, n. 2; *Wenhui bao, Jiefang ribao, Renmin ribao,* 12 October 1974. For more information on the historical analogies, see Whiting, *Chinese Domestic Politics.*

36. Tong Xiaopeng, *Fengyu sishinian,* 2:535.

37. Ibid., 2:536.

38. ZELNP, 3:679; Tong Xiaopeng, *Fengyu sishinian,* 2:536. Note the discrepancy in accounts between Zhou's *Chronology* and Li Zhisui, *Private Life,* 588–89. Also see Wang Hongmo, *1949–1989 nian,* 3:506–10.

39. ZELNP, 3:680–81.

40. ZRGJGD, 286.

41. Li Zhisui, *Private Life,* 580–86. Following a January 1975 medical examination, Li reports that "Mao had cataracts, amyotrophic lateral sclerosis, coronary heart disease, pulmonary heart disease, and infection in the lower half of both lungs, three bullae in

his left lung, bedsores on his left hip, and a shortage of oxygen in his blood (anoxia)." Li Zhisui, *Private Life,* 592.

42. Ibid., 601, 605.

43. "Guanyu yange luxing chukou shangpin hetong de tongzhi" [Circular on strict compliance with export product contracts], issued by the State Council on 26 June 1973, in ZRGJGD, 277.

44. "Guanyu zuzhi yanhai gangkou tuji zhuangxie de jinji tongzhi" [An emergency circular on organizing an assault on loading and unloading goods in coastal ports], issued by the State Council on 18 September 1973, in ZRGJGD, 278–79.

45. "Guanyu niuzhuan dangqian gangkou yanzhong yachuan qingkuang de qingshi baogao" [Report and request for instructions on turning around the current serious situation in harbor shipping], issued by the Ministry of Communications and the MFT and approved by the State Council and Central Military Commission on 4 April 1974, in ZRGJGD, 283; ZRGJD, 524–25.

46. ZRGJD, 525.

47. Ibid., 528–29.

48. "Guanyu zhua geming zu shengchan de tongzhi" [Circular on grasping the revolution and promoting production], issued by the CCP Central Committee on 1 July 1974, in ZRGJD, 284; ZRGJGD, 528–29. Parenthetical section originally from ZRGJD.

49. ZRGJGD, 284.

50. Ibid.

51. ZRGJD, 529.

52. Chen Yun, "Liyong," in *Wenxuan,* 3:224.

53. Richard Solomon, who was Kissinger's aide at the National Security Council and later in the Reagan and Bush State Departments, completed in 1985 the two-volume study on Sino-American relations between 1969 and 1984 for the National Intelligence Council. See Jim Mann, "Long-Secret Document Details How China Manipulated U.S.," *Los Angeles Times,* 13 June 1994.

54. ZRGJD, 531; Wang Hongmo, *1949–1989 nian,* 506–10.

55. Ashbrook, "China," 221.

56. "Yijiuqisi nian waihui shouzhi pingheng wenti de baogao" [Report on the foreign exchange revenue and expenditure problem], submitted by the SPC on 12 September 1974 and approved by the State Council on 30 September 1974, in ZRGJGD, 285; ZRGJD, 531–32.

57. ZRGJD, 532. This selection was not included in Li Xiannian's 1992 collected speeches.

58. Zhou Enlai, "Xiang sige xiandaihua de hongwei mubiao qianjin" [Forging toward the magnificent goal of the Four Modernizations], a portion of the government work report presented to the first meeting of the Fourth NPC on 13 January 1975, in ZELJJWX, 652; translated in *Peking Review* 4 (24 January 1975): 23, as cited in Barnett, *China's Economy,* 13–14.

59. ZELJJWX, 652–53.

60. Li Zhisui, *Private Life,* 609.

61. ZELNP, 3:693–94; ZRGJD, 288; ZRGJD, 540. Also see MacFarquhar, "Succession," 347–51. MacFarquhar's source differs slightly on the date of Deng's assumption of day-to-day control as January 1975. See 351, n. 166.

62. See Deng Xiaoping, *Wenxuan,* 4–11, 25–27; Dangdai Zhongguo Congshu, *Dangdai Zhongguo de jingji,* 154–56; Zheng Derong, *Zhongguo jingji tizhi,* 128–29; MacFarquhar, "Succession," 351–55.

63. *ZRGJD*, 557; for more detailed statistics of the recovery, see Guojia Tongjiju, ed., *Zhongguo tongji nianjian, 1984.*

64. *DXPSXNP*, 5, 7, 10.

65. Ibid., 16.

66. Deng Xiaoping, "Guanyu fazhan gongye de jidian yijian" [Several opinions on industrial development], in *Wenxuan,* 28–31; also see Lieberthal and Oksenberg, *Policy Making,* 201.

67. Guojia Tongjiju, ed., *Zhongguo tongji nianjian, 1984,* 420.

68. Deng Xiaoping, "Guanyu fazhan gongye de jidian yijian," *Wenxuan; DXPSXNP,* 15, 18; Lieberthal and Oksenberg, *Policy Making,* 201.

69. For more information, see *ZRGJGD,* 268, 290; *ZRGJD,* 484, 544.

70. *ZELNP,* 3:703.

71. Ibid., 697, 701.

72. Ibid., 704, 709, 713; Barnett, *China's Economy,* 124.

73. Li Zhisui, *Private Life,* 606.

74. *ZRGJD,* 554–55; Wang Hongmo, *1949–1989 nian,* 3:551–59.

75. MacFarquhar, "Succession," 356.

76. *ZRGJD,* 556–57.

77. Ibid., 555.

78. *ZRGJD,* 559; *ZRGJGD,* 295.

79. *ZRGJD,* 561; *ZRGJGD,* 295.

80. Li Zhisui, *Private Life,* 632.

81. *ZRGJD,* 561. In "Guanyu fazhan gongye de jidian yijian," Deng supported the idea of compensation trade to develop China's vast coal reserves.

82. *ZRGJD,* 563. This was a compilation of talks with Mao's nephew, Mao Yuanxin, which occurred between October 1975 and January 1976. Included was a reaffirmation of the Cultural Revolution and a criticism of capitalist-roaders still within the government.

83. After articles critical of Zhou Enlai appeared in March, a major demonstration in support of Zhou was staged on 5 April in Beijing's Tiananmen Square; more than a million people participated. Demanding that Zhou's memory be honored properly, the crowd eventually set ablaze a militia command post and vehicles. By nightfall, the militia moved in, and many people were killed. For details, see MacFarquhar, "Succession," 361–65.

84. "Xingzhi bianle"; "Kaichu Deng de yiqie zhiwu." In *ZRGJD,* 563–64.

85. *ZRGJD,* 559–60.

86. The two meetings were held to discuss the SPC's report on the implementation of Industrial Production and the National Economic Plan. It is unclear at which meeting Jiang Qing et al. made their criticisms. See *ZRGJGD,* 296; *ZRGJD,* 559–60.

87. Chen Donglin, "*Chen Yun,*" 1102.

88. *ZRGJD,* 560.

89. Fewsmith, *Dilemmas,* 58–59.

7. The Great Leap Outward, 1977–1979

1. Wang Hongmo, *1949–1989 nian,* 3:606–16; Li Zhisui, *Private Life,* 629–36; MacFarquhar, "Succession," 367–70.

2. "Guanyu dongjie ge danwei cunkuan de jinji tongzhi" [Emergency circular on the freezing of each unit's bank accounts], issued by the CCP Central Committee on 28 October

1976, in ZRGJGD, 297; ZRGJD, 570–71; "Guanyu jianjue yasuo he yange kongzhi shehui jituan goumaili de qingshi baogao" [Report and request for instructions on strictly reducing and controlling the buying power of social groups], issued by the SPC et al. and approved by the State Council on 28 March 1977, in ZRGJGD, 300; ZRGJD, 579. One major exception was an increase in wages, which had been postponed in 1974 and 1975. See "Guanyu tiaozheng bufen zhigong gongzi de tongzhi" [Circular on adjusting certain wages for staff and workers], issued by the State Council on 10 August 1977, in ZRGJGD, 307; ZRGJD, 585–86.

3. "Guanyu jinyibu zuohao yuanwai gongzuo de baogao" [Report on further improving foreign aid work], submitted by the MFT on 23 August 1977 and approved by the CCP Central Committee on 25 September 1977, in ZRGJGD, 307; ZRGJD, 586–87.

4. "Quanguo jiben jianshe huiyi jiyao" [Summary of the Conference on Capital Construction] and the accompanying circular issued by the State Council on 3 April 1977, in ZRGJGD, 301; "Guanyu pizhuan quanguo yejin gongye gongzuo huiyi jiyao de tongzhi" [Circular on the approval and summary of the National Conference on the Metallurgical Industry], issued by the State Council on 15 April 1977, in ZRGJGD, 302; ZRGJD, 579–80.

5. "Quanguo jieyu ranliao, dianli jingyan jiaoliu huiyi jiyao" [Summary of the Conference on Conserving Fuel and Energy], issued by the State Council on 9 April 1977, in ZRGJGD, 301; "Quanguo tielu gongzuo huiyi jiyao" [Summary of the National Work Conference on the Railroads], issued by the CCP Central Committee on 22 February 1977, in ZRGJGD, 299–300, ZRGJD, 575–76.

6. "Guanyu dali kaizhan niuzhuan qiye kuisun, zengjia yingli gongzuo de tongzhi" [Circular on emphasizing the turnabout of industrial losses and increasing profits], issued by the State Council on 8 July 1977, in ZRGJGD, 305; ZRGJD, 582–83.

7. ZRGJD, 594. Also see "Guanyu jinnian shangbannian gongye shengchan qingkuang de baogao" [Report on the industrial production situation during the first half of this year], submitted by the State Council and agreed upon and issued by the CCP Central Committee on 30 July 1977, in ZRGJGD, 306; ZRGJD, 584.

8. "Guanyu jinnian yilai waimao shougou jihua zhixing qingkuang he wenti de baogao" [Report on problems in fulfilling the foreign trade procurement plan since the beginning of this year], issued by the SPC and MFT and approved by the State Council on 15 May 1977, in ZRGJGD, 303–304.

9. Li Xiannian, "Jiji zengjia chukou," in *Li Xiannian,* 2:310–11.

10. Zhonggong Zhongyang Dangshi, *Zhonggong dangshi dashi,* 405; MacFarquhar, "Succession," 372.

11. Dangdai Zhongguo Congshu, *Dangdai Zhongguo de jingji,* 159–61; Nai-ruenn Chen, "Economic Modernization," 165–203.

12. Zhang Zerong, ed., *Zhongguo jingji tizhi gaige jishi,* 139; ZRGJD, 595–96.

13. Chen Yun, "Jingji xingshi yu jingyan jiaoxun" [The economic situation and the lessons from experience], in SQYZWX, 606. For more information about the goals of the Ten-Year Plan, see Hua Guofeng, "Report on the Work of the Government" as reprinted in *Peking Review,* 10 March 1978, 7–41; Naughton, *Growing,* 67–74.

14. Riskin, *China's Political Economy,* 220–22, 260.

15. ZRGJD, 583; also see Fewsmith, *Dilemmas,* 58; Brown, "China's Program," 161–64. The 17 July 1977 import substitution program approved by the Political Bureau probably was included in the State Council's Ten-Year Plan (draft plan) of February 1978. This is difficult to verify since the draft plan has not been published. Yet the program seems corroborated by Hua's work report.

16. For more on cost estimates of the import substitution program, see Barnett, *China's Economy,* 132–39.

17. "Guanyu Shanghai xinjian gangtiechang de changzhi xuanze, jianshe guimo he youguan wenti de qingshi baogao" [Report and request for instructions concerning the site selection and construction scale of Shanghai's new steel mill], submitted by the SPC et al. and approved by the State Council on 11 March 1978, in ZRGJD, 597. Also see Shanghai Shehui Kexueyuan, *Shanghai jingji,* 339–40; C. Lee, *China and Japan,* 30–75.

18. ZRGJD, 505.

19. Ibid., 605–606.

20. Long Chucai, *Liyong waizi gailun,* 232.

21. Ibid.; ZRGJD, 506.

22. ZRGJD, 496–97; ZRGJGD, 270.

23. Chen Yun, "Tiaozheng guomin jingji, jianchi anbili fazhan" [Readjust the national economy, support proportional development], in SQYZWX, 76; MacDougall, "Policy Changes," 158–59; Chen Yun, "Zai caijing weiyuanhui zhaokai de huibaoshang de fayan" [Speech to the report-back meeting of the Finance and Economic Commission], in SQYZWX, 174.

24. "Letter by Deng Xiaoping to Chairman Hua Guofeng and the Party Central Committee," 10 April 1977, Central Committee document 77.15, as cited in Ruan Ming, *Deng Xiaoping,* 39–40. For analysis, see MacFarquhar, "Succession," 373–76.

25. Deng Xiaoping, " 'Liangge fangshi' bu fuhe Makesi zhuyi" [The "Two Whatevers" do not conform to Marxism]; "Wanzhengde zhunquede lijie Mao Zedong tongzhi" [Completely and correctly understanding Comrade Mao Zedong]; "Zai quanjun zhengzhi gongzuo huiyi shang de jianghua" [Speech to the Military Work Conference]; "Gaoju Mao Zedong sixiang qizhi, jianchi shishi qiushi de yuanze" [Fly high the banner of Mao Zedong, uphold the principles of seeking truth from fact], in Deng Xiaoping, *Wenxuan,* 35–38, 40, 103–23. Also see Hu Qiaomu, "Act in Accordance with Economic Laws, Step up the Four Modernizations," 5 October 1987, in FBIS, *China,* 11 October 1978, E1-22; Hu Fuming, "Practice." For an excellent analysis of Hu Qiaomu, see Fewsmith, *Dilemmas,* 58–62.

26. Chen Yun, "Tiaozheng," in SQYZWX, 76; Wang Hongmo, *1949–1989 nian,* 89–90.

27. Nai-Ruenn Chen, "China's Foreign Trade," 121–22; Naughton, *Growing,* chap. 2. For an opposing view, see Shirk, *How China Opened Its Door,* 10–11.

28. For more information on 1978 imports, especially the buying spree of December 1978, see Davie and Carver, "China's International Trade," 26.

29. Li Xiannian, "Zai zhongyang gongzuo huiyishang de jianghua" [Speech to the central work conference), in SQYZWX, 117.

30. Zhao Ziyang, "Dangqian de jingji xingshi he jinhou jianshe fangzhen" [The current economic situation and future development plans], delivered on 30 November 1981 and 1 December 1981 to the Fourth Plenary Session of the Fifth NPC; Cheng Chu-yuan, "Modernization of Chinese Industry," 37; Brown, "China's Program," 165–68.

31. Zou Chuntai and Song Xingzhong, eds., *Zhongguo shehui zhuyi,* 426–427.

32. Chen Yun, "Tiaozheng," in SQYZWX, 76–77.

33. Zhu Jiamu, "Shiyijie sanzhong quanhui ji qi zhuyao wenjian xingcheng de ruogan qingkuang," 33–50; Wang Hongmo, *1949–1989 nian,* 120–35, and Ruan Ming, *Deng Xiaoping,* 47–49.

34. "Zhonggong zhongyang zhengzhiju huiyi tongbao" [Notification of the Political Bureau meeting of the CCP Central Committee], in SQYZWX, 596–97.

35. Hu Yaobang was appointed head of the Political Bureau Secretariat and eventually as chairman of the Party Central Committee in November 1980. See ibid., 598–99. The reform-minded leader of Sichuan and future premier, Zhao Ziyang, was appointed to the Political Bureau at the Fourth Party Plenum held 25–28 September 1979. In March 1980, he was appointed to head the important Central Government Small Leadership Group on Finance and Economics (Zhongyang Caizheng Jingji Lingdao Xiaozu), which replaced the Finance and Economic Commission. See Zhonggong Zhongyang Wenxian, *Zhonggong dangshi dashi,* 431; Zheng Derong, *Zhongguo jingji tizhi,* 81.

36. "Zhongguo Gongchandang Dishiyijie Zhongyang Weiyuanhui Disanci Quanti Huiyi gongbao" [Communiqué of the Third Plenum of the Eleventh CCP Central Committee], in Zhonggong Zhongyang Wenxian Yanjiushi, *Xin shiqi,* 6–10.

37. "Jiefang sixiang, shishi qiushi, tuanjie yizhi xiangqiankan" [Liberate thinking, seek truth from facts, unite and look to the future], in Deng Xiaoping, *Wenxuan,* 130–43.

38. "Zai quanjun zhengzhi gongzuo huiyishang de jianghua," ibid., 109. This speech, according to Hu Yaobang, was "to raise to a higher plane the level of discussions [about alternate approaches]." See Hu Yaobang, "Lilun gongzuo wuxuhui yinyan," 49–50. For a fascinating account of Hu Yaobang's role in promoting this approach, see Ruan Ming, *Deng Xiaoping,* 29–37.

39. Chen Yun, "Tiaozheng." in *SQYZWX,* 76.

40. Zheng Derong, *Zhongguo jingji tizhi,* 7, 711; ZRGJD, 614; ZRGJGD, 328. Also see Deng Xiaoping, "Guanche tiaozheng fangzhen, baozheng anding tuanjie" [Implement the readjustment of plans, guarantee stability and unity], in *Wenxuan,* 313.

41. Chen Yun, "Tiaozheng," in *SQYZWX,* 75; ZRGJD, 624; ZRGJGD, 340.

42. Li Xiannian, "Zai zhongyang," in *SQYZWX,* 1:109, 121.

43. Chen Yun, "Tiaozheng," 77; "Gaoji ganbu daitou fayang dangde youliang chuantong" [Upper-level cadre should take the lead in carrying forward the fine traditions of the party], in Deng Xiaoping, *Wenxuan,* 189.

44. Li Xiannian, "Zai zhongyang," in *SQYZWX,* 1:109; Zhonggong Zhongyang Dangshi, *Zhonggong dangshi dashi,* 428; Zheng Derong et al., *Zhongguo jingji tizhi,* 26; ZRGJD, 622; Chen Yun, "Tiaozheng," in *SQYZWX,* 74–79. For a listing of meetings and an excellent analysis of the Wuxi conference, which brought together Chinese economists to discuss reforming the relationship between the plan and the market, see Fewsmith, *Dilemmas,* 62–68.

45. Circular issued by the CCP Central Committee approving and transmitting the 5 April 1979 document "Li Xiannian zai zhongyang gongzuo huiyishang de jianghua" [Li Xiannian's speech to the central work conference], in ZRGJGD, 340; Chen Yun's speech at 25 March 1979 meeting of the Finance and Economy Commission, ibid., 333.

46. Zheng Derong, *Zhongguo jingji tizhi,* 26; Li Xiannian, "Zai quanguo jihua huiyishang de jianghua" [Speech to the national planning conference], in *SQYZWX,* 300.

47. Li Xiannian and Chen Yun, "Guanyu caijing gongzuo gei zhongyang de yifengxin" [A letter to the Central Committee on finance and economics work], in *SQYZWX,* 72.

48. The commission was replaced on 17 March 1980 with the Central Government Small Leadership Group on Finance and Economics. Zhao Ziyang was put in charge of the group. See Zheng Derong, *Zhongguo jingji tizhi,* 81.

49. "Guanyu xiada 1979 nian guomin jingji jihua de tongzhi." For actual figures in parentheses, see ZRGJGD, 640.

50. Chen Yun, "Tiaozheng," in *SQYZWX,* 75–78.

51. Li Xiannian, "Zai zhongyang," in *SQYZWX,* 112–15.

52. Accumulation is "the amassing of capital, for purposes of either investment or expenditure. If there is to be a 'means of production' over and above what is provided by nature, then there must be accumulation, in the form of 'produced means of production.'" See Scruton, *Dictionary,* 3.

53. Li Xiannian, "Zai zhongyang," in *SQYZWX,* 116–17.

54. In 1977, the accumulation rate was 32.3 percent; it rose to 36.5 percent in 1978. The highest rates were 43.8 percent in 1959 and 39.6 percent in 1960. See Zou Chuntai and Song Xingzhong, *Zhongguo shehui zhuyi,* 426.

55. Li Xiannian, "Zai zhongyang," in *SQYZWX,* 129–32.

56. Deng Xiaoping, "Guanche tiaozheng fangzhen," in *Wenxuan;* "Guanyu jinsuo jiben jianshe zhichu de jinji tongzhi" [Emergency circular on reducing capital construction expenditures], issued by the State Council on 30 November 1980, in *ZRGJFX,* 1:315–16.

57. Chen Yun, "Tiaozheng," in *SQYZWX,* 78.

58. "Guanyu banfa jixu yinjin he shebei jinkou gongzuo zhanxing tiaoli de tongzhi" [Circular on the issuance of the temporary regulations on technology and equipment importation], State Council document 81.12, issued 21 January 1981, in Zhongguo Renmin Yinhang Bangongshi, *1981 jinrong guizhang zhidu xuanbian,* 2:311–14.

59. Li Xiannian, "Zai zhongyang," in *SQYZWX,* 130.

60. Li Ming, "Huiyi Xiaoping tongzhi," 75; Baogang Gongsi, "Lishi zhengming," 36–37.

61. In "Guanche tiaozheng," Deng Xiaoping publicly admitted the existence of opposition to the readjustment policy. Citing an 8 May 1979 editorial on import substitution plant imports, Nai-ruenn Chen also acknowledges the existence of internal debates concerning the import substitution strategy. See Nai-ruenn Chen, "China's Foreign Trade," 124.

62. Fewsmith, *Dilemmas,* 96.

63. Lieberthal and Oksenberg, *Policy Making,* 169–268; Zhonggong Renminglu, *Zhonggong,* 305; Weil, "Baoshan Steel Mill," p. 1,377; Fewsmith, *Dilemmas,* 87–90; Ju Zhongyi, "'New Economic Group,'" 192–97.

64. Davie and Carter, "China's International Trade," 26–29.

65. Chen Yun, "Tiaozheng," in *SQYZWX,* 131; "Guanyu guojia tongjie waihui yinjin jijian shebei youguan caizheng, caiwu chuli de juti guiding" [Several specific regulations on resolving the financing of capital construction equipment that utilizes state unified foreign exchange], Caiyuzi 80.52, issued by the MOF on 24 May 1980, in Zhonghua Renmin Gongheguo Caizhengbu Bangongshi, ed., *Caizheng,* 68–76. The new regulations were designed for capital construction projects that borrowed foreign exchange for importing complete plants and equipment starting in 1980. See "Guanyu shiyong guowai daikuan yinjin jishu he jinkou shebei de jiben jianshe xiangmu zai waihui, caizheng, jijian jihuashang de chuli banfa" [Methods to solve the problems in foreign exchange, financing, and capital construction plans for capital construction projects that utilize foreign loans to import technology and equipment], State Council document 79.297, issued by the MOF on 21 December 1979, in *DJFZH,* 1:491–94.

66. *ZRGJGD,* 316, 332, 355; Li Yongchun, *Shiyijie,* 55; Zheng Derong, *Zhongguo jingji tizhi,* 43; *ZRGJD,* 632. Gu Mu was previously associated with the Petroleum Group and had joined Yu Qiuli on Mao's Small Planning Commission in the mid-1960s. See Lieberthal and Oksenberg, *Policy Making,* 189.

67. For more on the need of technology imports, see Hua Guofeng's government work

report, presented to the fifth NPC meeting and approved on 1 July 1979, in *Beijing Review,* 6 July 1979, 5–13.

68. Li Xiannian, "Zai zhongyang," in *SQYZWX,* 124–125.

69. Ibid., 123.

70. "Guanyu banfa 'Yinjin jishu youhui waihui huijia juti banfa' de tongzhi" [Circular on the promulgation of "The Specific Measures for Preferential Exchange Rates for Imported Technology"], Jinchuyinzi 81.046, issued by the SIEAC and the State General Administration of Foreign Exchange Control on 20 March 1981, in *DJFZH,* 1:469–71.

71. "Guanyu yinjin jishu de guonei zuojia banfa de tongzhi" [Circular on domestic pricing methods for imported technology], State Council document 79.197, issued on 9 August 1979, in *DJFZH,* 1:468. This was a supplement to "Guanyu jinkou shangpin shixing tongyi zuojia banfa de zhanxing guiding" [Provisional regulations on implementing unified pricing measures for imported commodities], issued on 17 December 1963, later updated by Jinchuyinzi 81.046, ibid.

72. "Guanyu qiye yinjin zhizao jishu suoxuyao feiyong kaizhi wenti de guiding" [Regulations concerning expenses and outlays needed by industries to import manufacturing technology], Caiqizi 80.208, issued by the MOF et al. on 28 June 1980, in Zhongguo Renmin Yinhang Jihuasi, *Lilü,* 777. Also see "Guanyu banfa 'Yinjin guowai jishu shebei guonei peitao daikuan banfa' de tongzhi" [Circular on the promulgation of the "Procedures for Issuing Domestic Auxiliary Loans for Importing Foreign Technology and Equipment"], Jianzongdizi 80.498, issued by the PBOC et al. on 11 September 1980, ibid., 780–82.

73. "Guanyu woguo jianli zhuanli zhidu de qingshi baogao" [Report and request for instructions on our country establishing a patent system], approved and transmitted by the State Council on 14 January 1980, in *ZRGJGD,* 374; "Guanyu shangpin shiyong shangbiao wenti de lianhe tongzhi" [Joint circular on problems of the use of commodity trademarks], issued by the SIEAC et al. on 4 February 1980, in Zheng Derong, *Zhongguo jingji tizhi,* 71.

74. Zhang Peiji, "Development of China's Foreign Trade," 118.

75. Chen Yun, "Tiaozheng," in *SQYZWX,* 78–79.

76. Li Xiannian, "Zai zhongyang," in *SQYZWX,* 131.

77. Reardon, "China's Coastal Development Strategy, 1979–1984, I," 9–18.

78. "Guanyu chukou gongyepin gongying zuojia jige wenti de qingshi baogao de tongzhi" [Circular on the report and request for instructions on the pricing of supplies of export industrial products], State Council document 79.206, submitted by the State Bureau of Material Pricing and approved on 21 August 1979, in Zhonghua Renmin Gongheguo Guowuyuan Fazhiju, *Zhonghua Renmin Gongheguo xianxing fagui,* 704–708 (for document number, see *DJFZH,* 2:1070).

79. According to "Guanyu shangpin fenji guanli banfa de baogao" [Report on the managing procedures for commodity classification] of 12 February 1959, commodities were divided into three different categories: commodities whose export was restricted (for instance, cotton and vegetable oil); commodities demanded by both the domestic and export markets, yet whose supplies were limited (for example, tea and pork); and all others. On 17 October 1979 the State Council approved the MOC's "Guanyu dangqian shangye gongzuo jidian yijian de baogao" [Report on several opinions on current commerce work], which reaffirmed the 12 February 1959 classification. See *ZRGJFX,* 2:131.

80. *WFSS,* 55.

81. Waimao Fuchi Chukou Shangpin Shengchan Zhouzhuan Zijin was first implemented

in 1975. The Ministry of Finance lent funds to the Ministry of Foreign Trade, which in turn lent the money to provincial or local governments or foreign trade corporations to encourage agricultural sideline and local specialty production for export. See *WFSS*, 83; Duiwai Jingji Maoyibu Renshi, *Chukou huoyuan gailun,* 87.

82. Chukou Chanpin Shengchan Cuoshi Touzi originated in 1973 and distributed close to RMB 800 million between 1973 to 1981 for 615 export production projects. See *WFSS*, 111; Duiwai Jingji Maoyibu Renshi, *Chukou huoyuan gailun,* 91.

83. The Specialized Loan Program for Industrial Export Production was instituted in 1964 to increase industrial export quality and variety and to improve packaging. Between 1972 and 1980, the loan financed the acquisition of 110,000 pieces of equipment at a total cost of RMB 1.84 billion. See *WFSS*, 69; Duiwai Jingji Maoyibu Renshi, *Chukou huoyuan gailun,* 86.

84. *WFSS*, 120.

85. Li Xiannian, "Jiejuehao renmin de chuanyi wenti" [Find a solution to clothing the masses], speech delivered on 23 May 1978 to the National Conference on the Textile Industry Studying Daqing, in *Li Xiannian,* 2:333.

86. The Administrative Measures (Chukou Xinshangpin Shizhifei) were combined in 1981 with the State Science Commission's Supplementary Funds for Scientific Research Used for Foreign Trade (Waimao Keyan Buzhufei) to form the MFT's Trial Management Procedures for Science and Technology Used for Foreign Trade (Waimao Keji Guanli Shixing Banfa). Between 1979 and 1981, the two original funds issued RMB 18.95 million to more than four hundred successful projects. See Duiwai Jingji Maoyibu Renshi, *Chukou huoyuan gailun,* 93; Wang Shouchun, *Zhongguo duiwai,* 43; *WFSS*, 115–18.

87. "Chukou shangpin shengchan zhongduanqi zhuanxiang daikuan shixing banfa" [Temporary methods for specialized medium- and short-term loans for export commodity production], Zhongxinzi 80.186, issued by the BOC on 11 October 1980, in Zhongguo Renmin Yinhang Jihuasi, *Lilü,* 895.

88. "Jixie shebei chukou zhongchangqi daikuan shixing banfa" [Temporary methods for specialized medium- and short-term loans for mechanical equipment production], Zhongxinzi 80.186, issued by the BOC on 11 October 1980, in Zhongguo Renmin Yinhang Jihuasi, *Lilü,* 700–701.

89. "Guanyu chukou shangpin waihui liucheng shixing banfa" [Trial procedures of the foreign exchange retention scheme earned from export commodities], issued on 13 August 1979 by the State Council under "Guanyu dali fazhan duiwai maoyi zengjia waihui shouru ruogan wenti de guiding" [Regulations regarding problems in putting great effort in developing foreign trade and increasing foreign exchange revenue], State Council document 79.202, in Reardon, " China's Coastal Development Strategy, 1979–1984, I," 9–18.

90. "Guanyu feimaoyi waihui liucheng shixing banfa" [Trial procedures of the foreign exchange retention scheme earned from nontrade activities], issued under State Council document 79.202, ibid. "Feimaoyi waihui liucheng shishi xize" [Detailed rules and regulations concerning the foreign exchange retention scheme earned from nontrade activities], Huizongzi 80.869; Jinchuzongzi 80.46; Caiwaizi 80.237, issued by the State General Administration of Foreign Exchange Control, the Committee of Import/Export Control and the MOF on 29 September 1980, in Caizhengbu, *Feimaoyi waihui zhidu huibian,* 86–92.

91. Li Xiannian, "Shangye he waimao ruogan gongzuo wenti," in *Li Xiannian,*

2:254–55. Li Xiannian actually praised a revised version of the foreign exchange retention scheme proposed by the Ministry of Foreign Trade in August 1965, which apparently eliminated the non-discriminate distribution of foreign exchange funds.

92. Zhongguo Guoji Jinrong Xuehui, ed., *Waihui tizhi gaige taolun wenji,* 146.

93. "Gongshang tongyishui tiaoli (caoan)" [Regulations of the unified industrial and commercial tax (draft)], issued on 13 September 1958, and "Gongshang tongyishui tiaoli shixing xize (caoan)" [Detailed rules and regulations of the unified industrial and commercial tax (draft)], Caishuizi 58.52, in *YCKTGWX,* 2:610–23. The tax is the primary source of government revenue and is assessed on enterprises and individuals involved in industrial or commercial dealings.

94. Wang Shouchun, *Zhongguo duiwai,* 51; *WFSS,* 51.

95. "Guanyu jinchukou shangpin zhengmian gongshang shuishou de guiding de tongzhi" [Circular on the regulations on reduction or elimination of the industrial and commercial taxes on import and export products], State Council document 80.315, submitted by the MOF and approved by the State Council on 30 December 1980, in Zhonghua Renmin Gongheguo Caizhengbu Bangongshi, *Caizheng,* 355–360; *WFSS,* 58–59.

96. *WFSS,* 60. Export taxes were re-imposed on 30 April 1982 with "Guanyu ruogan shangpin zhengshou chukou guanshui de qingshi" [Request for instructions concerning the imposition of export taxes on certain commodities], submitted by the MOF et al. and approved by the State Council on 30 April 1982, in *ZRGJGD,* 470.

97. "Dui jiagong zhuangpei he zhongxiaoxing buchang maoyi jinchukou huowu jianguan he zhengmianshui shishi xize (shixing)" [Detailed regulations concerning the supervision and control of and the imposition and exemption of taxes on import and export materials for processing and assembly and medium- and small-scale compensation trade (trial regulations)], issued by the General Customs Administration on 6 February 1980, in *ZRGJFX,* 2:300–302.

98. The devaluation finally was implemented in February 1981, when the RMB value dropped from RMB 1.5487 to RMB 1.6106. Daily settlement rates were only provided after 28 May 1981. See Guojia Waihui Guanliju, ed. *Huijia shouce,* 352–53; "Guanyu duiwaimao danwei jiehui yilu gaiyong dangtian jiage de tongzhi" [Circular on the changeover to a daily foreign exchange settlement rate for units dealing in foreign trade], Zhongzongzi 81.623, issued by the BOC on 28 May 1981, in Zhongguo Renmin Yinhang Bangongshi, *1981 jinrong guizhang zhidu xuanbian,* 2:381.

99. "Guanyu maoyi waihui neibu jiesuan jiage shixing banfa," State Council document 80.196, cited in "Guanyu yinfa guanyu maoyi waihui neibu jiesuan jiage shixing banfa de shishi xize de tongzhi" [Circular on the publication of the detailed regulations for the trial procedures of the internal settlement rate for foreign exchange earned from trade], Jinchukouweizongzi 81.018, Huizongzi 81.226, issued by SIEAC et al. after 27 March 1981, in *YCKTGWX,* 1:450–65.

100. *WFSS,* 50.

101. "Yijin yangchu shixing banfa" [Trial procedures for the importation of materials to develop exports], issued on 26 March 1979 by the State Council, in *YCKTGWX,* 1:175–78. Processing and assembly activities were greatly expanded, including the importation of major pieces of equipment such as boat motors and instrumentation. The *yijin yangchu* program was included within the plan and thus differed from the processing and assembly activities and compensation trade (*sanlai yibu*) first initially approved by State Council document 78.139 in July 1928. See *WFSS,* 4; Wu Jikun, *Duiwai Maoyi,* 119–26.

102. *WFSS,* 48.

103. "If either the RMB price of imported raw and supplementary materials or the profit/tax rate is too high and causes large export losses, and if there is a foreign market [for the product] and a reasonable rate of return of foreign exchange, then imported materials will be priced according to the actual import cost (*jinkou chengben*) and a 3 percent administrative fee." See State Council document 79:206 in Guowuyuan Fazhiju, *Zhonghua Renmin Gongheguo*, 704 (for document number, see YCKTGWX, 2:1070).

104. "Guanyu yinfa chukou gongyepin zhuanchang shixing banfa he chukou nongfu chanpin shengchan jidi shixing banfa de tongzhi" [Circular concerning the publication of the trial procedures for specialized factories for industrial product exports and the trial procedures for export commodity production bases for agricultural sideline products], Jinchuchuzi 80.041, approved by the State Council and issued by the SIEAC on 10 August 1980, in YCKTGWX, 2:1066–76.

105. New comprehensive bases were established in Heilongjiang Province, Suihua Prefecture (October 1980); Liaoning's Lüda City (1979) and Yingkou Prefecture (March 1981); Xinjiang's Tulufan Prefecture (1979); Shandong's Qingdao Municipality (October 1979) and Heze Prefecture (October 1980); Jiangsu's Xuzhou Prefecture (October 1980) and Nantong Prefecture (November 1980); Zhejiang's Taizhou Prefecture (1980); and Hubei's Shijiazhuang Prefecture (August 1981). See WFSS, 140–54.

106. The Chukou Shangpin Shengchan Jidi, Zhuanchang Fuchi Zhuanxiang Waihui (Specialized Foreign Exchange Funds to Promote Export Commodity Production Bases and Specialized Factories), a nonrepayable central government allocation of foreign exchange used for ECPB construction, was raised in 1980 to 20.45 million and in 1982 to $24.30 million. See WFSS, 69, 118. The ECPBS also could retain 1–2 percent more of foreign exchange funds than "normal" units.

107. In 1980, the SIEAC and the SPC guaranteed a steady supply of foreign exchange funds for the ECPBS and specialized factories by granting them 5 percent of the previous year's export trade revenue. See WFSS, 118.

108. Shanghai Shehui Kexueyuan, *Shanghai jingji*, 761.

109. "Da yidali jizhe Aolinaina Falaqi wen" [Answers to the questions of Oriana Fallaci], in Deng Xiaoping, *Wenxuan*, 310.

110. For background on past joint ventures with the Soviets, Poles, and Czechs, see Liu Xiangdong, ed., *Liyong*, 7–8.

111. Wang Shouchun, *Zhongguo duiwai*, 103.

112. Usually foreign countries extended sellers' credit to finance transactions with China. China would pay 10–15 percent of the cost in convertible currency and the rest over an extended period. This is not to be confused with buyers' credit. In the Chinese case, buyers' credit was only used at the end of 1978 in the form of officially supported credit extended by foreign export/import banks. See Wang Shouchun, *Zhongguo duiwai*, 108; World Bank, *China: Socialist Economic Development*, 2:462. For a cryptic description by Li Xiannian, see "Shichang qingkuang haozhuanhou xuyao jixu jiejue de wenti" [Problems that must continue to be resolved after the improvement of market conditions], in *Li Xiannian*, 2:171.

113. Youngson, ed., *China and Hong Kong*, 26. The leadership's definition of foreign debt is revealed in Chen Yun's 18 September 1979 speech to the Finance and Economics Commission: "Basically speaking, there are only two types of foreign debt: the first type is buyers' credit. . . . The second is convertible foreign exchange loans." See Chen Yun, "Zai caijing," in SQYZWX, 172–73. He thus doesn't consider sellers' credit to be a form of foreign debt.

114. "Guanyu jiji zhengqu qiaohui de yijian" [Opinion on actively striving for overseas Chinese remittances], State Council document 78.29, issued in early 1978, cited in "Guanyu juban waibi dingqi cunkuan de tongzhi" [Circular on conducting foreign currency time deposits], Zhongzongzi 79.2004, issued by the BOC on 31 October 1979, in Zhongguo Renmin Yinhang Jihuasi, *Lilü*, 674.

115. "Huaqiao touzi xingban xuexiao banfa" [Procedures for overseas Chinese to invest in establishing schools] and "Huaqiao touzi yu guoying huaqiao touzi gongsi de youdai banfa" [Preferential measures for overseas Chinese investment in state-owned overseas Chinese investment enterprises], submitted by the State Council and approved by the 78th meeting of the NPC Standing Committee on 1 August 1957, in *ZRGJD*, 194.

116. On 13 August 1978, the Central Committee established a Small Group on Hong Kong and Macao (Zhongyang Gang'ao Xiaozu). See Zhonggong Zhongyang Dangshi, *Zhonggong dangshi dashi*, 418. The State Council also reopened its Office of Overseas Chinese Affairs (Qiaowu Bangongshi), which had been closed since 1970; Jinan University (Guangzhou) and the Overseas Chinese University (Xiamen) reopened. Meetings of various overseas Chinese groups were held in December 1978 and overseas Chinese associations established. See Yuan Lizhou, ed., *Tongzhan zhishi yu zhengce*, 476–77; Li Yongchun, *Shiyijie*, 42; *Renmin ribao*, 21 October 1985.

117. MacDougall, "Policy Changes," 159. Also see Davie and Carver, "China's International Trade," 24; Nai-ruenn Chen, "China's Capital Construction," pt. 2, 61.

118. The Central Committee presumably arrived at the initial decision to use foreign capital, which was then discussed during the State Council Ideological Discussion Conference. An allusion to the Central Committee decision was made by Chen Yun in his 21 March 1979 speech. See Chen Yun, "Tiaozheng," in *SQYZWX*, 76. Both Zou Chuntai, *Zhongguo shehui zhuyi* (425) and *ZRGJD* (603) state that the decision to use foreign capital was adopted during the 1978 ideological conference. Thus, it is a "chicken and egg" problem. The Taiwanese analyst Tun Yung states the new foreign trade principles were formulated during the Learning from Daqing and Dazhai Conference. This appears inaccurate, and the author fails to provide an attribution. See Tun Yung, "Controversies," 33.

119. In August 1978, the Export Credit Guarantee Department (ECGD), which is the British government department providing officially supported credit (buyers' credit), "negotiated a deal with the BOC under which British banks would make deposits with the BOC under terms guaranteed by the ECGD." MacDougall, "Policy Changes," 160. In December 1978 a $1.2 billion loan agreement was signed with seven British banks. The British ECGD "provided 85% of the cover and subsidized the interest rate." World Bank, *China: Socialist Economic Development*, 2:462. For the Chinese definition of buyers' credit, see Chen Yun, "Zai caijing," in *SQYZWX*, 172.

120. "Kaizhan duiwai jiagong zhuangpei yewu shixing banfa" [Trial procedures for developing processing and assembly operations for the foreign market], State Council document 78.139, issued on 15 July 1978, cited in "Yinfa duiwai jiagong zhuangpei yewu de waihui jiesuan shixing banfa de tongzhi" [Circular on the publication of the trial procedures of foreign exchange settlement for processing and assembly operations for the foreign market], Maozonghuizi 78.203/Yinwaizi 78.399, issued by the MFT et al. on 28 August 1978, in *YCKTGWX*, 1:475–77.

121. State Council document 78.139 did not include regulations for compensation trade, which was considered more controversial. See the description in chapter 5 of Deng Xiaoping's 18 August 1975 speech. Yet compensation trade agreements were signed, such as the 31 August 1978 agreement establishing the Xiangzhou Woolen Factory north of

Macao. See Xianggang, *Zhongguo jingji,* 250. Li Xiannian also strongly supported compensation trade during the State Council Ideological Conference; he justified his decision as a way to "reduce domestic investment in such projects." See Li Xiannian, "Zai guowuyuan wuxuhuishang de jianghua" [Speech to the State Council Ideological Conference], 9 September 1978, in *Li Xiannian,* 2:370.

122. "Guanyu xishou huaqiao, waijiren deng zijin xingjian lüyou lüguan wenti de baogao" [Report on the problem of absorbing capital from overseas Chinese, foreigners, and others to construct tourist hotels], Jiji 78.583, submitted by the SPC on 26 August 1978, as cited in "Guanyu xishou qiaozi, waizi jianshe lüyou lüguan jinkou wuzi zhengmianshui wenti de qingshi" [Request for instruction on the problem of reduction or elimination of taxes on imported materials for tourist hotels constructed with capital from overseas Chinese and foreigners], Maoguanshuizi 79.498, submitted by the MFT, to the State Council on 30 October 1979, in *YCKTGWX,* 2:787–89.

123. Chen Yun, "Tiaozheng," in *SQYZWX,* 79.

124. See n. 120; MacDougall, "Policy Changes," 160–62.

125. Deng Xiaoping, "Gaoju Mao Zedong sixiang qizhi, jianchi shishi qiushi de yuanze" [Raise high the banner of Mao Zedong Thought, uphold the principle of seeking truth from fact], in Deng Xiaoping, *Wenxuan,* 123.

126. Li Xiannian, "Zai quanguo," in *SQYZWX,* 303.

127. Hu Yaobang, "Guanyu duiwai jingji guanxi wenti" [The problem of foreign economic relations], in *SQYZWX,* 1113.

128. "Gao zichan jieji ziyouhua jiushi zou zibenzhuyi daolu" [Carrying out bourgeois liberalism is taking the capitalist road], in Deng Xiaoping, *Jianshe,* 110. Huan Xiang and Dai Lunzhang date the "opening" policy as "formally defined in the communiqué of the Third Plenary Session." See FBIS, *China,* 5 April 1984, K5.

129. Chen Yun, "Jingji xingshi yu jingyan jiaoxun" [The economic situation and lessons from experience], in *SQYZWX,* 601. Considering its importance, this probably was a "decision" originating from the Party's Standing Committee. Wang Shouchun, *Zhongguo duiwai,* 109, states that the decision was "explicitly put forward" after the Third Plenum. It possibly was adopted during the post-Third Plenum Central Committee meeting held on 25 December 1978. See Sun Weiben, ed., *Zhongguo Gongchandang dangwu gongzuo dacidian,* 567. Otherwise, it was decided upon in January 1979 concurrent with the decision to readjust the economy. Whatever the case, the decision was finalized by February 1979 when Deng and other top leaders asked Rong Yiren to find a new way to use foreign capital.

130. Chen Yun, "Jingji xingshi," in *SQYZWX,* 601.

131. The term is fully coined by 1984 in Deng Xiaoping, "Shixian sige xiandaihua de hongwei mubiao he genben zhengce" [The magnificent goal and basic policy of bringing about the Four Modernizations], in 65–67. For a more in-depth analysis, see Guo Zhenying, *Deng Xiaoping,* 148–49.

132. Hu Yaobang, "Guanyu duiwai," in *SQYZWX,* 1119.

133. LIBOR (London Interbank Offer Rate) is the standard by which international banks set foreign commercial loan interest rates. In May 1979, the rate was set at 10.5 percent and was to jump to 17 percent by August. As for the Japanese nongovernmental loans, the interest rate the Chinese would have to pay was set at .25 percent to .5 percent over the LIBOR rate.

134. This amount included $8.2 billion in Eurodollar credits arranged by thirty-one Japanese nongovernmental banks and twenty-two companies. For details, see "Guanyu

he riben minjian yinhang qianding xindai xicyi de qingkuang ji shiyong gaixiang xindai ying zhuyi youguan shixiang de tongzhi" [Circular on the conditions under which a credit agreement was signed with the Japanese nongovernmental banks and the relevant matters that must be paid attention to in utilizing this credit], Zhongyezi 79.1624, issued by the BOC on 5 September 1979, in Zhongguo Renmin Yinhang Jihuasi, *Lilü*, 672–74.

135. Chen Yun, "Zai caijing," in *SQYZWX*, 172, 173.

136. Chen Yun, "Jingji xingshi," in *SQYZWX*, 601–602.

137. Hu Yaobang, "Guanyu duiwai," in *SQYZWX*, 1120.

138. On 18 December 1981, the agreement was adjusted to finance commodity purchases for two New Great Leap Forward projects, the Daqing Petrochemical Complex and the Baoshan Steel Complex. See Long Chucai, *Liyong waizi gailun*, 253, 288, 300; Kokubun, "Politics," 19–44; Davie and Carver, "China's International Trade," 27.

139. "Throughout 1979 they continued to arrange large lines of credit in anticipation of major capital purchases to follow. Thus by the end of 1979 the Chinese had amassed over $17 billion worth of officially supported export credits from France ($7.3 billion) [$7 billion], Britain ($5 billion) [$1.2 billion], Japan ($1.8 billion) [$2 billion], Canada ($1.7 billion) [$2 billion], and Italy ($1 billion), with smaller amounts from Belgium ($170 million), Sweden ($350 million), and Australia ($45 million)." Davie and Carver, "China's International Trade," 28; bracketed figures from World Bank, *China: Socialist Economic Development*, 2:462.

140. "Guanyu shiyong ying, fa, yi yinhang maifang xindai jinkou chengtao shebei youguan wenti de tongzhi" [Circular concerning the problems of using sellers' credit from English, French, and Italian banks to import turnkey factories], Zhongyezi 79.1417, issued by the BOC on 5 September 1979, in Zhongguo Renmin Yinhang Jihuasi, *Lilü*, 670–72.

141. Chen Yun, "Zai caijing," in *SQYZWX*, 172.

142. In 1980, the Chinese recovered their seat in both the World Bank and the IMF. During 1981, the World Bank agreed to lend China $800 million; the IMF lent SDR 759 million to help cover a foreign exchange deficit; the International Agricultural Development Fund lent $35 million to be paid back over a fifty-year period at a 1 percent interest rate.

143. Chen Yun, "Jingji xingshi," in *SQYZWX*, 601–2.

144. "Guanyu zhongwai hcying qiyc jigc wenti de qingshi baogao" [A report and request for instructions concerning several problems involving joint venture problems with foreign countries], Central Committee document 80.14, submitted by the Foreign Investment Management Commission and approved in principle on 6 February 1980, in *ZRGJGD*, 377 (for document number, see *YCKTGWX*, 2:533, 534).

145. See "Guanyu duiwai jiagong zhuangpei yewu kaizhan qingkuang de baogao" [Report on developing processing and assembly operations for the foreign market], State Council document 79.135, submitted by the SPC on 10 April 1979 and approved on 21 May 1979, in *DJFZH*, 2:932–40.

146. "Guanyu buchong xiuding kaizhan jiagong zhuangpei yewu shixing banfa de qingshi baogao" [Report and request for instructions on supplementing and revising the trial procedures for developing processing and assembly operations for the foreign market], submitted to the State Council by the SPC, the SEC, the SIEAC, and the MFT on 4 August 1979, ibid., 925–29.

147. "Kaizhan duiwai jiagong zhuangpei he zhongxiaoxing buchang maoyi banfa de tongzhi" [Circular on procedures for developing processing and assembly operations for

the foreign market and medium- to small-scale compensation trade], State Council document 79.220, issued on 3 September 1979, in *YCKTGWX*, 1:353–57.

148. Renmin Ribaoshe Gongshangbu, ed., *Zhongguo duiwai kaifang,* 916.

149. "Guanyu buchong xiuding kaizhan jiagong zhuangpei yewu shixing banfa de qingshi baogao," in *DJFZH*, 2:925–29.

150. Chen Yun, "Tiaozheng," in *SQYZWX*, 79. Discussions for joint offshore exploration had already begun by the summer of 1978, and letters of intent were signed in April 1979. For more information, see Lieberthal and Oksenberg, *Policy Making,* 169–268; MacDougall, "Policy Changes," 158; Davie and Carver, "China's International Trade," 29.

151. "Jianyi sheli guoji touzi xintuo gongsi de yixie chubu yijian" [A few initial opinions on recommending the establishment of an international trust and investment corporation], submitted by Rong Yiren to the Central Committee and the State Council in March 1979, cited in Guojia Jingji Tizhi, *Zongguo jingji tizhi,* 751.

152. For an excellent analysis of CITIC's origins, see ibid., 750–54.

153. Central Committee document 80.14, in Reardon, "China's Coastal Development Strategy, 1979–1984, I."

154. Undated letter enclosed in Central Committee document 80.14, ibid.

155. "Zhongwai hezi jingying qiye laodong guanli guiding" [Labor management regulations for equity joint ventures between China and foreign businessmen], State Council document 80.199, issued on 26 July 1980, in Guojia Jingwei Jishu Gaizaoju, *Jishu gaizao,* 417–19.

156. "Guanyu zhongwai hezi qiye jianshe yongdi guanli banfa" [The temporary regulations for the use of land in constructing equity joint ventures between China and foreign businessmen], State Council document 80.201, issued on 26 July 1980, in *YCKTGWX*, 1:328–30.

157. "Zhongwai hezi jingying qiye dengji guanli banfa" [Management procedures for the registration of equity joint ventures between China and foreign businessmen], State Council document 80.200, issued on 26 July 1980, in Guojia Jingwei Jishu Gaizaoju, *Jishu gaizao,* 420–21.

158. "Zhongwai hezi jingying qiye suodeshui fa" [The equity joint venture enterprises income tax law], approved and issued by the National Peoples' Congress on 10 September 1980, in *YCKTGWX*, 2:587–89; "Geren suodeshui fa" [The individual income tax law] approved and issued by the National People's Congress on 10 September 1980, in *YCKTGWX*, 2:603–605.

159. Originally, the term "export special zone" (*chukou tequ*) was adopted. A change in nomenclature was authorized by Central Committee document 80.41 of 16 May 1980. See "Guanyu 'Guangdong, Fujian liangsheng huiyi jiyao' de pishi" [Comment on the "Summary of the Conference on Guangdong and Fujian Provinces"], Central Committee document 80.14, approved and transmitted on 16 May 1980, trans. in Reardon, "China's Coastal Development Strategy, 1979–1984, I," 45–58. To avoid confusion, the term "special economic zone" (SEZ) has been adopted.

160. For instance, see Chossudovsky, *Towards Capitalist Restoration?* 132–33.

161. Stoltenberg, "China's Special Economic Zones," 638; Shaw, *Mainland China,* 368–370; and Oborne, *China's Special Economic Zones.*

162. Yao Yilin, "Tongxin xieli zuohao jingji gaige," 3–4.

163. Guo Tewen, "Juban jingji," 10.

164. Jinan Daxue Tequ, *Shijie jingjixing tequ yaolan,* 46–85.

165. Basile and Germidis, *Investing,* 44.

166. Zhonggong Shenzhen, *"Shenzhen,"* 5–6.

167. Stepanek, "China's Special Economic Zones," 38.

168. Wang Wenyang, ed., *Jingji tequ,* 10; also see Zhonggong Shenzhen, *"Shenzhen,"* 6.

169. Keohane and Nye, *Power,* chap. 1.

170. Weiss, "Economic Zones," 21–24; Basile and Germidis, *Investing,* 21–23; Tang Huozhao, *Shenzhen jingjimian mianguan,* 29.

171. Tang Huozhao, *Shenzhen,* 29, Zhongshan Daxue Jingjixi, ed., *Jingjixue luncong,* 296.

172. Sklair, "Shenzhen," 593–94.

173. Basile and Germidis, *Investing,* 19; Jao and Leung, ed., *China's Special Economic Zones,* 76.

174. World Bank, *China: External Trade,* vii–ix.

175. Zhonggong Shenzhen, *"Shenzhen,"* 6.

176. For more information on "political frontier defense" proposed by Lin Biao in August 1966, see *Jiefangjun bao,* 15 October 1978; Vogel, *One Step Ahead,* 341.

177. Shenzhenshi Renmin, *Shenzhen,* 21. Western estimates are much higher; see Youngson, *China and Hongkong,* 4–5.

178. *Shenzhen fengcai,* 1 July 1986, 2.

179. For more information on the Pearl River Delta region, see Sit, ed., *Resources;* Vogel, *One Step Ahead,* 125–250.

180. *WFSS,* 136; interview with SEZ official in Zhuhai in September 1987; "Guanyu fazhan bianfang jingji de ruogan guiding" [Several regulations regarding the development of the border economy], issued by the Shenzhen Municipal. Committee on 6 March 1979, cited in Shenzhen Jingji Tequ Nianjian Bianji Weiyuanhui, *1985,* 615.

181. "Guanyu jinnian yilai waimao shougou jihua zhixing qingkuang he wenti de baogao," in *ZRGJGD,* 303–4.

182. Li Xiannian, "Nuli zuohao dui Xiang'ao shichang de gongying" [Work hard to complete supplies to the Hong Kong-Macao markets], a comment (*piyu*) on a clipping from the National Foreign Trade Planning Conference, written on 28 October 1977, in *Li Xiannian,* 2:319.

183. "Guanyu Baoan, Zhuhai liangxian waimao jidi he shizheng jianshe guihua shexian de pifu," State Council document 79.38, issued on 14 February 1979. The actual document has yet to be located. For document title reference, see Xianggang, *Zhongguo jingji,* 381; for State Council document number reference, see Guangdongsheng Jiage Xuehui, *Jingji tequ,* 5; also see Shenzhen Jingji Tequ Nianjian Bianji Weiyuanhui, *Shenzhen,* 52. Several Hong Kong scholars contributing to Jao and Leung have stated that document 38 was issued in 1978. The 1979 dating is based on the opening speech of Vice-Mayor Zhou Xiwu given in February 1983 at a discussion conference on theories on pricing in the SEZs.

184. Guangdongsheng Jiage Xuehui, *Jingji tequ,* 5; Sun Ru, ed., *Qianjinzhong,* 13; Shenzhenshi Renmin, *Shenzhen,* 1; Shenzhen Jingji Tequ Nianjian Bianji Weiyuanhui, *Shenzhen,* 615.

185. *ZRGJD,* 617.

186. Interview with SEZ official in Zhuhai in September 1987; "Guanyu fazhan bianfang jingji de ruogan guiding" [Several regulations regarding the development of the border economy], issued by the Shenzhen Municipal Committee on 6 March 1979, cited in Shenzhen Jingji Tequ Nianjian Bianji Weiyuanhui, *Shenzhen,* 615.

187. For more background, see Zhonggong Renminglu, *Zhonggong,* 669–70 for Xi

Zhongxun and 757–58 for Yang Shangkun. Xi was also appointed chair of the Guangdong Provincial Revolutionary Committee, and Yang was named one of several vice-chairmen on 11 December 1978; after nearly twelve years in existence, the Revolutionary Committee's name was changed on 1 January 1980 back to the Guangdong Provincial People's Government. See Guangdong Nianjian Bianji, *Guangdong,* 84–90.

188. Sun Ru, *Qianjinzhong,* 12–13. For more on the March proposal, see Lei Qiang et al., "Shenzhen," 268; Zhao Yuanjie, *Zhongguo tequ jingji,* 56; *Shenzhen tequbao,* 9 August 1982.

189. *Shijie jingji daobao,* 18 May 1982; Barson, "Special Economic Zones," 464.

190. For instance, see Zhou Enlai's comments during his Shanghai trip of July 1961, in *ZELNP,* 2:424–25.

191. Chi Hsin, *Teng Hsiao-Ping,* 3.

192. Mamo and Upson, *Dizionario,* 411. Ezra Vogel reported that by the late 1980s, "about twenty high officials in Beijing of deputy minister rank or above were of Hakka extraction." Vogel, *One Step Ahead,* 245. For more on Ye Jianying's views on economic modernization, see Cao Yingwang, "Ye Jianying," 87–90.

193. Reardon, "China's Coastal Development Strategy 1979–1982, I ," 19–44.

194. Guangdong Jingji Xuehui, ed., *Guangdong jingji tizhi,* 117.

195. Crane, *Political Economy,* 26.

196. Ho and Huenemann, *China's Open Door Policy,* 49.

197. Both submitted sez proposals on 16 October 1979. See Xianggang, *Zhongguo jingji,* 366.

198. Zhonggong Zhongyang Shujichu Yanjiushi Lilunzu, ed., *Diaocha,* 5–6.

199. Ibid., 5.

200. Zhang Ge, "Guanyu jingji," 254; and Lei Qiang et al., "Shenzhen jingji tequ," 268.

201. Zhang Ge, "Guanyu jingji"; and Barnett, *Making of Foreign Policy,* 20–25.

202. "Keyi huachu yikuai difang, jiaozuo tequ."

203. Zhang Ge, "Guanyu jingji tequ," 256.

204. Liang Wensen, *Zhongguo jingji tequ,* 4–5.

205. The Shaanxi-Gansu-Ningxia border area was formally set up in 1937 with Yan'an as its government center. The leadership experimented with various economic and political reforms (the *sansan zhi* of political participation, rent and interest reduction, etc.) and led Communist forces against the Japanese and Chiang Kai-shek. See Xing Guohua, ed., *Zhongguo gemingshi xuexi shouce,* 418, 783, 784; Watson, *Mao Zedong.*

206. Chen Yun, "Zai caijing," in *SQYZWX,* 173.

207. Ibid.

8. Conclusion

1. Deng Xiaoping, "Gaoju Mao Zedong sixiang qizhi, jianchi shishi qiushi de yuanze," in *Wenxuan,* 123.

2. Deng Xiaoping, "Jianchi sixiang jiben yuanze," ibid., 146.

3. Li Zhongjie, *Shehui zhuyi gaigeshi,* 563.

4. Zhonghua Renmin Gongheguo Guowuyuan, *Zhonghua Renmin Gongheguo xian-xing fagui,* 275; *ZRGJFX,* 1:551.

5. Davie and Carver, "China's International Trade," pt. 2, 24; Nai-Ruenn Chen, "China's Capital Construction," 61.

6. Wang Shouchun, *Zhongguo duiwai,* 105.

7. Nai-Ruenn Chen, "China's Capital Construction," 61.

8. For a complete listing of export credit agreements between 1978 and 1980, see World Bank, *China, Socialist Economic Development,* 2:462.

9. Reardon, "China's Coastal Development Strategy, 1979–1982, II," Introduction. For a more detailed analysis, see Fewsmith, *Dilemmas,* chap. 5.

10. World Bank, *World Development Report 1987,* chap. 5; Sheahan, *Alternative Strategies,* 12–26.

11. For instance, see the perils of SOE reforms in *Washington Post,* 16 November 1999.

12. Nathan, "Policy Oscillations," 728.

13. For a recent discussion of linear and cyclical process models, Puchala, "History," 177–202.

14. In contrast to organizational theorists such as James March, most of the recent foreign policy research on learning has focused on international security issues at the decision-maker level of analysis, starting with Robert Jervis, *Perception,* chap. 6. For a comprehensive literature review, see Levy, "Learning," 279–312; as applied to the China security field, see Johnston, "Learning"; Hu Weixing, "Medium Nuclear Powers"; as applied to the nonsecurity China field, see Oksenberg, "Policy Formulation," and Petrick, "Policy Cycles."

15. The work of David Kolb, who conducts research in the education field, suggests one possible venue for future research in Chinese elite learning. Kolb has extensively tested his Experiential Learning Model, which suggests that learning itself goes through four stages: concrete experience, reflective observation, abstract conceptualization, and active experimentation. He further suggests that individuals emphasize particular stages of learning. See Kolb, *Experiential Learning;* idem, "Learning Styles."

16. Nye, "Nuclear Learning," 380; also see Argyris and Schon, *Organizational Learning,* 20–26; Levy, "Learning," 286–87.

17. Nye, "Nuclear Learning," 380.

18. See the discussion in chapter 2 of Lardy's and Heymann's periodization of agricultural and foreign technology policies.

19. Robert H. Bates, as quoted in Collins, "Report." Also see Bates, "Area Studies"; Walt, "Rigor," 5. Bates restricts his definition of rational choice to mostly game theory, which he believes can accommodate more empirically based approaches (Bates, de Figueredo, Weingast). However, his belief that "true" social scientists must promote the rational choice agenda appears as dogmatic as the assertions of those who promote Marxist paradigms.

APPENDIX A

1. Oksenberg, "Politics," 543–90.

2. "Guanyu jianguo yilai dang de ruogan lishi wenti de jueyi" [Resolution on certain historical problems since the founding of the PRC], approved at the Sixth Plenum of the Eleventh Party Congress, on 27 June 1981.

3. For a discussion of this problem, see Mao Zedong, *Writings,* 1:xxviii.

4. Interview with Yang Chengxu, director of the China Institute of International Studies, 17 April 1996.

5. For a comprehensive analysis of pre-1979 sources, see E. Wu, "Contemporary China Studies," 59–73. The Central Committee Archives also has issued *Zhonggong*

zhongyang wenjian xuanbian, a vast collection of documents and speeches covering the pre-1949 period. In 1981 the Party Secretariat issued a restricted collection, *Liuda yilai dangnei mimi wenjian.* Analysis of these works might reveal new insight on China's attitude toward the international economy.

6. Lieberthal and Dickson, *Research Guide,* xviii.

7. Ibid.

8. For Mao Zedong: *Jianguo; Writings,* 1–2; *Secret Speeches.* For Chen Yun: *Tongzhi wengao xuanbian; Wenxian, 1956–1985.* For Li Xiannian: *Lun caizheng jinrong maoyi, 1950–1991.* For Deng Xiaoping: *Wenxuan, 1975–1982; Jianshe you Zhongguo tese de shehui zhuyi.*

9. Lieberthal, *Central Documents;* Lieberthal and Oksenberg, *Policy Making,* 152–53.

10. "Guojia xingzheng jiguan gongwen chuli banfa" [The methods to handle official documents from state administrative organizations], issued by the State Council Office in February 1987, cited in Chen Hongbin, Wu Ge, Tong Yiquan, and Liu Yangyun, eds., *Jianming wenmi gongzuo shouce,* 181. The following description of the categories and types of Chinese official documents is taken from ibid., 181–89; and Waimao Yingyong-wen Bianxiezu, ed., *Waimao yingyongwen,* 140–55, 182–219.

11. Mao Zedong, "Speech at Conference of Provincial and Municipal Committee Secretaries," 2 February 1959, in *Miscellany,* 152.

APPENDIX B

1. "Emergency Directive to Make Great Efforts to Fulfill the Foreign Trade Procurement and Export Responsibilities," ZRGJGD 131.

APPENDIX C

1. "A Report and Request for Instructions for Establishing Export Commodity Production Bases," ZRGJGD, 143. This report was submitted by the Party Committee of the Ministry of Foreign Trade and approved and transmitted by the CCP Central Committee on 30 June 1960.

2. Another characteristic of the GLF was a large-scale decentralization of the bureaucracy.

3. *Fazhan zengchan jieyue yundong* was a long-term movement started 15 February 1957 to readjust the scale of 1957 capital construction due in part to a fiscal shortfall. See ZRGJD, 94, 257; ZRGJGD, 184–85.

4. Mishan is in southeast Heilongjiang Province, Hejiang is in southeast Sichuan, and Xingjiang reclamation area is in China's northwesternmost province, Xinjiang.

5. Text in brackets, ZRGJD, 273.

APPENDIX D

1. "Emergency Directive for the Whole Party to Make Great Efforts in the Campaign for Foreign Trade Procurement and Exports" ZRGJGD, 144–45.

Bibliography

Ahn, Byung-joon. *Chinese Politics and the Cultural Revolution.* Seattle: University of Washington Press, 1976.

Allison, Graham. "Conceptual Models and the Cuban Missile Crisis." *American Political Science Review,* 63, 3 (September 1969): 698–718.

Almond, Gabriel A., and Scott C. Flanagan, eds. *Crisis, Choice and Change: Historical Studies of Political Development.* Boston: Little, Brown, 1973.

Amsden, Alice H. *Asia's Next Giant: South Korea and Late Industrialization.* New York: Oxford University Press, 1989.

Argyris, Chris, and Donald Schon. *Organizational Learning: A Theory of Action Perspective.* Reading, Mass.: Addison-Wesley, 1978.

Ashbrook, Arthur G., Jr. "China: Shift of Economic Gears in Mid-1970s." In U.S. Congress, Joint Economic Committee, *Chinese Economy,* 204–35.

Bachman, David. *Bureaucracy, Economy, and Leadership in China.* Cambridge: Cambridge University Press, 1991.

———. *Chen Yun and the Chinese Political System.* Berkeley: Institute of East Asian Studies, University of California, 1985.

———. "Chinese Bureaucratic Politics and the Origins of the Great Leap Forward." *Journal of Contemporary China* 9 (Summer 1995): 35–55.

Balassa, Bela. "Comment." *Pioneers in Development,* ed. G. M. Meier and D. Seers, 304 11. New York: Oxford University Press, 1984.

———. *Development Strategies in Semi-Industrial Economies.* Baltimore, Md.: Johns Hopkins University Press, 1982.

———. *The Process of Industrial Development and Alternative Development Strategies.* Princeton N.J.: International Finance Section, Department of Economics, Princeton University, 1981.

Baldwin, David. "Neoliberalism, Neorealism and World Politics." In *Neorealism and Neoliberalism: The Contemporary Debate,* ed. David Baldwin, 3–59. New York: Columbia University Press, 1993.

Baogang Gongsi Dangwei Xuanchuanbu, *Baogangzhi* Bangongshi. "Lishi zhengming jianshe Baogang shi zhengque de" [History proves that the building of Baoshan steel complex was correct]. *Dang de wenxian* 60 (1997), 36–40.

Barnett, A. Doak. *China's Economy in Global Perspective.* Washington, D.C.: Brookings, 1981.

———. *The Making of Foreign Policy in China: Structure and Process.* Boulder, Colo.: Westview Press, 1985.

307

Barson, Joy. "Special Economic Zones in the People's Republic Of China." *China—International Business* 4 (1981): 461–94.

Basile, Antoine, and Dimitri Germidis. *Investing in Free Export Processing Zones.* Paris: OECD, 1984.

Bates, Robert H. "Area Studies and Political Science: Rupture and Possible Synthesis." *Africa Today* 44, 2 (April/June 1997); 123–31.

Bates, Robert H.; J. P. de Figueredo, and Barry R. Weingast. "The Politics of Interpretation: Rationality, Culture and Transition." *Politics and Society* 26, 4 (December 1998): 603–42.

Batsavage, Richard E., and John L. Davie. "China's International Trade and Finance." In U.S. Congress, Joint Economic Committee, *Chinese Economy,* 707–41.

Baum, Richard. *Burying Mao.* Princeton, N.J.: Princeton University Press, 1994.

———. "The Road to Tiananmen: Chinese Politics in the 1980s." In *The Politics of China, 1949–1989,* ed. Roderick MacFarquhar, 340–471. New York: Cambridge University Press, 1993.

———, ed. *China's Four Modernizations.* Boulder, Colo.: Westview Press, 1980.

Baum, Richard. Review of *From Bandwagon to Balance-of-Politics,* by Avery Goldstein. *American Political Science Review* 87, 1 (March 1993): 237–39.

Bennett, Gordon M. *Yundong: Mass Campaigns in Chinese Communist Leadership.* Berkeley: Center for Chinese Studies, University of California, 1976.

Bernard, Mitchell, and John Ravenhill. "Beyond Product Cycles and Flying Geese: Regionalization, Hierarchy, and the Industrialization of East Asia." *World Politics* 47, 2 (January 1995): 171–209.

Bernstein, Richard J. *Beyond Objectivism and Relativism.* Philadelphia: University of Pennsylvania Press, 1983.

Bernstein, Thomas P. "Cadre and Peasant Behavior under Conditions of Insecurity and Deprivation: The Grain Supply Crisis of the Spring of 1955." In *Chinese Communist Politics in Action,* ed. A. Doak Barnett, 365–99. Seattle: University of Washington Press, 1969.

———. "Stalinism, Famine and Chinese Peasants: Grain Procurement during the Great Leap Forward." *Theory and Society* 13, 3 (1984): 339–77.

Berry, Brian J. L. *Long-wave Rhythms in Economic Development and Political Behavior.* Baltimore, Md.: Johns Hopkins University Press, 1991.

Bhagwati, Jagdish N. *Foreign Trade Regimes and Economic Development: Anatomy and Consequences of Exchange Control Regimes.* Cambridge: Ballinger, 1978.

Binder, Leonard; James S. Coleman; Joseph LaPalombara; Lucian W. Pye; Sidney Verba; and Sidney Weiner. *Crises and Sequences in Political Development.* Princeton, N.J.: Princeton University Press, 1971.

Bo Yibo. "Guanyu yijiuliusinian jihua de wenti" [Problems with the 1964 plan]. *Dang de wenxian* 64 (1998): 5–7.

———. *Ruogan zhongda juece yu shijian de huigu* [Looking back on certain important decisions and events]. Vols. 1 and 2. Beijing: Zhonggong Zhongyang Dangxiao Chubanshe, 1991, 1993.

Bolt, Paul J. "China's Development and the Chinese Overseas, 1979–1994: State and Diaspora in the Contemporary World Order." Ph.D. diss., University of Illinois at Urbana–Champaign, 1996.

Brown, Shannon R. "China's Program of Technology Acquisition." In Baum, ed. *China's Four Modernizations,* 153–73.

Buchanan, James M.; Robert D. Tollison; and Gordon Tullock, eds. *Toward a Theory of the Rent-Seeking Society.* College Station: Texas A & M University Press, 1980.

Caizhengbu Waihui Waishi Caiwusi, ed. *Feimaoyi waihui zhidu huibian* [Collection of documents concerning the noncommercially earned foreign exchange system]. Beijing: Zhongguo Caizheng Jingji Chubanshe, 1991.

Calder, Kent E. *Crisis and Compensation.* Princeton, N.J.: Princeton University Press, 1988.

Cao Yingwang. "Ye Jianying de sige xiandaihua sixiang" [Ye Jianying's concept of the Four Modernizations]. *Dang de wenxian* 56 (1997): 87–90.

———. "Zhou Enlai duiwai jingji guanxi sixiang shulüe" [A brief summary of Zhou Enlai's thinking on foreign economic relations]. *Dang de wenxian* 29 (1992): 47–53.

Carnoy, Martin. *The State and Political Theory.* Princeton, N.J.: Princeton University Press, 1984.

Castells, Manuel. *The Economic Crisis and American Society.* Princeton, N.J.: Princeton University Press, 1980.

Chan, Alfred L. "Leaders, Coalition Politics and Policy-Formulation in China: The Great Leap Forward Revisited." *Journal of Contemporary China* 8 (Winter–Spring, 1995): 57–78.

Chang, King-yuh, ed. *Perspectives on Development in Mainland China.* Boulder, Colo.: Westview Press, 1985.

Chang, Parris H. *Power and Policy in China.* 1st and 2d eds. University Park: Pennsylvania State University Press, 1975, 1978.

Chen Dacai. "Zhou Enlai guanyu xuexi he liyong ziben zhuyi de renshi yu shijian" [Zhou Enlai's understanding and practice of studying and utilizing capitalism]. *Dang de wenxian* 41 (1994): 62–66.

Chen Donglin. "Chen Yun yu 70 niandai duiwai jingji gongzuo de xin kaituo" [Chen Yun and the new opening in foreign economic work in the 1970s]. In Zhu Jiamu, ed., *Chen Yun he tade shiye,* 2:1092–1103.

Chen, Edward K. Y. *Hypergrowth in Asian Economies: A Comparative Survey of Hong Kong, Japan, Korea, Singapore and Taiwan.* London: Macmillan, 1979.

Chen Hongbin, Wu Ge, Tong Yiquan, and Liu Yangyun, eds. *Jianming wenmi gongzuo shouce* [A concise handbook on document secretarial work]. Shenyang: Liaoning Jiaoyu Chubanshe, 1987.

Chen, Nai-Ruenn. "China's Capital Construction: Current Retrenchment and Prospects for Foreign Participation." In *China under the Four Modernizations:* Selected Papers Submitted to the Joint Economic Committee, U.S. Congress, 48–62. Washington, D.C.: Government Printing Office, 1982.

———. "China's Foreign Trade in Global Perspective." *China in the Global Community,* ed. James C. Hsiung and Samuel S. Kim, 120–39. New York: Praeger, 1980.

———. "Economic Modernization in Post-Mao China: Policies, Problems, and Prospects." In U.S. Congress, Joint Economic Committee, *Chinese Economy,* 165–203.

Chen Yun. *Chen Yun tongzhi wengao xuanbian* [Selections of Comrade Chen Yun's manuscripts (1956–1962)]. Beijing: Renmin Chubanshe, 1981.

———. *Chen Yun wenxuan, 1956–1985* [Chen Yun's selected works]. Beijing: Renmin Chubanshe, 1986.

———. *Chen Yun wenxuan* [Chen Yun's selected works]. Vol. 3. Beijing: Renmin Chubanshe, 1995.

————. "Guanyu xibei xiezuoqu jiben jianshe gongzuo de jige wenti" [Several problems in basic construction work in the northwest coordinate region]. *Dang de wenxian* 3 (1998): 8–13.

Cheng Chu-yuan. *China's Economic Development.* Boulder, Colo.: Westview Press, 1982.

————. "China's Industry: Advances and Dilemma." *Current History* 61, 361 (September 1971): 154–59.

————. *Economic Relations between Peking and Moscow: 1949–63.* N.Y.: Praeger, 1964.

————. "The Modernization of Chinese Industry." In Baum, ed., *China's Four Modernizations,* 120–39.

Cheng, J. Chester, ed. *The Politics of the Chinese Red Army.* Stanford, Calif.: Hoover Institution on War, Revolution, and Peace, 1966.

Cheng, Tun-jeng. "Political Regimes and Development Strategies: South Korea and Taiwan." In Gereffi and Wyman, eds., *Manufacturing Miracles,* 139–78.

Chi, Hsin. *Teng Hsiao-ping: A Political Biography.* Kowloon: Chung Hwa, 1978.

Chossudovsky, Michel. *Towards Capitalist Restoration?* London: Macmillan, 1986.

Cohen, Warren I., and Akira Iriye, eds. *The Great Powers in East Asia, 1953–1960.* New York: Columbia University Press, 1990.

Collins, Steven. "Report of the National Council of Area Studies Associations (NCASA) Meeting on Area Studies, Washington, D.C., 28 September 1996." *Asian Studies Newsletter* 41, 5 (Winter 1996): 12.

Conybeare, John A. C. *Trade Wars.* New York: Columbia University Press, 1987.

Crane, George T. *The Political Economy of China's Special Economic Zones.* Armonk, N.Y.: M. E. Sharpe, 1990.

Cumings, Bruce. "The Political Economy of Chinese Foreign Policy." *Modern China* 5 (October 1979): 411–61.

Dangdai Zhongguo Congshu Bianjibu, ed. *Dangdai Zhongguo de jingji tizhi gaige* [The economic structural reforms of contemporary China]. Beijing: Zhongguo Shehui Kexueyuan Chubanshe, 1984.

————. *Dangdai Zhongguo waijiao* [China's contemporary foreign relations]. Beijing: Zhongguo Shehui Kexueyuan Chubanshe, 1988.

Dangdai Zhongguo de Jingji Guanli Bianjibu, ed. *Zhonghua Renmin Gongheguo jingji guanli dashiji* [A chronology of the major events in the PRC's economy and management]. Beijing: Zhongguo Jingji Chubanshe, 1986.

Dangdai Zhongguo Shangye Bianjibu, ed. *Zhonghua Renmin Gongheguo shangye dashiji* [A chronology of the PRC's commerce]. Beijing: Zhongguo Shangye Chubanshe, 1990.

Davie, John L., and Dean W. Carver. "China's International Trade And Finance." In U.S. Congress, Joint Economic Committee, *China under the Four Modernizations,* 19–47. 97th Cong., 2d sess., 1982.

Deng Xiaoping. *Deng Xiaoping wenxuan, 1975–1982* [Selected works of Deng Xiaoping]. Beijing: Renmin Chubanshe, 1983.

————. *Jianshe you Zhongguo tese de shehui zhuyi (zengdingben)* [The construction of socialism with Chinese characteristics]. Beijing: Renmin Chubanshe, 1987.

Dernberger, Robert F., ed. *China's Development Experience in Comparative Perspective.* Cambridge: Harvard University Press, 1980.

Deyo, Frederic C., ed. *The Political Economy of the New Asian Industrialism.* Ithaca, N.Y.: Cornell University Press, 1987.

Díaz-Alejandro, Carlos F. *Foreign Trade Regimes and Economic Development.* Vol. 9: Columbia. New York: National Bureau of Economic Research, 1976.

Dittmer, Lowell. *Liu Shaoqi and the Chinese Cultural Revolution.* Berkeley: University of California Press, 1974.

————. "Patterns of Elite Strife and Succession in Chinese Politics." *China Quarterly* 123 (September 1990): 405–30.

Dong Zhikai. "Wushi niandai fan 'fengsuo, jinyun' de douzheng ji qi qishi" [Inspirations from the 1950s struggle against the "blockade" and "embargo"]. *Dang de wenxian* 28 (1992): 85–87.

Duiwai Jingji Maoyibu Renshi Jiaoyuju, Chukou Huoyuan Gailun Bianxiezu, ed. *Chukou huoyuan gailun* [An introduction to export sourcing]. Beijing: Zhongguo Duiwai Jingji Maoyi Chubanshe, 1986.

Eckstein, Alexander. *China's Economic Revolution.* New York: Cambridge University Press, 1977.

————. "The Chinese Development Model." In U.S. Congress, Joint Economic Committee, ed., *Chinese Economy,* 80–114.

————. *Communist China's Economic Growth and Foreign Trade.* New York: Columbia University Press, 1966.

————. "Economic Fluctuations in Communist China's Domestic Development." In *China in Crisis: China's Heritage and the Communist Political System,* ed. Ping-ti Ho and Tang Tsou, 691–729. Chicago: University of Chicago Press, 1968.

Eighth National Congress of the Communist Party of China. Vols. 1 and 2. Beijing: Foreign Languages Press, 1956.

Ellison, Christopher, and Gary Gereffi. "Explaining Strategies and Patterns of Industrial Development." In Gereffi and Wyman, eds., *Manufacturing Miracles,* 368–403.

Ellison, Herbert J., ed. *The Sino-Soviet Conflict.* Seattle: University of Washington Press, 1982.

Emmanuel, Arghiri. *Unequal Exchange: A Study of the Imperialism of Trade.* New York: Monthly Review Press, 1972.

Evans, Peter; Dietrich Rueschemeyer; and Theda Skocpol, eds. *Bringing the State Back In.* New York: Cambridge University Press, 1985.

Fairbank, John King; Edwin Reischauer; and Albert Craig. *East Asia: Tradition and Transformation.* Boston: Houghton Mifflin, 1989.

————. *The United States and China.* Boston: Harvard University Press, 1972.

Fang Weizhong, ed. *Zhonghua Renmin Gongheguo jingji dashiji (1949–1980)* [A chronology of major events in the PRC's economy (1949–1980)]. Beijing: Zhongguo Shehui Kexue Chubanshe, 1984.

Fei, John C. H.; Kazushi Ohkawa; and Gustav Ranis. "Economic Development in Historical Perspective: Japan, Korea, and Taiwan." In *Japan and the Developing Countries,* ed. Kazushi Ohkawa, Gustav Ranis, and Larry Meissner, 35–64. New York: Basil Blackwell, 1985.

Fewsmith, Joseph. *Dilemmas of Reform in China.* Armonk, N.Y.: M. E. Sharpe, 1994.

Foot, Rosemary. "The Search for a Modus Vivendi: Anglo-American Relations and China Policy in the Eisenhower Era." In Cohen and Iriye, eds., *Great Powers,* 143–63.

Friedman, Edward. "Maoist Conceptualizations of the Capitalist World-System." In *Processes of the World-System,* ed. Terence Hopkins and Immanuel Wallerstein, Beverly Hills, Calif.: Sage, 1980.

Friedman, Milton, and Rose Friedman. *Free to Choose.* New York: Harcourt Brace Jovanovich, 1980.

Fukuyama, Francis. "Confucianism and Democracy." *Journal of Democracy* 6, 2 (April 1995): 20–33.

Gadamer, Hans-Georg. "The Problem of Historical Consciousness." In *Interpretive Social Science: A Reader,* ed. Paul Rabinow and William M. Sullivan. Berkeley: University of California Press, 1979: 103–60.

Gasiorowski, Mark. "Economic Crisis and Political Regime Change: An Event History Analysis." *American Political Science Review* 89, 4 (December 1995): 882–97.

Gereffi, Gary, and Donald Wyman, eds. *Manufacturing Miracles.* Princeton, N.J.: Princeton University Press, 1990.

Gerschenkron, Alexander. *Economic Backwardness in Historical Perspective.* Cambridge: Harvard University Press, 1962.

Gillis, Malcom, and David Dapice. "Indonesia." In *The Open Economy,* ed. Rudiger Dornbusch and F. L. C. H. Helmers, 307–35. New York: Oxford University Press, 1988.

Gillis, Malcolm; Dwight H. Perkins; Michael Roemer; and Donald R. Snodgrass. *Economics of Development.* 3d ed. New York: W. W. Norton, 1992.

Gilpin, Robert. "Three Models of the Future." *International Organization,* Winter 1975, 37–60.

———. *War and Change in World Politics.* Cambridge: Cambridge University Press, 1981.

Goldman, Merle. "The Party and the Intellectuals." In MacFarquhar and Fairbank, eds., *Cambridge History,* 14:218–58.

———. "Party Policies toward the Intellectuals: The Unique Blooming and Contending of 1961–2." In Lewis, ed., *Party Leaderships,* 268–303.

Goldstein, Avery. *From Bandwagon to Balance-of-Politics.* Stanford, Calif.: Stanford University Press, 1991.

Goncharov, Sergei N.; John W. Lewis; and Xue Litai. *Uncertain Partners: Stalin, Mao and the Korean War.* Stanford, Calif.: Stanford University Press, 1993.

Gongheguo Lingxiu Dacidian Bianweihui, ed. *Gongheguo lingxiu dacidian—Zhu De* [A dictionary of the Republic's leaders—Zhu De]. Chengdu: Chengdu Chubanshe, 1993.

Gourevitch, Peter. *Politics in Hard Times: Comparative Responses to International Economic Crises.* Ithaca, N.Y.: Cornell University Press, 1986.

Grabowski, Richard. "Import Substitution, Export Promotion and the State in Economic Development." *Journal of Developing Areas* 28, 4 (July 1994): 535–54.

Green, Donald P., and Ian Shapiro. *Pathologies of Rational Choice Theory: A Critique of Application in Political Science.* New Haven, Conn.: Yale University Press, 1994.

Grew, Raymond, ed. *Crises of Political Development in Europe and the United States.* Princeton, N.J.: Princeton University Press, 1978.

Griffiths, Franklyn. "A Tendency Analysis of Soviet Policy-Making." In *Interest Groups in Soviet Politics,* ed. H. Gordon Skilling and Franklyn Griffiths, 335–77. Princeton, N.J.: Princeton University Press, 1971.

Griffith, William E. *Sino-Soviet Relations, 1964–1965.* Cambridge: MIT Press, 1967.

———. *The Sino-Soviet Rift.* Cambridge: MIT Press, 1964.

Grindle, Merilee S. "The New Political Economy: Positive Economics and Negative Politics." In *Politics and Policy Making in Developing Countries,* ed. Gerald Meier, 4–67. San Francisco: ICS Press, 1991.

Grindle, Merilee S., and John W. Thomas. *Public Choices and Policy Change: The Political Economy of Reform in Developing Countries.* Baltimore, Md.: Johns Hopkins University Press, 1991.

Ground, Richard Lynn. "The Genesis of Import Substitution in Latin America." *CEPAL Review* 36 (December 1988): 179–203.

Guangdong Jingji Xuehui, ed. *Guangdong jingji tizhi gaige yanjiu* [Studies on Guangdong economic structural reforms]. Guangzhou: Zhongshan Daxue Chubanshe, 1986.

Guangdong Nianjian Bianji Weiyuanhui, ed. *Guangdong nianjian, 1987* [The Guangdong yearbook, 1987]. Guangzhou: Guangdong Renmin Chubanshe, 1987.

Guangdongsheng Jiage Xuehui, Gangao Jingji Yanjiusuo, Shenzhenshi Jingji Xuehui, Shenzhenshi Wujiaju, ed. *Jinji tequ jiage lilun taolunhui wenxuan* [Selected papers from the theoretical conference on SEZ pricing]. Guangzhou: N.d., 1983.

Guo Tewen. "Juban jingji tequ sixiang de tichu yu shijian" [The proposal and practice of running SEZs]. *Dang de wenxian* 27 (1992): 9–14.

Guo Zhenying and Ma Benxiang, eds. *Deng Xiaoping jingji sixiang yanjiu* [A study of Deng Xiaoping's economic ideas]. Tianjin: Tianjin Shehui Kexueyuan Chubanshe, 1988.

Guojia Jihua Weiyuanhui Dangzu. "Shi shengchan he jianshe zai fazhanzhong dedao tiaozheng, gonggu, chongshi he tigao" [Bring about readjusted, consolidated, supplemented and higher expectations of success while carrying out production and construction]. *Dang de wenxian* 6 (1990): 3–4.

Guojia Jingji Tizhi Gaige Weiyuanhui, ed. *Zhongguo jingji tizhi gaige shinian* [Ten years of economic system reform in China]. Beijing: Jingji Guanli Chubanshe, Gaige Chubanshe, 1988.

Guojia Jingwei Jishu Gaizaoju, Guojia Jingwei Guanli Yanjiusuo, Guojia Jingwei Jinchukouju, ed. *Jishu gaizao jishu yinjin wenjian huibian* [A collection of documents relating to technological transformation and importation]. Beijing: Zhongguo Jingji Chubanshe, 1985.

Guojia Tongjiju, ed. *Zhongguo tongji nianjian, 1983* [The Chinese statistical yearbook, 1983]. Beijing: Zhongguo Tongji Chubanshe, 1983.

———. *Zhongguo tongji nianjian, 1984* [The Chinese statistical yearbook, 1984]. Beijing: Zhongguo Tongji Chubanshe, 1984.

Guojia Waihui Guanliju, ed. *Huijia shouce* [Handbook of currency values]. Beijing: Zhongguo Jinrong Chubanshe, 1986.

Guowuyuan Tequ Bangongshi, Bangongting Mishuju, ed. *Yanhai chengshi kaifang he tequ gongzuo wenjian xuanbian* [A selection of public documents relating to the opening of the coastal cities and the special economic zones]. Beijing: Guowuyuan Tequ Bangongshi, Bangongting Mishuju, May 1986.

Gurley, John G. *China's Economy and the Maoist Strategy.* New York: Monthly Review Press, 1976.

Haggard, Stephan. *Pathways from the Periphery.* Ithaca, N.Y.: Cornell University Press, 1990.

Haggard, Stephen, and Tun-jen Cheng. "State and Foreign Capital in the East Asian NICs." In Deyo, ed., *Political Economy,* 84–135.

Haggard, Stephan, and Pang Chien-Kuo. "The Transition to Export-Led Growth in Taiwan." In *The Role of the State in Taiwan's Development,* ed. Yu-Hsia Chen, Joel D. Aberbach, David Dollar, and Kenneth L. Sokoloff, 47–89. Armonk, N.Y.: M. E. Sharpe, 1994.

Harding, Harry. *China's Second Revolution*. Washington, D.C.: Brookings, 1987.
———. "The Chinese State in Crisis." In MacFarquhar and Fairbank, eds., *Cambridge History*, 15: 107–217.
———. "Competing Models of the Chinese Policy Process: Toward a Sorting and Evaluation." In Chang King-yuh, ed., *Perspectives*, 61–84.
———. *Organizing China*. Stanford, Calif.: Stanford University Press, 1981.
Harwit, Eric. *China's Automobile Industry: Policies, Problems and Prospects*. Armonk, N.Y.: M. E. Sharpe, 1995.
Hawes, Gary. *The Philippine State and the Marcos Regime: The Politics of Export*. Ithaca, N.Y.: Cornell University Press, 1987.
He Xinhao. "Yijin yangchu shi woguo fazhan duiwai maoyi de yixiang zhanlüexing cuoshi" [Importing materials to develop exports is a strategic measure to develop China's foreign trade]. In Wu Jikun, *Duiwai maoyi*, 119–26.
Herschman, A. O. "The Political Economy of Import Substituting Industrialization in Latin America." *Quarterly Journal of Economics* 82, 1 (February 1968): 1–32.
Heymann, Hans, Jr. "Acquisition and Diffusion of Technology in China." In U.S. Congress, Joint Economic Committee, ed., *China: A Reassessment of the Economy*, 678–729. Washington D.C.: Government Printing Office, 1975.
Ho, Samuel P. S., and Ralph W. Huenemann. *China's Open Door Policy*. Vancouver: University of British Columbia Press, 1984.
Holdridge, John H. *Crossing the Divide*. Lanham, Md.: Rowman & Littlefield, 1997.
———. Former assistant secretary of state. Interview, 13 January 1997.
Hou, Chi-ming. *Foreign Investment and Economic Development in China, 1840–1937*. Cambridge: Harvard University Press, 1965.
Howell, Jude. *China Opens Its Doors*. Boulder, Colo.: Lynne Rienner, 1993.
Hsu, John. *China's Foreign Trade Reforms: Impact on Growth and Stability*. Cambridge: Cambridge University Press, 1989.
Hu Fuming. "Practice Is the Sole Criterion of Truth." *Lilun dongtai*, 60 (10 May 1978).
Hu, Weixing. "The Medium Nuclear Powers and Nuclear Stability." Ph.D. diss. University of Maryland, College Park, 1992.
Hua Guofeng. "Government Work Report." *Beijing Review*, 6 July 1979, 5–31.
———. "Report on the Work of the Government." *Peking Review*, 10 March 1978, 7–41.
Hughes, T. J., and D. E. T. Luard. *The Economic Development of Communist China, 1949–1960*. New York: Oxford University Press, 1959.
Huntington, Samuel P. "The Lonely Superpower." *Foreign Affairs* 78, 2 (March/April 1999): 35–49.
Imai, Hiroyuki. "China's Endogenous Investment Cycle." *Journal of Comparative Economics* 19 (October 1994): 188–216.
———. "Explaining China's Business Cycles." *Developing Economies* 24, 2 (June 1966): 154–85.
Inman, Robert P. "Markets, Governments and the 'New' Political Economy." In *Handbook of Public Economics*, ed. A. J. Auerbach and M. Feldstein, 2: 647–777. New York: Elsevier, 1987.
Jachtenfuchs, Markus. *International Policy-Making as a Learning Process?* Brookfield, Vt.: Ashgate, 1996.
Jacobson, Harold K., and Michel Oksenberg. *China's Participation in the IMF, the World Bank and GATT*. Ann Arbor: University of Michigan Press, 1990.

Jao, Y. C., and C. K. Leung, ed. *China's Special Economic Zones.* Hong Kong: Oxford University Press, 1986.

Jervis, Robert. *Perception and Misperception in International Politics.* Princeton N.J.: Princeton University Press, 1976.

Jiang Siyi, ed. *Zhongguo Renmin Jiefangjun dashidian* [The chronicle of major events of the Chinese People's Liberation Army]. Tianjin: Tianjin Renmin Chubanshe, 1992.

Jin Chongji. "Mao Zedong de duli zizhu sixiang" [Mao Zedong's thinking on self-reliance]. *Dang de wenxian* 37 (1994): 21–24.

Jinan Daxue Tequ, Gangao Jingji Yanjiusuo, ed. *Shijie jingjixing tequ yaolan* [A handbook on the world's special zones with economic features]. Guangzhou: N.p., 1984.

Johnson, Chalmers. "Political Institutions and Economic Performance: The Government-Business Relationship in Japan, South Korea, and Taiwan." In Deyo, ed., *Political Economy.*

———. "Preconception vs. Observation, or the Contributions of Rational Choice Theory and Area Studies to Contemporary Political Science." *PS: Political Science and Politics* 30, 2 (June 1997): 170–74.

Johnson, Chalmers, and Keehn, E. B. "A Disaster in the Making. Rational Choice and Asian Studies." *National Interest* 36 (Summer 1994): 14–22.

Johnston, Alastair Iain. "Learning versus Adaptation: Explaining Change in Chinese Arms Control Policy in the 1980s and 1990s." *China Journal* 35 (January 1996): 27–61.

Joseph, William A. *The Critique of Ultra-Leftism in China, 1958–1981.* Stanford, Calif.: Stanford University Press, 1984.

Joseph, William A.; Christine Wong; and David Zweig, ed. *New Perspectives on the Cultural Revolution.* Cambridge: Harvard University Press, 1991.

Ju, Zhongyi, "'New Economic Group' versus 'Petroleum Group.'" In *Policy Conflicts in Post-Mao China,* ed. John P. Burns and Stanley Rosen. Armonk N.Y.: M. E. Sharpe, 1986.

Katzenstein, Peter. "Introduction: Domestic and International Forces and Strategies of Foreign Economic Policy"; "Conclusion: Domestic Structures and Strategies of Foreign Economic Policy." In *Between Power and Plenty: Foreign Economic Policies of Advanced Industrial States,* ed. Peter Katzenstein, 3–22; 295–336. Madison: University of Wisconsin Press, 1978.

Kaufman, Burton. "Eisenhower's Foreign Economic Policy with Respect to East Asia." In Cohen and Iriye, eds., *Great Powers,* 104–20.

Keohane, Robert. *After Hegemony: Cooperation and Discord in the World Political Economy.* Princeton N.J.: Princeton University Press, 1984.

———. ed. *Neorealism and Its Critics.* New York: Columbia University Press, 1986.

Keohane, Robert, and J. S. Nye. *Power and Interdependence.* Boston: Little, Brown, 1977.

Kim, Samuel S. "China as a Great Power." *Current History* 96 (September 1997): 246–51.

Kindleberger, C. P. *World in Depression.* Berkeley: University of California Press, 1973.

Kleinberg, Robert. *China's "Opening" to the Outside World: The Experiment with Foreign Capitalism.* Boulder, Colo.: Westview Press, 1990.

Klochko, Mikhail A. *Soviet Scientist in Red China.* New York: Praeger, 1964.

Kokubun, Ryosei. "The Politics of Foreign Economic Policy-Making in China: The Case of Plant Cancellations with Japan." *China Quarterly* 105 (March 1986): 19–44.

Kolb, David. *Experiential Learning: Experience as the Source of Learning and Development.* Englewood Cliffs, N. J.: Prentice-Hall, 1984.

————. "Learning Styles and Disciplinary Differences." In *The Modern American College,* ed. A. W. Chickering and Associates, 232–55. San Francisco: Jossey-Bass, 1981.

Krasner, Stephen D. "State Power and the Structure of Foreign Trade." *World Politics* 28 (1976): 317–47.

————. *Structural Conflict: The Third World against Global Liberalism.* Berkeley: University of California Press, 1985.

Krueger, Anne O. *Foreign Trade Regimes and Economic Development.* Vol. 10: *Liberalization Attempts and Consequences.* Cambridge: Ballinger, 1978.

————. *Trade Policy and Developing Nations.* Washington, D.C.: Brookings, 1995.

————. "Trade Policy and Economic Development: How We Learn." *American Economic Review* 87, 1 (March 1997): 1–22.

————. "Why Trade Liberalization Is Good for Growth." *Economic Journal,* September 1998, 1513–22.

Khrushchev, Nikita. *Khrushchev Remembers.* Boston: Little, Brown, 1970.

Kurth, James. "Political Consequences of the Product Cycle." *International Organization* 33 (Winter 1979): 1–34.

Lardy, Nicolas R. *Agriculture in China's Modern Economic Development.* Cambridge: Cambridge University Press, 1983.

————. "The Chinese Economy under Stress, 1958–1965." In MacFarquhar and Fairbank, eds., *Cambridge History,* 14:360–97.

————. "Economic Developments in the PRC." In *Two Societies in Opposition,* ed. Raymon Myers, 180–97. Stanford, Calif.: Hoover Institution Press, 1991.

————. "Economic Recovery and the First Five-Year Plan." In MacFarquhar and Fairbank, eds., *Cambridge History,* 14:144–84.

————. *Foreign Trade and Economic Reform in China, 1978–1990.* Cambridge: Cambridge University Press, 1992.

Lardy, Nicholas R., ed. *Chinese Economic Planning.* White Plains, N.Y.: M. E. Sharpe, 1977.

Lardy, Nicholas R., and Kenneth Lieberthal. *Chen Yun's Strategy for China's Development: A Non-Maoist Alternative.* Armonk, N.Y.: M. E. Sharpe, 1983.

Lee, Chae-jin. *Japan Faces China.* Baltimore, Md.: Johns Hopkins University Press, 1976.

————. *Zhou Enlai: The Early years.* Stanford, Calif.: Stanford University Press, 1994.

Lee, Oliver M. "U.S. Trade Policy toward China: From Economic Warfare to Summit Diplomacy." In Stahnke, ed., *China's Trade,* 33–87.

Lei Qiang et al. "Shenzhen jingji tequ shangye fazhan tantao" [A discussion on industrial development within the Shenzhen SEZ]. In *Jingjixue luncong* [A collection of views on economics studies], ed. Zhongshan Daxue Jingjixi. Guangzhou: N.p., 1983.

Levine, Marilyn A. *The Found Generation: Chinese Communists in Europe during the Twenties.* Seattle: University of Washington Press, 1993.

Levine, Steven I. *Anvil of Victory.* New York: Columbia University Press, 1987.

Levy, Jack S. "Learning and Foreign Policy: Sweeping a Conceptual Minefield." *International Organization* 48, 2 (Spring 1994): 279–312.

Lewis, John Wilson, ed. *Party Leadership and Revolutionary Power in China.* New York: Cambridge University Press, 1970.

Lewis, John Wilson, and Xue Litai. *China Builds the Bomb.* Stanford, Calif.: Stanford University Press, 1988.

————. *China's Strategic Seapower.* Stanford, Calif.: Stanford University Press, 1994.

Li Fuchun. *Li Fuchun xuanji* [The collected works of Li Fuchun]. Beijing: Zhongguo Jihua Chubanshe, 1992.

———. "March On! Hold High the Red Flag of the General Line!" *Hongqi,* 16 August 1960.

———. "Woguo guomin jingji yijing kaishi quanmian haozhuan" [China's national economy is already beginning to make a comprehensive turn for the better]. *Dang de wenxian* 64 (1998): 7–12.

Li Fuchun, Bo Yibo, and Luo Ruiqing. "Guanyu guojia jingji jianshe ruhe fangbei diren turan xiji wenti de baogao" [Report on how national economic construction can be prepared against sudden surprise attacks by the enemy]. *Dang de wenxian* 45 (1995): 33–34.

Li Hongcai. "Zhu De dui woguo shehui zhuyi jingji jianshe de yixie sikao" [Some reflections on Zhu De's views of China's socialist economic construction]. *Dang de wenxian* 34 (1993): 27–32.

Li Jie. "Dui Mao Zedong fangzhi heping yanbian sixiang de huigu he sikao" [Reflections and thoughts on Mao Zedong's thoughts on preventing peaceful evolution]. *Dang de wenxian* 21 (1991): 39–45.

Li, Linda Chelan. *Centre and Provinces: China 1978–1993.* Oxford: Clarendon Press, 1998.

Li Ming. "Huiyi Xiaoping tongzhi dui Baogang ji zhijin gongye de guanhuai" [Remembering the great attention paid—by Comrade Xiaoping to the Baoshan steel complex and the metallurgical industry]. *Dang de wenxian* 57 (1997): 75–77.

Li Ruizhen and Yao Yuanyang. "Chen Yun zaoqi geming huodong shulüe" [A brief account of Chen Yun's early revolutionary activities]. In Zhu Jiamu, *Chen Yun,* 2:977–87.

Li Xiannian. *Li Xiannian lun caizheng jinrong maoyi, 1950–1991* [Li Xiannian's discussions on finance and trade, 1950–1991]. Vols. 1 and 2. Beijing: Zhongguo Caizheng Jingji Chubanshe, 1992.

Li Xiaoxian, ed. *Duiwai maoyi yuanli yu shiwu jiaocheng.* [Text on the principles and practices of foreign trade]. Shanghai: Shanghai Renmin Chubanshe, 1986.

Li Yongchun, Shi Yuanqin, and Guo Xiuzhi. *Shiyijie sanzhong quanhui yilai zhengzhi tizhi gaige dashiji* [Chronicle of political structural reforms since the Eleventh Plenum]. Beijing: Chunqiu Chubanshe, 1987.

Li, Zhisui, with the editorial assistance of Anne F. Thurston. *The Private Life of Chairman Mao: The Memoirs of Mao's Personal Physician.* New York: Random House 1994.

Li Zhongjie, Xu Yaoxin, and Wu Li. *Shehui zhuyi gaigeshi* [A history of socialist reforms]. Beijing: Chunqiu Chubanshe, 1988.

Liang Wensen. *Zhongguo jingji tequ de jinxi he weilai* [The current and future prospects of the Chinese SEZ economies]. Hong Kong: Xianggang Jingji Daobaoshe, Shenzhen Daxue Tequ Jingji Yanjiusuo, 1988.

Liao Gailong, ed. *Zhongguo Gongchandang lishi dacidian, shehui zhuyi shiqi* [The historical encyclopedia of China's Communist Party, socialist period]. Beijing: Zhonggong Zhongyang Dangxiao Chubanshe, 1991.

Lieberthal, Kenneth. *Central Documents and Politburo Politics in China.* Ann Arbor: Center for Chinese Studies, University of Michigan, 1978.

———. *Governing China.* New York: Norton, 1995.

———. "The Great Leap Forward and the Split in the Yan'an Leadership." In MacFarquhar and Fairbank, *Cambridge History,* 14:293–359.

Lieberthal, Kenneth, and Bruce Dickson. *A Research Guide to Central Party and*

Government Meetings in China, 1949–1986. Rev. expanded ed. Armonk, N.Y.: M. E. Sharpe, 1989.

Lieberthal, Kenneth; Joyce Kallgren; Roderick MacFarquhar; and Frederic Wakeman, eds. *Perspectives on Modern China.* Armonk, N.Y.: M. E. Sharpe, 1991.

Lieberthal, Kenneth, and Michel Oksenberg. *Policy Making in China: Leaders, Structures and Processes.* Princeton, N.J.: Princeton University Press, 1988.

Lin Jinzhi, ed. *Huaqiao huaren yu Zhongguo geming he jianshe* [Overseas Chinese involvement in the revolution and construction of China]. Fuzhou: Fujian Renmin Chubanshe, 1993.

Lin Yunhui, Fan Shouxin, and Zhang Gong. *1949–1989 niande Zhongguo,* vol. 1: *Kaige xingjin de shiqi* [China 1949–1989: Period of triumphant songs of advancement]. Zhengzhou: Henan Renmin Chubanshe, 1989.

Little, Daniel. "Rational Choice Models and Asian Studies." *Journal of Asian Studies* 50 (February 1991): 35–52.

Little, Ian; Tibor Scitovsky; and Maurice Scott. *Industry and Trade in Some Developing Countries.* London: Oxford University Press for the OECD, 1970.

Liu Guoguang, ed. *Zhongguo jingji fazhan zhanlüe wenti yanjiu* [Research on China's economic development strategy]. Shanghai: Shanghai Renmin Chubanshe, 1984.

Liu Hua. "Jianguo chuqi qiaowu gongzuo shuping" [A commentary on overseas Chinese work during the early days of the PRC]. *Dangshi yanjiu ziliao* 193 (1993): 17–24.

Liu Shaoqi. *Liu Shaoqi lun xin Zhongguo jingji jianshe* [Liu Shaoqi's speeches on economic construction in New China]. Ed. Zhonggong Zhongyang Wenxian Yanjiushi. Beijing: Zhongyang Wenxian Chubanshe, 1993.

Liu Shufa, ed. *Chen Yi nianpu* [A chronicle of Chen Yi's Life]. Beijing: Renmin Chubanshe, 1995.

Liu Xiangdong. "Jicheng Mao Zedong duiwai jingji jiaoliu sixiang cujin woguo duiwai kaifang he duiwai jingji maoyi shiye de fazhan" [Inheriting Mao Zedong's ideas on foreign economic exchange to promote the development of China's opening and its foreign economic trade]. In Pei Jianzhang, ed., *Mao Zedong waijiao sixiang yanjiu* [Research on Mao Zedong's thoughts on foreign affairs]. Beijing: Shijie Zhishi Chubanshe, 1994.

———, ed. *Liyong waizi zhishi shouce* [Handbook of investment knowledge]. Beijing: Shijie Zhishi Chubanshe, 1986.

Long Chucai, ed. *Liyong waizi gailun* [An introduction to the use of foreign capital]. Beijing: Zhongguo Duiwai Jingji Maoyi Chubanshe, 1985.

Lowenthal, Richard. "Development vs. Utopia in Communist Policy." In *Change in Communist Systems,* ed. Chalmers Johnson, 33–116. Stanford, Calif.: Stanford University Press, 1970.

———. "The Postrevolutionary Phase in China and the Soviet Union." In Chang King-yuh, ed., *Perspectives,* 1–15.

Lupton, Colina MacDougall. "Hong Kong's Role in Sino-Western Trade." In Stahnke, ed., *China's Trade,* 175–208.

MacDougall, Colina. "Policy Changes in China's Foreign Trade since the Death of Mao, 1976–1980." In *China's New Development Strategy,* ed. Jack Gray and Gordon White. New York: Academic Press, 1982.

MacFarquhar, Roderick. *The Origins of the Cultural Revolution.* Vol. 1: *Contradictions among the People.* New York: Columbia University Press, 1974.

————. *The Origins of the Cultural Revolution.* Vol. 2: *The Great Leap Forward, 1958–1960.* New York: Columbia University Press, 1983.

————. *The Origins of the Cultural Revolution.* Vol. 3: *The Coming of the Cataclysm, 1961–1966.* New York: Columbia University Press, 1997.

————. "The Succession to Mao and the End of Maoism." In MacFarquhar and Fairbank, eds., *Cambridge History,* 15:305–401.

MacFarquhar, Roderick, and John K. Fairbank, eds. *The Cambridge History of China.* Vols. 14 and 15. Cambridge: Cambridge University Press, 1987, 1991.

Mah, Feng-hwa. *The Foreign Trade of Mainland China.* Chicago: Aldine, 1971.

Mamo, David, and Upson Laurie. *Dizionario Storico-Biografico Della Cina Moderna* [Historical biographical dictionary of modern China]. Florence: Vallecchi, 1977.

Manchester, William. *The Glory and the Dream: A Narrative History of America.* Boston: Little, Brown, 1973.

Mansbridge, Jane J. "The Rise and Fall of Self-Interest in the Explanation of Political Life." In Mansbridge, ed., *Beyond Self-Interest,* 3–22.

————, ed. *Beyond Self-Interest.* Chicago: University of Chicago Press, 1990.

Mao Zedong. "Ba woguo jianshe chengwei shehui zhuyi de xiandaihua de qiangguo" [To build China into a strong, socialist modernized country]. *Dang de wenxian* 49 (1996): 34.

————. *Chairman Mao Talks to the People: Talks and Letters 1956–1971.* Ed. Stuart Schram. New York: Pantheon Books, 1974.

————. *Jianguo yilai Mao Zedong wengao* [The post-1949 manuscripts of Mao Zedong]. Ed. Zhonggong Zhongyang Wenxian Yanjiushi. Vols. 1–. Beijing: Zhongyang Wenxian Chubanshe, 1990–.

————. Letter to Jiang Qing, 8 July 1966. *Issues and Studies* 9, 4 (January 1973): 94.

————. *Mao Zedong sixiang wansui* [Long live Mao Zedong Thought]. N.p., 1969.

————. *Mao Zedong waijiao wenxuan* [A selection of Mao Zedong's pronouncements on foreign policy]. Ed. Zhonghua Renmin Gongheguo Waijiaobu and Zhonggong Zhongyang Wenxian Yanjiushi. Beijing: Zhongyang Wenxian Chubanshe and Shijie Zhishi Chubanshe, 1994.

————. *Mao Zedong wenji* [The collected works of Mao Zedong]. Vols. 6–8. Ed. Zhonggong Zhongyang Wenxian Yanjiushi. Beijing: Renmin Chubanshe, 1999.

————. *Mao Zedong xuanji* [The selected works of Mao Zedong]. Vol. 5. Beijing: Renmin Chubanshe, 1977.

————. *Miscellany of Mao Tse-tung Thought (1949–1968).* 2 vols. Arlington, Va.: Joint Publications Research Service, 61 2690-1, 61269-2, 1974.

————. *The Secret Speeches of Chairman Mao.* Ed. Roderick MacFarquhar, Timothy Cheek, and Eugene Wu. Cambridge: Harvard University Press, 1989.

————. *The Selected Works of Mao Zedong.* 4 vols. Beijing: Foreign Languages Press, 1967, 1969, 1975.

————. *Selected Writings of Mao Tse-tung.* Vol. 4. Beijing: Foreign Languages Press, 1961.

————. *The Writings of Mao Zedong, 1949–1976.* Vols. 1–. Ed. Michael Y. M. Kau and John K. Leung. Armonk, N.Y.: M. E. Sharpe, 1986, 1992.

————. "Yao xia juexin gao jianrui jishu" [We must be determined to build cutting-edge technology]. *Dang de wenxian* 49 (1996): 10.

————. "Yige jiaoxun" [A lesson]. *Dang de wenxian* 4 (1990): 17.

————. "Zai di'erci Zhengzhou huiyishang de jianghua" [Speech at the second Zhengzhou meeting]. *Dang de wenxian* 4 (1990): 17–22.

Mastanduno, Michael. "The Management of Alliance Export Control Policy: American Leadership and the Politics of COCOM." In *Controlling East-West Trade and Techonology Transfer,* ed. Gary K. Bertsch, 241–79. Durham, N.C.: Duke University Press, 1988.

Mattick, Paul. *Economic Crisis and Crisis Theory.* White Plains, N.Y.: M. E. Sharpe, 1981.

Mayer, Peter. *Sino-Soviet Relations since the Death of Stalin.* Kowloon: Union Research Institute, 1962.

McKeown, Timothy. "Tariffs and Hegemonic Stability." *International Organization* 32, 4 (Autumn 1978): 73–91.

Meier, Gerald M. "Policy Lessons and Policy Formation." In *Politics and Policy Making in Developing Countries,* ed. Gerald M. Meier, 3–12. San Francisco: ICS Press, 1991.

Meisner, Maurice. *Mao's China.* New York: Free Press, 1977.

Meng Xianzhang, ed. *Zhongsu maoyishi ziliao* [Materials on Sino-Soviet trade history]. Beijing: Zhongguo Duiwai Jingji Maoyi Chubanshe, 1991.

Meskill, John, ed. *The Pattern of Chinese History: Cycles, Development, or Stagnation?* Boston: D. C. Heath, 1965.

Modelski, G. "The Long Cycle of Global Politics and the Nation-State." *Comparative Studies in Society and History* 20, 2 (April 1978): 214–35.

Moore, Thomas G. "China as a Latecomer: Toward a Global Logic of the Open Policy." *Journal of Contemporary China* 5, 12 (July 1996): 187–208.

Myers, Raymon, ed. *Two Societies in Opposition.* Stanford, Calif.: Hoover Institution Press, 1991.

Myint, Hla. "The 'Classical Theory' of International Trade and the Underdeveloped Countries." *Economic Journal* 68 (1959): 317–37.

———. *Exports and Economic Development of Less Developed Countries.* London: Macmillan, 1979.

———. "Infant Industry Argument for Assistance to Industries in the Setting of Dynamic Trade Theory." In *International Trade Theory in a Developing World,* ed. R. F. Harrod and D. C. Hague, 173–93. New York: St. Martin's Press, 1963.

Myrdal, Gunnar. *An International Economy.* New York: Harper, 1956.

Nakajima, Mineo. "Foreign Relations: From the Korean War to the Bandung Conference." In MacFarquhar and Fairbank, eds., *Cambridge History,* 14:259–89.

Nathan, Andrew. "A Factionalism Model for CCP Politics." *China Quarterly* 53 (January/March 1973): 34–66.

———. "Policy Oscillations in the People's Republic of China: A Critique." *China Quarterly* 68 (December 1976): 720–33.

———. Preface. In Li Zhisui, *Private Life.*

National Bureau on Statistics. *China Foreign Economic Statistical Yearbook, 1998.* Beijing: China Statistics Press, 1999.

———. *China Statistical Yearbook.* Beijing: China Statistical Publishing House, 1995.

Naughton, Barry. *Growing Out of the Plan: Chinese Economic Reform, 1978–1993.* New York: Cambridge University Press, 1995.

———. "Industrial Policy during the Cultural Revolution: Military Preparation, Decentralization and Leaps Forward." In Joseph, Wong, and Zweig, eds., *New Perspective,* 153–81.

———. "The Pattern and Legacy of Economic Growth in the Mao Era." In Lieberthal et al., eds., *Perspectives on Modern China,* 226–54.

———. "The Third Front." *China Quarterly* 115 (September 1988): 351–86.

Nelson, Joan M. *Economic Crisis and Policy Choice*. Princeton, N.J.: Princeton University Press, 1990.

Nie Rongzhen. "Guanyu lizu guonei fazhan keji deng wenti xiang zhonggong bing Mao Zedong de baogao" [A report to the central committee and Mao Zedong on developing a domestically based science and technology]. *Dang de wenxian* 49 (1996): 8–9.

Nye, Joseph. "Nuclear Learning and U.S.-Soviet Security Regimes." *International Organization* 41, 3 (Summer 1987): 371–402.

Oborne, Michael. *China's Special Economic Zones*. Paris: OECD, 1986.

Oksenberg, Michel. "Policy Formulation in Communist China: The Case of the Mass Irrigation Campaign, 1957–1958." Ph.D. diss., Columbia University, 1969.

———. "Politics Takes Command: An Essay on the Study of Post-1949 China." In MacFarquhar and Fairbank, eds., *Cambridge History*, 14:543–90.

Oksenberg, Michel, and Steven Goldstein. "The Chinese Political Spectrum." *Issues of Communism* 23, 2 (March–April 1974): 1–13.

Olson, Mancur. *The Rise and Decline of Nations*. New Haven, Conn.: Yale University Press, 1982.

Oye, Kenneth A. "Explaining Cooperation under Anarchy: Hypotheses and Strategies." *World Politics* 38, 1 (October 1985): 1–24.

Pang Xianzhi. "Chongwen Mao Zedong guanyu fangzhi heping yanbian de jiaodao," [Revisiting Mao Zedong's Teachings on Preventing Peaceful Evolution]. *Dang de wenxian* 15 (1990): 12–19.

Pangestu, Mari. "Indonesia: From Dutch Disease to Manufactured Exports." In Yang Shu-Chin, ed., *Manufactured Exports*, 217–30.

Pearson, Margaret. *Joint Ventures in the People's Republic of China: The Control of Foreign Direct Investment under Socialism*. Princeton, N.J.: Princeton University Press, 1991.

Pei Jianzhang, ed. *Mao Zedong waijiao sixiang yanjiu* [Research on Mao Zedong's thoughts on foreign affairs]. Beijing: Shijie Zhishi Chubanshe, 1994.

Peng Jianxin. "Zhou Enlai yu Guangjiaohui" [Zhou Enlai and the Guangzhou Trade Fair]. *Dangshi yanjiu ziliao* 232 (1996): 28–31.

Pepper, Suzanne. *Radicalism and Education Reform in Twentieth Century China*. New York: Cambridge University Press, 1996.

Perkins, Dwight H. "The Central Features of China's Economic Development." In Dernberger, ed., *China's Development*, 120–50.

———. "China's Economic Policy and Performance." In MacFarquhar and Fairbank, eds., *Cambridge History*, 15:475–539.

———. "Reforming China's Economic System." *Journal of Economic Literature* 26 (June 1988): 601–45.

Petrick, Richard L. "Policy Cycles and Policy Learning in the People's Republic of China." *Comparative Political Studies* 14, 1 (April 1981): 101–22.

Polsby, Nelson W. *Political Innovation in America: The Politics of Policy Initiation*. New Haven, Conn.: Yale University Press, 1984.

Prebisch, Raul. *The Economic Development of Latin America and Its Principal Problems*. New York: United Nations Economic Commission for Latin America, 1950.

Price, Robert L. "International Trade of Communist China, 1950–65." In U.S. Congress,

Joint Economic Committee, *An Economic Profile of Mainland China,* 90th Cong., 1st sess., 1967; 579–608.

Prybyla, Jan S. "On the PRC and the WTO: Threat or Promise of Good Things to Come?" *Issues and Studies* 36, 1 (January/February 2000): 143–60.

———. *Reform in China and Other Socialist Economies.* Washington, D.C.: American Enterprise Institute, 1990.

Puchala, Donald J. "The History of the Future of International Relations." *Ethics and International Affairs,* 8 (1994): 177–202.

Pye, Lucian. *China: An Introduction.* New York: HarperCollins, 1991.

———. *The Dynamics of Chinese Politics.* Cambridge, Mass.: Oelgeschlager, Gunn and Hain, 1981.

———. *The Dynamics of Factions and Consensus in Chinese Politics: A Model and Some Propositions.* R-2566-AF. Santa Monica, Calif.: Rand, 1980.

Qing, Simei. "The Eisenhower Administration and Changes in Western Embargo Policy against China, 1954–1958." In Cohen and Iriye, eds., *Great Powers,* 121–42.

Rawski, Thomas G. "Choice of Technology and Technological Innovation in China's Economic Development." In Dernberger, ed., *China's Development,* 191–228.

Ray, Dennis M. "Chinese Perceptions of Social Imperialism and Economic Dependency: The Impact of Soviet Aid." In *China's Changing Role in the World Economy,* ed. Bryant G. Garth, 38–82. New York: Praeger, 1975.

Reardon, Lawrence C. "Bird in the Cage: Chinese Export Promotion Policies and the Development of the Special Economic Zones, 1960–1982." Ph.D. diss., Columbia University, 1991.

———. "Learning How to Open the Door: A Reassessment of China's Opening Strategy." *China Quarterly* 155 (September 1998): 479–511.

———. "The Rise and Decline of China's Export Processing Zones." *Journal of Contemporary China* 5, 13 (November 1996): 281–303.

———. trans. and ed. "China's Coastal Development Strategy, 1979–1984, I." *China Law and Government* 27 (May/June, 1994): 1–95.

———. "China's Coastal Development Strategy, 1979–1984, II." *China Law and Government* 27 (July/August 1994):1–96.

Reardon-Anderson, James. *Yenan and the Great Powers.* New York: Columbia University Press, 1980.

Renmin Ribaoshe Gongshangbu, ed. *Zhongguo duiwai kaifang gongzuo shiwu shouce* [Practical handbook for China's opening to the outside]. Beijing: Gongshang Chubanshe, 1987.

Reynolds, Bruce. "China in the International Economy." In *China's Foreign Relations in the 1980s,* ed. Harry Harding, 71–106. New Haven, Conn.: Yale University Press, 1984.

Rhee, Yung Whee. "Managing Entry into International Markets: Lessons from the East Asian Experience." In Yang Shee-Chin, ed., *Manufactured Exports,* 53–83.

Riskin, Carl. *China's Political Economy.* Oxford: Oxford University Press, 1987.

———. "Neither Plan nor Market: Mao's Political Economy." In, Joseph, Wong, and Zweig, eds., *New Perspectives on the Cultural Revolution,* 133–52.

Roll, Eric. *A History of Economic Thought.* London: Faber, 1973.

Rozman, Gilbert. "China's Quest for Great Power Identity." *Orbis* 43, 3 (Summer 1999): 383–402.

Ruan Ming. *Deng Xiaoping.* Trans. Nancy Liu, Peter Rand, and Lawrence R. Sullivan. Boulder, Colo.: Westview Press, 1994.

Rueschemeyer, Dietrich, and Peter Evans. "The State and Economic Transformation: Toward an Analysis of the Conditions Underlying Effective Intervention." In Evans, Rueschemeyer, and Skocpol, eds., *Bringing the State Back In,* 44–77.

Ruggie, John G. "Continuity and Transformation in World Policy." *World Politics* 35, 2 (1983): 261–75.

Schoenhals, Michael, ed. *China's Cultural Revolution, 1966–1969.* Armonk, N.Y.: M. E. Sharpe, 1996.

Schram, Stuart R. "Mao Tse-tung's Thought from 1949 to 1976." In MacFarquhar and Fairbank, eds., Cambridge History, 15:1–104.

Schurmann-Franz. *Ideology and Organization in Communist China.* 2d ed. Berkeley: University of California Press, 1968.

Scruton, Roger. *A Dictionary of Political Thought.* London: Macmillan, 1982.

Segal, Gerald. "Does China Matter?" *Foreign Affairs* 78, 5 (September/October 1999): 24–36.

Sen, Amartya K. "Rational Fools: A Critique of the Behavioral Foundations of Economic Theory." In Mansbridge, ed., *Beyond Self Interest,* 25–43.

SEZ official. Interview. Zhuhai Special Economic Zone, September 1987.

Shang Pingshun and Yan Caijun, eds. *Zhongguo waihui tizhi gaige lilun yu shijian* [The theory and practice of China's foreign exchange system]. Beijing: Zhongguo Jingji Chubanshe, 1995.

Shanghai Shehui Kexueyuan. *Shanghai jingji (1949–1982)* [The Shanghai economy (1949–1982)]. Shanghai: Shanghai Shehui Kexueyuan Chubanshe, 1984.

Shanghai Shehui Kexueyuan Bumen Jingjisuo. *Jingji dacidian (gongye jingjijuan)* [Economic dictionary (industrial economy volume)]. Shanghai: Shanghai Cidian Chubanshe, 1983.

Shaw, Yu-ming, ed. *Mainland China: Politics, Economics and Reform.* Boulder, Colo.: Westview Press, 1986.

Sheahan, John B. *Alternative International Economic Strategies and Their Relevance for China.* Staff Working Papers, no. 759. Washington, D.C.: World Bank, 1986.

Shenzhen Jingji Tequ Nianjian Bianji Weiyuanhui. *Shenzhen jingji tequ nianjian, 1985* [Shenzhen Special Economic Zone yearbook, 1985]. Hong Kong: Xianggang Jingji Daobao Chubanshe, n.d.

Shenzhenshi Renmin Zhengfu Bangongting, ed. *Shenzhen jingji tequ jiben qingkuang jieshao* [An introduction to the basic conditions of the Shenzhen SEZ]. Shenzhen: N. p., 1983.

Shi Shi. "'Woniu shijian' shimo" [The beginning and the end of the "snail incident"]. *Dang de wenxian* 1 (1991): 52–53.

Shi Zhe. "'Zhongsu youhao tongmeng huzhu tiaoyue' qianding shimo" [The entire story of signing the "Sino-Soviet Treaty of Friendship, Alliance, and Mutual Assistance"]. *Dang de wenxian* 25 (1992): 52–57.

Shirk, Susan L. *How China Opened Its Door.* Washington, D.C.: Brookings, 1994.

———. "The Political Price of Reform Cycles: Elite Politics in Chinese-Style Economic Reforms." As cited in Baum, *Mao,* 6–7.

Shive, Chi. "The Next Stage of Industrialization in Taiwan and South Korea." In Gereffi and Wyman, eds., *Manufacturing Miracles,* 267–91.

Singer, David J. "The Level-of-Analysis Problem in International Relations." The *International System: Theoretical Essays,* ed. David J. Singer, Klaus Knorr, and Sidney Verba, Princeton, N.J: Princeton University Press, 1961. 77–92.

Singer, Hans W. "The Distribution of Gains between Investing and Borrowing Countries." *American Economic Review* 40, (May 1950): 473–85.

Singh, Ajit, and Hamid Tabatabai. *Economic Crisis and Third World Agriculture.* Cambridge: Cambridge University Press, 1993.

Sit, Victor F. S., ed. *Resources and Development of the Pearl River Delta.* Hong Kong: Wide Angle Press, 1988.

Skinner, G. William, and Edwin A. Winckler. "Compliance Succession in Rural Communist China: A Cyclical Theory." In *A Sociological Reader on Complex Organizations,* ed. Amitai Etzioni, 410–38. New York: Holt, Rinehart and Winston, 1969.

Sklair, Leslie. "Shenzhen: A Chinese 'Development Zone.'" *Development and Change* 16 (1985): 571–602.

Skocpol, Theda. "Bringing the State Back In: Strategies of Analysis in Current Research." In Evans, Rueschemeyer, and Skocpol, eds., *Bringing the State Back In,* 3–37.

Skowronek, Steven. *Building a New American State: The Expansion of National Administrative Capacities, 1870–1920.* Cambridge: Cambridge University Press, 1982.

Sladkovskii, M. I. *Istoriia Torgovo-ekonomickeskikh Otnoshenii SSSR s Kitai (1917–1974)* [History of Sino-Soviet economic relations (1917–1974)]. Moscow: N. p., 1977.

Solinger, Dorothy J. *Chinese Business under Socialism.* Berkeley: University of California Press, 1984.

———. "Commerce: The Petty Private Sector and the Three Lines in the Early 1980s." In *Three Visions of Chinese Socialism,* ed. Dorothy J. Solinger, 73–111. Boulder, Colo: Westview, 1984.

———. *From Lathes to Looms: China's Industrial Policy in Comparative Perspective, 1979–1982.* Stanford, Calif.: Stanford University Press, 1991.

Solomon, Richard. *Mao's Revolution and the Chinese Political Culture.* Berkeley: University of California Press, 1971.

Spence, Jonathan D. *The Search for Modern China.* New York: Norton, 1989.

Spero, Joan Edelman. *The Politics of International Economic Relations.* London: George Allen & Unwin, 1981.

Stahnke, Arthur A. "The Political Context of Sino-West German Trade." In Stahnke, ed., *China's Trade,* 135–73.

———, ed. *China's Trade with the West.* New York: Praeger, 1972.

Stepanek, James B. "China's Special Economic Zones." *China Business Review* 9, 2 (March/April 1982):38–9.

Stevenson, Adlai E. "Stevenson Notes Red China's Rise." *New York Times,* 2 October 1958. In Mayer, *Sino-Soviet Relations.*

Stoltenberg, Clyde D. "China's Special Economic Zones: Their Development and Prospects." *Asian Survey* 24 (June 1984): 637–54.

Sun Dongsheng. "Woguo jingji jianshe zhanlüe buju de da zhuanbian" [The major transformation in the strategic layout of China's economic construction]. *Dang de wenxian* 45 (1995): 42–48.

Sun Ru, ed. *Qianjinzhong de Zhongguo jingji tequ* [The Chinese SEZs on the move]. Beijing: Zhongguo Caizheng Jingji Chubanshe, 1983.

Sun Weiben, ed. *Zhongguo Gongchandang dangwu gongzuo dacidian* [Encyclopedia of Chinese Communist Party affairs]. Beijing: Zhongguo Zhanwang Chubanshe, 1989.

Sun Yeli. "Wenge houqi Chen Yun guanyu dui ziben zhuyi guojia maoyi wenti de jidian sikao" [Some of Chen Yun's reflections during the latter period of the Cultural Revolution on the problem of trade with capitalist countries]. In Zhu Jiamu, *Chen Yun,* 1080–91.

———. "Women zuo gongzuo buyao bei neixie laodongxi shufuzhu" [We cannot be fettered by those old things when doing our work]. *Dang de wenxian* 45 (1995): 29–32.

Sutton, Anthony. *Western Technology and Soviet Economic Development, 1917 to 1930.* Stanford, Calif.: Hoover Institution on War, Revolution and Peace, 1968.

Szczepanik, Edward. *The Economic Growth of Hong Kong.* New York: Oxford University Press, 1958; reprint ed., Westport, Conn.: Greenwood Press, 1986.

Tan Qingfeng. "Jianli chukou shangpin shengchan tixi chutan" [An initial investigation in establishing an export commodity production structure]. *Guoji maoyi* 4 (1986): 4–35.

Tan Qingfeng Yao Xuecong, and Li Shusen, eds. *Waimao fuchi shengchan shijian* [The practice of supporting foreign trade production]. Beijing: Zhongguo Duiwai Jingji Maoyi Chubanshe, 1984.

Tang Huozhao. *Shenzhen jingjimian mianguan* [Views on the Shenzhen economic situation]. Shenzhen: Haitian Chubanshe, 1987.

Teiwes, Frederick C. *China's Road to Disaster.* With Warren Sun. Armonk, N.Y.: M. E. Sharpe, 1999.

———. "Establishment and Consolidation of the New Regime." In MacFarquhar and Fairbank, eds., *Cambridge History,* 14:51–143.

———. *Leadership, Legitimacy, and Conflict in China.* Armonk, N.Y: M. E. Sharpe, 1994.

———. *Politics and Purges in China.* 2d ed. Armonk, N.Y.: M. E. Sharpe, 1993.

Theroux, Eugene A. "Legal and Practical Problems in the China Trade." In U.S. Congress, Joint Economic Committee, ed., *China: A Reassessment of the Economy,* 535–99. Washington, D.C.: Government Printing Office, 1975.

Thompson, Willie. *The Good Old Cause: British Communism, 1920–1991.* London: Pluto Press, 1992.

Toffler, Alvin. *The Third Wave.* New York: Morrow, 1980.

Tong Xiaopeng. *Fengyu sishinian* [The forty-year storm]. Beijing: Zhongyang Wenxian Chubanshe, 1996.

Tsang, Steve. *Hong Kong: Appointment with China.* New York: I. B. Tauris, 1997.

Tsou Tang. *The Cultural Revolution and Post-Mao Reforms.* Chicago: University of Chicago Press, 1986.

Tucker, Nancy Bernkopf. "A House Divided: The United States, the Department of State and China." In Cohen and Iriye, eds., *Great Powers,* 35–62.

Tun, Yung. "Controversies over the CCPCC's Current Political and Economic Lines." *Issues and Studies* 15 (November 1979):15–32.

U.S. Congress. Joint Economic Committee, ed. *China: A Reassessment of the Economy.* Washington, D.C.: Government Printing Office, 1975.

———. Joint Economic Committee, ed. *The Chinese Economy Post-Mao.* Washington, D.C.: Government Printing Office, 1978.

———. Department of State. *Foreign Relations of the United States, 1955–1957.* Vol 3. Washington, D.C.: Government Printing Office, 1986.

———. Bureau of Intelligence and Research. *Chinese Communist World Outlook.* Washington, D.C.: Government Printing Office, 1962.

Union Research Institute, ed. *CCP Documents of the Great Proletarian Cultural Revolution, 1966–1967.* Kowloon: Union Research Institute, 1968.

van Eekelen, W. F. *Indian Foreign Policy and the Border Dispute with China.* The Hague: Martinus Nijhoff, 1967.

Van Ness, Peter. "Three Lines in Chinese Foreign Relations, 1950–1983." In *Three Visions of Chinese Socialism,* Ed. Dorothy J. Solinger, 113–42. Boulder, Colo.: Westview, 1984.

Van Ness, Peter, and Satish Raichur. "Dilemmas of Socialist Development: An Analysis of Strategic Lines in China." In *Market Reform in Socialist Countries,* ed. Peter Van Ness, 143–69. Boulder, Colo.: Lynne Rienner, 1989.

Vernon, Raymond. *Sovereignty at Bay.* New York: Basic Books, 1971.

Vogel, Ezra. *Canton under Communism.* New York: Harper and Row, 1969.

———. *One Step Ahead in China.* Cambridge: Harvard University Press, 1989.

Wade, Robert. "Industrial Policy in East Asia: Does It Lead or Follow the Market?" In Gereffi and Wyman, eds., *Manufacturing Miracles,* 23–66.

Waimao Yingyongwen Bianxiezu, ed. *Waimao yingyongwen* [Practical writing in foreign trade]. Beijing: Duiwai Maoyi Jiaoyu Chubanshe, 1985.

Walt, Stephen. "Rigor or Rigor Mortis: Rational Choice and Security Studies." *International Security* 23, 4 (Spring 1999): 5–48.

Waltz, Kenneth. *Man, the State and War.* New York: Columbia University Press, 1959.

———. *Theories of International Relations.* Reading, Mass.: Addison-Wesley, 1979.

Wang Hongmo. *1949–1989 nian de Zhongguo.* Vol. 3: *Da dongluan de niandai* [China 1949–1989: The course of reform and opening]. Zhengzhou: Henan Renmin Chubanshe, 1989.

Wang Jun. "'Wenge' houqi Zhou Enlai zai duiwai jingji gongzuozhong de gongxian" [Zhou Enlai's contribution to foreign economic policy work during the latter period of the "Cultural Revolution"]. *Dang de wenxian* 67 (1999): 70–75.

Wang, Nora. "Deng Xiaoping: The Years in France." *China Quarterly* 92 (December 1982): 698–705.

Wang Shouchun and Li Kanghua. *Zhongguo duiwai jingji maoyi de xinfazhan* [The new developments of China's foreign economic trade]. Beijing: Duiwai Maoyi Jiaoyu Chubanshe, 1986.

Wang Wenyang, ed. *Jingji tequ* [The special economic zones]. Beijing: Zhongguo Zhanwang Chubanshe, 1983.

Wang Xiangli. "Zhu De jingji sixiang xuexi biji (xia)" [Study notes on Zhu De's economic thinking, (part 2)]. *Dang de wenxian* 12 (1989): 44–48.

Ward, Benjamin. "The Chinese Approach to Economic Development." In Dernberger, *China's Development Experience,* 91–119.

Watson, Andrew. *Mao Zedong and the Political Economy of the Border Region.* Cambridge: Cambridge University Press, 1980.

Weil, Martin. "The Baoshan Steel Mill: A Symbol of Change in China's Industrial Development Strategy." In U.S. Congress, Joint Economic Committee, *Modernizations,* Part 1, 377.

Weisskopf, Thomas. "Patterns of Economic Development in India, Pakistan, and Indonesia." In Dernberger, ed., *China's Development Experience,* 38–90.

Whiting, Allen S. *Chinese Domestic Politics and Foreign Policy in the 1970s.* Ann Arbor: Center for Chinese Studies, University of Michigan, 1979.

————. "The Sino-Soviet Split." In MacFarquhar and Fairbank, eds., *Cambridge History,* 14:478–538.

Winckler, Edwin A. "Policy Oscillations in the People's Republic of China: A Reply." *China Quarterly* 68 (December 1976): 734–50.

Witke, Roxanne. *Comrade Chiang Ch'ing.* Boston: Little, Brown, 1977.

Woetzel, Jonathan. *China's Economic Opening to the Outside World.* New York: Praeger, 1989.

World Bank, The. *China: External Trade and Capital.* Washington D.C.: World Bank, 1988.

————. *China, Socialist Economic Development.* Vols. 1–3. Washington, D.C.: World Bank, 1983.

————. *The East Asian Miracle: Economic Growth and Public Policy.* New York: Oxford University Press, 1993.

————. *World Development Report 1987.* New York: Oxford University Press, 1987.

Wu, Chun-Hsi. *Dollars, Dependents, and Dogma: Overseas Chinese Remittances to Communist China.* Stanford, Calif.: Hoover Institution on War, Revolution, and Peace, 1967.

Wu, Eugene. "Contemporary China Studies: The Question of Sources." In Mao Zedong, *Secret Speeches,* 59–73.

Wu Jikun, ed. *Duiwai maoyi fazhan zhanlüe* [Foreign trade development strategy]. Beijing: Zhongguo Duiwai Jingji Maoyi Chubanshe, 1984.

Wu Qungan. "Guanyu Zhou Enlai yijiuliulingnian shending tiaozheng jingji fangzhen de kaozheng" [Research on Zhou Enlai's 1960 decision to readjust the economy]. *Dang de wenxian* 6 (1990): 15–16.

Wu, Tien-wei. *Lin Biao and the Gang of Four.* Carbondale: Southern Illinois University Press, 1983.

Wu Wutong. *Duiwai maoyi jichu zhishi gailun* [Introduction to the basics of foreign trade]. Beijing: Duiwai Maoyi Jiaoyu Chubanshe, 1986.

Wu, Yuan-li. *An Economic Survey of Communist China.* New York: Bookman Associates, 1956.

Xianggang Zhongguo Jingji Tequ Nianjian Bianjibu. *Zhongguo jingji tequ nianjian, 1983* [The yearbook of China's special economic zones, 1983]. Hong Kong: Xianggang "Zhongguo Jingji Tequ Nianjian" Chubanshe, n.d.

Xin, Jianfei. *Mao Zedong's World View: From Youth to Yanan.* Lanham, Md.: University Press of America, 1998.

Xing Guohua, ed. *Zhongguo gemingshi xuexi shouce* [A review handbook on China's revolutionary history]. Nanchang: Jiangsu Renmin Chubanshe, 1987.

Xiong Huayuan. "Lun Zhou Enlai zai fan maojin zhong de tansuo" [A thorough analysis of Zhou Enlai during the Anti-Rash Advance period]. *Dang de wenxian* 2 (1988): 9–16.

Xu Dixin. *Zhengzhi jingjixue cidian* [A dictionary of political economy]. Beijing: Renmin Chubanshe, 1981.

Yahuda, Michael. *Towards the End of Isolationism: China's Foreign Policy after Mao.* New York: St. Martin's Press, 1983.

Yan, Sun. *The Chinese Reassessment of Socialism, 1976–1992.* Princeton, N.J.: Princeton University Press, 1995.

Yan Wen. "Jiu 'zuo' de qibu" [The first steps in rectifying "leftism"]. *Dang de wenxian* 4 (1990): 28–37.

Yang Chengxu. Director, China Institute of International Studies. Interview, April 1996.

Yang, Dali. *Calamity and Reform in China.* Stanford, Calif.: Stanford University Press, 1996.

Yang Ruiguang. "Zongguan Mao Zedong de duiwai jingji jiaowang sixiang" [A long-range view of Mao Zedong's thoughts on foreign economic contacts]. *Dang de wenxian* 20 (1991): 73–78.

Yang, Shu-Chin, ed. *Manufactured Exports of East Asian Industrializing Economies.* Armonk, N.Y.: M. E. Sharpe, 1994.

Yao Yilin. "Tongxin xieli zuohao jingji gaige de diaocha yanjiu." *In Jingji wenti yanjiu ziliao, 1979* [Research materials on economic problems, 1979], ed. Zhonggong Zhongyang Shujichu Yanjiushi Jingjizu, n.d.

Yeh, K. C. "Soviet and Communist Chinese Industrialization Strategies." In *Soviet and Chinese Communism,* ed. Donald W. Treadgold, 327–63. Seattle: University of Washington Press, 1967.

Youngson, A. J., ed. *China and Hong Kong: The Economic Nexus.* Hong Kong: Oxford University Press, 1984.

Yu Shicheng. *Deng Xiaoping yu Mao Zedong* [Deng Xiaoping and Mao Zedong]. Beijing: Zhonggong Zhongyang Dangxiao Chubanshe, 1995.

Yuan Lizhou, ed. *Tongzhan zhishi yu zhengce* [Knowledge and policy of the United Front]. Harbin: Harbin Gongye Daxue Chubanshe, 1985.

Zhang Feihong. "Liu Shaoqi yu xin Zhongguo de duiwai maoyi gongzuo" [Liu Shaoqi and New China's foreign trade]. *Dang de wenxian* 37 (1994): 69–72.

Zhang Ge. "Guanyu jingji tequ he yanhai chengshi jinyibu kaifang de ruogan qingkuang" [Certain conditions for the SEZs and the coastal cities to further opening their economies]. In *Jingji gaige yu duiwai kaifang (shang)* [Economic reform and opening to the outside world (vol. 1)], ed. Zhongguo Jingjixue Tuanti Lianhehui Jingji Kexue Peixun Zhongxin. N.p., 1985?.

Zhang, Guotao. Introduction to *Collected Works of Liu Shao-ch'i before 1944.* Hong Kong: Union Research Institute, 1969.

Zhang, Peiji. "Development of China's Foreign Trade and Its Prospects." In *Economic Reform in the PRC,* ed. and trans. George C. Wang, 115–23. Boulder, Colo.: Westview, 1982.

———. "Guanyu woguo duiwai maoyi fazhan zhanlüe de tantao" [A discussion of China's foreign trade development strategy]. In Wu Jikun, *Duiwai maoyi,* 26–36.

Zhang Tianrong et al. *Zhongguo gaige dacidian* [The major dictionary on Chinese reforms]. Beijing: Zhongguo Guoji Guangbo Chubanshe, 1992.

Zhang Tianyu, ed. *Shiji zhijiao de zhongxing zhanlüe* [Practical comments on major strategy]. Beijing: Zhongguo Qingnian Chubanshe, 1993.

Zhang Wenru. *Mao Zedong yu Zhongguo xiandaihua* [Mao Zedong and China's modernization]. Beijing: Dangdai Zhongguo Chubanshe, 1993.

Zhang Zerong, ed. *Zhongguo jingji tizhi gaige jishi (Sichuan)* [Chronology of China's economic structural reforms (Sichuan)]. Chengdu: Sichuan Kexue Jishu Chubanshe, 1986.

Zhang Zhi'an. "Lüelun Chen Yun duiwai kaifang de jingji sixiang" [A brief account of Chen Yun's thinking on opening to the outside]. In Zhu Jiamu, *Chen Yun,* 526–36.

Zhao Yuanjie and Chen Zhaobin, eds. *Zhongguo tequ jingji* [The economy of China's special economic zones]. Guangzhou: Kexue Puji Chubanshe Guangzhou Fenshe, 1984.

Zhao Ziyang. "Dangqian de jingji xingshi he jinhou jianshi fangzhen" [The current economic situation and future development plans]. Speech delivered on 30 November 1981 and 1 December 1981 to the fourth plenary session of the Fifth NPC.

Zhejiangsheng Jingji Yanjiu Zhongxin. *Zhejiang shengqing gaiyao* [Outline of the conditions of Zhejiang Province]. Hangzhou: Zhejiang Renmin Chubanshe, 1986.

Zhejiangsheng Sifating, Zhejiangsheng Duiwai Jingji Maoyiting, ed. *Duiwai jingji falü zhengce huibian* [A selection of foreign economic laws and policies]. Zhejiang: Zhejiangsheng Sifating, Zhejiangsheng Duiwai Jingji Maoyiting, March 1985.

Zheng Derong, Han Mingxi, and Zheng Xiaoliang. *Zhongguo jingji tizhi gaige jishi* [Chronology of China's economic structural reforms]. Beijing: Chunqiu Chubanshe, 1987.

Zhong, Jifu. "Methods in Formulating National Economic Plans." In *Chinese Economic Planning*, ed. and trans. Nicholas R. Lardy, 3–11. White Plains, N.Y.: M. E. Sharpe, 1977.

Zhonggong Renminglu Bianxiu Weiyuanhui, ed. *Zhonggong renming lu* [Biographies of Chinese Communist personages]. Taibei: Guoli Zhengzhi Daxue Guoji Guanxi Yanjiu Zhongxin, 1983.

Zhonggong Shenzhen Shiwei Jiangshituan, Zhonggong Shenzhen Shiwei Jiangshituan. *"Shenzhen tequ jingji lilun wenti jiangzuo" cailiao* [Materials from "The Lectures on Theoretical Problems of the Shenzhen SEZ"]. Shenzhen, 1986.

Zhonggong Zhongyang Dangshi Yanjiushi. *Zhonggong dangshi dashi nianbiao* [Chronology of major historical events of the Chinese Communist Party]. Beijing: Renmin Chubanshe, 1987.

Zhonggong Zhongyang Shujichu, ed. *Liuda yilai dangnei mimi wenjian* [Internal secret Party documents since the Sixth Congress]. Beijing: Renmin Chubanshe, 1981.

Zhonggong Zhongyang Shujichu Yanjiushi Jingjizu. *Jingji wenti yanjiu ziliao, 1979* [Research materials on economic problems, 1979], 3–4. N.p.: N.d.

Zhonggong Zhongyang Shujichu Yanjiushi Lilunzu, ed. *Diaocha yanjiu, 1979–1980* [Investigation and research, 1979–1980]. Beijing: Zhonggong Zhongyang Dangxiao Chubanshe, 1983.

Zhonggong Zhongyang Weiyuanhui. "Guanyu jiaqiang yierxian de houfang jianshe he beizhan gongzuo de zhishi" [Directive to strengthen the first and second line's rear area construction and preparations for war]. *Dang de wenxian* 45 (1995): 35–36.

Zhonggong Zhongyang Wenxian Yanjiushi. *Deng Xiaoping sixiang nianpu (1975–1997)* [A chronicle of Deng Xiaoping's Thought (1975–1997)]. Beijing: Zhongyang Wenxian Chubanshe, 1998.

———. *Liu Shaoqi nianpu (1898–1969)* [A chronicle of Liu Shaoqi's life (1898–1969)]. Beijing: Zhongyang Wenxian Chubanshe, 1996.

———. *Xin shiqi jingji tizhi gaige zhongyao wenxian xuanbian* [Selected important documents on economic structural reforms during the new period]. Beijing: Zhonggong Wenxian Chubanshe, 1998.

———. *Zhonggong dangshi dashi nianbiao* [A chronicle of major events in central Party history]. Beijing: Renmin Chubanshe, 1987.

———. *Zhou Enlai jingji wenxuan* [A Selection of Zhou Enlai's economic works]. Beijing: Zhongyang Wenxian Chubanshe, 1993.

———. *Zhou Enlai nianpu (1949–1976)* [A chronicle of Zhou Enlai's life (1949–1976)]. Beijing: Zhongyang Wenxian Chubanshe, 1997.

———. *Zhu De nianpu* [A chronicle of Zhu De's life]. Beijing: Renmin Chubanshe, 1986.

————. *Zhu De zhuan* [A biography of Zhu De]. Beijing: Zhongyang Wenxian Chubanshe, 1993.

————, ed. *Jianguo yilai zhongyao wenxian xuanbian, diyice* [Selected important documents issued since the establishment of the PRC, vol. 1–]. Beijing: Zhongyang Wenxian Chubanshe, 1992.

————. *Sanzhong quanhui yilai zhongyao wenxian xuanbian* [Selected important documents issued since the Third Plenum]. Beijing: Renmin Chubanshe, 1982.

Zhongguo Duiwai Jingji Maoyi Nianjian Bianji Weiyuanhui. *Zhongguo duiwai jingji maoyi nianjian, 1984* [China's foreign economic trade yearbook, 1984]. Beijing: Zhongguo Duiwai Jingji Maoyi Chubanshe, 1984.

Zhongguo Duiwai Maoyi Gailun Bianxiezu, ed. *Zhongguo duiwai maoyi gailun* [An introduction to China's foreign trade]. Beijing: Duiwai Maoyi Jiaoyu Chubanshe, 1985.

"Zhongguo Gongchandang dishiyijie zhongyang weiyuanhui disanci quanti huiyi gongbao" [Communiqué of the Third Plenum of the Eleventh CCP Central Committee]. In Zhonggong Zhongyang Wenxian Yanjiushi, *Xin shiqi,* 6–10.

Zhongguo Guoji Jinrong Xuehui, ed. *Waihui tizhi gaige taolun wenji* [Collected works on discussions of foreign exchange structural reforms]. Beijing: Zhongguo Jinrong Chubanshe, 1986.

Zhongguo Jingji Tizhi Gaige Shiyong Cidian Bianxiezu. *Zhongguo jingji tizhi gaige shiyong cidian* [A practical dictionary of Chinese economic structural reforms]. Beijing: Haiqiao Chubanshe, 1989.

Zhongguo Jingjixue Tuanti Lianhehui Jingji Kexue Peixun Zhongxin, ed. *Jingji gaige yu duiwai kaifang (shang)* [Economic reform and opening to the outside world, vol. 1]. N.p., 1985?

Zhongguo Renmin Yinhang Bangongshi, ed. *1981 jinrong guizhang zhidu xuanbian* [A selection of rules and regulations concerning the 1981 financial system]. Beijing: Zhongguo Jinrong Chubanshe, 1983.

Zhongguo Renmin Yinhang Jihuasi, ed. *Lilü wenjian huibian* [A collection of documents on interest rates]. Beijing: Zhongguo Jinrong Chubanshe, 1986.

Zhongguo Shehui Kexueyuan, Faxue Yanjiusuo, ed. *Zhongguo jingji guanli fagui wenjian huibian, xiace* [Laws, regulations, and documents relating to China's economic management, vol. 2]. Jilin: Jilin Renmin Chubanshe, 1987.

————. *Zhonghua Renmin Gongheguo jingji fagui xuanbian, 1979. 10–1981.12.* [Collection of economic laws and regulations of the People's Republic of China, October 1979–December 1981]. 2 Vols. Beijing: Zhongguo Caizheng Jingji Chubanshe, 1983.

Zhongguo Shehui Kexueyuan, Zhongyang Danganguan, ed. *Caizheng guizhang zhidu xuanbian, 1980* [A selection of 1981 financial rules and regulations]. Beijing: Zhongguo Caizheng Jingji Chubanshe, 1983.

————. *Zhonghua Renmin Gongheguo jingji dangan ziliao xuanbian: Gongshang tizhi juan, 1949–1952* [A collection of archival materials on the PRC economy, industrial and commerce structures, 1949–1952]. Beijing: Zhongguo Shehui Kexue Chubanshe, 1993.

————. *Zhonghua Renmin Gongheguo jingji dangan ziliao xuanbian: Gongye juan, 1949–1952* [A collection of archival materials on the PRC economy: Industry, 1949–1952]. Beijing: Zhongguo Wuzi Chubanshe, 1996.

————. *Zhonghua Renmin Gongheguo jingji dangan ziliao xuanbian: Jinrong juan,*

1949–1952 [A collection of archival materials on the PRC economy: Finance, 1949–1952]. Beijing: Zhongguo Wuzi Chubanshe, 1996.

Zhonghua Renmin Gongheguo Caizhengbu Bangongshi, ed. *Caizheng guizhang zhidu xuanbian, 1980* [A selection of 1980 financial rules and regulations]. Beijing: Zhongguo Caizheng Jingji Chubanshe, 1982.

Zhonghua Renmin Gongheguo Guowuyuan Fazhiju. *Zhonghua Renmin Gongheguo xianxing fagui huibian, 1945–1985 (caimao juan)* [Collection of current PRC laws and regulations (finance and trade volume)]. Beijing: Renmin Chubanshe, 1987.

Zhongshan Daxue Jingjixi, ed. *Jingjixue luncong* [A collection of views on economics studies]. Guangzhou: N.p., 1983.

"Zhong-Su maoyi" [Sino-Soviet trade]. *Guojimaoyi 10* (1985): 13–18.

Zhou Enlai. "Guanyu jiben jianshe de jige wenti" [Several problems in basic construction]. *Dang de wenxian* 45 (1995): 39.

———. "Zai disanjie quanguo renmin daibiao dahui diyicishang de 'Zhengfu gongzuo baogao' (jiexuan)" [The "Government Work Report" presented at the first session of the third National People's Congress (selections)]. *Dang de wenxian* 64 (1998): 14–20.

———. "Zai Nie Rongzhen 'Guanyu lizu guonei fazhan keji deng wenti xiang zhonggong bing Mao Zedong de baogao' de jiduan piyu" [Several comments on Nie Rongzhen's "A Report to the Central Committee and Mao Zedong on Developing a Domestically Based Science and Technology"]. *Dang de wenxian* 49 (1996): 10.

Zhou Xiaoquan and Ma Jianqun. *Zouxiang kaifangxing jingji* [Moving toward an open economy]. Tianjin: Tianjin Renmin Chubanshe, 1993.

Zhu De. "Cengjia chukou chanpin, fazhan Hainan jingji" [Increase export products, develop Hainan's economy]. *Dang de wenxian* 53 (1996): 34–35.

———. "Zai quanguo caizheng huiyishang de jianghua" [Speech to the national finance conference]. *Dang de wenxian* 3 (1988): 32.

———. *Zhu De xuanji* [Selected works of Zhu De]. Beijing: Renmin Chubanshe, 1983.

Zhu Jiamu. "Chen Yun yu Zhongguo gongyehua de qibu" [Chen Yun and the initial moves toward Chinese industrialization]. In Zhu Jiamu, ed., *Chen Yun,* 286–304.

———. "Shiyijie Sanzhong quanhui ji qi zhuyao wenjian xingcheng de ruogan qingquang—wo suozhidao de Shiyijie Sanzhong quanhui (xia)" [Certain situations that shaped the Eleventh Party Congress' Third Plenum and its important documents—what I know of the Eleventh Party Congress' Third Plenum (part 2)]. *Dang de wenxian* 67 (1999): 33–50.

———. "Zai quanguo caizheng huiyishang de jianghua" [Speech to the National Finance Conference]. *Dang de wenxian* 3 (1988): 30–35.

———, ed. *Chen Yun he tade shiye* [Chen Yun and his career]. Beijing: Zhongyang Wenxian Chubanshe, 1996.

Zhu Yuanshi. "Liu Shaoqi yijiusijiunian mimi fangsu" [Liu Shaoqi's secret 1949 trip to the Soviet Union]. *Dang de wenxian* 21 (1991): 74–89.

Zongcanmoubu Zuozhanbu. "Zongcan zuozhanbu de baogao" [Report of the War Preparations Department of the General Staff headquarters]. *Dang de wenxian* 45 (1995): 34–35.

Zou Chuntai and Song Xingzhong, eds. *Zhongguo shehui zhuyi caizheng jianshi* [Simplified history of Chinese socialist financial affairs]. Beijing: Zhongguo Caizheng Jingji Chubanshe, 1988.

Index

accompanying reports (*baosong*), 222
accumulation rate, 122–23, 188–89, 294n52
aerospace industry, 155
Afro-Asian states, 19, 20, 46, 66, 75–76, 91, 137, 177
Agricultural People's Communes, Articles on, 31
agriculture: and famines and natural disasters, 21, 29, 38, 106; producer's role in, 28, 120–23; and communes, 28, 31, 122, 126, 134; responsibility systems in, 31; and Great Leap, 97–98, 122; and Eight-Character Plan (1960), 106; and Four Modernizations, 112, 114; remunerative measures in, 122–25, 162; sideline production bases in, 126–27; during Cultural Revolution, 130, 149, 275n5; and "Four Guarantees," 142; during post-Mao period, 182–83; and Eight-Character Plan (1979), 187; to finance imports, 191; and reform experimentation, 204. *See also* export commodity processing bases; export promotion measures; grains
Albania, 104, 177
Allied American Corporation, 18
altruism, 26, 137
Anhui Province, 106, 204
Anshan charter, 99
Anti-Lin, Anti-Confucius Campaign (1973–74): analysis of, 9, 167–73, 287n8, 287n16; and glass snail incident, 168–69, 288n19; and *Fengqing* incident, 169–72; economic impact of,

169, 172–73, 184; and Zhou Enlai's health, 287n4
Anti-Rightist Campaign (1957): and Mao Zedong, 62; and overseas Chinese/ Hong Kong, 81; and development strategy, 85–6, 98, 99; ending of, 100; Zhou Enlai on, 112
Anti-Rightist Campaign (1975), 74, 172, 177–79, 182, 184
approval and transmission (*pizhuan*) of documents, 223
Arkhipov, Ivan, 56, 262n281
arts and handicrafts, 64, 82, 122, 124, 157, 159, 208
Asia: economic crisis in (1997), 4; industrialization of, 16–20
autarky. *See* semiautarky
automobile industry, 155
autonomy and capacity: and World Trade Organization admission, 3; enjoyed by elites, 11, 25–26, 45–46, 216; lack of, 46, 119, 174, 189–90, 205, 260n255, 294n61, 301n138
Azalea Mountain, 170

Bachman, David, 7
backyard furnaces, 86, 105, 214, 243n150, 260n261, 262n281
Balassa, Bela, 236n11
Bandung Conference (1955), 75–76
bandwagoning, 32, 99, 213
Bank of China: Hong Kong study, 147; ties with Chase Manhattan Bank, 154–55; use of Hong Kong assets, 161;